Project Management Planning

This book is part of the Peter Lang Education list.
Every volume is peer reviewed and meets
the highest quality standards for content and production.

PETER LANG
New York • Berlin • Brussels • Lausanne • Oxford

Muhamed Abdomerovic

Project Management Planning

From Practice to Applied Research

PETER LANG
New York • Berlin • Brussels • Lausanne • Oxford

Library of Congress Cataloging-in-Publication Control Number: 2022015750

Bibliographic information published by **Die Deutsche Nationalbibliothek.**
Die Deutsche Nationalbibliothek lists this publication in the "Deutsche Nationalbibliografie"; detailed bibliographic data are available on the Internet at http://dnb.d-nb.de/.

ISBN 978-1-4331-8934-0 (hardcover)
ISBN 978-1-4331-8935-7 (paperback)
ISBN 978-1-4331-8931-9 (ebook pdf)
ISBN 978-1-4331-8932-6 (epub)
DOI 10.3726/b19696

80 Broad Street, 5th floor, New York, NY 10004
www.peterlang.com

For my family, friends, and readers

Contents

List of Illustrations

Acknowledgments

We may consider project management planning (PMP) as an analytical setting for arranging daily requirements, changes, and decisions related to project scope, time, resources, cost, quality, risk, benefits, satisfaction, and other attributes. Tough decisions are required sometimes in a situation where many unknowns and limitations in PMP exist. Yet the project manager must move forward, whether the action will work out or not, and live with the consequences.

I learned the above knowledge consistently and continuously while living in Sarajevo and working as a construction management trainee for Vranica and reporting to the Construction Director Dz. Muhamedagic; as a department manager in Energoinvest-ERC and reporting to the CEO M. Cico; and as vice-president in Energoinves-IDV and reporting to the CEO Z. Selmanagic.

Then happened the siege of Sarajevo, which led to the massive destruction of lives, environments, and social structures in Sarajevo. Energoinvest was in flame. I was assigned by the Premier of RBiH (Republic Bosnia and Hercegovina) J. Pelivan to the Government Commission for Estimating the War Damages. In an extraordinarily complex situation, M. Dizdarevic supervised the commission, the RBiH's Secretary of the Construction Industry, whose management style and attitude could not have been more pleasing. After 30 months of wartime, I ended my last assignment in Bosnia. I took off into unknown roads. I felt so gratified and attached to where I am from as my life was to change soon.

I settled in the United States in November 1994, with solid experience and the particular knowledge and realization that each project manager must be responsible for developing and implementing a project management plan.

My first professional job in the United States was with Luckett and Farley Engineering. I was hired as program manager for a multi-project planning work. I got the privilege to help develop and update project management plan weekly for 7 to 12 project managers and build an integrated program plan. It was an exciting experience to communicate the general approach of PMP to a diversified group of general managers, architects, construction managers, accountants, estimators, and others. I learned a lot during that period, especially about the role of project management planning in case of an uprising, and downsizing of architect and construction engineering organization, and rightsizing of derivative startups. I appreciate the exemplary support and professional commitment extended by J. Stewart, vice-president, and G, Blackmore, department manager of Luckett and Farley. I also wish to express my special thanks to team members and my friends and peers, Project Managers T. Mihaljevic, H. R. Guyton, T. Smith, P. Newman, M. Mazeika, P. Burkhead. J. Sugars, J. Dortch, and others for their advice and for accommodating, accepting, and supporting me as one of the team and providing me with valuable inputs and wisdom about my work.

Several years later, I joined the FKI Logistex Integration Division and met a team of experienced engineers and project managers. It was the time when the FKI Logistex project team was working to tie-in the technology management processes and project management processes for better accomplishment of contracts. We confronted situations where strategic technological decisions emerged outside the project manager's influence, threatening to derail the effort of the project team and project's success. During this endeavor, I worked closely with R. Crawford, vice-president; T. Brennan, department manager; Project Managers M. Hockensmith, V. Williams, R. Stoess, K. Anderson, P. Mankowski, and others. I want to express my most profound appreciation for their help while learning new technologies and communicating possible solutions. I recall the priceless moments in my professional life when I had the chance to work with an inspired team and received extraordinary management support. Then, my whole work, including the reconstruction of information between technology management and project management processes, grew to a higher level and made the project manager's views heard.

Next, I joined Vanderlande Industries as a Project Planner, primarily motivated by the success of Vanderlande's big project, the UPS World Project, completed on time. Several moments helped develop and communicate the plan that matched the site work and covered the payment application process for numerous contractors. At the same time, the plan served as a top-level project performance report. Thanks to the silent and continuous support from J. Broeksteeg, project director; W. Vos, construction manager; and my peers and friends, E. Cengic, C. van Gog, T. Davidson, J. Connell, T. Grant, M. Walker, and other professionals—the development, update, and communication of the integrated project management plan became a common interest.

All the above experiences felt like a cultural cohesion among professional people benefiting from PMP.

Several others offered suggestions and clarifications during the course of publishing my previous books about system logic, something which I have also accommodated to strengthen the present books' discussions on the innovations in the development of PMP. In this sense, I am deeply grateful to R. Archibald for his endorsement and M. Wideman for his continuous support of the system logic idea. Without their support and encouragement, this textbook would not have come into fruition.

The book is also benefitted greatly from a highly devoted Acquisition Editor D. Green, who was helped and supported me at all the stages of the writing this book, and the Production Editor N. Palani who patiently managed the final touch of the book.

Special thanks are due to several anonymous reviewers for their effort to ensure that this book turned out to be a good-quality text for students and budding professionals.

Finally, I wish to thank my chronically busy family for their understanding while I was collecting materials and formatting and writing the draft versions of this book.

But this story has to reach students, practitioners, and scholars since writing in our society has to be endorsed by readers. Suppose this book helps educators introduce the values and limitations of PMP and prepare readers to advance their project management knowledge. In that case, many readers will see how project management experiences and concerns rise to a higher level and more stories follow.

Foreword

In this book, I describe new perspectives on the principles of project management planning (PMP) that apply to a subject whose components can be identified, quantified, related, implemented, controlled, and updated. The book shows integration and compatibility among principles of PMP and how we can use those principles for most development, research, or maintenance projects in construction, information technology, production, and others. This part of the book is fundamental for professional PMP.

I use the same principles of PMP to reveal and explain the system logic hidden within a collection of project management knowledge. Applying PMP principles to an empirical cluster of project management knowledge creates a positive condition that facilitates and supports the development and incorporation of critical outputs sequences in project management system knowledge. The book shows how the critical outputs sequence can be used as a textbook outline to develop a project management plan by augmenting the project management system knowledge. This part of the book is ahead of time and essential for understanding the project management system logic and the system approach to PMP.

To clearly express a complicated theme in simple terms, I first explain the genesis and application of fundamental theories and resulting methodologies for PMP. Then I derive the symmetric tools that help reveal and explain the logic of a project management system. Having the system logic of a recognized project management system, I select real-life projects and demonstrate the steps involved in the system approach to PMP. The book shows how:

- a model of project management system knowledge can expose its hypothetical meaning.
- to establish the critical links within the contents of the project management system and reveal its system logic.
- to debug and sense the system logic.
- to modify the system logic to better express the requirements and conditions of the specific project management plan.
- the system logic helps the practitioner or the reader to advance the contents and the application process of PMP.

Besides, I demonstrate how understanding the project or system contents can be considerably simplified when explaining the principles of PMP. The book shows that such an approach provides a measurable basis for comparing project management systems and enhances the contents and processes of the systems. I demonstrate how this line of reasoning should improve both the project management system logic and project management plan.

The above idea of the system approach to PMP originates from my works published earlier. It complements the understanding about project management system and its role in project management.

Preface

Project management planning is the science and art of handling planned responsibility and unexpected conditions. But evidence shows two massive gaps in PMP, across the community. The first gap is between current PMP and its potential as a practical discipline. The second gap is between project management system knowledge and its potential as an applied research discipline.

What do the project management scholars, students, practitioners, managers, or management trainees need to overcome these gaps? How does an individual realize the practical and research potentials of PMP? Suppose we do not understand both the current PMP and project management system knowledge. In that case, the gaps will get wider and mess up the project's development. If we have understood them well, then how should we manage these gaps?

Let's begin with facts. Each project is different when it comes to its technology, size, conditions, and objectives or whether it is related to types of activities and services such as construction, information technology, product development. However, the attributes, for example, scope, time, cost, quality, risk, benefits, and others, are generally shared across projects. For that reason, comprehensive PMP principles can be applied across all types of projects. Otherwise, we cannot identify the differences and commonalities between how different projects are planned and completed, and think about integrated project management for projects, programs, or project businesses.

Therefore, it is not about how to modify an existing method or create a new method to suit a project but about how to improve PMP potential to accommodate any project. It is about a simple, comprehensive explanation of the continuous path from practice and applied research to a system for PMP. Such an approach makes a difference since it promotes new perspectives that help to constantly improve project management system knowledge and, consequently, PMP. Suppose a specific teaching strategy links the PMP project management system knowledge. In that case, the teaching strategy's implementation takes advantage of both and reveals the system for PMP. Why should it work and how?

Project management planning has to be specific in terms of developing and implementing the project management plan. For this purpose, we must:

- Define, communicate, and explain the PMP objectives.
- Evaluate decision processes and actions to ensure support for PMP objectives.
- Motivate project stakeholders to accomplish PMP objectives.

This part of the book simplifies the learning and application of PMP essential for students and project management trainees interested in understanding PMP. Figure 4.2 illustrates a simple, sufficient, and reliable management summary report for the project valued at US$350 million, completed in 36 months, and described by 8,000 activities and about a 100,000 activity attributes. The weekly updated report helps top managers to assess the status, progress, and forecasts of the project and central contracts and make responsible decisions. The forms, selection, organization, usage, and update of PMP data and reports are transparent to any team or teams involved in the implementation of the whole project or the project programs' components. Understanding this part of the book (Chapters 1, 2, 3, and 4) is a precondition for and key to project management's success in contemporary times.

Project management system knowledge has to be explicit in developing and implementing project management system logic. For this purpose, we must:

- Display the system logic in a relative timeframe and discuss the meaning of the system logic.
- Give a good reason for adapting the system logic to specific planning objectives.

- Apply the system logic for the improvement of planning objectives.

This part of the book simplifies the process of understanding and applying project management system knowledge for scholars and professionals studying the system logic. Figure 5.2 illustrates the part of system logic discussed in the PMBOK Guide, Fourth Edition. A reader can use the sequence for various purposes, including for further analysis and updating project management system knowledge and system logic and processes to develop and implement the project management plan. We can use an identical approach to reveal, explain, and apply the unique system logic of any periodically updated project management system knowledge. Understanding this part of the book (Chapters 1, 5, and 6) is necessary for PMP in the 21st century.

A proven theoretical and methodological framework explains how to understand, apply, and continuously improve PMP and system knowledge. The book presents PMP and system knowledge as analytical processes supported by narrative rationality and continuous improvement. Such an approach is an essential component of the skill sets of a project manager. Besides, the book has substance that encourages readers worldwide to share global project management's prosperity as well as to read the book. Here are examples:

- Scholars in project management can gain new perspectives about the general collection of project management system knowledge and how to study, compile, and improve project management system logic.
- Professionals in project management can gain new perspectives about the fundamental methodologies of PMP and how to improve professional competence in PMP.
- A project management student can understand the theoretical and methodological framework and the necessary skills needed for project management research or trainee position.
- A project team member can understand the integrated methods and steps of best practice to develop and implement a project management plan. They can also learn how to use the project management system logic to improve the system approach to developing and implementing the project management plan.
- A project manager can better understand their role by learning how each project, regardless of its size, complexities, stakeholder relationships, and interests, and get a comprehensive, updated, and applicable project

management plan. They can also improve their understanding of PMP principles and better communicate their responsibilities to the PMP team.
- Project business executives can understand the integration and unity of strategic and operational PMP, extending their global influence and improving the results of both the project and the company's project business.

Project management, including PMP, is widely taught and researched. The readership of this book may include those affiliated with management schools, professional associations, or organizations closely related to PMP. For example:

- Schools and organizations with project management programs (e.g., George Washington University, Stanford University, DeVry University, Harvard University, Texas University, Cpella.edu, Keller.edu)
- National and international project management organizations that include professional education, development, and certification programs (e.g., Government Accountability Office [GAO], Project Management Institute [PMI], International Project Management Association [IPMA], American Society for the Advancement of Project Management [ASAPM], Association of Project Management [APM, UK], Project Management Association of Japan [PMAJ]).
- Organizations and companies tied with project business (e.g., American Institute of Architects [AIA], Construction Specification Institute [CSI], American Institute of Constructors [AIC], American Association of Cost Engineers [AACE], American Society of Civil Engineers [ASCE], Construction Management Association of America [CMAA], Associated General Contractors [AGC], American Society of Mechanical Engineers [ASME], Institute of Electrical and Electronics Engineers '[IEEE])

Besides, the reader of the book may meet the requirements as an active member of world-class project management websites. For example:

- *Project Management Journal* (www.pmi.org)
- *International Journal for Project Management* (www.elsevier.com)
- The U.S. Member Association of the IPMA (www.ipma-usa.org)
- *Project Management World Journal* (www.pmworldjournal.net)
- Project Management Wisdom (www.maxwideman.com)
- College of Performance Management (www.mycpm.org)
- Agile Alliance (www.agilealliance.org)

- Planning Planet (www.planningplanet.com)
- Other websites, including mass media, which relate to project management discussions, education, and services.

The book is the primary material for the PMP course or supplementary material for a project management course. It covers the following:

- Fundamental theories and generally accepted methodologies for PMP.
- Subjects open for study and application of project management system knowledge.
- Needs at different levels, including that of colleges, education seminars, and practice of PMP.

There is no sustainable trend or paradigm change that affects one stabilized component for managing diverse projects and applying the ever-growing project management system knowledge. Yet, there are not as many PMP books as we need. Here are some common deficiencies in existing books, pointing to common gaps in PMP literature. Namely:

- The gap between PMP and its potentials has to be clarified. Insufficient explanation of PMP inhibits the usage of its distinguished patterns. For example, the competing books show: weak descriptions or absence of descriptions about project management feedback, ambiguous explanations or no explanation provided at all for overlaps among project phases; weak or insufficient answers or no answers at all that explain the relationships between strategic and operational project management; subjectivism in clarifications about PMP pattern; sporadic descriptions or no descriptions at all about the relationship between the technology management and project management. Can we still learn substantially from such works despite the obvious lacks described?
- The gap between project management system knowledge and its potentials is far from being closed. Inadequate handling of project management system knowledge inhibits the recognition and the usage of project management system logic. Even if we continue to pile information and explain the already impressive project management system knowledge, the problems do not stop. For example, without project management system logic, users cannot systematically add new components to project management system knowledge. They will not be able to move project management system

knowledge from the education stage to the application stage; they will have no opportunity to visualize the development sequence of project management system knowledge. Can we afford to let such issues persist?

Then, I asked myself, what are the distinct features of my book? Perhaps, the book is more oriented to PMP than are its competing books. This notion can be supported by at least three reasons:

- First, the book clarifies and supplements the theoretical and methodological framework for PMP.
- Second, the book contains a comprehensive explanation of project management system logic that readers can use in basic and applied research for improving the contents and processes of a collection of general project management system knowledge.
- Third, the book shows how the system logic of an empirical collection of project management system knowledge helps move the reader from the stage of visions about and motivation to engage in project management to the stage where they can learn comprehensive processes of system approach to project management plan.

Thus, *Project Management Planning*, the present book, first explains the current practice for PMP. This notion clears the way for applied research that helps explain the system logic of a vast collection of project management system knowledge, consequently improving the system approach to the project management plan. What else?

The PMP community has always needed improvements. Today, we may think about breaking new ground with some evidence and exercise caution in approach to applying current PMP to corporate management planning. That is my vision for the evolution of PMP.

This book points toward the needs of scholars, students, professionals, trainees, managers, and others interested in PMP. They are looking for comprehensive theories and methodologies to develop ideas and plan and implement them in various project management areas, based on a common set of project management attributes. For this purpose, a short description of book chapters and education courses shows how this book meets readers' interest in PMP.

Chapter 1—Overview of the Project Management Planning—introduces the link between the practical achievements and research views in PMP. The chapter explains the frameworks, processes, theoretical origins, and methodological principles for practical PMP. It also shows the arguments and methods for research in PMP by understanding and using an updated collection of a general project management system.

Chapter 2—Time and Resource Project Management Plan—describes the required processes to complete the project within the planned time and allocated resources. The time management plan shows duration, start date, finish dates, and other time attributes for project activities, work packages, deliverables, and other structural constructs of the project. The resource management plan shows what resources we need and when and how much resources to utilize in any of the project's structural constructs and within the planned time.

Chapter 3—Cost Project Management Plan—aids the understanding of time–cost links and their attributes pointing to the high predictability of project success. In mature settings, the cost management data of the project plan show the status, progress, changes, and forecast for the time and cost of any project's structural constructs.

Chapter 4—Best Practice in Project Management Planning—provides a selection of available best processes in a company with a history of trust and commitment in PMP. The chapter shows an overview of the understanding and skills needed to cope with the company's best practice and successfully develop and decisively implement the various steps in the project management plan.

Chapter 5—Project Management System Logic—presents an analysis of the hypothetical meanings and potentials for the general project management system collection. The chapter essential parts provide guidelines and methods to analyze, relate, and synthesize project management system knowledge and reveals its logic. We can use such system logic to debug and understand the collection of general project management system knowledge and improve the efficacy and quality of PMP.

Chapter 6—Where Is Planning in (Project) Management Going Next? Over the past seven decades, scientific PMP has contributed to developing human's most successful adventures. Now is the time to clarify the gap between the project management system knowledge's proclamations and logic. The reader can find here how structural simplicity and integrity of PMP, enhanced by narrative rationality described in earlier chapters, help to see where is management planning, including project management, going next.

Chapter 7—Derivative Project Management Planning—iIs the derivative project management planning the case for a paradigm shift in PMP? The chapter explains emerging businesses' common intention to simplify PMP and derive something simple, easy to learn, and which will be endorsed by customers. The most heralded derivatives, such as the Critical Chain Method and Agile, are discussed in light of how they are incorporated into or can be compared with current PMP.

Chapter 8—Notes, Integrated Definitions, and Readings—brings supporting evidence for some statements in the book and challenges the readers to think critically and innovatively. The chapter delivers more facts about the book topics and explains some puzzling PMP ideas that have been used on and off for decades and some ideas that did not reach readers. Yet, their source form may lead to a solution for some persistent PMP problems.

Based on the recognized theories and applied research, the PMP discipline and proven practice could fulfill a purposeful project's and system's objectives.

Finally, consider the audience that sparks the author's intentions to write a widely accepted book. So, prospective education courses within PMP must be comprehensive, scalable, and cohesive to help students understand better the curriculum being taught and fully engage and immerse themselves with greater interest in the learning process. For this purpose, the course's framework consists of proven theories, generally accepted methodologies, and established practices. The courses rely on the scientific process of ever-improving unified themes of project management system knowledge and PMP. They have clear divisions of responsibilities for book topics, which are especially important in large-scale projects, where goals are stable and everyone has to understand the project mission. Here are the details of some of the courses specific to the topics covered in this book:

Undergraduate students learn:

- Introduction to project management planning (PMP); the theoretical backgrounds, related methods, and communication patterns
- Contents of the project management plan; from project phases as the interface between the project and the project business to project activities that indicate the type of works carried out, for example, to install hardware and software, provide services, execute processes, or facilitate the flow of information between different stakeholders
- Processes of the project management plan; technological process groups and management process groups
- Interactions and overlaps within a process group and among the process groups
- Interactions and overlaps in a project management plan

- Structures and relationships among structures in a project management plan the Work Breakdown Structure, Organizational Breakdown Structure, Virtual Breakdown Sstructures
- Planning networks and methods for handling a project management plan; the Critical Path Method, Program Evaluation and Review Technique, Precedence Diagramming Method
- Activity types in planning networks; task activity, independent activity, meeting activity, hammock activity, dummy activity, lead/lag activity, milestones, flags
- Activity attributes—identifications, relationships, durations, dates, constraints, floats, resources, codes
- Activity role in shaping interactions and overlaps between higher-level project components and their attributes
- Forms of the project management plan—the original, baseline, and current project management plans
- Development of project network diagram—primary, secondary, and hammock logic
- Characteristics of project time and resource management plan—the balance between time and resources, time and resources alternatives, essential calculations, activity calendar, resource calendars
- Identification, collection, estimation, and assignment of required time and resource attributes for project activities
- Resource availability, deployment, aggregation, leveling, smoothing, and allocation for the project or project business
- The calculation, production, and assessment of project time and resource management plan to comply with project requirements, objectives, and conditions
- Setting the project management plan baseline
- Compilation and distribution of the reports on time and resource planning
- Implementing the project management plan by performing project activities
- Controlling the implementation of project management plan through status, progress, and forecast of project activities
- Controlling what has been achieved and what should have been achieved at the moment by assessing, approving, paying, securing, using, and maintaining completed works
- Functions and features of project management software needed for time and resource planning

- Project management planning derivatives
- Chapters 1, 2, 7, and 8 of the book cover the undergraduate course

Graduate students learn the following in addition to what they have learned at the undergraduate level:

- Introduction to project cost management
- Cost types, definitions, and relationships
- Cost values and calculation elements
- Developing and maintaining cost estimation databases or using commercially available cost estimation databases
- Cost-estimating process
- Time–cost relationships—planned value, earned value, actual value, cost estimate to complete, cost estimate at completion
- Planning direct and indirect project costs
- Establishing cost account codes and cost category codes
- Earned value management
- Earned schedule management
- Cost variances and indexes
- Project cost and time performance management
- Cost management constraints
- The payment process for project works
- Introduction to best practice in project management planning (PMP)
- Steps involved in implementing best practice in PMP
- Reports and records in PMP
- Quality assessment of project management plan
- Maturity path in PMP
- Career path in PMP
- Functions and features of project management software needed for cost management in PMP
- Chapters 1, 2, 3, 4, 7, and 8 of the book present details on the curricula covered in the graduate course

Postgraduate students learn the following, in addition to the undergraduate and graduate curricula:

- Introduction to system approach to PMP

- Introduction to a general collection of project management system knowledge
- Introduction to project management system logic
- Rules for the handling of project management system logic; rules for relating particles of system logic, rules for developing sequence of particles, rules for verification of system logic
- Steps in determining and following the project management system logic
- Disambiguation process of system components
- Steps in the implementation of project management system logic
- Changes to project management system logic
- Process groups in a project management system
- Relationships among the various process groups of a project management system
- Impact of system logic on the development and application of a general collection of project management system knowledge
- Impact of system logic on the compilation of global project management system knowledge and affirmation of project management profession
- Details that scholars need to increase the impact of their research on system logic by moving a general collection of project management system knowledge from education to application.
- Information that the average manager needs to make its work better and easier by using the system logic—a simple, sufficient, and credible form of a general collection of project management system knowledge
- Chapters 1, 2, 3, 4, 5, 6, 7, 8, and the bibliography of the book present details of the postgraduate course

All courses spring from the same concept and methodological base; therefore, the courses are integrated and applicable for planning any project, program, or project business.

1

Overview of Project Management Planning

Introduction

Since the early days of humanity, people have made plans for the development of their ideas. Important documents of this kind have been in existence from 5th century BC. The documents were used to develop the towns, Piraeus and Rhodes (White 1971, 11).[1] Urbanized societies of early civilization were receptive to planning. From the fascinating project of that time, people have understood the plan's regulatory characteristic, which implies developing and implementing the plan.

Management professionals consider planning in different ways today. Here are some planning divisions and associated extents that help us see the route to project management planning (henceforth specified as PMP, a well-known acronym for project management planning):

- Planning policies (state-dominated economy, state-engaged investment, or mixed)

1 White, Brenda. *Sourcebook of planning information*. London, UK: Clive Bingley, 1971.

- Owners of planning (those with assigned rights and responsibilities to develop and implement the plan)
- Organizational areas of planning (complete business, or a specific area of business, including project business)
- Professional areas of planning (feasibility, sustainability, stakeholders, finance, investment, organization, growth, employment, payment, security, usage, maintenance, or other)
- The timespan of the planning period (short-term, medium-term, long-term, open-end, or combined)
- Attributes of planning (scope, time, resource, cost, quality, risk, benefits, other measurable attributes)
- Planning stages (preliminary, strategic, master, contract, as-built, or other)
- Aspects of planning (socioeconomic and methodological-economic)

Most divisions are open for consideration when developing or implementing the planning objectives. Nearly any division or combination of divisions expresses anticipated characteristics through various aspects of planning, the knowledge of which has been evolving continuously and shared among generations of scientists and practitioners.

Within management planning, we can recognize three situations: the discrete production management planning, mass production planning, and PMP:

- Discrete production management planning occurs when a repetitive sequence of operations competing for resources, multipurpose machines, or trades are carried out in a flexible manner. This situation requires carrying out operations in such a way that succeeding operations are not delayed. We can successfully manage this type of planning by the Line of Balance (LOB) method designed for production planning. However, there are excellent applications of the LOB in repetitive construction projects. For example, building a series of assisted-living apartments with phased operations, including a phased occupation of apartments, has much in common with discrete production planning.
- Mass production management planning occurs when a repetitive sequence of operations competing for resources, the single-purpose, or high-speed machines are carried out in a stable manner. This situation requires performing operations in such a way that machines work optimally. This type of planning typically orients itself to the Manufacturing Resource Planning (MRP II) process that includes operational planning and control

of customer orders or completing the manufacture of product to meet a specific quantity. For example, establishing limits of manufacturing operations at a conveyor production plant requires optimal use of each machine with the minimum or zero stock of unfinished conveyors, as illustrated in Figures 2.7 and 2.8.

- PMP occurs in a situation where a unique sequence of activities competing for human, material, and other resources are carried out dynamically. This situation requires allocating resources in such a way that the series of activities planned are completed on time. Such an objective shows how PMP makes an exception within a mutually acceptable planning world. The notion implicitly confirms the editorials of the PMI's *Project Management Journal*, 2006–2012, where Bredillet clarifies why project management's unique history and remarkable development emerge as a management branch.

We often hear that project management problems should be solved by production management, as summed up in the first or second management planning situations presented earlier. PMP has theoretical and methodological foundations applicable to general management planning, including production management planning; however, using production management techniques to resolve problems in PMP is not a good idea.

It is not possible to draw an analogy between production management planning and PMP. The development phase of a production project—the prototype stage—consists of a unique set of activities performed one time only. In contrast, the mass production phase of a production project consists of a repetitive set of operations to be carried out for each product. The difference is substantial. We manage any project, including its development phase, by PMP, and the production phase by production management planning.

Basis for Project Management Planning

Project management planning (PMP) is the science and art of handling planned responsibility and unexpected conditions. PMP contents differ from man-made endeavors to study humanity and explore the universe. However, the processes of planning contents (initiating, planning, executing, controlling, closing) and the attributes of planning contents (scope, time, resource, cost, quality, risk, benefits, others) are generally common. For that reason, comprehensive PMP will apply across all types of projects, and all kinds of planning situations, including the agile sequence of short-term investments or the critical-chain buffers management. This concept is essential; otherwise, we cannot connect differences and commonalities or think about integrated project management for a program, project business, company, or corporate.

I emphasize the science and art notions about PMP discussed in several book chapters. The core of PMP—its scope, time, resources, cost, benefits, and related performance—is scientific. Besides, the project manager must have various leadership talents, skills, and contingencies to make sense of the plan's conditions. General sense-making tools help deal with complications and complexities by understanding and relaxing assumptions and developing predictive actions (Kurtz and Snowden 2003).[2] Both the science and art sides of the PMP depend on structured and narrative communication methods.

PMP is an indispensable component of the project, project management, and competence of a project manager. Here are some pieces of evidence:

- The relationship between the project and project management planning has been recognized many decades ago, for example, in PMI's PMBOK Guide—the PMI 1996, 167; PMI 2000, 204; PMI 2004, 368; PMI 2008, 434; PMI 2013, 553; and PMI 2017, 715.[3]
- The relationship between project management and project management planning is a close one, too. The visions, amd most project management schools of thought include project management planning (Bredillet 2010, 10–12).[4]
- The relationship between the project manager's competence and PMP portrays the professional who plans and controls a project (ICB 2006, Preface) or has a wider range of skills that modern project managers are expected to possess (ICB 2015, Foreword).[5]

2 Kurtz, Cynthia, and David Snowden. *The new dynamics of strategy: Sense-making in a complex and complicated world.* IBM System Journal. Volume 42. No. 3 (2003): 462–483.

3 PMI 2017. *A Guide to the Project Management Body of Knowledge (PMBOK® Guide) Sixth Edition.* Newtown Square PA: Project Management Institute, 2017.

4 Bredillet, Christophe. "Blowing Hot and Cold on Project Management." *Project Management Journal* Volume 41, Number 3 (June 2010): 4–20. www.pmi.org.

5 ICB 2015. *ICB – IPMA Competence Baseline. Version 4.0.* IPMA – International Project Management Association, 2015. www.ipma.ch.

- Representative project management systems assert the meaning of the project, project management, and project manager's work through PMP (PMBOK Guide; GAPPS 2020[6]; EIA-748D 2019[7]; ISO AS 4817:2019[8]).
- Leading project management software shows that all we do in project management is planning (Microsoft Project 2019[9]; Primavera/Oracle 2019[10]).

Besides, the substance of PMP raises new perspectives for project management system knowledge. It explains how PMP should be the first instrument for handling a massive collection of general project management system knowledge. For this purpose, the book consists of two virtual but complementary parts:

- The first part of the book covers the overview of current or prevailing forms of PMP. Although PMP has been in existence since 1962, it has never been disputed, superseded, or explained in an integrated form. While at the same time, most existing planning books reiterate network planning rules described in detail five decades ago (Woodgate 1968)[11]; none of the books show an application of feedback in PMP. The first part of the book simplifies the learning and application of PMP essential for students and project management trainees interested in understanding PMP. Within this part the reader learns details about the time, resource, cost, and performance parameters in PMP. I complete the first part of the book by presenting the best practices in PMP.
- The book's second part depends on the first part and covers the project management system logic of a general collection of project management system knowledge. This idea has been floating around for almost two

6 GAPPS 2020. *A Guide Framework for Leaderships in Complexity—Exposure Draft.* Sydney, Australia: Global Alliance for Project Performance Standards, September 2020. www.globalpmstandards.org.

7 EIA-748D-2019. *EIA-748D Earned Value Management Standard.* NDIA, January 2019

8 ISO/AS 4817 2019. *Earned Value Management in Project and Programme Management.* Sydney, Australia: Standards Australia, August 2019.

9 Microsoft Project. *Project Management Solutions.* Microsoft, 2019. http://microsoft.com/project.

10 Primavera P6 2019. *Project Portfolio Management.* Primavera / Oracle, 2019. http://www.oracle.com/primavera.

11 Woodgate, Samuel. *Planning by network: Project planning and control using network techniques,* 2nd Edition. London UK: Brandon System Press, 1968.

decades; however, only a small group of researchers have even heard of it. The book's second part simplifies the process of understanding and applying project management system knowledge essential for scholars and professionals interested in studying and improving project management system logic. The book's principal success is its presentation of new opportunities to study and use a massive collection of general project management system knowledge for practical purposes.

I conclude this journey with a series of questions and suggestions on project management's status and perspectives, including exciting ideas that can secure for project management a primary role in management planning science.

Before explaining the two complementary parts of the book, I would like to introduce the reader to seemingly unconnected but fundamental subjects for understanding PMP. The introductory subjects are as follows:

- Current PMP—summarizes the development and implementation of the project management plan.
- System knowledge in PMP—emphasizes the importance of a general collection of project management system knowledge to develop and implement project management plans.
- Details in PMP important for comprehensive development and implementation of the project management plan.
- The narrative communication method, which relates to modeling a problematic situation that few masters can produce; the problem model looks logical and straightforward, has high appeal, and keeps stakeholders well-informed about the problem and its solution.
- The structural communication method details a problematic situation that many professionals can produce; the problem model looks sophisticated and automatic, does not captivate, and stakeholders feel over-informed about the problem and its solution.

Let's look at the above subjects; it will help us distinguish between the facts that matter and those that do not when dealing with PMP and project management system knowledge.

Current PMP.

The current form of PMP has been a result of efforts that commenced seven decades ago when scientists and practitioners from different fields discovered the relationship in the classical theories and initiated the ongoing development of PMP. Scientific PMP is articulated through analysis, relationships, synthesis, and updating of PMP contents based especially on knowledge from the following sources:

- From Descartes' *Rules for the Direction of the Mind* published in 1629 to the *Work Breakdown Structure* method which we use today primarily for analyzing PMP content.
- From Euler's *The Seven Bridges of Konigsberg* published in 1735 to the Network Diagramming Methods we use today primarily for relating PMP content.
- From Maxwell's *On Governors* published in 1868 to the Management Feedback method we use today to update PMP content.

The above methods are central to the process of PMP. The process consists of two stages:

- Developing the project management plan by analyzing and estimating details of project contents, relating and sequencing details of project contents, aligning content details, approving content attributes, and setting up a baseline project plan.
- Implementing the project management plan by controlling project contents through assessing status, progress, changes, and forecast of the project plan, comparing what has been achieved with what should have been achieved at the moment through assessing, accepting, paying, securing, using, benefiting, and maintaining completed works, and the project plan.

The development of a project management plan starts when the project is formally authorized, along with the scope statement written in the form of objectives and deliverables for work on hardware, software, service, process, or information. It ends when the project management plan is approved and disseminated. The development of a project management plan consists of analyzing, relating, and synthesizing PMP contents.

In general, the development of a project management plan starts with a top-down analysis of PMP contents arbitrarily defined by a series of project phases, for example, sales, design, procurement, installation, commissioning, and handover. Each phase is broken down successively into more detailed contents, all the way to the level of discrete pieces of work defined by activities. When the content's structure reaches the most detailed level, the project's activity level, we can identify the project management plan's contents. It means that we can understand project management's contents as well as know its structure.

To complete the first phase of the top-down analysis, we break down project scope from project phases to project activities, using the Work Breakdown Structure (WBS) method and defining relationships among activities using the Critical Path Method (CPM) or similar network methods. The first phase of the project management plan's development is finalized by adding measurable attributes to project activities.

Then comes the bottom-up verification, a synthesis of PMP contents and contents' relationships to more abstract contents, the work packages, deliverables, project phases, and the project conclusion. The bottom-up synthesis uses both WBS and CPM and may change the initial assumptions about PMP contents. We may need to review PMP contents multiple times to identify all of the attributes of PMP contents.

The above methods, in addition to many supplementary methods, such as the assessment of requirements and conditions, quantity takeoff, estimation of time and resource, financing, safety planning, quality planning, risks analysis, procurement planning, benefits planning, or acceptance of project plan, are fundamental for the development of a project management plan.

Implementing the project management plan starts when the general project contract is signed, and work conditions for the client and performing organizations meet requirements. It ends when all project contracts are complete, warranties expire, and all books close. Implementation of a project management plan consists of continuous processes for managing and accomplishing PMP contents and updating and approving the most current version of project management plan.

In general, implementing a project management plan starts with executing project activities and ends when all project activities are concluded. The systematic and sequential management processes, known as feedback processes, the planning, executing, controlling, and back to planning, occur at project data date. We use the feedback processes to update the activities in progress on the data date and, as a result, update succeeding activities after the data date.

The feedback processes include the initiating and closing processes to update major activities or a group of activities from time to time. The update for activities builds a dynamic and integrated picture of project status, progress, changes, forecasts, and causes. It shows how project activities' results change the outcomes for higher project contents, including project phases. The implementation of the project management plan is accomplished using the Feedback Method (FM).

The FM, in addition to many supplementary methods during the update procedure, such as safety surveying, benefit measuring, quantity surveying, quality control, risk assessment, change controls, earned value management, payment request processing, or claims processing, is fundamental for the implementation of a project management plan.

The development and implementation of the project management plan have to be specific primarily in terms of providing support to the project manager. This part of the book belongs to Project Management First Order (PM-1). For this purpose, we must do the following:

- Define planning contents and understand what influences planning objectives by evaluating alternatives for attributes associated with the project management plan's components.
- Communicate planning contents to stakeholders and build trust in planning objectives by instructing each stakeholder to understand the project management plan's integrity and results.
- Motivate project stakeholders to accomplish the planning objectives by developing and maintaining incentive schemes consistent with the project management plan's accomplishments and trends.
- Control the dynamism of planning contents, process, and impact on planning objectives by updating and measuring status, progress, changes, and forecasts of the project management plan.
- Evaluate decision processes and actions to support planning objectives by cooperating with each stakeholder to assess contents, requirements, and responsibilities defined in the project management plan.

During the project management plan development and implementation, we must maintain interactive relationships with project business or strategic management that facilitates an integrated approach to project and organization objectives. In addition to the project objective, this helps achieve the organization's strategic objectives (Stretton 2019a)[12] that are managed outside the project (Stretton

12 Stretton, Alan. "Representing 'other strategic work' in addition to projects in an organizational strategic management context." *PM World Journal* Volume VIII, Issue I (January 2019a). www.pmworldtoday.com.

2019).[13]

System knowledge in PMP.

The theoretical and methodological integrity of PMP simplifies and unlocks new project management perspectives. For example, now, a collection of general project management system contents can be considered a project. It means that a project management system's contents can be analyzed, related, and updated to get system logic and use it for practical purposes.

The project management systems knowledge grows faster than the average user can absorb. But the real problem is that most project management plans are developed and implemented outside the available systems. Besides, in the past two decades, the collections of general project management system knowledge show extraordinary improvement; however, we still need to explain why such improvements are not seen in PMP practice.

The definition of system idea, in general, has been stable over the decades. Here are some views:

- A system is "all elements, including hardware, software facilities, personnel; an organized or complex whole, a group of interrelated activities, which that work together to accomplish results" (Cleland and Kerzner 1985, 245).[14]
- A system is "a set of interrelated elements, each of which is related directly or indirectly to every other element and no subset of which is unrelated to any other subset" (Ackoff and Emery 2008, 18).[15]
- A system is the "aggregation of the processes, tools, techniques, methodologies, resources, and procedures to manage a project" (PMI 2017, 716, 42–44).

13 Stretton, Alan. "A perspective on project success levels in an organizational strategic management context." *PM World Journal* Volume VIII, Issue II (February 2019). www.pmworldtoday.com.

14 Cleland, David, and Harold Kerzner. *A Project Management Dictionary of Terms.* New York, NY: Van Nostrand Reinhold Company, 1985.

15 Ackoff, Russel, and Fred Emery. *On Purposeful Systems: An Interdisciplinary Analysis of Individual and Social Behavior as a System of Purposeful Events.* New Brunswick, NJ: Transaction Publishers, 2008.

Consequently, project management system knowledge and its logic become essential for PMP. Here are some reasons for this vision.

- Each project management plan may start with the same phases; however, the phases' structure is different for each project and ends with different sets of activities and sequences that cannot be copied for use in other projects. Quite contrastingly, each project management system logic may have different areas of knowledge; however, the structure of the selected system knowledge areas is the same or similar for each project management system. Such structure ends with identical or interchangeable particles; hence, their sequence, or the system logic, can be copied and modified to improve various projects' contents and relationships. It is a great opportunity, but can we get there?
- Each system shows the contents of elements in each group and relationships between elements within a group and among groups. As we know, the project management plan must be based on the contents of activities in work packages and relationships of activities within a work package and among work packages. Analogically, project management system logic must be based on particles' contents in project management processes and relationships of particles within a process and among processes. Therefore, the symmetry between the project management plan and system logic creates credible conditions to use PMP and reveal the logic of project management system knowledge.

Before deciding about the systematic approach to PMP, we must select a recognized, well-structured project management system. It should address all relevant, known, and knowable subjects of project management system knowledge. Let's consider the system as a project and system particles as project activities. We look for methodological symmetry that controls or governs both the project management and the system management by their most detailed elements. In that case, we analyze, relate, and synthesize the system particles, as we do with project activities. This approach allows for arriving at definite knowledge of selected project management systems that reveal project management system logic. Such system logic can be methodically analyzed and modified in an outline to aid the development and implementation of a project management plan consistent with the selected project management system.

Therefore, project management system knowledge has to be specific in developing and implementing project management system logic. A carefully chosen project management system must have the potential for continuous and comprehensive updating of its contents. Consequently, it is the best choice for the development and implementation of applicable system logic. Whenever the project management system updates and improves its logic, the PMP outline improves. For this purpose, the system logic must get a complete explanation. This part of the book belongs to Project Management Second Order (PM-2). Here, we carry out the following:

- Display system logic in a relative time frame by revealing relationships and sequential positions of each particle of the project management system.
- Discuss the meaning of the system logic and detect and fix errors in system logic development caused by interruptions of relationships or inaccurate, unusual, or impossible sequences among system particles.
- Adopt and sense the system logic for specific requirements by revealing different conditions and requirements for system processes and, consequently, for the system's particles.
- Assign each particle of the system logic by codes for higher system knowledge levels and connect system logic to the company's system structure and external organizational entities.
- Apply system logic to improve planning objectives because the contents of system logic represent the generally accepted meaning of project management system knowledge.

Details in PMP.

I intended to explore the causes behind the lack of understanding about the project management system knowledge and its enormous potential by drawing an outline for developing and implementing the project management plan. For this purpose, we must reassess the flawed assumption that a detailed project management plan or system logic is a waste of time and won't pay back or may undermine the evolution of the whole project or a system.

In real life, we perform various elements of the work through operations of the technological process (definition, procurement, installation, usage, maintenance, dissolution) and manage work elements with operations of the management process (initiate, plan, execute, control, and closeout). Accordingly, each operation of the technological process passes through operations of management processes. If a single performer works on two or more work elements, then we must cut each work element into parts. Then, the corresponding relationships between parts of the work reveal the sequence in which the various parts of work elements are carried out. Regardless of our impression, a real project of any size certainly is performed through executing various work elements, where each work element defines an activity or part of an activity. Such an approach helps with creating reliable estimate and controlling, measuring, and accepting work elements that are part of the project management plan and contract. Otherwise, we cannot explain decisions about the status, progress, changes, forecasts, or causes for project components and the whole project.

Suppose there are more work elements open for processing. In that case, more performers can work simultaneously, which causes overlaps among work elements and intensifies interactions between technological and management attributes of work elements. The explanation of overlaps among project components, in general, comes from the understanding of development logic among work elements. The answer to interactions between technological processes and management processes comes from information exchange between performers and managers of work elements. The magnitude of overlaps and interactions among work elements automatically reflects the higher-level project components.

To endeavor toward "simplifying a system" by considering only its holistic levels while ignoring the system details is rather counterproductive. Imagine a biologist who thinks about whole living organisms and avoids talking about the DNA, or a structural engineer who studies the architecture and functionality of a bridge without using the concept of Finite Elements, or a project manager who considers a contract bid without analyzing the Schedule of Values items. For example, when management discusses the company's balance sheet, cash flows, and other items on the balance sheet, they use only a summary of data from cost accounting that presents most detailed transactions. It is not different for a project. When management discusses the status, progress, or forecasts of the company's project business, they ask cost accounting to summarize project costs based on the detailed schedule value items and their cost accounts and cost categories.

Still we handle project management system contents based on narratives or the structural method of human communication. Although the method may seem to support a common purpose, it is rarely accepted in that way.

Narrative Communication Method.

The narrative method can deliver a likable description of a hypothetical project management system model; however, the method alone is inadequate for explaining the project management plan or project management system logic.

The narrative approach shows the incomplete structure of system contents since the system structure components do not expand to the system particles' level. Unfinished structure causes the formation of circular loops and experimental parallel paths of system components. Consequently, the narrative system, in reality, may become complicated and provoke many questions. For example, how can assumptions of a narrative system be proven before facts arrive? What does the system logic look like? Can changes to system components change our perception of the system? Can we explain relationships, interactions, and overlaps between elements of the narrative system? Can we use system contents to improve a project management plan? Components of the narrative system relate to one another in many ways, and, when connected, they imply subjective, ambiguous, incomplete, and impractical system logic. Similar outcomes are apparent for the narrative view of the project management plan.

The problems connected with a narrative system can be much more profound in practice. A successful narrative approach to a project management plan cannot be repeated because each story has a unique project management form that cannot be copied for use in other projects (Muirhead and Simon 1999).[16] But it does not mean that research in narrative project management should slow down, regardless of whether it is possible to directly integrate and use its messages for project management plan or project management system logic. The value of the narrative method is essential in setting a framework for narrative databases and soft skills that are an undisputable side of PMP, including the following:

- Social environment—the economic, cultural, educational, behavioral, political, organizational factors (Parsons 2012, 1–15, 42–43, 46–57, 56–57, 71, 97–101, 126–132, 138–145)[17]
- Communication between participants and project owners that contributes to a broader consensus on project value (Chow and Leiringer 2020, 3, 24)[18]
- Social clusters, including organizational structures, project office and teams, stakeholders, educators, public, trainees, and others (Kerzner 2017, 89–108, 117–138, 317–334)[19]

16 Muirhead, Brian, and William Simon. *High Velocity Leadership: The Mars Pathfinder Approach to Faster, Bette, Cheaper.* New York, NY: HarperCollins Publishers, 1999.

17 Parsons, Talcott. *The social system.* New Orleans, LA: Quid Pro Books, 2012.

18 Chow, Vivien, and Roine Leiringer. "Public Engagement Events and the Management of External Stakeholders: Artifacts as Boundary Objects or Tools of Discipline and Control?" *Project Management Journal* (August 2020): https://journals.sagepub.com. 2020. www.pmi.org.

19 Kerzner, Harold. *Project management: A Systems Approach to Planning. Scheduling and Controlling,* 12th edition. Hoboken, NJ: John Wiley & Sons, 2017.

- Social and behavioral aspects of values in project studies tested by the subjectivity and plurality of stakeholders' values (Martinsuo 2020, 1, 23)[20]
- Social entities—the individuals, teams, and formal and informal groups (Dalcher 2018, 1–11)[21]
- Narrative capital derived from experience and added to accumulated knowledge reflecting an individual's way of living (Carlsen and Pitsis 2020)[22]
- The interactions between different narratives and how they remain contestable over time (Greene and Sergeeva 2019, Abstract)[23]
- Relationships between the amount of investment and related changes of social structure (Soderlund, Sankaran, and Biesenthal 2017, 1)[24]
- Project value types and strategic choices for the owner, project-based firm, and temporary project organization in the project (Zerjav 2021)[25]
- Management of qualitative data (McLaren and Loosemoro 2019, 979)[26]
- Soft skills needed to succeed in project business (Arumugam 2019, 9–12)[27]

20 Martinsuo, Miia. "The Management of Values in Project Business: Adjusting Beliefs to Transform Project Practice and Outcomes." *Project Management Journal* (June 3. 2020). https://journals.sagepub.com.

21 Dalcher, Darren. "The wisdom of teams revisited: Teamwork, teaming and working for the common good." *PM World Journal* Volume VII, Issue IX (September 2018): www.pmworldjournal.net.

22 Carlsen, Arne, and Tyrone Pitsis. "We are projects: Narrative Capital and Meaning Making in Projects." *Project Management Journal* (June 2020): Abstract. https://journals.sagepub.com.

23 Greene, Stuart, and Natalya Sergeeva. "Value creation in projects: Towards a narrative perspective." *International Journal of Project Management* Volume 37, Issue 5 (July 2019): 636-651. www.elsevier.com/locate/ijproman.

24 Soderlund, Jonas, and Shankar Sankaran, and Christopher Biesenthal. "The past and present of megaprojects." *Project Management Journal* Volume 48, Number 6 (2017): 5-16. www.pmi.org.

25 Zerjav, Vedran. "Why Do Business Organization Participate in Projects? Toward a Typology of Project Value Domains." *Project Management Journal* Volume 52 Issue 3 (April 2021): 287-297. www.pmi.org.

26 McLaren, Matthew, and Martin Loosemoro. "Swift trust formation in multinational disaster project management teams." *International Journal of Project Management* Volume 37, Issue 8 (November 2019): 979-988. www.elsevier.com/locate/ijproman.

27 Arumugam, Ramkumar. "Skills Every PM Needs in Managing a Millennial Workforce." *The Measurable News*, Issue 01 (2019): www.mycpm.org.

- Relationships between large-scale projects and their institutional fields (Hetemi, Marrewijk, Jerbrant, and Bosch-Rekveldt 2021)[28]
- Project narratives as the tool for promoting or resisting changes in organizational identity (Sergeeva and Winch 2021)[29]

While many scholars and practitioners acknowledge the above reality and show when and how to use the narrative method, the primary role of the structural approach for PMP and project management system logic is not in dispute.

Structural Communication Method.

The structural method is fundamental for comprehensive analysis, relationships, synthesis, and updating PMP and system contents. Forrester emphasizes that "structure is essential if we are to effectively interrelate and interpret our observations in any field of knowledge" (Forrester 1968, 1/2–1/3).[30] It follows that developing a structure, its components, and the relationships between components is crucial for understanding a project management plan and system logic.

For example, to develop a comprehensive structure of system contents, we must formulate the equivalent contents of knowledge for each level in the system structure. Levels of system structure could be the system, system functions, function processes, individual processes, and particles of each process. In all cases, we must ensure that each level in the system structure includes developing all steps necessary to achieve outcomes assumed in the preceding system level. The same contents of knowledge develop further to succeeding levels in more detail. When the system structure reaches the particle level of the system, regardless of how we organize the intermediate levels of system structure, it always ends with the same set of unique particles. Consequently, the following changes happen:

- Each particle from the set can relate in one way at the moment.
- A related set of unique particles reveals unique system logic.

28 Hetemi, Ermal, and Alfons van Marrewijk, and Anna Jerbrant, and Marian Bosch-Rekveldt. "The recursive interaction of institutional fields and managerial legitimation in large-scale projects." *International Journal of Project Management* Volume 39, Issue 3 (April 2021): 295–307. https://sciencedirect.com.

29 Sergeeva, Natalya, and Graham Winch. "Project Narratives That Potentially Perform and Change Future." *Project Management Journal* (March 2021): https://doi.org/10.1177/8756972821995340.

30 Forrester, Jay. *Principles of Systems*. Cambridge, MA: Productivity Press, 1968.

- System logic becomes an integrative object of project management system structure.

The above observations for the three editions of the PMBOK Guide show the path for further study. I realize that particles of each edition can relate in one way at the moment. When related, they reveal the unique and integrative system logic of a particular PMBOK Guide edition (Abdomerovic 2002).[31] Let's take a look at some of the details.

Why should the particles of a project management system be related in one way at the moment? Since each process output particle is unique and other process identifies it as an input required to develop a succeeding process, such a relational particle fills in the input needed for the subsequent process. Therefore, for a well-documented system, we rather reveal than construct the system relationships; in fact, unique particles' relationships evolve in one way and almost entirely without our intervention or direction. The idea is important. The well-structured system contents allow particles from different processes to disclose their ultimate relationships and combine and transform them into logical strings.

Why do particles of a project management system reveal unique system logic? The top-down analysis of contents and contents relationships always results in more simple and unique components. Each component is described by unique succeeding components, which exclude repeating components in a system's contents. Once the system contents reach the process level of system structure, each process relates to preceding and succeeding processes by one or more unique particles. Such unique and relational particles create a network of relationships for a project management system's given contents and show precisely how the system logic evolves. It follows that there are no alternative relationships between particles but only those relationships that form the unique system logic.

Why is system logic an integrative object of project management system structure? The higher levels of system logic result from the bottom-up synthesis of system particles and their relationships into higher components. Once the system logic gets synthesized at the process level by relational particles, each process is synthesized indirectly at a higher level, covering the whole system structure. Therefore, the network of relationships between system content's unique components is analyzed top-down, from the topmost to the lowest system structure, and synthesized bottom-up to encompass the whole system. So, the network

31 Abdomerovic, Muhamed. *Brainstorming The PMBOK® Guide 2000 Edition.* Louisville, KY: Project Management Publications, 2002.

of relationships stays integrated at each level and across all levels of the system structure.

We may acknowledge now that system particles relate in one way only at the time, which results in the unique and integrative system logic. We can then use this view of the general collection of project management system knowledge and improve the project management plan's contents.

The big picture of project management shows a mix of structural and narrative perspectives. However, when we look at some project management areas in more detail, the picture looks different. For example, PMP is overwhelmingly structural, with narrative thinking providing insight into why projects fail (Shore 2008).[32] Quite contrastingly, project governance is a traditional narrative area that adopts structural rationality by introducing risk-sharing capacity that provides the basis for assessing organizational, contractual, and financial opportunity and design of project governance (Chang 2015).[33]

The above sections help us think systematically, act logically, and bring seemingly unrelated perspectives into our experience. It shows the simplicity and practicality of structural communication and the valuable impact of narrative research to handle the ever-growing project management system knowledge. We will use the sections consistently and continuously through the book.

Development of Project Management Plan

PMP is primarily supported today by the best-practice systems. Such a system may depend on fragmented theoretical and methodological contents, characterized by the technology and size of the project and the user's understanding and experience. The best-practice system may also result from the planning processes of various project management knowledge bases or derivatives.

Disagreements about PMP usually come after steady requests for something "simple" and "flexible" to cope with "uncertainty" in PMP. But new theories usually fail to explain why most of the project's uncertainty is related to a poor understanding of PMP. In this respect, it would be best to recount the

32 Shore, Barry. "Systematic Biases and Culture in Project Failures." *Project Management Journal* Volume 39. Number 4 (December 2008): 5–16. www.pmi.org.

33 Chang, Chen-Yu. 2015. "Risk-beating capacity as a new dimension to the analysis of project governance." *International Journal of Project Management* Volume 33, Issue 6 (August 2015): 1195-1205. https://sciencedirect.com.

theoretical and methodological bases for developing and implementing the project management plan.

The PMP concept is being enthusiastically applied in major engineering and construction companies since the past 60 years. Many have disputed the concept in social science, information technology, and new and fast-growing industries. While current methodologies have not always been adequately presented and applied, which created many adversaries, new suggestions are challenging rhetoric that does not work well for developing and implementing the project management plan. Confusion and polarized viewpoints may look significant and meaningful. The successful application of PMP in its current form, including its application in information technology, is a reality (Fleming and Koppelman 2000, 141–143).[34] Some scholars call for a paradigm shift, the reconstruction and replacement of the concept, or trading its comprehensiveness for uncreative simplicity (Goldratt 1997, 113, 172, 231[35]; Hatfield 2013, 1–5[36]).

However, "to break the rules, you must first master them" (Audemar 2016, 11).[37] It means dealing with ideas presented in the section Basis for Project Management Planning; we must understand the theoretical and methodological foundations for the development and implementation of the project management plan. For this purpose, I will clarify on the following:

- Two frameworks which are in existence for centuries—the Technological Contents and Management Processes that define the project.
- Three principal, ever-evolving methods—the Work Breakdown Structure, Critical Path, and Feedback that help operate the frameworks.

Besides, there are many supplementary frameworks and methods, and most of them, except the Critical Path Method, have been earlier adopted in some form by general management.

Before we start developing the project management plan, we assume that major risks are cleared and that project feasibility study, scope statement,

34 Fleming, Quentin, and Joel Koppelman. *Earned Value Project Management*, Second Edition. Newton Square PA: Project Management Institute, 2000.

35 Goldratt, Eliyahu. *Critical Chain.* Great Barrington MA: The North River Press Publishing Corporation, 1997. www.northriverpress.com.

36 Hatfield, Michael. "The Coming Sea-Change in Project Management Science." *PM World Journal* Volume II, Issue I (January 2013); www.pmworldjournal.net.

37 Audemar, Piguet. The Economist. December 19th 2015 – January 1st 2016. Ad.

authorization, layout, bill of materials, tender documents, and master plan have been completed. We may also have answers to tender documents and drawings and, eventually, the quotes from potential contractors. These documents help understand the project and PMP contents.

Contents in Project Management Planning

We focus primarily on project's technological contents during PMP and less on functional governance, leadership, and responsibility to meet technological requirements.

The project's technological contents are different for each type of technology and are chosen based on how they fit with product development procedures. Technological contents remain scattered over a business structure and the sectors, divisions, or types of projects. Top-level technological contents may identify with a project phase (e.g., quotation, negotiation, contracting, design, production, installation, commissioning, warranty). The lowest level in technological content consists of steps and decision points arranged within a product flow chart that shows how project work is defined to achieve product objectives. The steps of a product flow chart forming part of a product development procedure may reproduce, modify, relate, revise, and transform the network diagram activities.

Project phases define the overall project contents and the link between the project management plan and the project business management plan. Phases mostly show a set of overlapping top-level components of the project. Some companies use the same term, phases, to display a set of subprojects or deliverables.

In a well-established project management organization, we may find standard phases that serve as a top management tool for project and business management. Such sets of phases may have a design according to the type of the project—for example, construction projects (Wideman 2004, 54),[38] industrial product development projects (Halbertsma 1972, 201–214),[39] software development projects (PMI 1996, 15–16),[40] reengineering projects (Champy 1995, 111–148)[41]—or

38 Wideman, Max. *A Management Framework for Project, Program and Portfolio Integration*. Vancouver, BC: Trafford Publishing (UK), 2004.

39 Halbertsma, K. *The Phased Development of New Industrial Products*. In: Project Management and Project Control. Frascati: ESRO 10th Summer School, 1972.

40 PMI 1996. *A Guide to the Project Management Body of Knowledge (PMBOK® Guide) 1996 Edition*. Newtown Square PA: Project Management Institute, 1996.

41 Champy, James. *Reengineering Management: The Mandate for new leadership*. New York, NY: HarperCollins Publishers. 1995.

other structures of the project. Yet, all those project phases related to different projects are substructures bounded by higher-level general phases in the project management organization (PMI 2013, 39[42]; Arcidiacono 2014, 1[43]).

We can divide the general phases into three parts: project preparation, project development, and project follow-up:

- The preparation phase assesses the political, cultural, organizational, financial, environmental, and regulatory conditions for developing sustainable projects and project business objectives. The objectives of the preparation phase are accomplished mainly by the feasibility study, which indicates whether to continue with the project. The preparation phase may include activities such as preliminary analysis, conception, and feasibility study.
- The development phase defines the requirements of project business management and transform project management contents into reality. It starts after deciding to continue with the project and ends after the project is handed over to the client. It is accomplished by the development process and the implementation of the project management plan. It may include negotiation, design, procurement, commissioning, and handover phases.
- The follow-up phase comprises continuous operation, maintenance, and development of project and project stakeholders' long-term objectives. It starts after the project is transferred to the client and may last all the way up to transforming the project into another business opportunity. The follow-up phase may also include usage, benefits, and dissolution phases.

An important cohesive factor between project phases and general phases is the strategic organizational management that starts from the front end of the preparation phase and ends with the completion of the development phase. But it does not stop there. The general project phase, and thus the project phase, may expand during the follow-up phase to include internal and external broader strategic support services for the customer (Stretton 2020).[44]

42 PMI 2013. *A Guide to the Project Management Body of Knowledge (PMBOK® Guide) Fifth Edition.* Newtown Square PA: Project Management Institute, 2013.
43 Arcidiacono, Giuseppe. 2014. "Use of Project Cycle Management in Project Selection Process: Evaluation of European Commission approach." *PM World Journal* Volume III, Issue III (March. 2014): www.pmworldjournal.net.
44 Stretton, Alan. "Expanding from conventional project management into broader types of services in an organizational strategic management context." *PM World Journal* Volume IX, Issue VII (July 2020). www.pmworldtoday.com.

There are other strategic considerations to extend the traditional developmental phase of the project to the other phases in the project. By understanding the benefits and natural meaning of project phases and their transformative perspectives, we may find that the project phases do not end with project development but encompass contents from the start of the project to the concluding phase where the operation and values of the project are transferred to the client (Dalcher 2019).[45]

Some researchers build on existing knowledge and attempt to define what project strategy is as well as the project strategy's constructs. They call for changes in traditional strategic project management based not only on managing the project's scope, time, cost, and quality constraints but also on assuming the responsibility for project business results and consequences. This includes three major components—the perspective that clarifies project business rationale and objectives, the position that clarifies technical and functional requirements, and the plan that clarifies how to manage and accomplish the project (Patankul and Shenhar, 2012).[46]

The project team should supply top management with simple, reliable, and sufficient information at any time and for any project component. A comprehensive report on project phases is usually the most critical and exclusive document for the company's managers at the highest level of the management hierarchy (Figure 4.2). For this purpose, we must provide and continuously update an integrated and real-time picture depicting the status on the various attributes of the project phases.

The number of project phases depends on project type and the ability of project managers to understand common project business phases. In dislocated projects with drawbacks such as limited time frame and resources, the project management team must first determine which phases of the project can be distinguished and developed. What portion of each phase of the project can be accomplished within a specific time frame? What are the resources needed and when and where can such resources be most efficiently employed?

45 Dalcher, Darren. "Moving beyond project delivery: Reflecting on the life cycle concept as way for organizing project work." *PM World Journal* Volume VIII, Issue I (January 2019): www.pmworldjournal.net.

46 Patankul, Peerasit, and Aaron Shenhar. "What Project Strategy Really Is: The Fundamental Building Block in Strategic Project Management." *Project Management Journal* Volume 43, Number 1 (February 2012): 4-20. www.pmi.org.

We may need to work simultaneously with several sets of project, program, or portfolio phases in the coming years, including in the following scenarios:

- The permanent operational phases of the organization—sales, design, procurement, installation, commissioning, and handover
- The success and benefit realization phases—identification of benefits and delivering client requirements during different phases, such as project development, usage, and dissolution
- Short-term agile phases
- Virtual phases—include product design, production, distribution, maintenance, and dissolution
- Environment phases—market, political, social, financial, and regulatory environments
- Any other phases that help to successfully connect project attributes to the company structure

Managing of above complex phases facilitates reflects and entails effective orientation of project phases to the organizational structure and thus allows for adopting a comprehensive structural approach to PMP.

Terminology.

Each project contains specifications of work and product development that remain scattered throughout the project business structures and are included in the various project stages, periods, or phases. For example, a "Project Design" phase may consist of work products from several design departments of the performing company and its subcontractors.

The project phases define what technological and management work we should complete and who should be involved in each phase. Project phases can be arranged in linear or circular ways, depending on the intensity of feedback received about work conducted during the preceding phases of the project. The lineal model starts at the left and proceeds gradually to the right until the project is handed over to the customer, and the circular model runs clockwise.

Project phases are collectively known as the project lifecycle (PMI 1996, 11; PMI 2017, 19), project lifespan (Wideman 2004, 27–31, 49–71), project lifecycle phases (Archibald 2004, 1),[47] project life stages/cycle (Wearne 1973, 10–

47 Archibald, Russell. "Part 2 Project Life Cycle Models." *Max's Project Management*

16),[48] or project cycle management (Arcidiacono 2014).

The term project "lifespan" better describes the temporary nature of a project where project phases are considered short-term contractual opportunities and the design, build, and handover of the project, or a phase, or a contract to the customer (Wideman 2004, 27–31, 49–52). This model presents project management phases in linear form. The term project "lifecycle" better describes the project's sustainable nature. Here, the project phases reflect a long-term business opportunity, to initiate, design, procure, construct, install, commission, operate, maintain, and dissolve the customer's project (Wearne 1973, 10–16). This book uses the terms "phase" or "phases," regardless of how they are arranged in the model.

Characteristics.

The lineal and cyclic phases must include some comments received during the preceding phases in order to better use the future model. For example, PMI uses a linear model to describe four main phases—starting the project, organizing and preparing the project, carrying out the project work, and closing the project. This approach may encompass a set of general phases and provide a base for developing the future phases of the project (PMI 2013, 39). European Commission uses a cyclic model to describe five general phases: the programming, identification, formulation, implementation, and evaluation of a project. The approach aligns countries' needs and donors' expectations to improve project selection and results (Arcidiacono 2014, 3). The model, number, and definition of project phases bring up the following considerations:

- How do project phases show the functional management structures?
- How do functional managers understand project business structure and project requirements?

As project phases present the communication link between project management and project business or strategic management, we must understand:

- How do project phases show the objectives of project business or strategic management?

Wisdom, Guest Article, (2004): www.maxwideman.com.

48 Wearne, Stephen. *Principles of Engineering Organization.* London, UK: Edward Arnold Publishers, 1973.

- How are project phases supported by project business or strategic management?
- How is the decision process of project business or strategic management integrated into the project structure?
- How do we plan, manage, and update the phases and the intervals between phases?

Overlaps among Phases.

We view project phases as a sequence of stages during the development of project management plan; however, the project phases overlap during the implementation of the project management plan. For example, any project phase can be finished substantially before the next phase starts; however, the remaining work can still continue across several consecutive phases.

There are many debates about studying the overlaps by using a narrative form; however, few can use narrations in practice. A narrative explanation of overlaps among the different phases of a project can lead to disagreements in many ways. Sometimes, we call it a "flexible," "simplified" approach to overlaps among project phases, which does not explain the ambiguity in narratives. Besides, narrative views are mostly associated with derivative methods that pay no attention to project phases. Let's discuss the schematics of conventional and agile approaches for project phases, where the following happens:

- The "conventional" approach, illustrated in Figure 1.1, always assumes the whole project, the structure of its phases, and dynamic overlaps among its phases.
- The "Agile" approach, illustrated in Figure 1.2, carries only a short-term investment, the structure within the short-term investment phase, and the steady sequence of events between the current and upcoming short-term investment phases.

From the upper part of Figure 1.1, we can see the plan related to the project phases. This arrangement of project phases and the distribution of resources pass through the verification process to confirm the final model of the plan. Although some authors argue that concluding one phase means permission to start the next, we do need to consider that project phases do overlap during the implementation of the project management plan.

The consumption of time and resources during overlaps among project phases, whose causes may vary, cannot be defined at the beginning of the project.

We need to know the actual status and progress of time and resource consumption for project phases in progress as well as the time and resources forecasts in order to measure the scope for progress in the upcoming project phases. Other goals, such as maintaining a robust project information system and keeping project and project business dynamism under control, are a part of routine work. The basic assumption here is that in this way we will know what causes the overlaps between project phases.

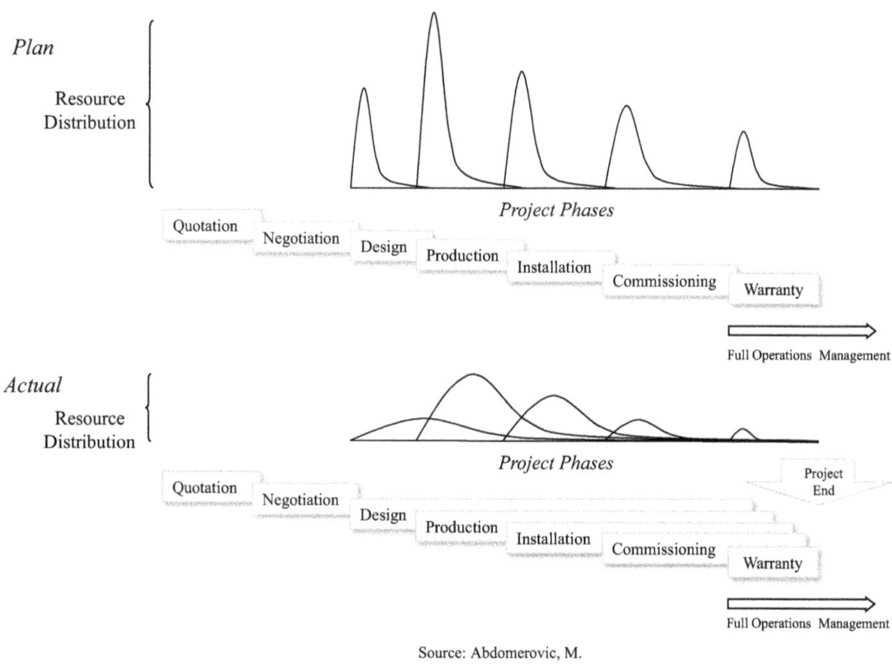

Figure 1.1: Project Phases—Conventional

From the lower part of Figure 1.1, we can see the actual arrangement of the project phases. The arrangement of project phases, related overlaps, as well as resource distribution acquires a firm shape during project implementation. The dynamics of project and project business which we observe at different project phases arise from the dynamics that emerge during project activities. Knowing this, we can control the source of overlapping among project phases and act early enough to ensure substantial accomplishment of phases as required and gradually finish the remaining works of phases and projects on time.

From Figure 1.1, we can see that the overwhelming proportion of work in each phase gets accomplished during its original duration. However, there will always be some outstanding work in each phase that lingers on even at the time the project approaches its end, and exceptional outcomes of succeeding phases follow the pattern. We can observe similar cases at any time, in any phase, and for any project. When the above schematic expresses time and cost metrics, then the relations and overlaps among the project phases are quantified and show the measurable form of the status, progress, and forecast for project and project business.

There are projects where the project management team focuses on the current, short-term investment, or short-term subproject.

From the upper part of Figure 1.2, we can see that the project management plan's development and implementation lose their meaning in an "Agile" environment. The agile practice manages short-term requirements, the concept which stayed real in the past, stays real today, and will stay real in the future.

The "Agile" view of upcoming project events differs sharply from the conventional system view; in a situation where the whole system is unknown or not needed at a time, some parts of the system can serve as a basis for a rapid development and then we talk about the agile environment. Consequently, "Agile" does not contain data essential for understanding the project or the project business in future; it cannot forecast the development of upcoming short-term investment phases and overlaps among phases. In such cases, the project scope's outstanding part is also unknown and has to be compiled incrementally and attached to the upcoming short-term requirements. Since the project's end is indefinite, the project transforms into a sequence of short-term needs and continuous development.

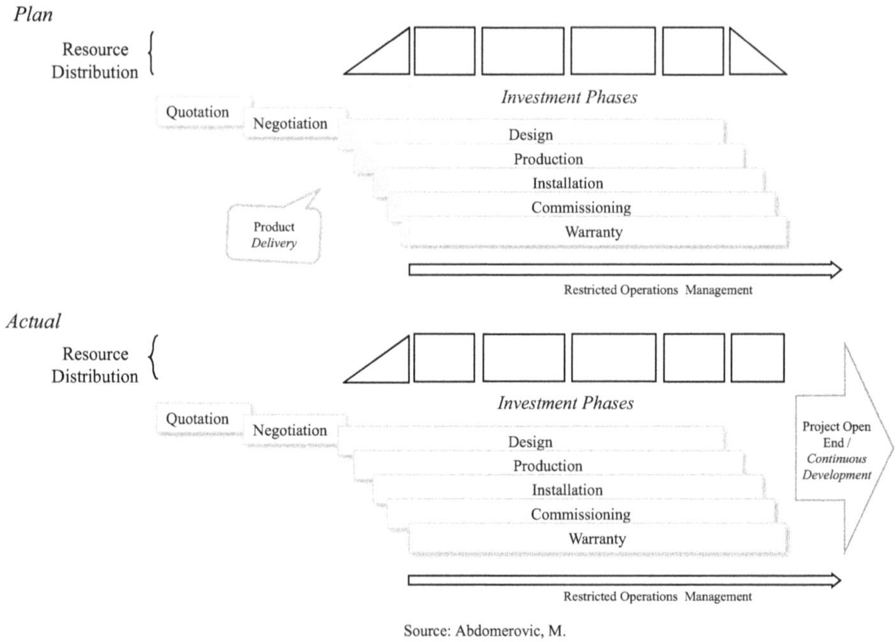

Figure 1.2: Project Phases—Agile

From the lower part of Figure 1.2, we can see the project phases' actual arrangement. As the project scope for upcoming investment phases is unknown, vital project parameters such as time and cost are indefinite.

Accordingly, understanding the outstanding work, time and resource consumption, and overlaps among the agile project phases becomes meaningless; the Agile project management system changes into assessing short-term development and associated "level of efforts." We can come to a simple conclusion that "Agile" has a short-term plan for technological steps within the current investment phase, for which the development time is 4–6 weeks. Therefore, agile investment phases are a set of short-term, sequentially related subprojects. Each subproject passes through the analysis, relationships, synthesis, and updating of its contents. Although we know that long-term investors do better than short-term investors, agile promoters still have sufficient arguments in their favor to keep their experiments floating.

The above approaches and understanding of project contents and communicating overlaps among project phases or other components of a project contents are not generally applied. If the decision for outstanding work of a project comes from the top management level and lacks a detailed structure, then verification of the decision is impossible. Simply because the real damage for scope, time, and cost appears first at the activity level and does not get attention from the upper management until such time when correcting the wrong decisions becomes expensive; let's discuss further.

The project management plan is gradually developed from project phases to discrete pieces of project work defined by activities and then gets updated as the project progresses. By understanding the function of details and how all build up from the elements, we can synthesize the contents and get a comprehensive view of any structural construct in the project, including the agile investment phases. We realize that a unique set of updated activities build a realistic and integrated picture of the project plan and make known the overlaps between components at any level of any project, program, or project business structure. The process can include overlaps between projects, works, organizations, contracts, agreements, processes, phases, deliverables, stages, or any other structural breakdown immanent in project, program, or project business management. Finally, the overlaps among higher elements of the project management structure may have an impact only on the ideas or concepts proposed in the project management plan. Nevertheless, overlaps can be verified by status, progress, changes, and forecasts of project activities.

The same logic applies to the project management system; if we need to know how project management processes or process groups overlap, we must understand the most detailed and relational elements of the system's contents.

In all cases, we must understand a unique set of activities or particles that define the contents and contents' interrelationships that consequently explain the overlaps among components of a project or system and, in turn, the causes behind the "problem" of overlaps simply evaporate.

Processes in Project Management Planning

During PMP, we focus primarily on project management processes and less on project management governance, leadership, and responsibility to manage project management requirements.

Project management processes are mostly the same for most technologies and are associated with project management procedures (initiating, planning, executing, controlling, and closing). Project management's central processes (planning, executing, controlling, and back to planning) are performed at the activity level and update activity attributes at the start of the project, and closing processes are used periodically to start or close different groups of activities. The results of this management procedure reflect on all business structures, sectors, companies, divisions, and different types of projects, programs, or portfolios, depending on the company's project business structure.

Terminology.

There are different terms used to define project management process groups and their content:

- Project control cycle (plan, monitor/report, analyze, redirect/control, modify plan; Wideman 2004, 138)
- Management lifecycle (planning, organizing, implementing, controlling; Turner 2006, 94)[49]
- Central process groups (planning, executing, controlling; PMI 2000, 30),[50] and other terms

The above terms and their contents describe the feedback part of the project management processes which continuously happens during the implementation of the project management plan. Actually, "the same cycle is repeated over and over throughout the project life span" (Wideman 2004, 27, 137).

The project management processes are consistently used to control changes at the activity level and, consequently, to control changes at any higher level of the project or project business. I understand those project management process groups and their contents as the project management feedback.

Characteristics.

During the PMP, both the technology management and project management act seemingly independently. Although technology and project management may have a flexible form without rigid links, a comprehensive approach to PMP ensures a strong connection. But what is the thing that connects technology management and project management?

Technology management and project management are different in several key activities. Technology management is based on specific technical knowledge and

49 Turner, Rodney. "Towards a theory of project management: The nature of the project governance and project management." *International Journal of Project Management* Volume 24 (2006): 93–95. www.elsevier.com/locate/ijproman.

50 PMI 2000. *A Guide to the Project Management Body of Knowledge (PMBOK® Guide) 2000 Edition.* Newtown Square PA: Project Management Institute, 2000.

understanding of project's technical requirements, operations, and flowcharts. The technology manager is a leader primarily responsible for the specification and relationships of activities within technological content and accomplishing specialized work. Project management has a base in project management knowledge and understanding of project management requirements, contents, and processes. The project manager is the administrator responsible for developing and implementing the project management plan and related management works. For example, an activity titled "Foundation design" must include references for technological and management attributes:

- The design manager has to ensure that based on the "foundation design" technological attributes are defined and implemented according to the technical requirements, specifications, contracts, and conditions of the project.
- The project manager must ensure that the project management attributes for the "foundation design" are defined and implemented according to project management requirements, specifications, contracts, and conditions.

It looks like activity attributes divided the responsibilities into technology management and project management.

Interactions between Processes.

Analysis of technology management processes help us understand what level of control we should implement for a specific technology. It may start with a revision of activities' specifications because contractors of different products may organize their activities at different levels of details. For example, architectural design activities and construction work are usually managed by various contractors who operate at unpredictable levels of control, which complicates the relationship between design and construction work.

Analysis of project management processes helps us understand what level of control we should implement for project management. We must specify management requirements and project management processes, activities, and management attributes for each activity. This may entail a revision of the specification of activities since contractors of different products may plan their work at different levels of detail and understanding. For example, the sources of cost plan and actual cost may be organized at different levels and by various organization units, complicating the comparison between the cost planned for and the actual cost incurred.

As soon as the project plan gets approval, and the contract is signed, the implementation of the project plan starts, and the project management feedback takes the center stage. In uninterrupted project management feedback cycle (planning, executing, controlling, and back to planning), the project activities which represent the most detailed view of technology in the project are updated. This triggers automatic updates of technological aspects at various levels, including during the project phases.

To understand how technology management and project management interact, let's look at two figures that show some interactions between technology management and project management (Figures 1.3 and 1.4).

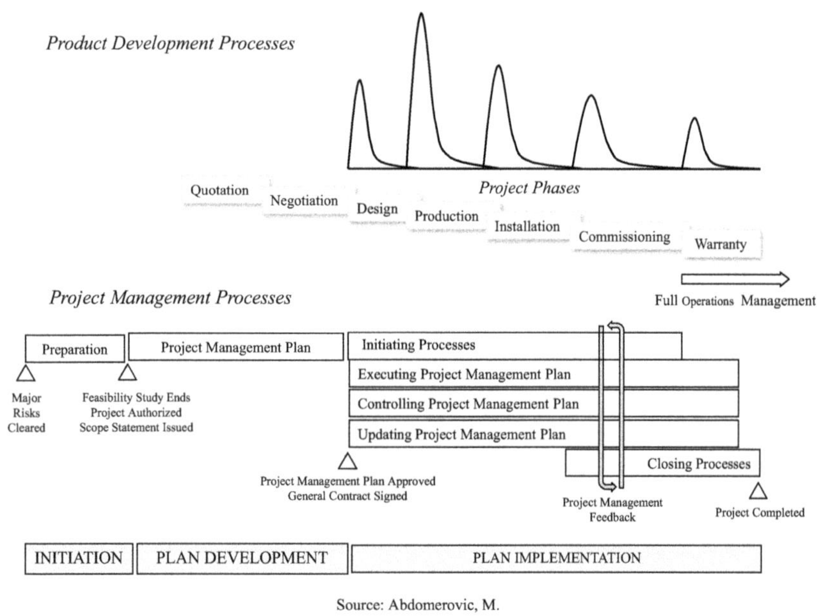

Figure 1.3: Processes in Project Management

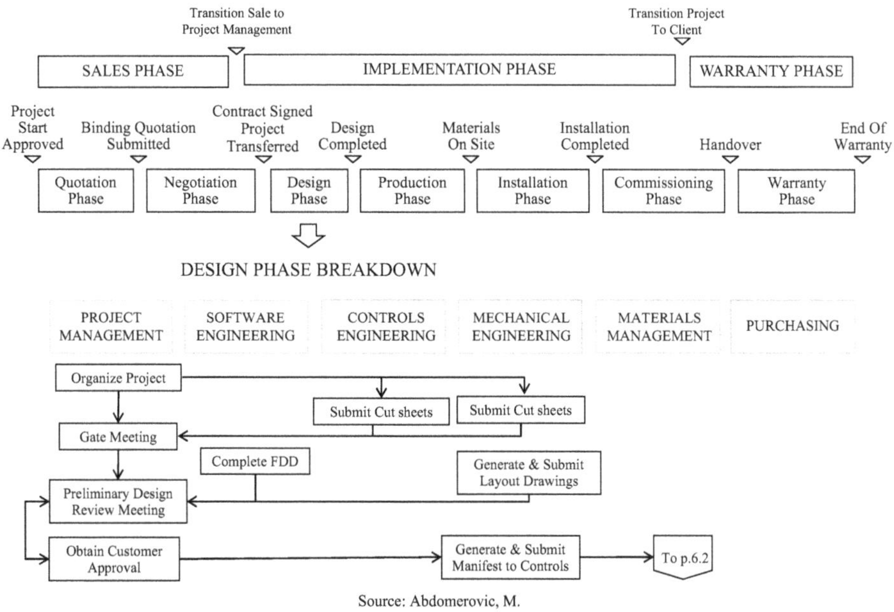

Figure 1.4: Relationships among Project Processes

Figure 1.3 shows a general model of relationships between project phases (technological processes) and project management feedback (project management processes). We can realize that each operation of the technological process—a discrete piece of project phase defined by activity or its part—passes through a series of operations of management processes.

Figure 1.4 shows specific relationships between project management and technology management. Project management and technology management processes are compiled here from a practice-oriented model.

The upper part of Figure 1.4 shows all project phases. The gates between the phases determine when a substantial accomplishment of the phase can transit to the next phase. The bottom part of Figure 1.4 shows only the “Design” process (software engineering, controls engineering, etc.) and the “Project management” process. The technology and management processes are in active collaboration to provide documentation for the production/purchase of material. On the first page of the “Design” phase of this multi-page model, we can see the excerpt of interactions between management activities and technological activities. We can also see how participants exchange information and interact during this continuous checking and decision-making process between the customer, project manager, suppliers, and designers. In all instances of this development, the participants focus on the source of information, a specific activity, and activity attributes.

We may now recap the interactions between technology management and project management. If we look at the problem holistically during the project phases, we will realize the difficulty is real because we speak about different contents, technological processes, and management processes. However, suppose we look at the problem details, which arise from the project activities. In that case, the problem exits the purview of technology management and project management and moves down to the technological and management aspects of a specific activity. When we reach the relevant point that allows for a comprehensive definition of the project work, we encounter the activities carried out to incorporate technological and management attributes. It causes the "problem" of interaction between technological processes and management processes to transform itself into responsibilities for technological and management attributes of the activity.

Structures in Project Management Planning

The work breakdown structure (WBS) has roots in the theory of reductionism (Descartes, *the Rules for the Direction of the Mind*, 1629, cited in Descartes 1952).[51] The WBS is a widely applied method for understanding project contents by orienting its predictable meaning to the most simple and clearly defined activities (DOD and NASA Guide 1962, Chapter II)[52]; Fleming 1988, 78–91[53]; PMI 1996, 171). Work breakdown structure, regardless of its organization, the number of series, and levels within a series of analyzed knowledge, ends with a unique base of the most detailed facts described by project activities and activity attributes.

The first step in structuring the PMP contents is distributing high-level attributes to identified project phases. By structuring project phases and related attributes in more detail, we further simplify PMP. Although this process starts by defining end items that can function as relatively independent units, that is, the project phases, the process continues to the most detailed components of project

51 Descartes, Rene. *Rules for the Direction of the Mind.* In: Hutchins, Robert, Editor in chief, Great Books of the Western World, Volume 31. Chicago, IL: Encyclopedia Britannica, 1952.

52 DOD and NASA Guide. *PERT COST: Systems Design.* Office of the Secretary of Defense and National Aeronautics and Space Administration. 1962.

53 Fleming, Quentin. *Cost/Schedule Control Systems Criteria: The Management Guide to C/SCSC.* Chicago, IL: Probus Publishing Company, 1988.

attributes in the project activities identified. This analysis of project contents is known as the work breakdown structure (WBS). At the very beginning, the process starts with the structuring of the project scope. Other attributes are systematically estimated for each activity and used in the next stage of PMP.

The first significant and applicable description for structuring the contents of a problem comes from Descartes' reductionism. Using his method for discovering truth in the science, known as the *Rules for the Direction of the Mind*, published in 1629, we can recognize a part of the general approach to developing a management plan (Descartes 1952, x, 1–40). The reason we think about top-down analysis of a project's contents today is mostly similar to the reason behind why Descartes had chosen such an approach (Descartes 1952, 7, Rule V).

In the top-down or deductive process, we rationally analyze an object, a project phase, to find out its basic components and then, step by step, reach those objects that are simple and clearly understood, that is, the project activities. In the deductive process, we move from the whole problem down to its most minute details by differentiating as many objects as possible and establishing their levels and relationships. Therefore, in this process, an object is revealed and related top-down, within a definite series, from a project phase to project activities.

In the bottom-up or intuitive process, we naturally synthesize an object to find out its higher component and continuously, passing from one level to another, reach the top object of the system. In the inductive process, we establish order and move from the simplest facts of the problem, the project activities, to its whole, the project phase, by tallying all of the differentiated intermediate objects. Therefore, objects are enumerated bottom-up within the definite series by its more detailed objects and established levels in this process.

Descartes was the first who understood that analysis of relationships between objects, the components, must be developed to the most detailed level of the problem, that is, to the level of facts. His "tree," which illustrates genealogical relations (Descartes 1952, 32), is one of the figures that Descartes used to present a part of his concept. Descartes' tree consists of objects and relations between objects, which evolve during the deduction process, "continuous and nowhere interrupted" (Rule VII), "in the series" (Rule VIII), moving from the recognized problem to reach its simplest account. His rules show how facts and their relationship to another which already has a definite magnitude can determine a material body possessing the figure of a resolved problem (Descartes 1952, 35). Descartes' approach to the synthesis of the problem is intuitive. Besides the "tree" developed during problem analysis, he uses the facts "to reflect their relations to one another" (Descartes 1952, 17) and then, by intuitive reasoning, climbs back up on the same tree and synthesizes the upper object.

From Reductionism to Breakdown Structure Method.

The "tree" model, which displays parenthood relationships, was later developed as a case of the tree graph, known as the arborescence graph (Berge 2001, 13, 152–164).[54] Arborescence graph is generally used as a Lead Time Chart (LTC), a technique commonly used in the job shop or when introducing new products into the factory (Santora 1963, 734–736)[55] or when processing an order and performing the manufacturing operations (Link 1963, 748–752).[56] The arborescence graph has also been developed to make it an essential management tool known as the Work Breakdown Structure (WBS).

In Figure 1.5 the heavy line shows the hierarchy of project contents in the form of "genealogical relations" for the single, horizontal, high-level component of the project work. The basic rule is to have more than one component at each level except the first level, that is, the project level. The WBS emerges from top-level components, followed by project deliverables, phases for each deliverable, contracts for each phase, and more work packages for each contract. The deduction process doesn't stop after reaching the level of work packages; next, we define each work package in schedule values, items, or activities. At this level of the project structure, we deal with the details and, in turn, with the recognizable components of the contract or agreement.

Each of the most detailed WBS elements, which is usually a work package, must have unique identification; defined scope of work for activities; attributes for each activity, including resources or cost of the resources or factored value as a part of the total project value; start date, data date, and end date; cost accounting; and specific responsibilities for accomplishment of activities in the work package. If we cannot identify work at the most detailed WBS level, we cannot determine which work activities and project contents to include in the project scope.

Therefore, WBS means breaking down unique project contents into more detailed unique components in order to orient them to the definition of the work that we intend to plan and accomplish. If a breakdown structure relates to a

54 Berge, Claude. *The Theory of Graphs.* Mineola, NY: Dover Publications, 2001.

55 Santora, A. V. *The Encyclopedia of Management*, Edited by Carl Heyel. New York: Reinhold Publishing Corporation, 1963, 732–739.

56 Link, Philip. *The Encyclopedia of Management*, Edited by Carl Heyel. New York, NY: Reinhold Publishing Corporation1, 1963, 748–752.

specific component, for example, work, contracts, organization, costs, stakeholders, or another component, we call it the work breakdown structure, contract breakdown structure, organizational breakdown structure, cost breakdown structure, and so on.

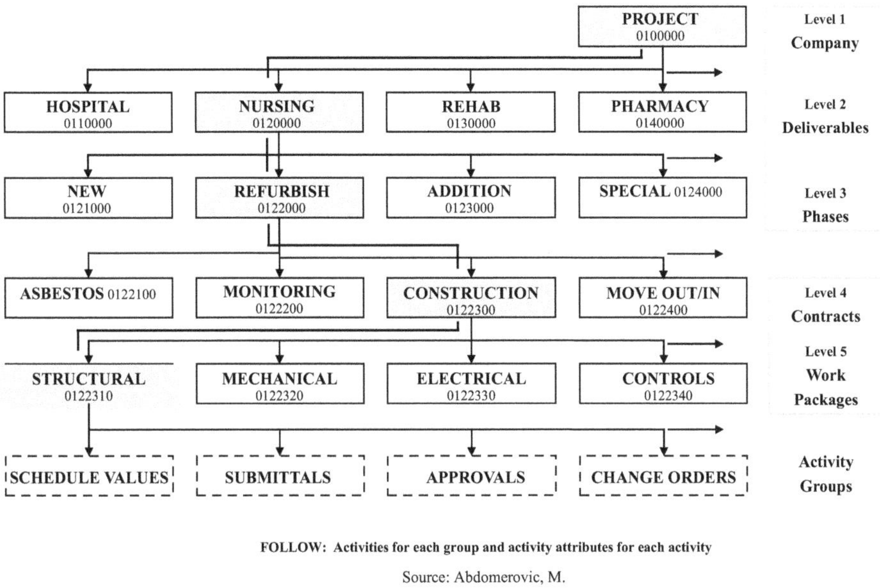

Figure 1.5: Work Breakdown Structure

Characteristics.

The work breakdown structure development does not start from the scratch; it comes after data collection and analysis of the following PMP documents:

- Scope statement for work and its objectives and deliverables
- Specification of project phases and works for each project phase
- Drawings and technical specifications for identified works
- Contractual conditions and guidelines for identified works
- Stakeholders' objectives and other documents related to project works

Many project phases and deliverables within contracts can vary depending on the project type, project condition, management requirements, and available information. In all cases, we can gradually develop the total project contents through intermediate levels to the most detailed work breakdown structure, that is, the work package level. Each work package is identified later by one activity and one cost account at a minimum. When the work breakdown structure of PMP contents is complete, the sum of activity attributes equals the total of a higher-level component's attributes. To get the total of a higher-level component's attributes, we must define the following:

- The activity attributes we want to summarize
- Unique relationships and codes for each activity and its attributes
- A responsible person capable of coordinating technological and management attributes for a set of activities

The use of a work breakdown structure is a universal tool for almost all areas of project management. It helps to accomplish the following tasks:

- Define management and technical objectives for project and project business
- Define management and technical objectives for PMP
- Develop project contents for various levels, from program and project phases to project activities
- Develop project code structure and assign codes to activities
- Estimate, contract, control, assess, update, and accept work defined by project activities
- Summarize activity data to higher structural levels of project and project business
- Manage integrated reporting from the lowest level of project activities to the project business level

The work breakdown structure shows how we organize project work. It can be achieved in many ways depending on the management's needs and how they see the project work structure. Here are some practical instructions to manage work breakdown structure:

- Work breakdown structure must be developed jointly by project team members, project stakeholders, and external consultants. They define the entire project scope as a base for other project structures, such as project organization, estimating, responsibility, accounting, contracting, and reporting.

- At the very beginning, we can start by developing a global, high-level structure, which can be developed in more detail as data become available. Work breakdown structure should comprise two levels to a maximum of nine levels and from two components to a maximum of nine components for each level.
- The development of the work breakdown structure may start from the project business phase. We have to show how work is instructed, including, for example, the internal work of a project-performing company. Project structure can be of various kinds. For example, project work can appear as project deliverables within each project phase, as work packages within each deliverable, and as schedule values, items, or activities within each work package.
- Work breakdown structure should be oriented to project works. The structure must show how the customer will manage the project (upper part of the structure, for example, project phases) and how the contractor will accomplish works (lower part of the structure, for example, work packages). Upper levels of the structure relate to the company's integrated project business units, whereas the lower levels relate to the project's specific functional contents and contracts.
- Part of the work breakdown structure developed by contractors usually shows work packages and related schedule value items. The activities should specify clear guidelines on how specific work packages should be contracted, accomplished, and paid. It follows that individual activities are already aligned to the total work envisaged for the project.
- Work packages must be proportional to the weight factor for the project's total scope and control requirements. For example, if project phases are the basis for developing a work breakdown structure, the conceptual project phase can contain five work packages; in comparison, the project design phase can have up to 30 work packages.
- The work package's volume and complexity must be understood, planned, and controlled by an individual. Also, the work package cannot be so small that higher-level management ignores its impact on the project.
- During the development of project management plan, the work package activities have to be shown in the project network diagram and be loaded with the direct cost for the work planned.
- Each activity that has a cost and related cost account must have a single responsibility for the cost. Each responsibility for the cost of activities must

be part of the control account management plan to allow performance measurements for activity and higher-level components.

- For most projects, a single cost account should be sufficient for a group of activities rather than for each work package's activity. Each activity usually includes many attributes that enable flexible estimating, tracking, selecting, sorting, grouping, and reporting.
- Work package should contain one cost account at least and one or more cost account categories that show the base classification for cost, material, labor, expenses, and subcontracts.

The arborescence graph has also been developed over time to become a vital management tool that is known as the Organizational Breakdown Structure (OBS). We use today's deductive process to develop the organizational breakdown structure and organize people for PMP. Here are some practical instructions to manage the organizational breakdown structure:

- Organizational breakdown structure is usually functionally oriented, but it can be matrix of functions as well. It helps to manage the performance in relation to the work contracted out for the project and in other processes such as internal procurement in the work breakdown structure.
- Organizational breakdown structure shows the hierarchy of project-performing organizations, or general contractors, from the organization's top management to its functional units responsible for the execution of specific activities. It starts from the top-level component to the more detailed components, such as departments, project teams for each department, and responsibilities for members within each project team.
- The lowest level of the organizational breakdown structure defines immediate responsibility for elements of the authorized work specified in the project's work breakdown structure. It means that defined responsibility relates to one or more cost accounts assigned for works forming part of the project activities specified in the work breakdown structure.
- The organizational breakdown structure helps at some point to assess the project organization's indirect costs—the costs not specific to any single activity of the defined project work. Those costs are planned, authorized, accrued, and controlled by the organization's procedures for project business. Indirect costs for a specific project are assigned at the organizational breakdown structure's appropriate management level and shown at corresponding hammock activities of the project management plan.

- Organizational breakdown structure shows the responsibilities for planning, controlling, and accomplishing the defined project work, and cost account code ties in the WBS and OBS structures, or work and people.

WBS and OBS development is a delicate effort and affects all PMP work that follows. Also, it is crucial to develop other project structures and make relationships among different structures. We can also develop a single breakdown structure and all other structures, including complex inter-organizational structures (Whyte and Davies 2021)[57] or multiple governance units of program organizations (Frederiksen, Gottlieb, Leiringer)[58] considered as virtual. In that case, the base structure must incorporate the level of details that can express any virtual structure. Such a system empowers the user to select, sort, format, present, and manage the project information by any virtual project structure and any structural constructs in the project and project business.

Relationships among Structures.

Each activity resulting from the WBS must relate to OBS by its cost account. This relationship shows how work and people are connected, who is responsible for performing or managing work, and where performance measurement occurs. It is an essential step in integrating technology and management processes in the project and outlining responsibilities for developing and implementing the plan. Usually, one or more work packages, including all cost accounts within a package, are assigned to individual responsibility. Assignment of work packages to personal responsibility follows after the attributes of work are accurately defined by technology and management professionals and before the cost account starts.

Cost accounts assure tie-in between WBS and OBS. If for some reason we are not able to obtain cost accounts, then project activities assume the tie-in role. If management decides that WBS' most detailed elements are work packages, then tie-in occurs at the work packages level. As a result, the dollar amount at the project level and summarized amount at the most detailed level are the same for

57 Whyte, Jennifer, and Andrew Davies. "Reframing System Integration: A Process Perspective on Project." *Project Management Journal* Volume 52 (March 2021). https://doi.org/10.1177/8756972821992246.

58 Frederiksen, Nicolaj, and Stefan Christoffer Gottlieb, and Roine Leiringer. "Organizing for infrastructure development programmes: Govering internal logic multiplicity across organizational spaces." *International Journal of Project Management* Volume 39, Issue 3 (April 2021): 223–235. https://sciencedirect.com.

both WBS and OBS structures; however, intermediate levels of both structures are different, and associated dollar values are different as well. To explain some tie-in issues between WBS and OBS, let's look at Figure 1.6.

Figure 1.6 illustrates how the company defines and manages the project's direct and indirect costs. We assign direct costs to a cost account that resides on task activity, whereas we assign indirect costs to a cost account that resides on hammock activity. For example, responsibility 51110 relates to work package 21110 by three cost accounts (21110-15, 21110-25, 21110-55) for the direct cost (labor, materials, subcontracts), and one cost account (21110-75) that measures the indirect cost (management fees, reimbursements, office expenses). Note that this example consists of ten task activities and one hammock activity.

A single responsibility must be assigned for each end-element of the project work breakdown structure. For example, the OBS responsibility 51110 is assigned to the WBS work package 21110; although the work package can contain many cost accounts, a specific cost account may be assigned to more activities; for example, the cost account 21110-15 is assigned to activities "C" and "F." Although individual responsibility may relate to more work packages, more activities, and more cost accounts, we must always assign a single responsibility to each activity and its attributes, including cost account.

The costs of the work package 21110 are further summarized, level by level, for both WBS and OBS. The WBS summarizes the cost of the work package 21110 for contract 21100. The cost of the contract 21100 is summarized for the project phase 21000. And the cost of phase 21000 is summarized for the project work breakdown structure 20000. The OBS summarizes the cost of responsibility 51110 into the project team 51100. The cost of project team 51100 is absorbed into the department 51000. And the cost of department 51000 is absorbed into the project organization structure 50000. Therefore, coding structures for WBS and OBS assure that a component's costs can only be integrated into a single component of its higher structure. The WBS and OBS structures also summarize other attributes for their higher-level components, like project duration, start, completion, costs, variances, indexes, and other attributes. By applying the above explanations, we can keep the integrity of project structures.

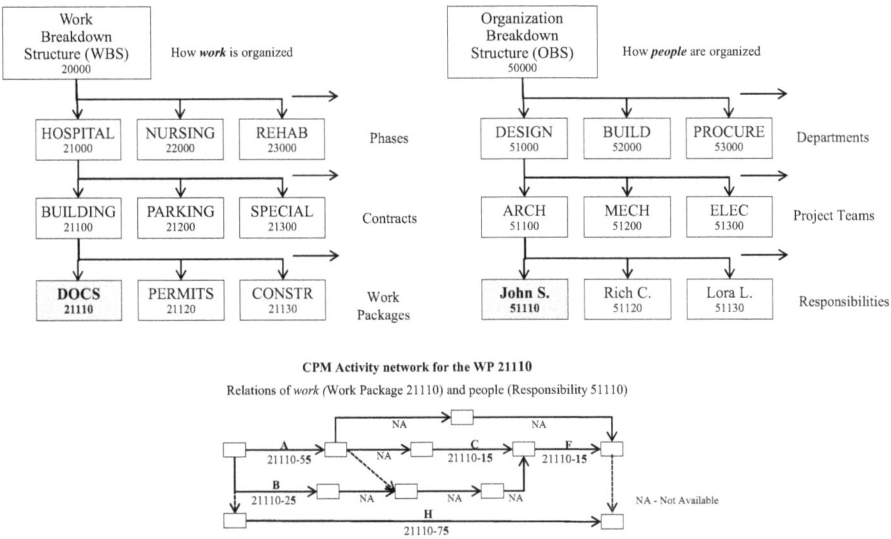

Source: Abdomerovic, M.

Figure 1.6: Cost Account Code

Descartes' "tree" is sufficient for top-down analysis of a complex system, different phases, disciplines within a project phase, including the most detailed elements for the system or the project. But the bottom-up integration of information cannot be handled by the "tree" alone. An attempt to transfer the knowledge of all objects of a higher level of particular series, by precisely similar steps established during the top-down analysis of particular series (Descartes 1952, 7), and reflect their relations to one another through intuitive reasoning (Descartes 1952, 17), even if a fictitious one among objects, which do not follow a natural sequence established by top-down analysis (Descartes 1952, 47), is not sufficient for bottom-up synthesis of some attributes of PMP contents. It means that we need, besides what has been said, a clear understanding of the relationships among the most detailed elements scattered throughout the different series of activities of a project or a system; we must have an explicit tool to handle the impact of relationships among the simplest facts within a series and among series of project activities and then proceed with the synthesis of objects at higher levels of the problem.

Networks in Project Management Planning

The Critical Path Method (CPM) has roots in Euler's graph theory (Roper 2012, 16).[59] Euler initiated the graph theory more than a century after Descartes' *Rules for the Direction of the Mind.* On the subject of the CPM's analysis of project relationships among its most detailed elements, the project activities, as well as the synthesis of project activities to higher project levels, the solution comes centuries later with the growth of graph theory and its transport network graph (Ford and Fulkerson 1956[60]; Kelley and Walker 1959; Malcolm et al. 1959[61]; Kelley 1961[62]; Berge 2001, 5–6, 71–85, 204).

Shortly after, the CPM was applied to develop project management plans by relating project activities into a network diagram and processing activity attributes (DOD and NASA Guide 1962; Woodgate 1968; O'Brien 1969[63]; Moder and Phillips 1969[64]; PMI 1996).

In general, the unique base of the most detailed elements from the WBS is related in the CPM network diagram to present the development logic of a system, project, program, or business and process the attributes of the CPM's network diagram elements.

Leonard Euler, mathematician and philosopher, started this journey in 1735 by committing himself to solve an old mathematical problem known as The Seven Bridges of Konigsberg (now Kaliningrad, Russia). The town is located on the mainland and has two islands surrounded by the Pregel River. At that time, islands and the mainland were linked by seven bridges. The question was whether it was possible to cross each of seven bridges once time only. Roper notes

59 Roper, Duncan. "Euler and the Konigsberg Bridges: Some Lessons for the Philosophy of Mathematics." *School of Quantitative Methods and Mathematical Science, University of Western Sydney Australia.* (Retrieved: April 2021).

60 Ford, Lester, and Delbert Fulkerson. "Maximal Flow through a Network." *Canadian Journal of Mathematics* Volume 8 (1956): 399–404.

61 Malcom. D. G., and Roseboom. J. H., and Clark. C. E, and Fazar. W. "Applications of a Technique for Research and Development Program Evaluation." *Operations Research 7* (1959): 646–669.

62 Kelley, James. "Critical-Path Planning and Scheduling: Mathematical Basis." *Operations Research* Volume 9, Number 3 (May–June 1961): 296–320.

63 O'Brien, James. *Scheduling Handbook.* New York, NY: McGraw-Hill Book Company, 1969.

64 Moder, Joseph, and Cecil Phillips. *Project Management with CPM and. PERT.* New York, NY: Van Nostrand Reinhold, 1964.

Euler's thinking was to find a theoretical approach first (Roper 2012, 18). Euler's approach shows that for the Konigsberg Bridges problem, the answer is negative. Euler's lemmas and theorems related to the bridge problem culminated in proposals of the first graph theorem and the path from a practical question to the theory, in this case graph theory (Roper 2012, 15–27).

Graph theory today is a recognized mathematical field that is advancing in application and theory. A range of disciplines, from PMP, structural modeling, and topology in engineering design, to flow networks in the infrastructure industry, circuit diagrams in the communication industry, systems and networks of social entities, games, and so on, with no end in sight, depend in one way or another on Euler's theory of graphs.

From Graph Theory to Critical Path Method.

A graph consists of a set of nodes or vertices and a set of lines called edges, arrows, or arcs, which connect pairs of vertices. There are different types of graphs for different types of problems in a specific discipline. Our interest is in the "tree/arborescence" and "transport" graphs concerning PMP. These graphs were developed over time to become vital project management tools. The arborescence graph evolved as a support tool for the definition of project contents, as we discussed in the Work Breakdown Structure (WBS) section. The transportation graph became a tool primarily for describing the relationships among project activities. It was later developed into what we is now known as the Critical Path Method. One of the earliest essays on the Critical Path Method (CPM) was Kelley's (1961),[65] which covered a wide range of methods, including the following:

- Fundamental algorithm and publication (Ford and Fulkerson 1957)[66] that preceded Kelly's paper
- List of significant results obtained by application of the CPM for a variety of projects
- Rules for relationships among the activities of a project
- Example of the project in the chemical processing plant that includes relationships, time, as well as cost attributes

65 Kelley, James. "Critical-Path Planning and Scheduling: Mathematical Basis." *Operations Research* Volume 9, Number 3 (May–June 1961): 296–320.

66 Ford, Lester, Delbert Fulkerson. "A Simple Algorithm for Finding Maximal Network Flows and an Application to the Hitchcock Problem." *Canadian Journal of Mathematics* Volume 9 (1957): 210–218.

- Percentage of critical activities in projects
- Variety of calculations for a project defined by the network diagram or other such tools

It took more than two centuries since the publication of Euler's work for scholars to even begin to apply network planning methods to develop and implement a project management plan (Chapter 8, Planning methods).

We also record the Program Evaluation and Review Technique (Malcom et al., 1959). Shortly after, the Precedence Diagraming Method became prominent in the management discipline and is actively used today (Fondahl 1961[67], 1962[68]). The CPM, PERT, and PDM methods use the same principles defined in graph theory; oriented lines or arcs connect the plane points or the vertices. In our case, we describe the arcs and vertices as follows:

- Vertices are for CPM, describing the events at the start and the end of an activity; for PERT, the events at the start and the end of an activity; and PDM, only the endpoints of an activity.
- Arcs are for CPM, the activities and relationships between the activities; for PERT, the activities and relationships between the activities; and PDM, activity relationships only.

Although the CPM, PERT, and PDM are similar, their differences are real.

- Critical Path Method (CPM) is also known as the activity-oriented method, because the development of work is orientated to project activities, or the i–j method, because each activity uses unique i–j pair of alphanumeric events for identification. The method may contain dummy activities to exclusively present the activity's relations to boundary pairs of events or other activities. Those conditions form only one activity between two unique pairs of events. Each activity, except for dummy activities,

67 Fondahl, John. "A Non-computer Approach to the Critical Path Method for the Construction Industry," 1st Ed. *Stanford University, Department of Civil Engineering* (1961).

68 Fondahl, John. "A Non-computer Approach to the Critical Path Method for the Construction Industry," 2nd Ed. *Stanford University, Department of Civil Engineering* (1962).

must have a description, a single timeframe, and may contain resources and other activity attributes.

- Program Evaluation and Review Technique (PERT)—it is also known as the event-oriented method because the development of work is oriented to project events, where a unique number and description identify each event. The method may contain dummy activities to uniquely present activity's relations to boundary pairs of events or other events. Those conditions form only one activity between two unique pairs of events. Each activity, except for dummy activities, must have a description, three durations (minimum, most likely, and maximum), and may contain resources and other activity attributes.
- Precedence Diagramming Method (PDM)—it is also known as the node-oriented method and orients work development to project activities. Each activity uses a unique alphanumeric code that denotes the activity's start and end points. The method may contain dummy activities that reflect unique relations among activities. Each activity must have a description, a single timeframe, and may contain resources and other activity attributes.

The CPM, PERT, or PDM can create various relationships between project activities to show the progress in project work. A relationship between activities that do not consume resources, for example, as in a dummy activity, may have zero duration because the start and end events or points of time in the trajectory of the activity have nil duration and thus need nil resources.

If the lead or lag time between events of CPM activities is nil, then we can delete such relationships between activities and tie in associated events. This notion is valid for CPM as long as different i–j pairs of alphanumeric events identify each activity and maintain the logic between activities. However, such handling of relationships between two PERT activities complicates and renders ambiguous the distinctive descriptions of PERT events. As for PDM, the transformation is not possible because its endpoints cannot be tied.

There are similarities in the ways network diagram is used to present the different elements of a project; however, the elements have different purposes. For example, a random alphanumeric identifier for the CPM event discreetly adopts both the inflow or outflow processes in project activities. In contrast, descriptions of PERT events must match the description of the inflow and outflow processes occurring in a set of activities which are carried out together to achieve goals common for all activities incorporated in that set of activities. We may require additional dummy activities and events to cope with the specific description of

PERT events. The same problem may also happen if we need to use other relationships between activities besides FS (Finish-to-Start) relationships. Also, the CPM activity has a deterministic duration, and the PERT activity has a stochastic duration. It necessitates the use of different calculations and, thus, different interpretations of results; the CPM dates for activities and events appear deterministic at some time point, and the PERT dates also appear stochastic at some time points. A comparison between other elements of methods and other network diagraming methods can reveal their similarities and differences. For example, a close comparison of the above network diagraming methods can show that PDM is essentially a hybrid of CPM and PERT; PDM has relationships similar to those that occur in CPM and the description of activity node resembles the PERT description of activity endpoints. Figure 1.7 shows general relationships between two activities, that is, "From" and "To" activities.

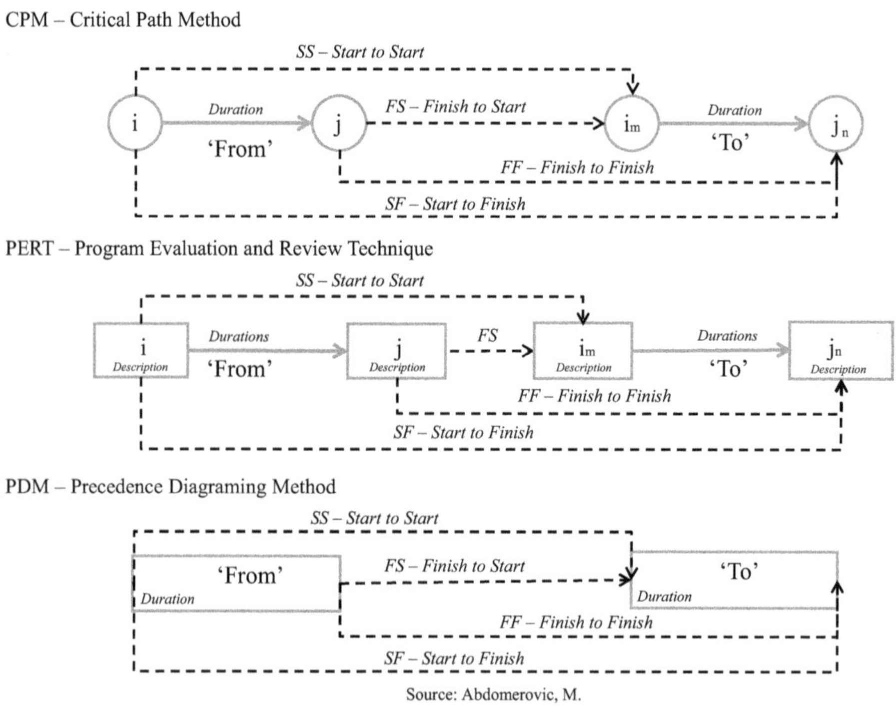

Figure 1.7: Network Diagramming Methods. Relationships between "From" and "To" activities—Logical View

For example, the relationships between CPM and PDM show the transparency in both methods, and help distinguish one relationship from another based on the characteristics determined as unique to each relationship:

- Finish-to-Start (FS) relationship shows that "To" or successor activity can start after "From" or after the conclusion of its predecessor activity.
- Start-to-Start (SS) relationship shows that "To" or successor activity can start after "From" or after its predecessor activity has started.
- Finish-to-Finish (FF) relationship shows that the "To" or successor activity comes to an end after the conclusion of "From" or its predecessor activity.
- Start-to-Finish (SF) relationship shows that "To" or successor activity cannot be concluded until "From" or its predecessor activity has begun. Note that none of these relationships can show a backward flow; therefore, the hypothetical SF relationship ties the end of the "To" activity to the start of the "From" activity.

Although many standard contracts use a CPM or PDM-based schedule as a contract management tool, the PDM is applied more exclusively in practice today.

To adapt the CPM network diagram to the PDM network diagram, we must show CPM activities as nodes that represent PDM activities; convert each I–J pair of CPM activities into a string to identity PDM activities; except for open–start and open–end relationships in CPM activities, take all relationships between the start and the end points of PDM network into consideration; remove dummy activities from PDM network and restore the flow of PDM activities.

To adapt the PDM network diagram to the CPM network diagram, we must append additional identifiers for each PDM activity's identification, for example, "S" (start point) and the "C" (completion point). Now each PDM activity is identified as a CPM activity by events at its starting point and events at its concluding point. Besides, we must add dummy activities in the CPM network and, if necessary, restore the flow of CPM activities. Whereas CPM and PDM look different from one another, their logic, functions, and results are essentially the same. We can see such similarities between CPM, PDM, and PERT methods as well.

A project network diagram can show a variety of relationships between two activities at the same time. Yet, only one relationship is usually sufficient to express the required conditions between two real and consistently structured project content activities. For details of activity relationships, the reader should primarily study a current manual of project management software or some earlier references from the 1960s or 1970s (Woodgate 1968; Moder and Phillips 1969).

Figure 1.8 shows the relationships between the "From" and "To" activities on a time scale. The figure presents the direct relationships between two activities in their earliest phase only, which is only one out of the many phases that activities go through in real-time situations. Activity time position often changes by the following:

- Constraint dates (activity's early start or its end, late start or its end, and mandatory start or its end)
- Resource constraints (resource availability and resource allocation criteria)
- Lead or lag time constraints (positive, negative)
- Constraints in predetermined flows (front, interruptible, or late)
- Constraints arising from related activities or from other constraints

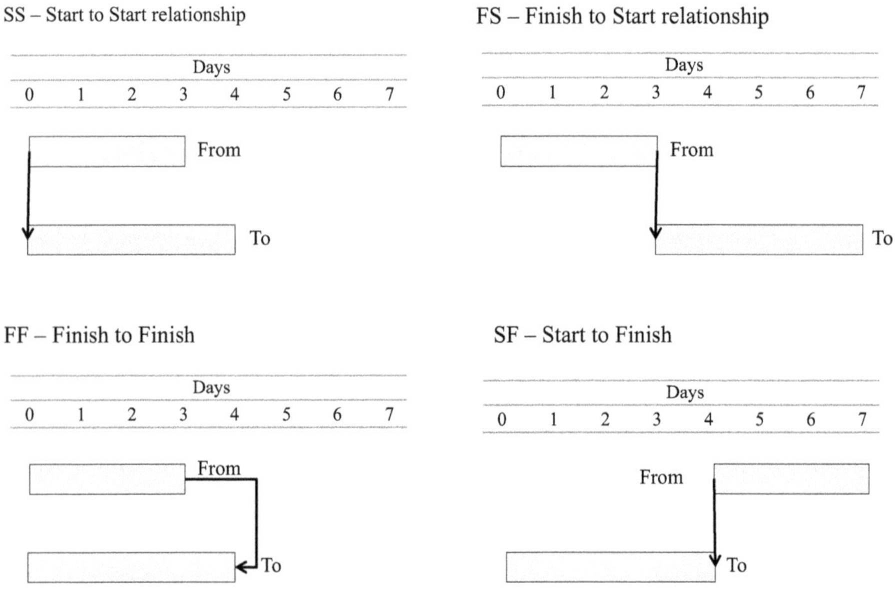

Source: Abdomerovic, M.

Figure 1.8: Network Diagramming Methods. Relationships between "From" and "To" activities—Time View

Characteristics.

Key elements of project network diagrams are project activities as well as their attributes. There are some of the basic and calculated attributes of an activity:

- Basic attributes of activity include the following: alphanumeric identification; description of contents; relationships; code and name of responsible person; duration; name and quantity for each resource or cost for each resource; cost account code and one or more related cost account categories; associated risk, quality, safety, priority codes; constraint dates; activity codes and other basic attributes needed for processing the activity's calculated attributes.
- The calculated attributes of activity are as follows: start and finish dates; floats; a variety of resource loadings and profiles; a variety of cost amounts and profiles; cost variances and indexes, associated progress, and other calculated attributes needed for the assessment of activity status, forecasts, as well as causes for the estimated results.

There are several types of activities, and most projects contain more than one type of activity. Here is how Primavera systems (Primavera P3, 1993)[69] describe the different types of activities:

- Task Activity—if you aren't assigning resources to the activity or assign only non-driving resources or schedule or assign resources according to the activity's basic timeframe, it is a task activity. So, task activity is commenced based on network logic and gets concluded when its duration has elapsed.
- Independent Activity—if you plan to use resource calendars and driving resources for the activity, then it is an independent activity. In a resource-driven schedule, you don't specify duration when you add an activity; the duration of each driving resource is determined based on the resource calendar. The time between the starting point of the first driving resources and the endpoint of the last driving resource's determines the duration of each independent activity.
- Meeting Activity—if you require that all resources work together simultaneously to complete the activity, this indicates a meeting activity. The duration of a meeting activity is defined by the driving resource with the longest duration. It uses a calendar that is a combination of the calendars for all driving resources.

69 Primavera P3 1993. *Project Planner for Windows – Reference.* Primavera System, 1993. www.primavera.com.

- Hammock Activity—if you need to monitor the lapse of the beginning-to-end duration of a group of activities, this indicates a hammock activity. The duration of hammock activity is calculated based on the duration of the segment of the plan it covers. A hammock activity must have one or more start-to-start predecessors and finish-to-finish successors.
- Dummy Activity—if you need to facilitate planning network relationships, then it indicates a dummy activity. A dummy activity generally has zero duration; however, it may still have a duration to show a lead or lag time between related points.
- Milestones, Start or Finish—if you need to indicate the beginning or the end of a major event or a phase in the project timeline, then you need to indicate a start or finish milestone. Milestone generally has zero duration.
- Flags, Start or Finish—if you need to signal the start or the end of the activity or group of activities based on the earliest start or the latest end points of its predecessors, then you indicate a start or finish flag. The flag generally has zero duration.

Although activity types' characteristics mostly stay the same, the name and definition of activity types are changing. For example, the Primavera P6 renames the Hammock Activity to the Level of Effort activity, introduces the WBS Summary activity, and adds more specific definitions for the activities (Primavera/Oracle 2019).[70]

If the project management team is capable of developing the lists of activities and associated basic attributes (where each list refers to a particular work package); can understand the rules for the relationship between activities (start to start, start to finish, finish to finish); can recognize the technological conditions for activities (sequence of work, skills, materials, output rate for available resources); can know the limitations for activities (available energy, space, documentation, critical situations, equipment, tools), as well as management requirements for activities (induced priorities, overlaps, constraints, out-of-sequence directions), then the development of reliable project network diagram is a certain venture.

Experience with using CPM, PERT, and PDM methods represents the step forward for general management science, particularly project management. The unique and lasting characteristics of these methods were observed as early as six decades ago. For example, according to Moder and Phillips, the methods

70 Primavera P6 2019. *Project Portfolio Management.* Primavera / Oracle, 2019. http://www.oracle.com/primavera.

- encourage a logical discipline in planning, scheduling, and control of the project
- encourage more long-range and detailed planning of projects
- provide a standard method of documenting and communicating project plans, schedules, and the time and cost performance
- identify the most critical elements in the plan, focusing management attention on the 10 to 20 percent of the project that is most constraining on the schedule, and
- Illustrate the effects of technical and procedural changes on the overall schedule. (Moder and Phillips 1969, 5–6)

Development of Project Network Diagram.

The project network diagram should be developed gradually by analyzing the relationships among project activities. Such an analysis should happen in a phased manner and focusing on the primary, secondary, and hammock relationships.

To develop a project network diagram, we should identify and use the primary logic for each work package. This part of the project network diagram is the backbone of the project management plan. It must show in sufficient detail and using minimum relations how major tasks will be accomplished, who is responsible for them, what resources are required, and for that purpose we may use the "finish-to-start" relationships only and reveal rather than construct relationships for a work package's activities. Relaxation of relationships between activities is possible using flexible lead/lag times as an alternative for the finish-to-start relationship between activities or applying progress override features for some activities. However, measurements for activity attributes, including the status, progress, variances, indexes, and float trends, cannot be compromised (Chapter 8, Causal Premise).

Primary relationships must develop in close communication between the project manager and the technical manager. The project manager is responsible for developing management conditions and requirements for creating a project management plan, including work packages' start and finish dates. The technology manager is responsible for developing technical directions, descriptions, relationships, durations, and resource requirements for activities. The communication between the project manager and technology manager defines the client, architect/engineer, and general contractor's involvement in PMP.

Let's see Figure 1.9, which shows the development stages, durations, and relationships of activities within the work package.

Primary relationships may call for rework of WBS. For example, the construction of a specific work package cannot start without approved documentation; however, we may find that release of design documentation is organized to happen during the different phases of the design process rather than by the construction of work packages. For example, the final phase of project design documentation may not be completed before constructing a specific work package. Such a situation ultimately requires a disambiguation process for design documentation. This process helps reveal a level of overlaps and simultaneous sequences among design and construction activities and prevents construction delays for the specific work package. However, we will not always reveal relationships among activities; particular requirements and conditions will impose new relationships; therefore, envisaging or forecasting the type of relations that might emerge over the project trajectory and construct relationships based on forecasts is a solution.

Next, we must add the secondary logic for each work package. This part of the project network diagram includes roughly 50–80% of the total number of activities for the work package; therefore, we must simplify the secondary-stage activities as much as possible. Usually, one relationship for each activity and eventually one constraint date are necessary. Secondary-stage activities typically have a one-time-unit duration, which also simplifies the process of handling the project network diagram. Such activities mostly present the following:

- List of outputs or control points for primary logic activities (level of definitions, accuracy, relevancy for released outputs, etc.)
- Submittals related to primary logic activities, including the safety manuals and safety instruction, list of project management team members and responsibilities, office manual, master schedule, inspection, testing program, estimated spare list, periodic maintenance manual, certification of workmanships compliance, stamped documentation, as-built drawings, and others
- Approvals related to some submittals, documentations, works, invoices, environmental requirements, working calendars, claims, and other activities not included in the primary logic activities
- Work with a flexible logic
- Work outside substantial completion

After required activities and relationships are completed for work packages and between work packages, we may proceed to creating preliminary calculations of the project time plan. And again, the relationships between work packages have to be revealed rather than constructed. However, suppose the work package doesn't have an immediate start or a clear relationship. In that case, we can impose an early start date or late finish date for the work package until we get more reliable data for the work package's relationships. When we reach a point that roughly expresses our expectations for the project plan's objectives, we can create hammock activities for work packages and higher project network diagram clusters.

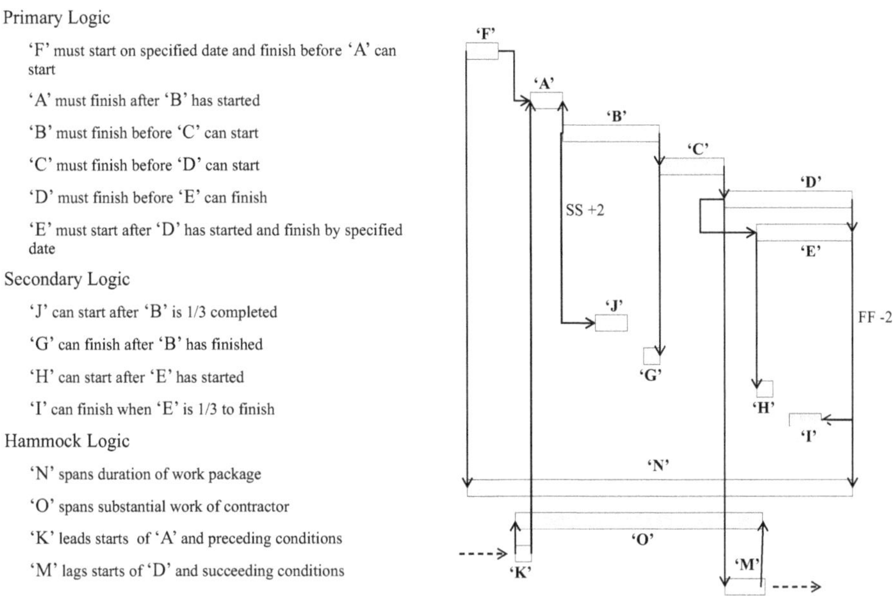

Source: Abdomerovic, M.

Figure 1.9: Network Diagramming Methods. Development of Relationships

We have to construct hammock relationships for each work package and beyond. This activity is also known as span activity, or level-of-effort activity. We use hammock activity to express different summaries among activities it spans. For example, Figure 1.9 shows how hammock activity "N" is constructed. The sequence of activities ("F" … "E") must start before the start of the hammock activity; therefore, the first activity in a particular sequence is related to hammock activity as a "start-to-start" relation, from the start of activity "F" to the start of activity "N." Hammock activity must finish after the conclusion of the last activity in the sequence ("F" … "E"); therefore, hammock activity is related to a particular sequence as a "finish-to-finish" relation, from the end of activity "E" to the end of activity "N."

There are some exceptional cases in the construction of hammock activity, including the activity "O." Suppose there is a need to start hammock activity "O" earlier than the first activity in a particular sequence ("A"–"B"–"C"). In that case, we must add a lead-time activity "K" at the beginning of the particular sequence. The start of the hammock activity "O" is now at the start of lead-time activity "K." Suppose the relationship between the beginning of a particular sequence and lead-time activity is negative or positive. In that case, the start of the lead-time activity and hammock activity is pushed to an earlier or later period, correspondingly. Suppose there is a need to finish hammock activity "O" later than the last activity in a particular sequence ("A"–"B"–"C"). In that case, we should add a lag-time activity at the end of a particular sequence. The end of the hammock activity "O" is now at the end stage of the lag-time activity. Suppose the relationship between the end point of a particular sequence and lag-time activity is negative or positive. In that case, the end point of the lag-time activity and the hammock activity is pushed to the earlier stage or the later stage, correspondingly.

Suppose we cannot assign a direct or indirect cost to the work package's task activities. In that case, we assign an associated value to the corresponding hammock activity or activities. This case is more typical in the indirect cost assignment identified in the organization breakdown structure (OBS) of the project-performing company; this happens when we use hammock activity to relate activities containing specific cost accounts and related responsibility.

Last, we must think about the planning of safety, quality, benefits, risk, and other attributes assigned to an activity in the project.

- Activities describing safety in the project belong to the secondary logic and must be accomplished before starting the primary-logic activities. The contractor must ensure that both upcoming and current work comply with safety requirements and the project's safety plan.
- Quality-related activities must comply with primary project relationships to allow the contractor's quality manager, client's quality supervisor, and quantity surveyor to coordinate quality-control procedures. In many cases, we can simply add the quality attributes to a set of existing activities, since quality management is an ongoing job of the project team.
- The activities related to project benefits management, or closing the gap between various perceptions about the success of the project, project business, stakeholders success, or investment success surrounded by different

perspectives and criteria, contribute to the success of both the project and the project business (Carlos and Kunc 2015).[71] We measure benefits usually after project completion, but this may not be the ideal stage where it is possible to understand how benefits are distributed to different entities in the project and its internal and external stakeholders. The better way is to calculate benefits during project plan implementation by adding them to the hammock activities spanning specific cost accounts. Before that, the reader must study the identification and delivery of benefits (Aba, Pells, and Shepherd 2018).[72]

- Risk management is different, since a highly critical risk management process occurs outside the project plan but earlier than the start of the project. A massive study of risk management practice shows that half of the severe incidents in complex projects occur before detecting the potential for such risks to occur. In contrast, successful risk management ensures that risk is addressed earlier and prevention mechanisms are implemented using sophisticated methods such as analytical risk management (Thamhain 2013).[73] There are good examples from practice that we must study before addressing the risks associated with the project (Chapman 2021).[74] In most cases, we can simplify risk calculations by using computer software and simulate different project risk management scenarios (Maharana 2020, 283–401).[75]

The above management subsets and other subsets (financial, social entities, social environment, sustainable development, security, uncertainties) are

71 Carlos Eduardo Martins Serra, and Martin Kunc. 2015. "Benefits Realization Management and its influence on project success and on the execution of business strategies." *International Journal of Project Management* Volume 33, Issue 1 (January 2015): 53–66. https://sciencedirect.com.

72 Aba, Wayne, and David Pells, and Miles Shepherd. "Program benefits management: an international best practice the US government could use." *PM World Journal* Volume VII, Issue VI (June 2018): www.pmworldjournal.net.

73 Thamhain, Hans. "Managing Risks in Complex Projects." *Project Management Journal* Volume 44, Number 2 (2013): 20–35. www.pmi.org.

74 Chapman, Robert. "Ineffective Risk Management and the collapse of Carillion - an update" *PM World Journal* Volume X, Issue III (March. 2021): www.pmworldjournal.com

75 Maharana, Dibyaranjan. *Oracle Primavera P6 Professional Project Management, Release 19.* Coppell, TX, 2020.

traditionally a part of general management; however, they are also the reality of each project. For a small project, the roles are part of the project manager's work; however, in a big project, the roles range from full-time jobs (safety manager, project quality managers) to part-time positions (project risk manager).

Before implementing the project management plan, we must understand its time and cost alternatives to validate the integrity of the project management plan. For this purpose, we have to assure that the following activities happen:

- Project management terminology, cost rules, and cost calculations have been described and practiced.
- The total direct and indirect cost estimates have been assigned to project activities.
- The first alternative for cost estimating, including estimates for contingencies, undistributed budgets, and management reserve, uses parameters for normal work conditions by excluding all thresholds.
- Conditions for each activity within a work package eventually allow a comparison between costs estimated and the costs actually incurred.
- The project budget is completed to provide the basis for the subsequent control of the project cost.
- An activity with assigned resources or costs is not modified or deleted from the plan until the resources or cost differences are transferred to other activities within the project and the change orders issued.
- Work specified and planned for an activity is not added to another activity.

The project manager is responsible for creating and maintaining an environment where reviews, maintenance, and approval of the plan will be of prime interest to stakeholders. For this purpose, we must always have a thorough understanding of the project management feedback.

Implementation of Project Management Plan

Implementation of a project management plan does not happen in an ideal reality where things always happen as planned. Like any analytical documentation, a project management plan, be it architectural, mechanical, electrical, software, or administrative documentation, can rarely be a reflection of how the planned project activities happen in real time—there's a plan, and the project activities planned for either deviate partly from the plan's specifications or totally contravene how they were envisaged in the plan. Consequently, professionals must update the project management plan according to regulations, requirements, issues, and best-practice procedures. The actual results that emerge during the implementation of project management plan may change the project activities and help develop an updated and integrated picture of project status, progress, changes, forecast, and causes.

Before we start implementing the project management plan, we must ensure that project contract documentation, project plan, payment procedure, and guarantees are approved and delivered to the contractor. Each contractor must get information about inclusions/exclusions related to the project neighbors, other contractors, site location, existing structures, space organization, access roads, access requirements for personnel, responsibilities, communication lines, insurances, use of site space, offices, facilities and services for people, and materials and equipment. Besides, each service provider must get approval for their short-term plan and plan alternatives, including a safety plan and a plan for emergency action. Those information help understand the project's contractual requirements, conditions, potential risks, problem-solving capacities, decision-making, and dealing with unforeseen emergencies and deviations in processes.

Feedback in Project Management Planning

The Feedback Method (FM) has its roots in dynamic, control, or feedback theory (Maxwell 1868).[76] More than a century after Euler's *The Seven Bridge of Konigsberg*, Maxwell published *On Governors* and explained the feedback mechanism. Feedback theory has been later broadly applied to govern the dynamic nature of the system in general, including implementing a project management plan (Wiener 1965, 95–115[77]; Doyle 1992, 31–43[78]; Wideman 1991, VII-3[79];

76 Maxwell, James. "On Governors." *Proceedings of the Royal Society* Volume XVI, Number 100 (1868): 270–283. Retrieved 10/2/2011. http://seit.unsw.adfa.edu.au/staff/sites/hrp/historicalpapers/ongovernors.pdf.

77 Wiener, Norbert. *Cybernetics or Control and Communication in the Animal and the Machine. Second edition.* Cambridge, MA: The MIT Press, 1965.

78 Doyle, John, and Bruce Francis, and Allen Tannenbaum. *Feedback Control Theory.* Mineola, NY: Dover Publications, 1992.

79 Wideman, Max. *A framework for project and program management integration.* The PMBOK handbook series Volume No 1. Upper Darby, PA: Project Management Institute, 1991. www.pmi.org.

Wideman 2004, 135–139; Abdel-Hamid 2011, 12–25[80]). The feedback method shows the results of sequential and recurring interactions between the planning, executing, controlling, and back-to-planning processes applied to the most detailed components of the project management plan, which usually are project activities.

We show project contents by a time-oriented network of activities and their attributes where each activity or its part presents a work element. A performer handles the work element or its parts in a step-by-step manner, doing only one part of work at one time. When work details change because of the emergence of unanticipated/nonconforming or unplanned outcomes from project activities carried out in real time that contradict the plan, the performer does not need to work on anything except an emergency case until the work gets completed or an output is used as input for succeeding work elements assigned to another performer. Such a work element passes through the feedback cycle of planning, executing, controlling, and back to planning. After each feedback cycle, the work element may stay unchanged, progress, or conclude. Erroneously performed or reported work is transferred to the next data date and reconsidered during the next feedback cycle.

Feedback is a sequential and recurring causality model. When we understand how feedback functions in general, we can grasp its role in PMP. Principally, if a process group of feedback is not complete for the work element or its part, then the succeeding process groups cannot happen. However, if a process group of feedback completes the work element or its part, the succeeding process groups must not follow immediately. On a data date, we should assess all activities under progress and complete the feedback cycle. Finally, we must provide and organize the results to show the status, progress, forecasts, changes, and causes for project activities, higher project components, the whole project, and the project business.

From Dynamic Theory to Feedback Method.

The most severe misunderstanding of project management today relates to handling the project management plan's dynamism. People usually anticipate the project management plan as a single document. However, to understand project dynamism and have an exact measurement of project performance, we must

80 Abdel-Hamid, Tarek K. "Single-Loop Project Controls: Reigning Paradigms or Straitjackets?" *Project Management Journal* Volume 42, Number 1 (February 2011): 17–30.

concurrently refer to three forms of project plan: the original project plan, the baseline project plan, and the current project plan.

- The original plan clarifies the scope, time, resource, and cost estimates for completing all project work. When the original plan is approved, has a timeframe, and is contracted out, it serves as the first picture of the baseline and current project plan. The original project plan changes hardly ever and is used in the future to compare the original plan's changes with the baseline project plan.
- The baseline plan comes to be the benchmark after the original plan gets completed and approved. From then on, the baseline plan changes through approved change orders only. If the project does not contain approved change orders, then a substantial number of baseline plan elements are equal to the original plan.
- The current plan always refers to the present time. It contains the most recent update of project data necessary to assess the project status, progress, causes, and forecasts to data date. So, it may contain approved change orders and pending change orders. As a result, the key difference between the baseline and current plans expresses the pending change orders.

Figure 1.10 shows the development and implementation of the project management plan; once a project management plan develops, we use project management feedback to implement and update the plan. Such a specific order of actions at the data date must be applied directly to each activity under progress, reflecting related succeeding activities of a project management plan. The total number of activities considered during each feedback procedure is usually less than 10% of the plan's total number of activities. During unique feedback iteration, an activity or a portion of an activity cannot feedback to the same or preceding process until it passes the feedback sequence. For example, when control for an activity is complete, the control process's information cannot feedback to the execution process because the activity must pass through the planning process and update.

The figure illustrating the project management feedback cycle shows the relationship between the different elements of the project management processes. If the implementation of project management plan is progressing, then the project management plan changes accordingly. Once the project management plan starts and the project plan migrates into the project management feedback cycle, we must have active reference to the current plan and the baseline plan, including the narrative databases and soft skills, to understand better the actual situation.

We always deal with different data sets during each period of project plan implementation than what we recorded in the earlier period; hence, we must understand the facts behind the changes.

Changes to plans are elaborate and are documented progressively using the project management feedback cycle, so we must save all versions of the original, the baseline, and the current plan for future analysis, use, and possible audit. A general form of project management feedback is discussed in Chapter 5 (see Figure 5.3 Management Feedback in Chapter 5).

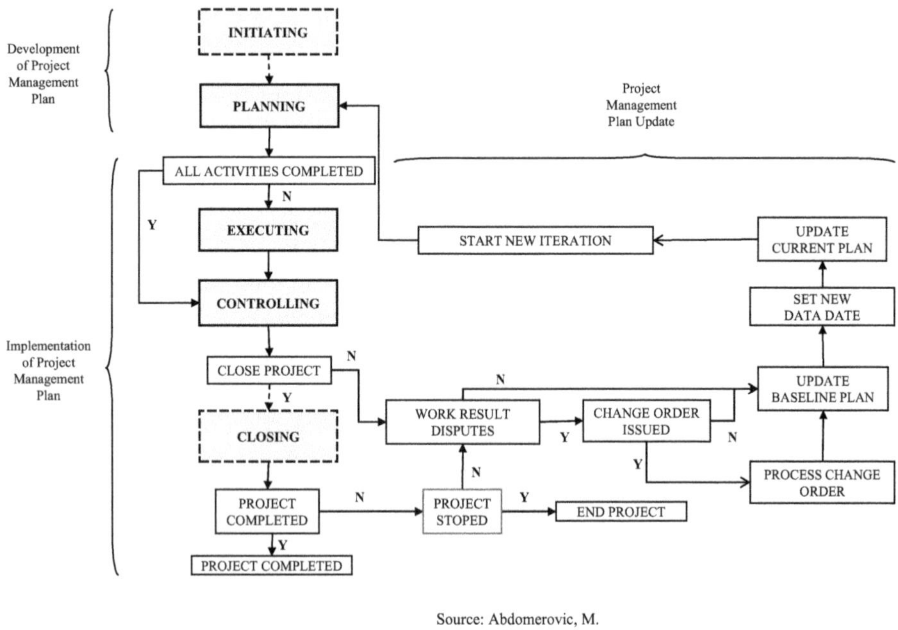

Figure 1.10: Project Management Feedback

Characteristics.

Implementing the project management plan assumes the documentation and actions that comply with contractual and management requirements and help update the project in an organized manner. A project management plan, like other plans, is always prescriptive and dynamic; there is always the awareness that the plan must precede actions and that any changes in the project's progress, including progress without any deviation from the plan, must be recorded.

Therefore, it is not news that the project is not completed according to the original project management plan since we have seen this happening for a long time; however, what would be news is that the project met the original plan. We know that actual events change the plan and the feedback method helps understand and manage project reality, particularly its dynamism and changes.

Each real project must contain activities, which we know as the schedule of value items, submittals, claims, change orders, approvals, and other activities (Means 1991).[81] For example, a $5 million-worth construction project may encompass a thousand activities, and a $500 million construction project may entail carrying out tens of thousands of activities. Small projects are planned in more detail and updated daily, whereas big projects allocate larger values to activity attributes which are updated weekly or frequently and regularly, depending on the project timeframe. We should regularly estimate and update the duration or time scale of project activities at least thrice and over three specific time periods when the project is going on, regardless of the project scale, large or small.

Although the level of detail for schedule value items is a relative category, we must ensure we deal with and negotiate on this issue because the details of schedule value items are key to understanding project contents and implementing the project management plan. For this purpose, we must do the following:

- Sufficiently define the project plan to identify the facts and relate with factual project documentation
- Maintain detail record of project quality control
- Simplify work estimates, measurement, and approvals of accomplished works and payment applications
- Assist in the preparation of claims among contracting parties and assessment of claims by the court
- Assess changes by professional authorities and project stakeholders

What follows immediately after the start of the implementation of the project management plan is the feedback cycle. From that point on, the current plan directs us from the most recently achieved point to the the next destination point. The activities at this point include assessing the project status, progress, changes, forecast, and causes for each activity positioned between the previous update and the project's current plan's next data date. The impacts and assessments of

81 Means. *Illustrated Construction Dictionary.* Kingston, MA: R. S. Means Company, 1991.

the outcomes of the activities results must be recorded, calculated, analyzed, approved, organized, and disseminated to project stakeholders to decide whether any changes are required to the plan to carry out future actions. The evaluation may initiate payment requests, claims, compilation of the current issues, and explain changes to scope, time, resource, cost, quality, procurement, and other project attributes.

Controlling Changes in Project Management Plan.

Perhaps the first step is to recognize that learning about project management is learning about a process—the process of managing change.

The issue is change which is carefully conceived, deliberately planned and expertly executed—all for someone's benefit. (Wideman 1991, ii, VII-3 to VII-5).

A similar notion is in circulation today; the IPMA's Competence Baseline states that "project management is established as the preeminent method for implementing change in the world and project, program and portfolio managers are leading the way" (ICB 2015, Forward).

The implementation of a project management plan requires intensive management of changes; once a project manager settles all conditions related to a particular issue, they move to discover and settle the next critical issue. This routine happens in an ongoing manner between the first day of the project completion and the stage where stakeholders deliberate on whether project management plan needs further, ongoing improvement. Although there is no guarantee that project will be concluded according to its original plan, we can still ensure that PMP control project status, progress, forecasts, and causes of changes. The contractor performs work according to the specifications provided and modified time and again in contract documents and their updates and publishes the project plan's results to let the stakeholders know whether the project has indeed been completed based on original requirements as well revisions made to the plan's goals. The basic rule here is we cannot change, add, or delete project activities' planned contents and relationships without the client and performing organization's agreement. The client and the performing organization agree that the project contract, scope, cost, and time, including all the milestones specified in the project plan, cannot be changed without change orders.

The contractor must know how to accomplish work and fulfil the contract's demand, while the project manager must know how to manage work and what they request and expect from the contractor. If a contractor fails to accomplish work planned for the current week, the project manager leads the action to get the required output by the middle of next week. But there are cases where time and cost contingency and liquidated damage have been exhausted, disputes and litigation between contractual parties emerge, which may even lead to the bankruptcy of the client or performing organization.

For example, a matter-of-fact, business-like statement such as "the project hasn't been completed according to the baseline plan" simply points to a failed project but still does not confirm the failure of the project in a straightforward manner. The truth is most projects are completed according to some version of the baseline plan that underwent changes via approved change orders, which again are a prominent feature of contracts and usually add value to the project. This notion is gaining ground, and the definition, data, reasons, and statistics of failed projects need new assessments. We should take into account in our review the complexity of environmental and social entities, unexpected conditions, the project lifespan from the idea-creation stage to the project dissolution phase, educational spectrum, motivation for skills-related careers in project management, and others.

Morris et al. add other factors that cause projects to either fail or succeed, including the commercial, initial requirements, and numerous references that become progressively gain more significance and impose revisions to the project goals and activities during the course of project implementation (Morris, Patel, and Wearne 2000, 156).[82] The Chartered Institute of Building's International Construction Contract emphasizes the dynamic character of the project and gives guidelines on how to manage the plan. In two of the related articles, the reader can find that a failure to update a baseline plan project cannot indicate project failures (Pickavance February 2013[83]; Pickavance March 2013[84]). Prieto notes that people's opinions in the project management community are close to understanding the meaning of "failed" projects (Prieto 2015, 1, 23, 26).[85]

82 Morris, Peter, and Marsh Patel, and Stephen Wearne. "Research into revising the APM project management body of knowledge." *International Journal of Project Management*, 18 (2000): 155–164. www.elsevier.com/locate/ijproman.

83 Pickavance, Keith. "A New Construction Contract for the 21st Century - Background." *PM World Journal* Volume II, Issue II (February 2013). www.pmworldjournal.net.

84 Pickavance, Keith. "A New Construction Contract for the 21st Century - Time management." *PM World Journal* Volume II, Issue III (March 2013). www.pmworldjournal.net.

85 Prieto, Bob. "Project Management Theory of Large Complex Projects." *PM World Journal* Volume IV, Issue VI (June 2015). www.pmworldtoday.net.

Stretton analyzes failed projects within the context of strategic management and found that approximately half the causes were not directly related to project management responsibility (Stretton 2018a[86], 2018k[87]). In a comprehensive analysis of the proposals made by Cooke-Davies (Coke-Davis, Terry. *Project success: The Wiley Guide to Managing Projects*, Eds Peter W. G. Morris & Jeffrey K. Pinto. Hoboken, NJ: John Wiley—Chapter 5, 2004, 99–122), Stretton has confirmed the notions from 2018a and 2018k (Stretton, 2019).

Managing real-time events, including unexpected conditions and misuse of existing know-how, are just normal project situations handled regularly. For example, suppose a customer decides to add a new ticket counter for a baggage-handling project in progress. In that case, project architect, mechanical, electrical, control, procurement, software, planning, and other professionals must update their documentation. It is just a systematic and continuous dealing with changes.

The key is to understand the requirements and limitations for project management and create an environment for the best available knowledge application. First, we must understand the project management plan's forms and meanings and distinguish the relationships between the original plan, baseline plan, and current plan. We must know how pending and approved scope changes add or subtract; how we use contingency; how we record and compare work accomplishments during the current period; how we estimate work forecast for the next reporting period; how recent and expected delays or acceleration impact the plans; how a change in relationships, addition, modified, or deletion for activities and milestones affect the plans and actions of stakeholders; how to relate the plan with approvals for the work done and payment process. We must also show how we handle requests for information, field orders, damage for delays, interruptions, claims, corrective measures, and how contract time and cost, including all contract milestones change.

Besides, we must mention how changes and associated information are managed in complex projects and the Big Data world. And again, a comprehensive structure, in the form of configuration management of complex product systems and associated information, may lead the way. Typical commonalities from

86 Stretton, Alan. "Relating causes of project failure to an organizational strategic business framework." *PM World Journal* Volume VII, Issue I (January 2018a). www.pmworldtoday.com.

87 Stretton, Alan. "Responsibilities for 'project' successes/failures?" *PM World Journal* Volume VII, Issue XI (November 2018k). www.pmworldtoday.com.

three industries (Airbus, CERN, and Crossrail) are examples of using a common approach to configuration management and managing change in complex projects (Whyte, Stasis, and Lindkvist 2016, 18).[88]

Sometimes, the company's project business manager allows for publishing the project cost's factored value instead of the actual cost amount. So, if we cannot provide performance measurements based on real costs of work, then we must use some physical units of measure for a product in order to assess its performance periodically. For example, if we want to install 26 km of conveyors in one year, the contractor must install approximately 500 meters of conveyors each week to achieve the required performance. Applying the same approach to other works, we can establish factored relations between them, measure the performance for each work package and related cost accounts, and summarize factored values and other attributes for higher-level components. There are some good things about this approach. The company manager and their close circle may be challenged with the exclusive privilege to convert factored values into the real values of status, progress, and forecast for each project and act in a timely manner to strike a balance in how the organization's resources are put to use vis-à-vis project execution.

In case of unexpected conditions, complexities, or complicated changes, the analytical approach alone may not be sufficient; therefore, we must also look at a theoretical and practical framework for managing such situations (Daniel and Daniel 2019, 1017–1033).[89]

More of the Same, only Bigger and Better

The structural communication method is vital for analysis, relationships, synthesis, and updating PMP and system contents. The method is essential for PMP contents whose components can be identified, quantified, planned, implemented, controlled, accomplished, selectively reported, paid, and updated. Most development, research, or maintenance projects in engineering, construction,

88 Whyte, Jennifer, and Angelos Stasis, and Carmel Lindkvist. "Managing change in the delivery of complex projects: Continuation management, asset information and 'big data'." *International Journal of Project Management* Volume 34, Issue 2 (February 2016): 339–351. https://sciencedirect.com.

89 Daniel, Eric, and Pierre Daniel. "Megaprojects as complex adaptive systems: The Hinkley point C case." *International Journal of Project Management* Volume 37. Issue 8 (November 2019): 1017–1033. www.elsevier.com/locate/ijproman.

information technology, production, or other areas need to consider these factors. The structural method is also indispensable for gathering knowledge about the project management system, whose components can be identified, collected, generalized, clustered, analyzed, related, synthesized, used, and updated as may be appropriate during the project execution. This scenario is typical with most national, international, institutional, company, or individual system knowledge collections.

We have gathered information on a successful application and advancing of the scientific PMP from its first-ever application, namely, the Du Pont de Nemours, Chemical plant, Louisville, Kentucky, 1957–1958 (O'Brien 1969), all way to my recent experience, the Vanderlande, the UPS World Project, Louisville Kentucky, 2007–2010 and beyond. Fortunately, regardless of problems caused by various factors, it does not look like a paradigm change, not even close to one steady and straightforward connected set of theoretical and methodological backgrounds and experiences in PMP. If we learn the approach in an integrated manner, we will prove again and again that "noting works better than good theories."

Archibald's comments on the chronology spanning five decades of scientific project management concepts, principles, methods, and supporting information systems are short, simple, yet decisive and final: "Where will this very important movement, with its continued development and broader application of PM concepts, methods, systems, and tools, be taking us during the coming decade? More of the same, only bigger and better (Archibald 2009).[90] Such a well-founded and stabilized path for the inclusion of diverse projects and the ever-growing project management system knowledge create a perfect environment where researchers and practitioners share valuable experiences, insights, and knowledge about the past, present, and, naturally, the future of global project management.

Finally, when the project is complete and actual data replace the plan's simulated data and projections, we can analyze the project's final performance and success and document the lessons learned. This analysis is outside the scope of this book.

90 Archibald, Russell. "Five Decades of Modern Project Management: Where It Comes from, Where It's Going." *PM World Today* Volume XI, Issue. X (October 2009): www.pmworldjournal.net.

2

Time and Resource in Project Management Planning

Introduction

The introduction of the concept of project management development in 1962 accelerated an already recognized need to improve large American organizations' project time, cost of resources, and performance indicators (DOD and NASA Guide 1962).[91] The increased emphasis on scientific project management planning (PMP) often concentrated on the evident progression of project size and complexity and the new opportunity to manage them. There is also a growing emphasis on searching for unique contributions to established knowledge, soft skills, efficiency, and future PMP stability.

Many textbooks brilliantly explain the role and the impact of time and resources in PMP for trainees. But this is not what I have in mind for the most popular subject of project management planning. I want to explain the critical contents of time and resources in PMP within the integrated book topics and help the student of any grade competently deal with PMP which is both a science and an art.

91 DOD and NASA Guide. *PERT COST: Systems Design*. Office of the Secretary of Defense and National Aeronautics and Space Administration. 1962.

While not many companies have a formal and comprehensive PMP structure or team, there is an intensifying need for the PMP's scope to include explanations based on new perspectives. We discussed earlier the basis, contents, processes, structures, and methods of PMP. We also dedicated sufficient attention to the origins of scientific time and resource project management planning and its leading practices, collectively bounded by project network diagrams. The project management software development, inclusion of narrative rationality, simplification of definite achievements, and project network diagrams have become a fundamental tool for project planning. Many classic textbooks referenced in the preceding chapter discuss in detail about project network diagrams. To avoid reiterating the well-covered matter, I focus first on the sources and fundamentals of project network diagrams and their generalization.

Planning for time and resource in project management is developed by studying client requirements, project technology, contents, processes, and conditions. The project planner uses project documentation to understand the project scope and learns about various technological and social systems, works, timeliness, resources, costs, and milestones across the project. They analyze the company's best practices and project requirements to define the specific steps for developing and implementing achievable project management plans with the most economical utilization of time and resources. Besides, they usually review a general collection of project management knowledge and journal articles to enhance the relevance of the contents of the project management plan.

The project's time management plan assists the user in fixing the appropriate timeframe for each of the project component. A time management plan answers questions about the timeframe decided for completing project activities and, consequently, for work packages, deliverables, phases, or other structural constructs of project and project business. At a minimum, the time management plan must cover the following aspects:

- Project works, including managing multiple contractors, work areas, material storage, equipment, and management of change orders, claims, incentive schemes, and others
- Project start date, and the date by which the conditions for the start of open-start project activity are to be concluded
- Duration or total development time assigned specifically to an activity
- Activity type, resource calendar for driving resources, and other constraints that define the activity
- Early and late dates for completing project activities

- Measurement of activity status, progress and forecast, and information development at various levels of technology management and project management
- Flexibilities in timeslots assigned to each project activity to signal the possibility of risks arising from delayed activity which may result in conflicts between parties and lead to claims and penalties
- Elapsed time from the start of the activity to data date of activity plan assessment
- Remaining time available for the completion of project activities under progress
- Critical path, to explain the longest chain of project activities and the shortest time for project completion

Project resource management deals with estimation and optimum allocation and use of project resources. In addition to people, we must estimate all resources necessary for each activity in the project, which assumes the estimate of anything measured by physical units, such as currency, work, equipment, material, people, space, and other resources that make the activity. Besides, scholars are experimenting with the soft approach across a social environment and social entities in the resource-estimating process to improve efficiency in project resource management. The resource management plan supplements the time management plan and, in due course, enhances the activity by specifying at a bare minimum the following parameters:

- Activity type—distinguishes a mechanism for handling time and resources for an activity
- Estimate of human and material resources needs for project activities
- Resources' names
- Resource calendar for each resource
- Unit measure for each resource
- Cost of unit measure for each resource
- Quantity of resources needed to complete an activity

The resource manager can specify each resource as total quantity for an activity or discrete quantity for each time unit of activity duration. The following equations show the balance between time and resource for task activity's total or remaining duration,

Duration = Resource Units (Total for Duration) / Resource Units (for Each Time Unit of Duration)

If you need to calculate a new duration for the activity in progress, then

New Duration = Actual Duration to Date + Remaining Duration

If we change or freeze one value, other values change correspondingly to balance the equation. All of these processes are highly automated today. For example, we can choose to work with the Fixed Duration and Units, Fixed Duration and Units/Time, Fixed Units, or Fixed Unite/Time (Maharana 2020, 181)[92]. Suppose we deal with an independent activity, that is, the resource-dependent activity. In that case, the time between the start of the first driving resources and the last driving resource's conclusion determines the duration of the independent activity. Project management software has many other automated routines based on planning network diagrams.

Project time and resource themes relate with substantial contents of other chapters in the book, but mostly Chapters 1, 3, and 8.

Time Management

The network planning diagrams and some other specifics of the project management plan have been described in Chapter 1, Network in Project Management Planning. In one part of the chapter, the reader can recall the description of project planning network diagrams known as the Critical Path Method (CPM), Program Evaluation and Review Technique (PERT), as well as the Precedence Diagramming Method (PDM). Some common elements of the above methods are activities and relationships between activities.

Before continuing this section, the reader should revisit Chapter 1, Networks in Project Management Planning and understand their descriptions, similarities, and adaptions. Besides, the reader should briefly examine Figure 3.4 and the section Cost Estimating in Chapter 3 to understand relationships between time and resources for activity and the estimating stages for the project. Close to the

92 Maharana, Dibyaranjan. *Oracle Primavera P6 Professional Project Management, Release 19.* Coppell, TX, 2020.

above, the reader can find within the contents of Chapters 4 and 8 some practical aspects of project time and resource management.

Characteristics

Each activity contains attributes that closely express activity specifics. While developing and implementing a project management plan, we continuously examine activities and related attributes to better integrate their specifics as a constituent of a project management plan. The following sections will discuss the essential characteristics and processes for calculations in the planning network diagram, which are fundamental for developing and implementing the time and resource project management plan.

Time in PMP mostly depends on realistic time estimates and the availability of type and skills of required human resources, the materials, equipment, space, and other resources and conditions to develop project activities. Time estimate for an activity must include an adjustment for adverse weather, vacations, training, injuries, innovative technology, and so on. Besides, temporary restrictions imposed on continuing with project working, delayed payment, changes in development logic, requirements, documentation, scope, workmanships, and others may disrupt the activity's planned estimate.

The planning network diagram and related methods for calculating and presenting activity attributes must be detailed enough to allow a quick and realistic updating of the following:

- Acceptable relationships for project works and alternative approaches for resources deployment
- Planned accomplishments, synchronization, and negotiation for work under different disciplines, long-lead items, milestones, contracts, and contractual parties' businesses
- Time position for project phases to connect with project business, solve challenging problems, or extend opportunities
- Dates approval for activities of common interests

Before we proceed to the application of project network diagrams for time and resource PMP, the following must happen:

- The reader should revisit the key elements of project network diagrams, activity types, relationships between two activities, activity's basic

attributes, calculated attributes, and development of project network diagrams.
- The educator should methodically understand upcoming examples and recognize time and resource management as the key factors that make the difference in the post-Gantt realm in theorizing and practicing workable systems for time and resource management components in PMP.

The calculation of the network planning diagram is known as forward and backward pass through the planning network diagram. It defines two sets of dates for each activity, the early and late start and finish dates.

All those calculations are computerized today and described in PMP software. We must be mindful here that the project management software creates an illusion of sufficiency in the knowledge about project's nature and needs. Therefore, the project management planner must first study the PMP processes and then choose the relevant software before starting the PMP practice.

I use the Precedence Diagramming Method (PDM) to explain the forward and backward calculations since this is almost the only planning network diagram we use today. Let's see Figure 2.1 Precedence Diagramming Method—Basic Calculations; we will understand and eventually memorize the contents and notations from the figure. The example consists of 11 activities only, yet looks challenging and complicated with various activity types, relationships, and conditions that help students simulate different inputs and understand results. Here are the names and durations for activities of the example which we will discuss using Figures 2.1, 2.2, and 2.3:

- Five task activities "A" d = 2, "B" d = 4, "C" d = 3, "D" d = 5, "E" d = 3
- One dummy time, start-to-start relationship—"SS" d = 0
- Three dummy times, finish-to-start relationships—"FS" d = 0
- One lead time, finish-to-start relationship—"FS+5" d = 5
- One lag time, finish-to-finish relationship—"FF+2" d = 2

Forward calculation.

This defines project activities' early start and finish dates—the earliest dates for an activity to start and finish. The calculation begins at each open-start activity that has no predecessors and moves forward to succeeding activities. The early start date of the activity comes from the largest sum of the activities within preceding paths completed by their early dates. The early finish date of the activity comes from adding its duration to its early start date. After completing the forward pass, the largest of the open-end activities' latest early finish date defines the project's duration. In particular, the following happens:

- The project's early start belongs to activity "A" with time unit "0"; forward pass takes the earliest early start of open-start activities as the early start of the project.
- Activity "A's" early finish comes from adding its duration "2" to its early start "0."
- The early start of activity "E" occurs at time unit "12" since this is the largest sum of durations of the preceding paths to the early start of the activity "E." We add to the early start of activity "E" its duration to define early completion of activity "E," as well as early completion of the project. Here are the details:
    - "A" + "FS" + "C" + "FS" = 2 + 0 + 3 + 0 = 5
    - "A" + "FS" + "D" + "FS+5" = 2 + 0 + 5 + 5 = 12; 12 + "E" = 12 + 3 = 15
    - "SS" + "B" + "FF+2" + "FS+5" = 0 + 4 + 2 +5 = 11
- Therefore, the latest early finish date, the longest sum of the duration of preceding paths, and completion of this project indicate or decide the early finish date of activity "E" that occurs at the time unit "15."
- The same calculation can be applied for the early start and early finish dates for any other activity in the project.

Backward calculation.

This defines the project activities' late start and finish dates—the latest dates on which an activity must be started and finished. The calculation begins at each open-end activity with no successors and moves back to preceding activities. The late finish date of the activity comes from the smallest sum of the activities within succeeding paths completed by their late dates. The late start date of activity comes from subtracting its duration from the late finish date. After completing the backward pass, the smallest of open-start activities' earliest late start date defines the project's start. Specifically, the following happens:

- The project's late finish belongs to activity "E" at time unit "15"; backward pass takes the latest late finish of open-end activities as the late finish of the project.
- Activity "E's" late start comes from subtracting its duration "3" from its late finish time unit "15."

- The late finish of activity "A" occurs at time unit "2" since this is the smallest sum of durations of the succeeding paths to late finish of activity "A." We subtract from the late finish of activity "A" its duration to define the late start of activity "A," as well as late start of project. Here are the details:
  - 15 – "E" – "FS" – "C" – "FS" = 15 – 3 – 0 – 3 – 0 = 9
  - 15 – "E" – "FS+5" – "D" – "FS" = 15 – 3 – 5 – 5 – 0 = 2; 2 – "A" = 2 – 2 = 0
  - 15 – "E" – "FS+5" – "FF+2" – "B" – "SS" = 15 – 3 – 5 – 2 – 4 – 0 = 1; note that this path relates to start of activity "A."
- Therefore, the earliest late start date, the smallest sum of the duration of succeeding paths, and the start of this project correspond to the late start of activity "A" that occurs at the time unit "0."
- The same calculation applies for the late start and late finish of any other activity in the project.

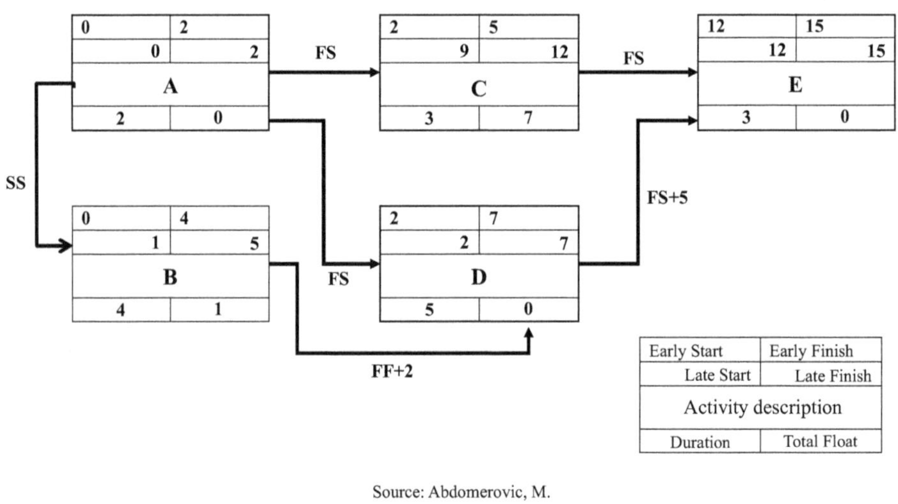

Figure 2.1: Precedence Diagramming Method
Basic Calculations

The same calculations for forward and backward passes apply to PDM, PERT, and CPM methods. In general, the forward and backward calculations tell us that activity can develop between its endpoints and between the earliest possible and latest allowed dates of its endpoints.

Processes

There are many processes related to planning network diagrams supporting the development and implementation of project management plans, such as activity relationships, activity coding, and activity dynamics. However, the most substantial part of the planning network diagram relates to understanding activity float or the amount of time an activity can safely delay the early start date to its late start date. For example, an update of the planning network diagram might display the time units available for delaying an activity in the project without delaying its latest allowed dates. Some paths in the planning network diagram have added flexibility for their development without delaying the project's duration. This flexibility for the development of an activity is known as activity float.

Float Management.

Not all activities start on early dates; some activities have different types of floats that allow them to start and complete later than their early dates without any impact on the project completion date. If we manage the float carefully, as we do with activities, it may help effectively manage project time and resources. For example, an activity may initially have high priority. Still, if we get deeper inside its structure, we may find that only a small part of the activity must be completed on an early planned date, and the rest of the activity has sufficient flexibility for its completion.

There are several types of activity float—total float, early free float or free float, late free float, and independent float. However, in practice, two floats, the total float, and the free float apply.

- Total float for activity comes from subtracting its earliest start date and duration from the earliest late start of successor activities. A total float shows the number of time units an activity can delay its start or finish without delaying the late start of succeeding activities. The same amount of total float is transferable to other activities of the related sequence; spending or earning total float or part of it decreases or increases the total float for that sequence.
- Free float for activity comes from subtracting its earliest start date and duration from the earliest early start of successor activities. A free float shows the number of time units by which an activity can delay its start or finish without delaying the early start of succeeding activities. The amount of free float is not transferable to any other activity.

A critical activity is one with zero total floats. It should start on time and finish on or before its planned completion; otherwise, project completion time may slip. Critical activities control the overall timing of the project. The chain of critical activities forms the critical path; the ultimate path from project data date to completion implies completing all other project activities. For example, Figure 2.1 Precedence Diagramming Method—Basic Calculations shows that the "critical path" consists of activities "A" + "FS" + "D" + "FS+5" + "E" = 2 + 0 + 5 + 5 + 3 = 15. Identification and visualization of the critical path help the user manage the project's logic better. Presentation of the critical path is essential for communication between project managers and technology managers and building consensus about project development.

Critical path or paths can temporarily have a negative total float during the development stage of the project management plan. It may change during the implementation of the project management plan. The number of critical activities of an actual project rarely exceeds 15% of the total number of project activities.

Some authors present a duration-based performance index to forecast project finish date based on total flow usage compared to traditional use of total float as an indicator of project completion at the project data date (Carter 2012).[93]

.

A noncritical activity is one with a positive float. It has flexibility for the activity's start and finish times without changing the project completion time. For example, Figure 2.1 Precedence Diagramming Method—Basic Calculations shows that activity "B" has early finish at time unit "4" and late finish at time unit "5." It means that the end limits and positive values of activity "B" are different, so the activity can delay the start or finish date within its end limits without changing the project's late finish date.

Primavera/Oracle project management software introduces the Relationship Float. It is the duration existing through a relationship that drives the successor activities and creates criticality. If the zero-relationship free float exists, that relationship is a driving relationship, as any delay with the predecessor will impact the successor (Maharana 2020, 212–214).

93 Carter, Carissa, "The Total Float Consumption Index (TFCI)." *The Measurable News*, Issue 4 (2012): 17–20. http://mycpm.org.

Progress Management.
As the project development progresses, we must understand and capture its dynamic and update the project plan.

We can follow the results of the project plan's update from Figure 2.2 Precedence Diagramming Method—Updating Project Progress. For example, we update the project at data date "2" and see that activity "A" undergoes planned progress and gets completed at time unit "2." However, activity "B" does not progress, and its start time changes from time unit "0" to time unit "2" (the actual start date of "B" is at the second time unit). As a consequence, the critical path of the project has changed; it consists now of the "Actual start of B" + "B" + "FF+2" + "FS+5" + "E" = 2 + 4 + 2 + 5 + 3 = 16 time units for total duration, which is "1" time unit more than the original project duration of 15 time units revealed by calculating the initial forward and backward passes between activities.

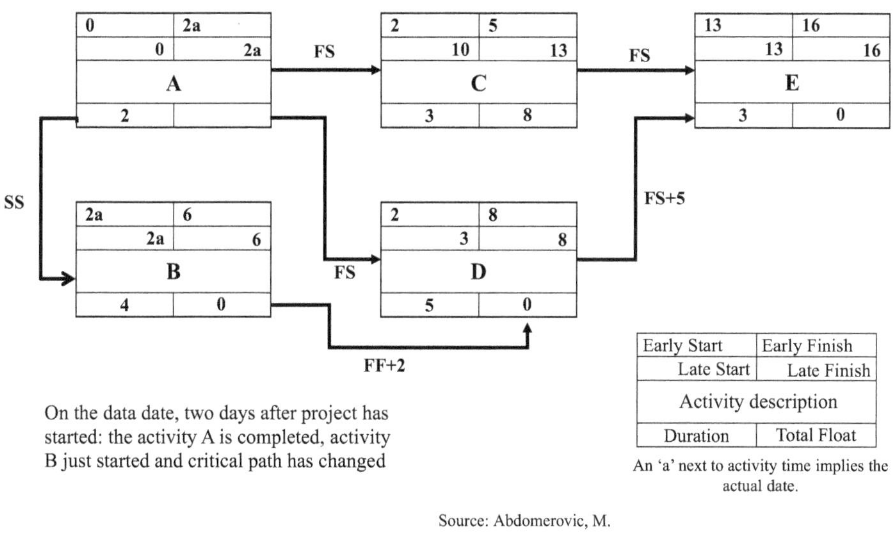

Figure 2.2: Precedence Diagramming Method
Updating Project Progress

After completing the process of project relationships and adjusting the attributes for activities, the preliminary calculation of the project plan can be fine-tuned by additional planning features as follows:

- Calendars, assigned to an activity or group of activities (project phases, work packages, periods), may carry out working units (hours, days, weeks,

months), working shifts, holidays, non-work units, or other calendar features. Calendars may relate to an activity's time or resources specific to that activity.
- Constraint dates, assigned to an activity or group of activities (project phases, work packages, periods), may impose early possible, late allowed, mandatory, or other constraint dates. Constraint dates may relate to the start or endpoint of the activity or different resources within the activity. The early constraint date relates to the start of an activity; it means the activity cannot start earlier than the specified constraint date. We consider the early constraint dates during the forward pass. The late constraint date relates to the conclusion of an activity; it means the activity cannot be finished later than the specified constraint date. We consider the late constraint dates during the backward pass.

Mandatory constraints date relates to the start or finish of an activity. It means that the activity must start or finish on a specified date. We consider the mandatory constraint dates during forward pass only after the activity's mandatory start date and backward pass before the mandatory finish date.

Constraint dates show a more convincing time position for project components regardless of time-based calculation. The most common use of the constraint date is to lock an activity's start or finish date or a common endpoint of activities. Consequently, it may define constraint dates for activity chains of significant deliverables, phases, or projects.

From Figure 2.3 Precedence Diagramming Method—Constraint Dates Effects, we learn that activity "D" cannot start before time unit "4" (early constraint start date for activity "D" is at the fourth time unit). As a consequence, the project cannot finish before time unit "17" ("Constraint start date of D" + "D" + "FS+5" + "E" = 4 + 5 +5 +3 = 17). Note that activity "B" is not critical at this time since activity "B" has "one" time unit of positive float, so it cannot affect completion of activity "D"—the "Actual start of B" + "B" + "FF+2" = 2 + 4 + 2 = 8—while "Constraint date of D" + "D" = 4 + 5 = 9.

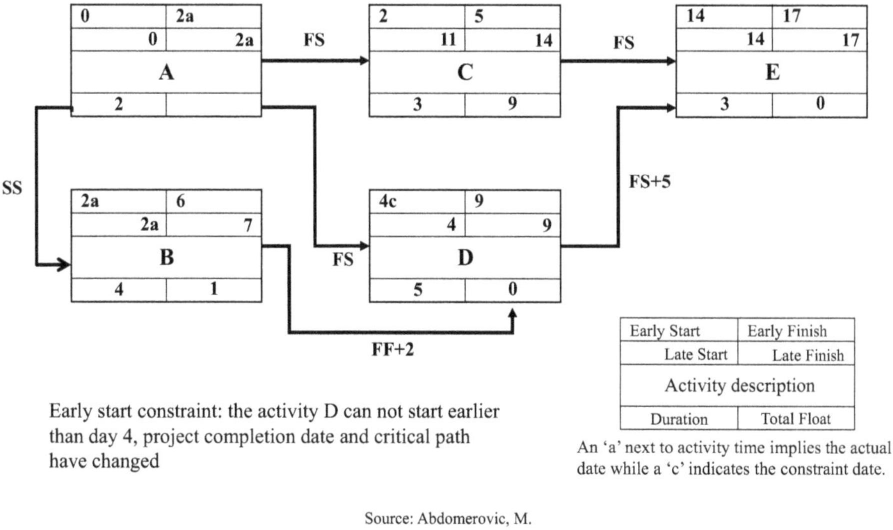

Figure 2.3: Precedence Diagramming Method
Constraint Dates Effects

Understanding the above calculations can create a wealth of information and alternatives to develop meaningful time management plans and emphasize our project, program, or business objectives. We can therefore do the following:

- Develop, use, and maintain project time management plan
- Explain alternatives and recommend a set of management actions
- Show the results of each decision and action that impacts any component of the project time management plan

Activity duration, available resources, and relationships often bind the activity. Also, there are situations, including the technological conditions (availability of workspace, skills, materials, equipment, tools, technical documentation), general conditions (political, environmental, contractual, organizational, weather, financial, management capability), or complexity and uncertainty of any kind, which disrupt the development of an activity.

The above and other conditions require the support of skilled planners and managers who understand the meaning of PMP and can deal with numerous specifics that surround PMP. For example, we must know how to:

- compile a project plan using a project template;
- structure, assign, and maintain a dictionary for project activity codes;

- define relations between continuous and interrupted activities;
- explain a project plan results when a change arises and affects numerous relationships, constraints, and other activity attributes;
- choose out-of-sequence progress for an activity or group of activities;
- handle open starts and open ends of activities;
- use a float trend chart and track the progress of activities outside primary logic;
- handle a complex of inter-project relationships and project group relationships;
- identity relationships between two activities that may additionally influence constraint dates, resources, use of floats, priority, and other activity's attributes and conditions.

Earlier, we learned that the critical path is the longest one out of many activities that occur sequentially. Simultaneously, a critical path defines the shortest possible sequence to complete network planning diagram activities. However, suppose we acknowledge the reality of the project's dynamics, including the possible risks and any uncertainty associated with the successful conclusion of the project. In that case, it can be concluded that the deterministic critical path is not necessarily steady and not the most likely path to the successful completion of a project schedule. Some authors suggest adding working units to address risk and uncertainty in the project plan over and above the planned duration estimates. The authors explain how added working units and probabilistic analysis determine the most likely critical path in the future (King and Smith 2019, 31–54).[94] The suggested approach is the step to address the possible risks and uncertainty in the project, but this approach gains acceptance only after sufficient time has been spent to get full coverage, testing, and results.

Resource Management

Time positions of task activities are often constrained by available resources, whereas time positions of independent or meeting activities are constrained by driving resources. If the volume of work for an activity is not in line with the

94 King, Michele, and Robin Smith. "Concurrently Verifying and Validating The Critical Path and Margin Allocation Using Probabilistic Analysis." *The Measurable News* (2019.01): 31–47. http://mycpm.org.

resources allocated, then the activity type, duration, or resources of the activity must be changed accordingly.

To achieve time management objectives, we must plan and control available project resources. This process starts with resource estimating, which defines the resources necessary to develop project activities.

Estimating activity duration requires assuming that resources are available to accomplish the activity. Consequently, the resource requirements of the project match the resource requirements for all activities of the project. If the project duration is longer than the combined duration of the project activities' time-frames, we must reduce the duration of the critical activities. Although each such activity retains the same total quantity of resources, the discrete quantity increases for each time unit in the activity timeframe. The procedure repeats until we achieve the time management objectives and ensure the resource requirements do not exceed the available resources.

There are many alternatives for the levels of resource requirements; however, there are two options that have distinct meanings:

- The first alternative assumes that all project activities start and get completed at their early dates; this means that this alternative is front-loaded or demands early resource aggregation; it uses resources as early as the rationale of the activities allows for it.
- The second alternative assumes that all project activities start and get completed at their late dates; this alternative is back-loaded or requires late resource aggregation; it delays the use of resources as much as the float of activities allows.

The above alternatives rarely happen in practice; however, those are starting steps before we learn how to allocate available resources and achieve the project management plan's time and resource objectives.

Characteristics

Resource-specific estimates in PMP are developed concurrently with time-specific estimates in PMP. Techniques for calculating and presenting project resource graphs and tables symbolize the resource management part of the PMP and allow resource management to take place at any level or any cluster of the project components. Graphs and tables help review the following:

- Resource selection, sorting, and formatting
- Resource limits for a particular period of the project
- Resource calendars for a particular period of the project
- Resource unit prices for a particular period of the project
- Resource amount for each time unit, or cumulative resource amount for any period of any cluster of project components, and other characteristics of resource graphs and tables.

There are various choices related to the calculation and presentation of project resource graphs and tables. The most common choices are known as resource aggregation and resource allocation.

Resource Aggregation.

The time position of project activities, supported by the planning network diagram, plays a crucial role in shaping resource graphs and tables. For the following example, we must understand the right side of Figure 2.5, the Logical View of project activities, the planning network diagram, since Figure 2.4 and the left side of Figure 2.5 depend on the logical view.

Figure 2.4 Resource Aggregation shows early and late resource aggregation. The figure's left side illustrates early resource aggregation, whereas the right side shows late resource aggregation. Each side of the figure has three parts:

- The upper part of the figure shows a Time View of project activities and their relationships. Each activity has a name, duration, and resources necessary to complete the activity. For example, activity "A" has a duration of "2" time units and needs "2" resources for each time unit to get completed on time. The sequence of activities "B," "C," and "D" defines the critical path of the project, whereas activities "A" and "E" encompass the float. Activity "A" can start at the beginning of the project and must be finished by the project is completed; therefore, this activity has "2" time units of float. Activity "E" can start at the beginning of the project and be concluded before starting activity "D"; therefore, this activity has a "1" time float unit.
- The middle part of the figure shows a resource graph for early and late resource aggregation or project resource requirements for each time unit. As we can see from the figure, the graph of resource histograms depends on each activity's resource requirements and time position. There are several alternatives to position activities "A" and "E"; however, each

alternative results in the same total amount and different graphs of resource requirements.

- The lower part of the figure shows the cumulative graphs of project resource requirements. Although both sides of the figure have the same cumulative amount of resource requirements and, consequently, the project's same cost, the cumulative curves' shapes are different. The cumulative curve for early resource aggregation shows that the project initially requires "6" resource units, and the requirements drop gradually by the end of the project. The cumulative curve for late resource aggregation shows that the project requires "1" resource unit at the beginning of the project and then requirements constantly increase until the end.

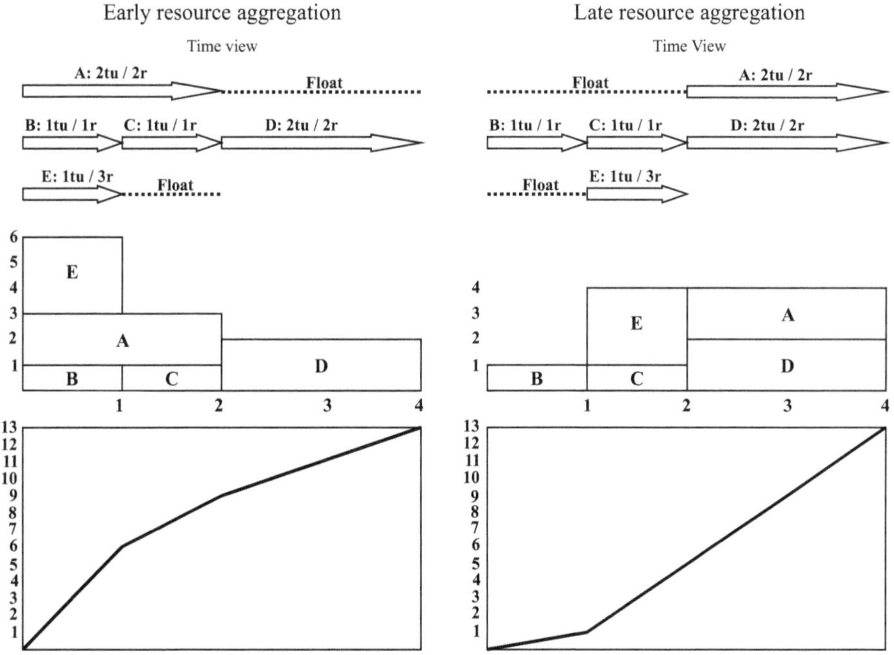

Source: Abdomerovic, M.

Figure 2.4: Resource Aggregation

Resource aggregation gives a first glimpse of the potential distribution of planned resources and serves as a base for negotiation among project stakeholders that aims to achieve best resource deployment.

Resource Allocation.

Since resources are usually limited, and neither flexible nor unlimited, the performing organization has to achieve project's conclusion within the contracted duration and within available resources. In this process, an activity moves between its earliest possible and latest allowed dates and defined normal and maximum resource limits until it comes to a position where it matches the resources made available to plan it. As soon as an activity gets resources and plan dates, the available resources for the project decrease.

The above process continues until the project team finds the best way to perform activities within the available resources and meet the project milestones and completion date. So, we talk about resource allocation when activities are placed between their early and late dates to get needed resources.

In practice, we should start by establishing plans and then simulate alternatives until we come to a strong time and resource plan for the project. If no option comes close to the histogram of available resources, we must delay the project completion date.

For example, the left side of Figure 2.5 shows the sequence of work when we have a Limited Level of Available Resources of "3" units maximum for each time unit. This situation requires the placement of activities between their early and late dates to determine the most efficient use of available resources.

The figure has the same parameters as the one described in Figure 2.4 Resource Aggregation, including the same activities, activity relationships, names, durations, resource requirements, and histogram square values. However, the resource allocation case has one significant difference: the level of available resources. To complete the project within a given condition, we cannot use more than "3" resources for each time unit. There are several alternatives to complete the project under this constraint; however, all other options result in project delay. Figure 2.5 Resource Allocation is one of those alternatives that illustrate how the level of limited resources and ultimate activity relationships affect project duration.

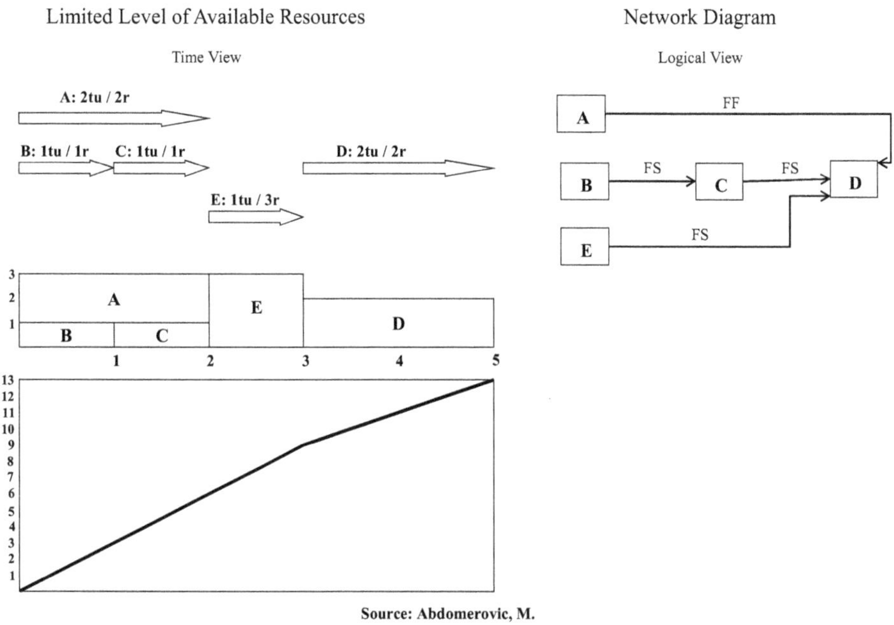

Figure 2.5: Resource Allocation

Processes

An average project, program, or business includes many activities, resources, and constraints. Therefore, we must have a selective approach to choosing resources and activities that result in the best resource allocation. In most cases, we should analyze resources that critically impact the project and then allocate such resources to activities with negative total float, high cost, or long duration. During this process, we must consider the following:

- What is the time position for the activity?
- What technologies and resources does the activity require?
- What are the total resource requirements and availability for a particular time position of an activity?
- How do we recognize and communicate process groups and share project time and resource information?
- How do we link and cope with responsibilities for task-driven activities?
- How do we define and manage resource calendars and profiles for resource-driven activities?

- How do we link, monitor, update, report, and record project time and resources?

In practice, we must consider the conditions when project dates overrun and resource availability exceeds the limits. We distinguish here two situations:

Time-Limited Schedule.

When project objectives are not flexible in relation to project milestones and completion dates and the time objectives must comply with a time-limited schedule, then we approach the problem of resource allocation by:

- allocating available resources to critical activities and then determining schedule dates for those activities
- allocating resources to other activities that are not on the critical path and determining schedule dates for those activities
- using threshold resources rather than a threshold time.

Resource-Limited Schedule.

When project objectives do not demonstrate flexibility in regards to resource availability and the resource objectives must comply with a resource-limited schedule, we approach the problem of resource allocation by:

- understanding when and under what conditions the project completion date, or accomplishment of a particular milestone, can overrun
- finding out if and under what conditions some resources can overrun limits
- using a threshold time rather than threshold resources.

Understanding the above limitations, we can simulate a dynamic allocation of resources in a multi-project environment. It may result in the optimal usage of available resources and substantial cost savings. Besides, many other processes support resource management planning during developing and implementing a project management plan. For example, resource codes and code values, resource estimating, resource timing, resource organization, resource shifts, resource leveling, resource deployment, resource updating, and other processes are part of project resource management planning.

If a company decides to manage available resources and complete its projects on time and within the budget cost, then it is important for it to address the following aspects:

- How do we manage resource databases and update periods for resource availability?
- How do we integrate resource management with the company's fundamental structures, cost estimating structure, cost accounting structure, work breakdown structure, and organizational breakdown structure?
- How should the company's project management office be organized to help integrate and update the resource database?
- How do we implement the policy and strategy for project business and usage of available resources in the company?
- How should the company's management distribute the responsibilities for resource allocation in a multi-project environment?

The best results occur if we use the above assessments to initiate a new project and then update it regularly by including data from other projects. As project business management is responsible for controlling resources at the company, department, or project levels, an updated picture of resource requirements and availability may be essential for management decisions. We will discuss the above ideas in the forthcoming chapters.

There is also another side to resource management that deals with complex issues. For example, we should examine the roles in developing and maintaining reliable estimating databases, product knowledge, resource management policy and strategy for deployment of resources, external influence, and decision-making processes in resource management.

Besides, we acknowledge the definition of a project as a temporary structure within a project business organization which is a permanent structure. This situation opens many questions about human resource management, including politics, organization, continuous education, optimal allocation, motivation, career orientation, and others and their orientation and alignment with individual projects and project business objectives (Dalcher 2015).[95]

Time and resources in PMP are mostly regulated matters. For this purpose, the reader should be well-informed about relevant standards, specifications, and guidelines. For example, the U.S. Government Accountability Office's (GAO)

95 Dalcher, Darren. "There is nothing so permanent as temporary: Some thoughts on adapting project structures." *PM World Journal* Volume IV, Issue VI (June 2015): www.pmworldjournal.net.

Best Practice for Project Schedule (Kurian 2019),[96] the Construction Specification Institute's (CSI) *Manual of Practice* (*CSI Manual of Practice* 2004),[97] and other tools and templates can help develop mature scheduling specifications and better organization of time and resources.

Case Study

This study aims to illustrate the project manager's role in developing and implementing a project management plan. The study results show that the project manager's early involvement in the project team's configuration and PMP process improves the project plan. The study also describes the project manager's role in bringing together project management and technology management. The presented example relates to a megaproject that includes massive construction works and procurement of equipment and organization and coordination of contractors for mechanical, electrical, and industrial control services and other such major contractors.

Knowledge of Project Manager

A project manager has a crucial impact on the project planning process. The project plan can be useful if the manager understands the general PMP process and can develop and implement the project management plan. For this purpose, we should understand:

How general project management knowledge of project manager complements

- technology management,
- project management best practice,
- standards and regulations practice,
- contract management,
- links between project planning structure and project business structures, and

96 Kurian, Tijo. "How to write a Model Scheduling Specification Incorporating the GAO's 'Best Practice in Scheduling' Appendices." *PM World Journal* Volume VIII, Issue XI (December 2019): www.pmworldjournal.net.

97 CSI Manual of practice. *Project Resource Manual: CSI Manual of Practice, 5th Edition.* New York: McGraw Hill, 2004.

- work of internal services and agreements in the company.

As well, the specific professional experience and competence of the project manager complements the

- project requirements and objectives,
- project contents' structure and organizational structure,
- software to be used for PMP,
- communication of project status, progress, payments, changes, causes, forecasts, and actions, and
- update of project and project business management plan.

Key reasons that inhibit the project manager from giving their full support to project planning are insufficient procedures for project planning in the company, diversified project planning experience of project team members, and lack of professional PMP knowledge. Those conditions create subjective approaches to project planning, making it difficult to organize and apply project planning processes.

At the beginning of the project, we usually hear that project planning is necessary. However, when the project plan's development begins, conflicting ideas about developing and updating the project plan surface. Most project team members try to explain personal experience on project planning processes, updating procedures, reporting structure, and others, resulting in poor commitment and communication among team members and suboptimal decisions (Manata, Garcia, Mollaoglu, and Miller 2021).[98] In such a situation, the project manager becomes concerned mainly with using and maintaining those portions of the project management plan that they consider important. It means some other areas with the same weight factor, cost, and number of schedule value items may not get the same attention from the project manager and may drive parts of the project to uncontrolled development. In contrast, good communication and exchange of information among team members improve learning, personal

98 Manata, Brian, and Angelo Joseph Garcia, and Sinem Mollaoglu, and Vernon Miller. "The effect of commitment differentiation on integrated project delivery team dynamics: The critical roles of goal alignment, communication behaviors, and decision quality." *International Journal of Project Management* Volume 39, Issue 3 (April 2021): 259–269. https://sciencedirect.com.

performances, and creative problem-solving in the project (Carmeli, Levi, and Peccei).[99]

Suppose the project manager develops a workable document that summarizes the plan, for example, Figure 4.1 Project Planning, Manager's View. In that case, the project team may develop a detailed plan. However, their view of the project plan may not be perfect, and the subsequent planner's work must show detailed alternatives and eventually reveal the glitches in the manager's view of the project plan. Assume a document created by the project manager describes only a certain portion of the project. In that case, the project planner has to act proactively and develop other supplementary documents, for example, a sketch of ultimate relationships of scope, which may motivate the project manager to work on different parts of the project plan. During that time, the project team must answer the following questions:

- How to check if the manager's view of the project plan is suitable enough to develop the project plan's overall sequence? For example, does a global view of the overlap between the mechanical and the electrical installations lead to the shortest project duration?
- How do we relate project plan documents from various stakeholders to project managers' global views of the project plan? For example, how do we relate a detailed mechanical installation guideline with a rough electrical installation plan?
- Can the project team members develop the required details for a sequence defined in managers' global view of the project plan? For example, does a summary duration for mechanical installation have enough flexibility to suit a detailed plan of activities to be performed to complete mechanical installation?
- Can the primary logic sequence be used to develop a secondary logic of the project plan? For example, how can we use the primary logic of mechanical installation to develop a detailed production plan to deliver mechanical equipment?
- How do we make similar conditions for different contractors? For example, how can we distribute the total float for mechanical insulation equally

99 Carmeli, Abraham, Avi Levi, Riccardo Peccei. "Resilience and creative problem-solving capacities in Project teams: A relational view." *International Journal of Project Management* In-Press Version (May 2021). https://sciencedirect.com.

to other contractors who either follow or avoid their work within a crushing schedule?

The project team members can answer the above questions if the project management plan's outline comes from extensive consultations with the project manager and team members. Besides, the project manager must work closely with functional managers, prospective contractors, and planning professionals to improve the value of their outline of the project plan. The project team must have proven databases of similar works, appropriate methodologies, and tools to simulate alternative project development plans during this period. It may include simulation of various conditions, assumptions, requirements, and alternatives for accomplishing the project objectives.

Involvement of Project Manager

Project management planning (PMP) needs the close involvement of the project manager since they are responsible for creating sustainable communication with project stakeholders and appropriately govern the project, in terms of the project contents, directions, and outcomes (Ziek and Anderson 2015).[100] For example, if the project is small, the manager becomes a one-person team that performs most project management work. Such a project manager has to perform the following activities in relation to implementing the project management plan:

- Provide support and play a coordinator role in the administration, development, and maintenance of the project.
- Keep daily progress logs and records of all events related to the project management plan.
- Assist in the acceptance of accomplished work, calculate the earned value, and control the payment applications process.

However, suppose it is a large-scale project. In that case, the project manager should employ an experienced system analyst/project planner to develop and continuously update the project management plan. In that case, the project manager retains a coordination role, creates a work environment based on project

100 Ziek, Paul, and Dwight Anderson. "Communication, dialogue and project management." *International Journal of Managing Project in Business* Volume 8, Issue 4 (September 2015): 788–803. https://doi.org/10.1108/ijmpb-04-2014-0034.

deliverables, and prepares guidelines for developing and implementing the project management plan. In this case, the project manager performs or is involved in completing the following activities:

- Study the best planning practice, project-related standards and regulations, planning frameworks, and methodologies.
- Explain project planning requirements and documents; dedicate special attention to contract with the performing organization, including the required details, schedule value items, coordination of works, and payment process.
- Understand the time required for the entire project and project milestones, including a preview of project time before initiating the project master plan. Here it is important to compile a list of procurements with a long lead time for major contracts, equipment, materials, and site machinery to be used for the project.
- Participate in the analysis of project scope and project contents for each major area of the work, including work contents of major contracts and internal agreements, and identification and quantification of major resource requirements for structural components.
- Visit prospective contractors to understand their interests, abilities, resource availability, cooperation pattern, and communication needs; participate in negotiating contents; ensure that prospective contractors understand requirements and submit contract management plans as required. It is of prime significance that each contractor specifies schedule value items showing how work will be accomplished and paid for, as well as constraints in supplying each schedule value item.
- Ensure that each stakeholder specifies a wish list for the PMP and reporting contents.
- Use the project master plan to develop the beginning and completion of significant contracts and internal agreements.
- Identify work interfaces and requirements within each work area and areas necessary to coordinate major works and continuously protect all completed works.
- Follow requests for information and clarification of requirements and discrepancies in existing documents and works.
- Assist clients in understanding the project planning requirements, actions, and results, including information on project progress, status, changes, causes, and forecasts.

- Understand and communicate with passion the processing of change orders, payments, and claims.

Soft Skills of Project Manager

Let's look at the practical side of the project manager's role in the planning of material-handling projects.

Work in material-handling projects involve intensive mechanical engineering, which counts for more than 55% of all works. Material-handling equipment manufacturing represents over $20 billion in the industry (Material Handling Industry of America [MHIA] 2010).[101] It is common to believe that overall project performance in the industry depends on sound planning and procurement of mechanical equipment, where equipment are procured in a timely manner and at best possible prices. The subsequent electrical or industrial control work will likely get delayed if there is delay in deciding which mechanical equipment to design and fabricate or to buy and delay in its delivery or installation.

Project layout areas are the primary structure of material-handling projects. In most cases, construction column lines determine sub-areas which we use for various purposes, for example, organization and execution of the process of design, procurement, and installation of mechanical equipment. A division by column lines does not have much meaning outside construction and mechanical works.

101 Material Handling Industry of America. *Material Handling Equipment Manufacturing.* MHEM Industry, 2010. www.mhia.org/learning/marketresearch/forecast.

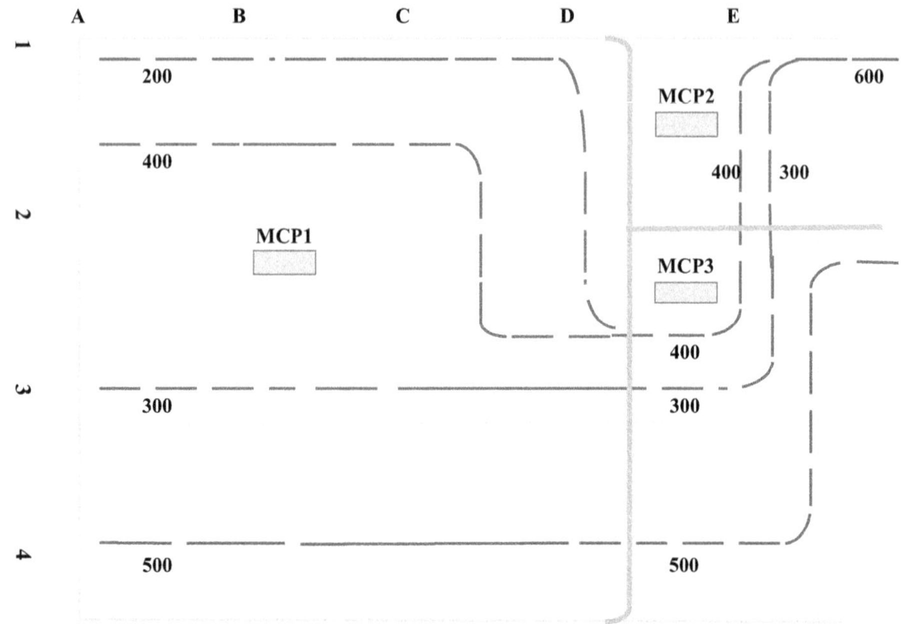

Source: Abdomerovic, M.

Figure 2.6: Project Planning
Equipment Layout

For example, electrical design analysis shows that the motor control panels (MCP) and associated mechanical components do not match the mechanical design areas. There can be several reasons for this situation:

- Single MCP (MCP1) or multiple MCPS (MCP1 and MCP3) may be necessary to run mechanical components (Conveyor 200) located in a single mechanical design area, the area A-D/1-3.
- Single MCP (MCP1) or multiple MCPs (MCP1, MCP2, MCP3) may be necessary to run mechanical components (Conveyor 400) located in multiple mechanical design areas, the areas A-D/1-3; D-E/2-3; D-E/1-2.

Therefore, before we hand over planning requirements to the planner, the project manager must explore in depth the scope of the project scope and understand the exchange of planning information between functional groups and contractors. For example, which level of mechanical design must be completed before electrical designers can allocate MCPs and add the mechanical equipment to the panels? To accomplish this task, the project manager must consider both mechanical and all other types of work to develop meaningful guidelines for the project plan. For example, they must analyze the relationship between mechanical work and electrical work and clarify the expectations envisaged in the overall project management plan:

- When, in logical terms, can a mechanical designer issue a general layout of mechanical equipment, including the list of conveyors?
- When, in logical terms, can an electrical designer locate MCPs so that each MCP is associated with the mechanical equipment that resides in a single mechanical design area or neighboring areas?
- When can mechanical and electrical engineering provide documentation for developing the project and equipment production plans?
- When can the project planning team start analyzing the tie-in relationships between areas and works, for example, the most detailed and definitive sequence that shows how to hand over the project to the client?

Analyzing the above questions helps the project manager realize that the production and project schedules should be based on the disposition of electrical equipment and associated mechanical equipment within neighboring areas. Figure 2.7 Project Planning—Mechanical Equipment—Project-Oriented Production illustrates this notion. In this final phase, the project manager opens the door to the project team in order for them to engage in the detailed development of the project management plan, including developing a detailed production plan for equipment.

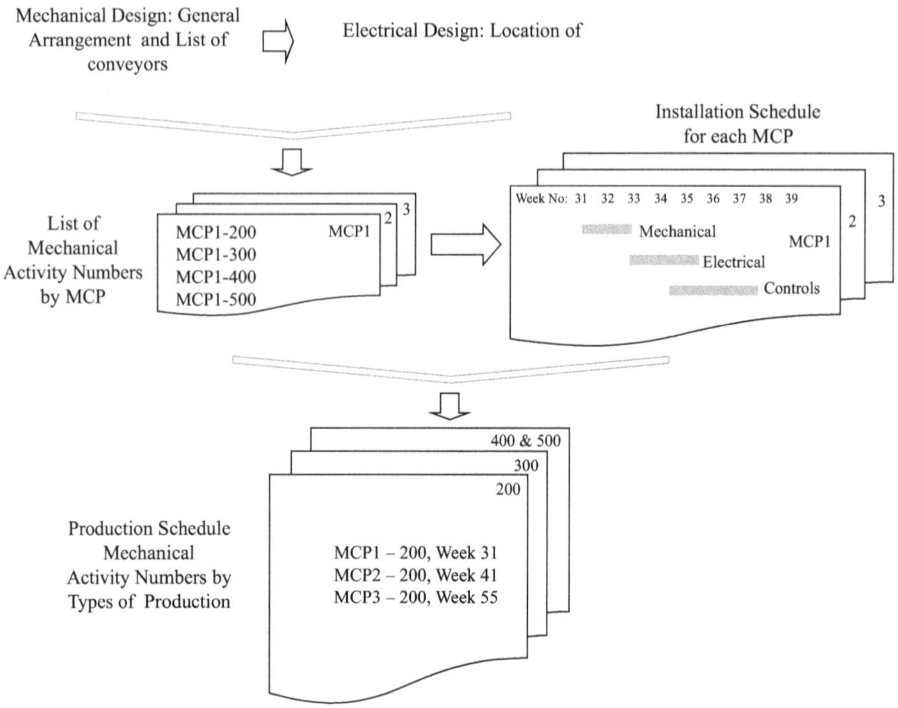

Source: Abdomerovic, M.

Figure 2.7: Project Planning
Mechanical Equipment—Project-Oriented Production

In addition to the company's best practice and standardized methodology for project planning, the project team also used Primavera project management software to help manage the timely delivery of special equipment and "just in time" delivery of standard equipment. One out of many reports, project-oriented production plan report, is shown in Figure 2.8 Project Planning, Connection Lines, Delivery, and Installation.

Activity Description	Activity Duration	Activity Start Date	Activity Finish Date	Activity Percent Completed	Activity Budgeted Quantity	Activity Earned Quantity	Activity Total Float
Mechanical Equipment On Site, Project 95, Building *E*							
Connection Lines, 53221	1	7Aug08	7Aug08	0	502	0.00	0
Connection Lines, 53223	1	29Aug08	29Aug08	0	528	0.00	3
Connection Lines, 53225	1	5Sep08	5Sep08	0	451	0.00	19
Connection Lines, 53227	1	11Sep08	11Sep08	0	437	0.00	25
Connection Lines, 53229	1	16Sep08	16Sep08	0	506	0.00	2
Connection Lines, 53231	1	20Oct08	20Oct08	0	1212	0.00	0
Connection Lines, 53233	1	29Oct08	29Oct08	0	857	0.00	4
Mechanical Installation, Project 95, Building E							
Connection Lines, 53221	5	8Aug08	14Aug08	0	209	0.00	0
Connection Lines, 53223	4	2Sep08	5Sep08	0	320	0.00	3
Connection Lines, 53225	4	8Sep08	11Sep08	0	188	0.00	19
Connection Lines, 53227	3	12Sep08	16Sep08	0	182	0.00	25
Connection Lines, 53229	5	17Sep08	23Sep08	0	211	0.00	2
Connection Lines, 53231	7	21Oct08	29Oct08	0	505	0.00	0
Connection Lines, 53233	5	30Oct08	5Nov08	0	357	0.00	4

Source: Abdomerovic, M.

Figure 2.8: Project Planning
Connection Lines–Delivery and Installation

A project management plan guided by the project manager and operated by the project team will be accepted and pushed project-wide; even a good plan that does not have the manager's hands around it is worthless. The project manager must consider simulation processes for at least two alternatives, a mechanical engineering–driven plan, and an electrical engineering–driven plan.

- In the first alternative, mechanical design determines the operational areas, which coincide with building column lines. In this case, the driving mechanism for all other disciplines becomes mechanical design.
- In the second alternative, electrical design determines the operational areas, which coincide with mechanical equipment sets in neighboring areas. In this case, the driving mechanism for all other disciplines becomes electrical design.

By simulation of project planning objectives and goals, as well as stakeholders' requirements, we observed the following:

- A project plan based on mechanical design, organized across construction column lines and oriented to conveyor trains, has continuous mechanical design, delivery, and installation results. However, electrical works cannot follow the same sequence because their work is organized by MCPs oriented to sets of conveyors located in neighboring areas with different completion schedules. The electrical installation related to a specific MCP was affected by a mechanical installation sequence oriented to conveyor trains, which produced delays and idle time for electrical work. Uninterrupted electrical work requires installing mechanical equipment in areas controlled by a specific MCP, which creates a scattered sequence of mechanical design, delivery, storage, and installation.
- A project plan based on electrical design is good for both mechanical and electrical work. For example, a single MCP located in a certain area controls mechanical equipment in several neighboring areas. A control panel is complete when all equipment belonging to a particular MCP are connected. Suppose the project team has planned a mechanical design by considering the areas controlled by a specific MCP. In that case, the project team can manage the mechanical design, equipment delivery, and installation with minimal interruptions, delay, or idle time. As a result, the sequence of electrical installation activities coincides with the sequence of mechanical installation activities.
- Consequently, the long lag time between mechanical installation and electrical installation is reduced, and the float used by electrical engineering in the previous (mechanical) scenario is evenly distributed between all disciplines. Also, the critical path was now more realistically distributed between more disciplines. Although this approach could require some additional cost for mechanical design and, eventually, store conveyors, it may be less expensive than squeezing or delaying electrical installation. It causes delays in control engineering work and handing over the completed areas to the client.

As we see, the problem of prioritizing mechanical installation adversely affects first the electrical engineering activities; second, the controls engineering; and, third, the handover of project deliverables to the client. In this situation even a slight increase in project cost for mechanical design and storing of conveyors can increase the idle time of electrical and controls resources and delay the project completion date.

By carefully studying the above example, we learn that the project plan should focus on concurrent development of both mechanical design and electrical design, with minimum lag time between the two disciplines. It should result in an early release of the conveyor list, early location for MCPs, early association of conveyors to the MCPs, and better convergence of subsequent mechanical, electrical, and controls works.

We can conclude from the above example that procurement and installation of mechanical equipment should not follow the sequence of mechanical design. It may seem controversial, but a project plan based on electrical design could more effectively determine the installation of mechanical and electrical devices. Of course, we should remember that the above example focuses only on the relationship between mechanical work and electrical work. However, to benefit from the project manager's involvement in project plan development, the project team must analyze the relationships between other disciplines, for example, electrical work and system control work. If this approach is systematically analyzed, it can lead to creating and following a standard that works best for project-oriented production, equipment installation and save both time and cost in material-handling projects.

We must assess the level of details present in a project plan. For example, mechanical equipment installation should be planned at the conveyor level, whereas other work should be planned for and carried out at higher levels, for example, a train or set of conveyors. By assigning a conveyor production number to corresponding mechanical installation activity, we can develop a very efficient database, where updating PMP information is limited to a single source and distribution of information automated. This part of the project plan must be discussed in more detail, especially its technological and management aspects, for example, details about the various steps involved in creating the project plan, including the project functions, features of the software application used for the project, projects costs, and project benefits and outcomes associated with the planning effort.

If the project plan's development proceeds without the close involvement of the project manager, then the project stakeholders will not support the project plan. Consequently, the project will not have a comprehensive plan. Uncontrollable events will become a reality and a daily story, excessively long meetings and storms of emails and memos are certain to occur, and, eventually, the project planning effort may become useless.

The early involvement of project manager in project planning is a pragmatic approach. It is based on the confirmation that the project's master plan for the key contract is sufficient for organizing the project activities. This concept may work well for key contracts. To make the planning concept widely acceptable, the project manager must have a vision of an integrated, all-inclusive project plan and must lead the activities in the development and implementation of project management plan, including the development of a detailed production plan.

3

Cost in Project Management Planning

Introduction

Before 1962, project cost management planning was operated by a standard costing system, a type of production cost management considered suboptimal for resolving project cost management problems. Project cost management is the most vibrant area of project management planning (PMP); its methodologies and practices are constantly growing, and project managers continue to reap the benefits of its unique characteristics.

Project cost management planning starts after an organization completes a project feasibility study and financial arrangements to conceptualize, develop, and, eventually, operate a project. To comply with the requirements for a cost project management plan, the project manager must be able to do the following:

- Build a cost project management structure that is equally useful for managers at the project's operational levels and the company's business levels.
- Establish relationships among the project cost accounts and the company's general cost accounts.
- Understand information about diverse project management costs, planned cost, actual cost, earned value cost, and estimated total cost at the time

of completion of the project, along with cost variances, cost indexes, and other metrics.
- Provide cost information for the status, progress, changes, forecasts, and causes of the project.
- Compile a narrative that supplements the project cost results for project and project business managers.
- Suggest possible actions for improving the results of the cost project management plan.

Cost management in project management plan is a vital feature to the already explained features such as the integrity of scope of the project and the time and resource needed to successfully manage the project.

Cost Management

The reader entering the cost management area encounters many new terms and requirements to comply with the cost management terminology.

Users of system knowledge for cost management in PMP usually operate the same set of cost data. However, the cost data are named differently by different users. For example, the primary cost name Planned Value also has synonyms known as Planned Value for Work Scheduled, Budgeted Cost for Work Scheduled, Contract Sum, Allocated Budget, or Budgeted Cost. As a result, the complex relationships between such terminologies (Haupt 2004, 34)[102] create a situation where project managers and cost planners, estimators, or accountants barely understand each other.

Let's examine the original, currently used, and perspective names for basic project cost management such as Actual Cost, Planned Value, and Earned Value. Those costs are the basis for understanding other costs, cost variances, and cost indexes.

The original names for basic cost management come from traditional production cost management known as standard costing. A description of the various routinely used terms in cost management is provided below:

102 Haupt, Eleonore. "The Wonderful World of Acronyms." *The Measurable News* (Summer 2004). www.mycpm.org.

- The actual cost in production management is known as the actual quantity produced at the actual cost per unit, whereas in project management it is identified as the actual cost or actual resource units at the actual unit price.
- Budgeted cost in production management is known as the budgeted quantity produced at standard cost per unit, whereas in project management it is identified as the planned value or baseline resource unit at the baseline unit price.
- Standard cost in production management is known as the actual quantity produced at the standard cost per unit, whereas in project management it is identified as earned value or the actual resource unit at the baseline unit price.

Therefore, regardless of cost application areas, production, or project, we always deal with the cost of resources or let the computer calculate the cost based on the resource quantity and resource unit price.

Besides, there are similarities between names for costs in production management and names for costs in project management. However, the differences between these two types of costs are substantial. Cost in production management creates only periodic relationships between groups of identical products and production time, where cost in project management creates continuous relationships between project activities and project time as well as the various attributes of time:

- Cost "To Date" of project performance measurement, assuming any date during project phases
- Cost "To Complete" from the date of project performance measurement to the date of project completion
- Cost "At Completion" from the date of project start to the estimated date of project completion

Whereas there are no relationships between cost and time in the context of the different names of costs in production management, the relationships between cost and time in terms of cost names in the original project management are evident. The following are some of the names for cost in production management vis-à-vis cost in original project management, such as cost as of "To Date" used for measuring project performance:

- "Actual Cost" (Brown and Howard 1969, 140)[103] versus Actual Cost (PMBOK Guide 2000, 197)[104] or "Actual Cost of Work Performed" (Fleming 1988, 501).[105]
- "Budgeted Cost" (Brown and Howard 1969, 140) versus Planned Value (PMBOK Guide 2000, 204) or "Budgeted Cost of Work Scheduled" (Fleming 1988, 504).
- "Standard Cost" (Brown and Howard 1969, 140) versus Earned Value (PMBOK Guide 2000, 201) or "Budgeted Cost for Work Performed" (Fleming 1988, 504).

As we can see, the original names for project management costs adopted by Fleming are profession-specific. Such costs are

- descriptive, since each name's meaning can be recognized from its description;
- consistent, since each name defines a single subject, the cost; and
- time-bound, since each name expresses a clear relationship between cost and time.

The meanings for terms used to denote different types of cost in basic project management have remained the same from the time they originated. However, efforts towards simplifying the names of cost has changed the names of cost in original project management to match those in current parlance:

- The original name, the "Actual Cost of Work Performed" (Fleming 1988, 501), is currently termed as the "Actual Cost" (PMBOK Guide 2000, 197).
- The original name, the "Budgeted Cost of Work Scheduled" (Fleming 1988, 504), is currently called the "Planned Value" (PMBOK Guide 2000, 204).

103 Brown, Lewis, and Leslie Howard. *Principle and Practice of Management Accountancy.* London, UK: McDonald and Evans, 1966.

104 PMI 2000. *A Guide to the Project Management Body of Knowledge (PMBOK® Guide) 2000 Edition.* Newtown Square PA: Project Management Institute, 2000.

105 Fleming, Quentin. *Cost/Schedule Control Systems Criteria: The Management Guide to C/SCSC.* Chicago, IL: Probus Publishing Company, 1988.

- The original name, the "Budgeted Cost for Work Performed" (Fleming 1988, 504), is currently called the "Earned Value" (PMBOK Guide 2000, 201).

Even though names of costs in current project management are simple and easy to remember, they lack subject consistency. If we use only the quantity for resources in project management plan, then current cost names must add a new subject. For example, the "Actual Cost" should become the "Actual Quantity," which increases the number of current cost names. Besides, the cost names in current project management do not show any relationship with project time.

As the subject "value" includes "cost" and "quantity," or anything that physical units can measure, we may also think about different names for project management costs. Such names should be simple, descriptive, consistent, time-related, and profession-specific:

- Planned value of work scheduled
- Planned value of work performed
- Actual value of work performed

The above issues will be clarified later after we gain general insights into project management plans and costs.

Characteristics

The project cost management plan consists of the Original plan, Baseline plan, and Current plan. Figure 3.1 shows the elements of time and project cost management plans covered in this chapter. While learning about project cost management, the reader may find it useful to revisit this pictorial summary of project cost management which illustrates numerous cost situations.

Cost Types.

Cost types, namely the Planned Value, Earned Value, Actual Cost, and Estimate to Complete Cost, characterize the project cost management plan. The first three types of cost have deterministic value, and the fourth type of cost has stochastic value. Here are brief descriptions of cost types:

- Planned Value—shows the cost, or cost of resources, for an activity that defines project work that should have been completed in a given period.

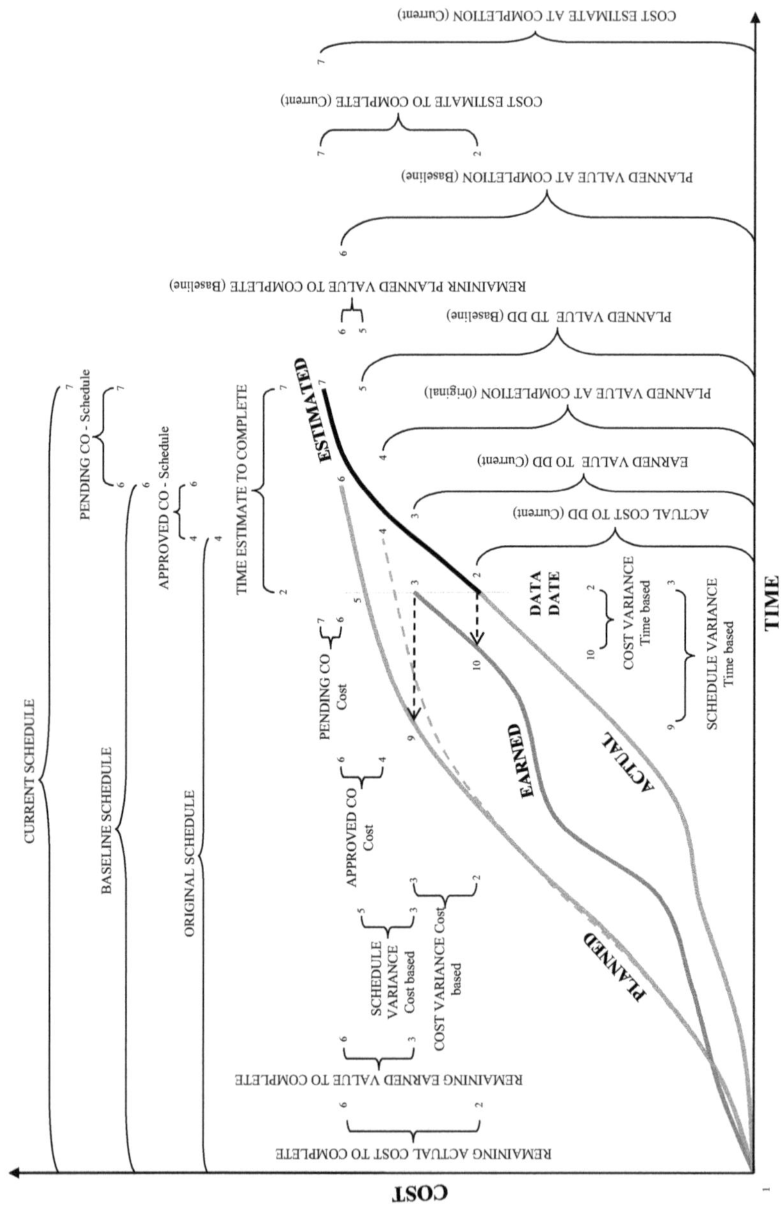

Source: Abdomerovic, M.

Figure 3.1: Project Schedule and Cost Plan Schematics

Planned value is deterministic, approved, and, in most instances, a contracted cost that must have the highest possible accuracy.

- Earned Value—shows cost, or cost of resources, for an activity that defines project work which has been completed within a given period. So, work can have earned value only if it is planned. Earned value needs approval if we use it for any financial decisions and records.
- Actual Cost—shows cost, or cost of resources, for an activity that defines project work and which has been paid for during a given period of the project. Actual cost is independent of earned value but can occur only if it is earned or anticipated as advance payment. The actual cost may be different from the amount billed to the client and must be approved.
- Cost Estimate to Completion—shows cost, or cost of resources, for an activity that defines project work which should occur from the date of project performance measurement to the date of completion of current schedule. Cost estimate to completion is mostly a stochastic value, which includes project activity performance by data date and may include pending change orders (PCOs). Cost estimate to completion is usually priced but not necessarily approved or contracted cost.
- Cost Estimate at Completion—shows the estimate of probable cost, or cost of resources, for project activity that defines work which has been completed plus contracted work that should have been completed plus forecasted work that probably should be completed from the project start to the estimated project completion. Usually, the cost estimate at completion is equal to the sum of the actual cost to date and the cost estimate at completion. The cost estimate to complete is not an approved cost, and the cost estimate at completion is not an approved cost either. However, it can serve in the early negotiation stage about achievable and reliable final project scope and cost.

Figure 3.2 Basic Costs shows cost types, brief definitions, synonyms, and practical calculations for project cost management plan.

Basic Calculations.

The most important aspect of the project cost management is understanding the logic behind calculation values and calculation elements. Let's have a look at the contents of Figure 3.3 Calculation Elements:

		Definitions and Synonyms	Time Periods	Practical Calculations
Deterministic	Planed Value (PV)	**Definition:** *Planned* resource units, or cost of the resource units for the activity that defines project works, which *should have been completed* to a given time period of project. **Synonyms:** Planned Value of Work Scheduled, Budgeted Cost of Work Scheduled, Performance Measurement Baseline, Approved Budget, Contact Sum, Scheduled Value, Allocated Budget, Planned Cost, or Budgeted Cost.	Planned Value at Completion (PVAC)	PVAC; Approved Planned Value at Completion. May include Approved Change Orders that reside in current and baseline project plan.
			Planned Value to Date (PVTD)	PVTD * Resource or Schedule % Complete to Date of the baseline plan.
			Planned Value to Complete (PVTC)	PVAC – PVTD; Remaining planned value to complete.
	Earned Value (EV)	**Definition:** *Planned* resource units, or cost of the resource units for the activity that defines project works, which *have been completed* to a given time period of project. **Synonyms:** Planned Value of Work Accomplished, Budgeted Cost of Work Performed, Completed and/or Stored Value, Earned Cost, or Standard Cost.	Earned Value at Completion (EVAC)	PVAC
			Earned Value to Date (EVTD)	PVAC * Resource or Schedule % Complete to Date of the current plan
			Earned Value to Complete (EVTC)	PVAC – EVTD; Remaining earned value to complete.
	Actual Value (AV)	**Definition:** *Actual* resource units, or cost of the resource units for the activity that defines project works, which *have been paid* to a given time period of the project. **Synonyms:** Actual Cost of Work Performed, Actual Cost Incurred, Actual Value, or Historical Cost.	Actual Value at Completion (AVAC)	PVAC
			Actual Value to Date (AVTD)	Comes from project cost accounting. Usually equal to approved EVTD from most recent period
			Actual Value to Complete (AVTC)	PVAC – AVTD; Remaining actual value to complete.
Stochastic	Estimated Value (EV)	**Definition:** *Forecast* of resource units, or cost of the resource units for the activity that defines works, which *will probably complete* to a given time period of project. **Synonyms:** Cost Forecast, Latest Revised Estimate, Statistical Estimate, Cost Estimate, or Estimated Expenses.	Estimated Value at Completion (EVAC)	AVTD + EVTC. A part of EVTC resides in current plan only and may include Pending Change Orders.
			Estimated Value to Date (EVTD)	It calculates a short term forecast for upcoming payment requests..
			Estimate Value to Complete (EVTC)	Estimate value to complete the remaining planned and forecasted works of project cost plan. Otherwise, PVAC – EVTD +/- PCO.

Source: Abdomerovic, M.

- Title row of the figure shows the different types of costs in project cost management—Planned Values, Earned Value, Actual Value, and Estimated Value to Complete.
- The first column in the figure shows calculation elements necessary to determine the resource units or cost of the resource units for different types of costs.
- In general, the figure shows the intersection between cost types in project cost management and calculation elements.

From Figure 3.3, Calculation Elements, we can draw many conclusions:

- There is no Earned Value cost for the baseline plan, or the Earned Value cost for the baseline plan is not significant. We can tell the same for Actual Value and Estimate Value to Complete.
- If only the resource unit expresses project work, then Earned Value and Actual Value are the same for a given period in the project trajectory. It is because both types of costs include the same calculation elements.
- If the resource unit expresses project work, then Actual Cost and Earned Value cost can be different since other calculation elements—the Baseline Resource Unit Price and Current Resource Unit Price—can be different.

Relationships between types of costs and cost calculation elements show what we must obtain to get a specific value. For example, we can see from Figure 3.3 that we must know the number of resource units for any calculation. Even if baseline resource units cannot or need not be counted in detail, we still need to perform some calculations.

	Baseline Plan		Current Plan		
Basic Calculation Values	Planned Value at Completion (PVAC)	Planned Value to Date (PVTD)	Earned Value to Date (EVTD)	Actual Value to Date (AVTD)	Estimated Value to Complete (EVTC)
Basic Calculation Elements					
Baseline Resource Units at Completion		■	■	■	
Baseline Resource Unit Price		■	■		
Baseline Resource Units % Complete					
Baseline Schedule % Complete		■			
Current Resource Unit Price				■	
Current Resource Units % Complete					
Current Schedule % Complete			■	■	
Remaining Duration to Complete					
Estimated Resource Units to Complete					■
Estimated Resource Units per Time Unit					
Estimated Resource Unit Price					■
From to Date to Current Plan Completion					■

Examples

Planned Value to Date = Baseline Resource Units at Completion * Baseline Schedule % Complete to Date * Baseline Unit Price
Earned Value to Date = Baseline Resource Units at Completion * Current Schedule % Complete to Date * Baseline Unit Price
Actual Value to Date = Baseline Resource Units at Completion * Current Schedule % Complete to Date * Current Unit Price
Estimate to Complete = Estimated Resource Units tp Complete * Estimated Resource Unit Price

Source: Abdomerovic, M.

Figure 3.3: Calculation Elements

The above costs serve as a base for the terminology and the calculation of other derivative costs, cost variances, and cost indexes.

The fundamental base for project cost management consists of cost-estimating and cost-planning processes. Cost estimating ensures that the calculation of cost is in the best interest of the client and contractor. Cost-planning processes empower the user to handle project costs according to contract and management requirements.

Processes

Project participants at different organizational and contractual levels estimate the cost or the cost of resources to complete project activities. Those who succeed in developing a reliable cost estimate achieve a basis for successful cost project management. It is of particular interest to clients who encounter this issue from the conceptual project phase when everything is in alternative conditions to project completion when all bills must be settled.

The client should prepare a preliminary cost estimate structured by bid packages and critical resources for each bid package. It will help avoid qualitative interpretation during the bidding process. The quality of a client's cost estimate determines their ability to manage project contracts. The contractor steps into the client's shoes when estimates of subcontractor cost are to be presented, since the most important cost estimates come from subcontractors and suppliers of material and equipment who participate in the bidding.

For a contractor, their basic objective in the cost-estimating process is to win the contract and make a profit. There are many solutions, and most of them depend on the reliability of the cost estimate. Increasing the cost-estimating process's reliability leads to better outcomes or results in project management for both the client and their contractors. In general, the cost estimate impacts the following issues (Fine 1969)[106]:

- An inaccurate estimate, big or small, will waste the bidder's resources even if the company wins the contract.
- A smaller but reliable bid is necessary to receive as many sub-bids as possible. It will increase the probability of selecting the best subcontractors who offer the lowest prices.
- Those who can make cost estimating reliable will also be able to estimate quickly and participate successfully in many bidding events.
- If the cost estimate is more reliable, then we can expect a bigger positive difference between the contractor's bid price and the client's allowed price for the job.
- If we want to keep the same revenue and permanent cost estimate reliability, then we must extend more invitations to the bidding process and facilitate an increase in the number of participants in the bidding process.
- A positive difference between the contractor's bid price and the client's allowed price for a job will be bigger when all participants present bids with more reliable estimates.

Cost Estimating.

The cost-estimating process correlates with the engineering process and evolves as the knowledge about project contents increases. During this sequence, cost estimates stay accurate within an acceptable 5–10% range. However, a difference in the cost estimate from the earliest project stage and the actual cost at project completion can be substantial and can even exceed by 100%; this is the

106 Fine, Brian. *Management Game (Lecture notes delivered at the University of Loughborough, UK).* Costain, Operational research department. London, UK: February 1969.

difference between the cost estimate and the actual cost decreasing toward later project phases. The following principal sequence illustrates cost-estimating stages and development of cost-estimating information:

- The order-of-magnitude stage is based on initial project data, technical requirements, and rough structure of related works, materials, expenses, and services for the project. This stage usually estimates total project cost by using the actual cost of similar projects. During this stage, the client describes the project's product and the project's characteristics and makes a macro decision about the project structure and content. In this cost-estimating stage, the client typically applies an analogous estimating technique. The difference between the cost estimate for this stage and the project's actual cost which can be above 100%.
- The conceptual stage is based on 30% of the documented data, conceptual design, feasibility studies, scope statement, defined specifications for major equipment, structural concept, alternatives, and long lead items. At this stage happens the measurement of the alternative balance between cost, duration, and performance by estimating quantifiable and scalable parameters for project deliverables and objectives. This stage must show a comprehensive structure of 20% of the most important works specifications, which encompasses about 80% of the total cost estimate. Here, the client typically applies the parametric modeling technique. The difference between cost estimate at this stage and the project's actual cost can be above 70%.
- The preliminary stage is based on 50% of the documented data, which includes the preliminary design comprising specifications for the various components of the project, including building foundations, supports, floors, and roof, purchase of special equipment, and estimating the cost for carrying out activities in relation to all of these requirements. At this stage, the total project cost is determined by preparing budgets based on which bidders are invited and orders issued for services that require long lead items. Here, the client concludes the process of taking principal material decisions and creating the overall contracting structure, that is, the contract in its final form. Client typically applies a bottom-up estimating technique. The difference between the cost estimate at this stage and the project's actual cost can be above 50%.
- The definitive stage is based on 90% of the documented data. The final design includes the final scope of the project, including the final technical

decisions, schematic drawings and specifications, submittal needs, and cost estimates from selected contractors and suppliers of work, materials, equipment, and services. It usually estimates total project cost by estimating a structured budget and negotiating the contracts. This stage must show different clauses oriented toward different contractors and regulation of their cost estimate submittals. The client typically asks bidders to apply bottom-up estimating techniques. The difference between the cost estimate at this stage and the project's actual cost should not exceed 20%.
- The control stage of cost estimate is based on the final design documentation and checks for bids, quotations, and proposal from contractors and suppliers of materials and equipment. In addition to the awarded contracts or external agreements, this cost-estimating stage must include detailed estimates for all internal commitments, risks, money to be spent, overheads, profits, contingency plans, and the end of the client–contractor negotiations. Also, this stage must estimate the management reserve, which is not part of the project budget. Finally, this stage must have a ready system for a cost estimate of internal and external change orders. The difference between the cost estimate for this stage and the project's actual cost can be above 10%.

The system of project cost estimating is carried out and concluded within a short duration, followed by a long period in which it can be second-guessed, criticized, and divided into three basis subsystems:

- Develop and maintain cost-estimating databases
- Identify and describe project work elements in cost estimate databases and specify the quantity or amount of resources, human and material, for each work element
- Calculate the bidding price

The subsystem of developing and maintaining cost-estimating databases relates to all projects within an organization. It is important for estimating costs in an organized and efficient way. Besides, well-developed and well-maintained cost-estimating databases improve the quality of decisions because both the team preparing the cost estimates and those carrying out the work based on those estimates use the same rationale in judging the feasibility of carrying out the work or activity as specified in the cost estimates. The most important attributes of general work elements include:

- Description of typical work elements for a technology division
- Unit of measure for each work element
- Classification codes for each work element
- Quantities of resources (labor, material, equipment) used to perform the unit of measure of work element
- Unit price for each resource to carry out and complete work in each of the work elements specified

The subsystem of identifying descriptions of work elements relates to a specific project. This subsystem's primary purpose is to make a detailed review of contract documents, define the required work elements for a specific project, and identify each work element within the estimating database.

The subsystem of calculating and defining the bidding price based on cost-estimating databases can combine the cost-estimating stages and simplify the cost-estimating processes. Cost-estimating professionals use project documentation; calculate quantity of resources at completion; add overheads and the cost of contingency plans; determine profits to be expected; and define the final bidding price for the work elements and for the project in totality. We use the same work elements to track the progress, status, changes, forecasts, and causes, reflecting all of the higher levels of project and project business structures. Some of the above costs—the overheads, contingency, and profit—are estimated at higher structural levels for work packages, deliverables as well as for the whole project. This estimating technique is known as activity-based costing or bottom-up cost estimating. If activity-based costing is not feasible, then we can apply analogous estimating or parametric modeling techniques. In each case, cost estimates must be detailed enough, identified by a single component of work breakdown structure, the activity, or work package, where cost is estimated for each component at its most detailed level. Otherwise, the work item for which cost estimates are to be prepared has to be broken down into more subcomponents.

Use of commercially available project cost–estimating database, such as Means 2019[107] or WinEst 2017,[108] is vital to the process of managing project costs in order to ensure smooth and timely flow of information between all stakeholders of the project, including between the client and the performing organization. Compilation of new databases containing detailed, well-organized, and all-inclusive contents for specific engineering division or construction work is a

107 Means. *Building construction cost data*. Kingston, MA: R. S. Means Company, 2019.

108 WinEst. *Cost estimating solution*. WinEstimator, 2017. www.winest.com

long process; in my experience, it exceeds seven thousand hours. With Artificial Intelligence in sight and its application in PMP, we can expect that data, processes, and opinions within pre-loaded technologies may heavily depend on project estimating databases—see Williams (2019, 10)[109] and Budeli (2020, 5).[110]

Cost Presentation.

Pictorial presentation of project cost or cost of resources is usually in the form of a cumulative curve. The purpose of cost accumulation is to get the total cost for each time unit over project duration. The process provides a visual basis for comparison among project's various durations and costs, which must be closely monitored by the performing company and its client.

To understand the development of a cumulative cost curve for any type of project cost, we must have cost specifications for project activities. Figure 3.4 Cost Account Baseline shows activities A1, A2, A3, and associated resources, as well the cost of resources. For example, activity A2 may have the following:

- Start cost (R2), which must not coincide with the start of the activity; some advance cost can be made a part of the activity well before the activity starts.
- Time unit cost (R3), which coincides with activity duration, is usually uniformly distributed and accumulated from the start of the activity start to the end of the activity.
- Finish cost (R4)—this must not coincide with the conclusion of the activity; some retention cost can be made a part of the activity well after the completion of the activity.

After finalizing the multi-line cost estimates for cumulative activities, we can arrive at an approximate cost value which usually is depicted by a single discrete curve as shown in Figure 3.4 Cost Account Baseline.

109 Williams, Rob. "Fortifying your career in 2020 and beyond." *The Measurable News* Volume 2019, Issue 02 (2019): 9-12. http://mycpm.org.

110 Budeli, Lalamani. "Data analytics to improve engineering project management office (PMO) performance: The predictive analytics approach." *PM World Journal* Volume X, Issue III (March 2021): www.pmworldjournal.net.

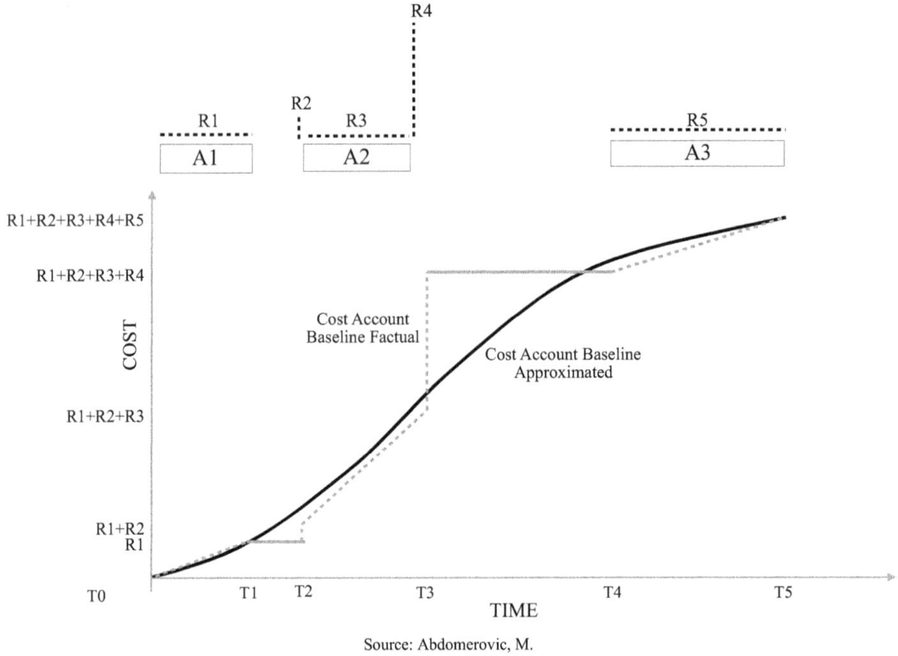

Figure 3.4: Cost Account Baseline

The process of aggregating costs or resources for individual activities produces a time-phased value for the higher structural component of the project, program, or project business. When the project's time–cost aggregation is accepted, it becomes a guideline for a project's financial plans and policies; the performing organization also endeavors to make such plans and policies suitable for and align them with the objectives of other projects within the organization. Let's have a closer look at the types of costs and their interrelationships.

Planned Value.

Planned value is a time-phase-specific cost estimate; therefore, its cumulative value is different for each time phase or point of time in the overall timeframe for completing of the project. Thus, planned value changes during project development and can be a part of reports for different periods, including the periods specified for project performance measurement, accounting, long-term results, and fiscal investments and expenditures. The planned value usually has two parts:

- The first part, the Planned Value to Date, displays a cumulative planned value cost that should have been in its final form right from the start of the

baseline schedule to the date on which the project performance measurement is carried out.
- The second part, the Planned Value to Complete, displays a cumulative planned value that should have been completed from the data date to the date the baseline schedule comes to an end. Planned Value to Complete is a synonym for Remaining Planned Value to Complete.

The sum of Planned Value to Date and Planned Value to Complete is equal to the Planned Value at Completion. Planned Value at Completion is a synonym for Baseline Planned Value at Completion.

Planned Value to Date is related to the date on which the project performance measurement is carried out. We can calculate Planned Value to Date in three ways:

- Accumulate baseline resource units that should have been completed "to date" as specified in baseline plan

Planned Value to Date (Resources) = Baseline Resource Units (To Date)

Planned Value to Date (Cost) = Baseline Resource Units (To Date) × Baseline Resource Unit Price

- Multiply the percentage of baseline resource units that should have been completed "to date" of the baseline plan by baseline resource units at the completion stage

Planned Value to Date (resource) = Baseline Resource Units Percentage Complete (To Date) × Baseline Resource Units at Completion

Planned Value to Date (Cost) = Baseline Resource Units Percentage of Completion (To Date) × Baseline Resource Units at Completion × Baseline Resource Unit Price

- Multiply the percentage of baseline schedule that should have been completed "to date" as per the baseline plan by baseline resource units at the completion stage

Planned Value to Date (resources) = Baseline Schedule, Percentage Complete (To Date) × Baseline Resource Units at Completion

Baseline Schedule, Percentage Complete = [(BD – BRD) / BD] × 100, where BD is Baseline Duration and BRD is Baseline Remaining Duration

Planned Value to Date (Cost) = Baseline Schedule, Percentage Complete (To Date) × Baseline Resource Units at Completion × Baseline Resource Unit Price

The above values are always associated with baseline dates and show the status in relation to the "should be" progress according to the percentage of completion of the baseline plan. It assumes that the baseline plan at the completion stage has been updated.

Planned Value at Completion may change over of the duration of the project. The changes emerge progressively, from the date the contract has been signed and the original Planned Value at Completion has been added to the contract's completion date when the current Planned Value at Completion is replaced by Actual Cost at Completion. The original Planned Value at Completion usually stays the same until the date of the project completion, and the baseline Planned Value at Completion changes based on Change Orders. Therefore, if we use an updated baseline Planned Value at Completion, it includes all approved Change Orders.

A comparison between the baseline plan cost and current plan costswill reveal the status, progress, and forecast of the project's scope, duration, and costs. Based on these findings, the current project plan gets approved and becomes the new baseline plan. Suppose there is a need to update the baseline plan more often. In that case, we can save as many baseline plans as necessary and use them to analyze trends in project performance in later periods during the course of the project. If contingency reserves have been spent, additional funding for the baseline plan must be borrowed from the management reserves since the baseline plan must serve as a reference for measuring the project's performance.

The baseline plan serves as a record for the most recent update of the budget and schedule for project activities. We should recall that the schedule or the budget should be updated to reflect changes stipulated and implemented based on change orders. If we need to make changes to the baseline plan based on existing data in the current plan, we must understand all of the effects and consequences of such an update. For example, changing the baseline resource schedule will affect the project's planned value and earned value. Therefore, before each update, we must protect the starting condition if a need arises to go back and change the recent assumptions.

After discussing the cost of changes, we can also calculate the Planned Value Variance, a synonym for Budget Variance. It refers to the difference between the baseline Planned Value at Completion and the original Planned Value at Completion. As mentioned earlier, Planned Value at Completion changes by

Change Orders, which could be positive or negative. Therefore, Planned Value Variance will show the magnitude of this change as follows:

Planned Value Variance = Planned Value at Completion (Baseline) – Planned Value at Completion (Original)

Cost planning is a simulation process performed until we get a satisfactory picture of costs to be incurred over various time points during the course of the project and to accommodate and implement changes in the overall project structure. Using this approach, we can prepare the initial but fully integrated plan that reflects the overall scope, schedule, and cost of the project. This leads to the question of how detailed should the project cost plan be. According to the prevailing views of practitioners, this job should be performed as follows:

- If resources or costs are assigned to each task activity, we can get a precise view of the project scope, cost, and schedule. This process requires skills related to many knowledge areas (management of organization, technology, project scope, time, and cost, including management of processes such as cost estimating, budgeting, control, and cost accounting). It works very well for expert users.
- For projects with a detailed structure of scope, it is acceptable to assign resources or costs to completing the task activity representing the work package or hammock activity, spanning from the start to the end of the work package. In that case, cost budgeting becomes simple. However, this alternative does not include a cost plan for each activity; therefore, group activity hides the reason for cost deviation within a work package. Even if we apply this simplified procedure, it is necessary to make detailed assessments of all work packages that show negative cost trends.

The cost project management plan assumes that each activity or group of activities becomes the time- and cost-planning center. When we have a cost project plan ready, the emphasis moves from planning and executing processes to controlling processes. Methodologies for controlling changes to project cost include features that help react to changes, determine the causes of variances, and improve project cost trends.

Earned Value.

Although there are many aspects to project cost control, we are mostly concerned with the progress of an activity that defines the project's work element. This progress is known as the *earned value*. It represents a portion of planned resource units or planned cost of the resource units of an activity that has been accomplished by a specific date. If the start of the activity is after the data date, its earned value is zero. The simplest way to calculate the earned value for activity in progress is to multiply its planned value by the percentage of completion of activities in the current schedule. If we estimate the time currently left to complete an activity, we can arrive at the earned value of the activity. The planned value here is the approved budget or performance measurement baseline used to assess performance in completing an activity. We must also assume that the approved budget is evenly distributed across the whole duration of the activity, allowing for identifying the link between the current percentage of completion of work and the current percentage of the utilization of the approved budget or earned value. We can calculate the Earned Value to Date in three ways:

- Accumulate planned resource units that have been completed "to date" as per the current plan; this is an alternative that is hardly ever practiced

Earned Value to Date (Resources) = Current Resource Units (To Date)

Earned Value to Date (Cost) = Current Resource Units (To Date) × Baseline Resource Unit Price

- Multiply the percentage of resource units completed "to date" by the percentage of completion of baseline resource units as specified in the current plan

Earned Value to Date (Resource) = Current Resource Units Percentage Complete (To Date) × Baseline Resource Units at Completion

Earned Value to Date (Cost) = Current Resource Units, Percentage Complete (To Date) × Baseline Resource Units at Completion × Baseline Resource Unit Price

- Multiply the percentage of completion of activity duration based on the date specified in the current plan by the percentage of completion of baseline resource units, where the resource units are distributed linearly across the duration of the activity

Earned Value to Date (resources) = Current Schedule Percentage Complete (To Date) × Baseline Resource Units at Completion

Current Schedule, Percentage Complete = [(CD – CRD) / CD] × 100, where CD is Current Duration, and CRD is Current Remaining Duration

Earned Value to Date (cost) = Current Schedule, Percentage Complete (To Date) × Baseline Resource Units at Completion (resource) × Baseline Resource Unit Price

The above values are always associated with current dates and show the progress that "has been" made according to the percentage of completion reflected in the current plan. It assumes that Planned Value at Completion is updated because the same Planned Value at Completion has to be used to calculate both the Planned Value to Date and Earned Value to Date. Consequently, Earned Value to Date will be different from Planned Value to Date if percentage of completion of the resources units differs from the percentage of completion reflected in the scheduled utilization of resources.

Both the baseline and the current plan contain cost and schedule data. These data are from the same source; after changes to the current plan are approved, the baseline plan is updated. However, the plans will be different if the baseline and current schedules are different. If we change the resource schedule, resource units, resource unit price, or resource loading type in the current plan, the planned value will change. If the project plan's update procedure changes the current plan's activity schedule, then planned value will not change. However, if we change the activity schedule in the baseline plan, then the planned value will change.

If we change the baseline percentage of completion for resource units or for the schedule, Earned Value to Date will change. Although the calculation of percentages of completion does not measure or take into account the amount of work accomplished or resource consumption for a work activity, it does provide results immediately which are sufficient and reliable for decision-makers. For example, people responsible for the approval of payment application can estimate either the percentage of work completed or the duration left to complete work and produce Earned Value to Date. Here, the base assumption is that we must have a scheduling system where the percentage of schedule completed and the duration left to complete activities have a direct relationship. It means the more percentage of completed, the less the duration left to complete an activity.

Although the "percentage completed" method is widely used, there is also a plethora of methods frequently used to plan and measure resource consumption as well as the specific requirements of the project and the performing company's practices (Fleming and Koppelman 2000, 88–99).[111]

111 Fleming, Quentin, and Joel Koppelman. *Earned Value Project Management,* Second Edition. Newton Square PA: Project Management Institute, 2000.

Managing the earned value is standard procedure and is updated regularly to deal with every new situation. For example, in the case of a science project, we may need to customize the techniques of management of the earned value in order to ensure the beneficial application of the said science project's exploratory characteristics, scientific collaboration as well as measure the general uncertainty surrounding the project (Xiaofeng 2019, 23–27).[112]

The readers interested in the study of earned value management may find a comprehensive article that describes the current three standards (and their structures) of earned value management known as the EIA 5/32, the ISO 2/11, and the ANSI 5/49 (Driessnack 2019-02, 34–38).[113]

Actual Cost.

This represents the actual resource units or the cost of resource units for the completion of an activity that has been paid by a specific date. Actual cost relates to work accomplished or money earned during a particular period, calculated usually on the same date by which the project performance is measured. The actual cost for work elements is calculated in three ways:

- Accumulate the actual resource units completed in line with the date specified in the current plan; this alternative is seldom used

Actual Value to Date (Resources) = Current Resource Units (To Date)

Actual Value to Date (Cost) = Current Resource Units (To Date) × Current Resource Unit Price

- Multiply the current percentage of resource units completed as per the date of the current plan by the percentage of completion of baseline resource units

112 Xiaofeng Guo. 2019. "Enabling EVM to benefit big science projects: Success in tailoring EVM." *The Measurable News*, Volume 2019, Issue 02 (2019): 23-27. http://mycpm.org.

113 Driessnack, John. "Earned value management standards structures: Part 1 – Why three" *The Measurable News* Volume 2019, Issue 02 (2019): 34–38. http://mycpm.org.

Actual Value to Date (Resource) = Current Resource Units Percentage Complete (To Date) × Baseline Resource Units at Completion

Actual Value to Date (Cost) = Current Resource Units, Percentage Complete (To Date) × Baseline Resource Units at Completion × Current Resource Unit Price

- Multiply the percentage of activity duration completed as per the date of the current plan by the percentage of completion of baseline resource units, where the resource units are distributed linearly across the activity duration

Actual Cost to Date (Resources) = Current Schedule Percentage Complete (To Date) × Baseline Resource Units at Completion

Current Schedule, Percentage Complete = [(CD – CRD) / CD] × 100, where CD is Current Duration, and CRD is Current Remaining Duration

Actual Cost to Date (Cost) = Current Schedule, Percentage Complete (To Date) × Baseline Resource Units at Completion (Resource) × Current Resource Unit Price

If only the resource units are involved, then Actual Resource Units and Earned Resource Units are the same. If Actual Unit Prices and Baseline Unit Prices are the same, then the Actual Cost to Date and Earned Value to Date are the same as well. However, if Actual Unit Prices and Baseline Unit Prices are different from one another, then Actual Cost and Earned Value to Date will also be different from one another.

Actual cost is the sum total of costs of actual labor, material, expenses, and subcontractors. Although we should provide the total actual cost from cost accounting functions, we must remember that this is a complicated job to perform in controlling processes due to potential difficulties in the following activities:

- Collecting and allocating actual cost of resources exactly at places where they have been planned, including the actual cost of change orders.
- Allocating the actual cost already recorded in project cost accounting but not planned and earned yet, which includes advance payment and material paid for, stored, but not utilized; we should remember that the actual cost can only be used for performance assessment if planned and earned by the data date.
- Recording the actual cost consistently with the cost accounting system of the company.

In some cases, we may look for a practical procedure that can be operated quickly and allows for using it with enough precision routinely. For example, the collection of actual costs for work elements may be simpler if we assume that most of the Actual Cost generate where they earn. Therefore, through the use of some global calculation, we can distribute Actual Cost proportionally to activities, where

Actual Cost (for Work Element) = Earned Value (for Work Element) × F

F = Actual Cost (for Project, or Selected Components) / Earned Value (for Project, or Selected Components)

The approach enables a reliable measurement of performance at the higher management levels. However, it is necessary to periodically make a detailed distribution of actual cost to work elements where they belong. It will help gain a better picture of the cost of the current project and use its cost structure to estimate future projects.

Some projects allow for the distribution of actual cost by calculating the percentage expended for the project or selected components, showing the proportion of the Planned Value at Completion that has been spent to date, where

Percentage Expended to Date = Actual Cost to Date / Planned Value at Completion.

Percent Expended to Date generally doesn't carry an indicative value; it does not tell anything about work accomplishments. However, it can be useful for repetitive projects with good statistics for project phases and actual cost and help ascertain whether a fair value has been received for the amount spent for a particular phase of the project.

The above text explains Planned Value, Earned Value, and Actual Cost related to task activities and associated direct costs. Note that indirect costs are usually related to hammock activities, where the

- planned value represents the indirect planned cost for a group of related task activities.
- earned value is calculated by multiplying the planned value at completion and weighted percentage of time-specific progress in related task activities.
- actual cost is usually set equal to total indirect actual cost for the group of task activities or to hammock activities' earned value.

Variances and Indicators.

We can calculate different variances and indexes for resources or cost of resources for a specific date using the Planned Value, Earned Value, and Actual Cost. This calculation will give us a more comprehensive picture of project development. The variances and indexes are defined as follows:

- Cost Variance (CV), or cost-efficiency variance, is a difference between the actual cost and earned value, or how much the cost paid for differs from the earned value for a specific date. It is kept higher or equal to the average monthly payment for the contract. If it has a negative value, then it means the current cost value is in excess of value specified in the plan; in such a scenario, it is advisable that we stop payment until we have carried out a detailed assessment of project's earned value and actual cost.

Cost Variance to Date = Earned Value to Date – Actual Cost to Date

- Schedule Variance (SV), or cost performance variance, is the difference between the planned value and the earned value, or how much does the planned value differ from the earned value on a specific date. We should not use schedule variance to assess a specific schedule position in the project plan. If the schedule variance is negative, it indicates that project work should speed up; it also does not mean delays are allowed in the completion of the project on the date specified in the project plan. In simpler terms, you cannot make delays an accepted part of the plan or redraw or amend the schedule to suit the delays just because we see those delays occurring routinely. Instead, we should eradicate the issues that cause delays and the potential for further delays. A negative schedule variance could result in a delay in activities with a positive float. If the schedule variance is positive, it indicates that project accomplishment, or earning, is ahead of schedule. However, it does not mean that the project will likely be completed on an earlier date just because we found a positive schedule variance could result from the acceleration of activities with a positive float.

Schedule Variance to Date = Earned Value to Date – Planned Value to Date

Figure 3.1 Project Schedule and Cost Plan shows the relationships between project cost management's key values, including cost variances. From this figure, we can see some of the major challenges to be anticipated during the course of the project:

- Schedule delay—shown on the time axes as a difference between current schedule and baseline schedule.

- Cost overrun—shown on the cost axes as a difference between cost estimate at completion and planned value at completion.
- The amount of work accomplished has been lower than the amount of work planned—this is shown as the schedule variance; the examination of this variance should be more detailed and thorough and specific to a project, in order to precisely measure the level of significance of this variance in that project.
- More work has been accomplished than what was already paid for or due to be paid—this is shown as a cost variance.

Also, the reader should understand the meaning of cost indexes, which attract a broader academic and professional audience than cost variance:

- Cost Performance Index (CPI) is the most important interpreter of project cost development; it is also known as the cost efficiency indicator and used to forecast whether a project will exceed the estimated costs and the timeframe for completion as specified in the project plan and to what extent. It is calculated as Earned Value against Actual Cost, or how many dollars have been earned against each dollar spent. It is favorable if the index value is greater than 1:

Cost Performance Index to Date = Earned Value to Date / Actual Cost to Date

Fleming and Koppelman go over the evidences (published in Beach, Chester Paul, Jr.1990. A-12 Administrative Inquiry memorandum, November 28. Studies by Gaylord E. Christie et al. Department of Navy, Office of the Under Secretary of Defense for Acquisitions) and (published in Christensen, Maj, David S., and Scott R. Heise, USAF, 1993. Cost Performance Index Stability, National Contract Management Association Journal) that show that as early as the phase of 15–20% completion of any project, the cumulative cost performance efficiency factor (earned value vs. costs) has been demonstrated to be stable. The data provided can be used to predict the final range of costs for any given project (Fleming and Koppelman 2000, 38–41).

- Schedule Performance Index (SPI), also known as the schedule efficiency indicator, is used to estimate the project completion date. It calculates as Earned Value against Planned Value or how many dollars have been accomplishedfor each dollar that has been planned. It is favorable if the SPI index value is greater than 1:

Schedule Performance Index to Date = Earned Value to Date / Planned Value to Date

The changing ratio of cost variances and indexes points to the changes in project schedule and cost. To determine the adequacy of changes, we must consistently use the base costs (Planned Value, Earned Value, and Actual Cost), including in the following situations which are likely to emerge during the course of the project:

- Suppose Earned Value and Actual Cost by data date of project performance measurement do not pertain to the same updating period, do not use the same percentage base, or do not contain updates for the same work elements. In that case, the Cost Variance and Cost Performance Index will not be realistic regardless of changes in the Current Schedule, Earned Value, or Actual Cost.
- Suppose Earned Value and Planned Value by data date of project performance measurement do not pertain to the same updating period; then, calculating these values doesn't require the use of the same Planned Value at Completion or use of the same base percentage. In that case, the Schedule Variance and Schedule Performance Index will not be realistic regardless of changes in the Baseline schedule, Planned Value, or Earned Value.
- If a project's Planned Value at Completion (baseline) and Planned Value at Completion (original) do not show identical cost records in the cost accounting subsystem, then Planned Value Variance will not be realistic.

Cost Estimate to Complete.

If the project works change, then we must estimate the cost of those changes. In most cases, we must calculate the Cost Estimate to Complete (CETC), which estimates probable resource units or the cost of resource units for activities that define the forecasted project works.

The best solution is to make a new estimate of the remaining costs for activities, especially if an assessment of those activities show that current performances are unique and cannot be used to predict Cost Estimate to Complete. The new "cost estimate to complete" is calculated as follows:

Cost Estimate to Complete (Resource) = Estimated Resource Units to Complete (from To Date to Current Plan Completion)

Estimated Resource Units to Complete = Estimated Resource Units per Time Period × Remaining Duration

Cost Estimate to Complete (Cost) = Estimated Resource Units to Complete (from To Date to Current Plan Completion) × Estimated Resource Unit Price

The most pragmatic solution is based on the assumption that Planned Value at Completion is regularly updated. It may include Approved Change Orders (ACO), if any; however, the Planned Value at Completion cannot include Pending Change Orders (PCO) that are a part of the Cost Estimate at Completion. It follows that we must first calculate the Cost Estimate to Complete. If a PCO has been issued, then the Cost Estimate to Complete is calculated as follows:

Cost Estimate to Complete = Remaining Earned Value to Complete ± PCO, where

Remaining Earned Value to Complete = Planned Value at Completion – Earned Value

Cost Estimate to Complete = Planned Value at Completion – Earned Value ± PCO

Suppose we have a consistently development of past project performances. In that case, we use the Cost Performance Index (CPI) to improve the calculation of Cost Estimate to Complete and, consequently, Cost Estimate at Completion. This calculation is more stochastic but can be a useful guide for better handling the Cost Estimate to Complete (Fleming and Koppelman, 2000, 132–134).

Cost Estimate at Completion = Actual Cost to Date + Cost Estimate to Complete / CPI ± PCO, where

Cost Estimate at Completion = Actual Cost to Date + (Planned Value at Completion – Earned Value) / CPI ± PCO

If change orders are frequent and released in a predictable manner, we should divide them using the CPI. Figure 3.1 Project Schedule and Cost Plan illustrates some of the project costs discussed above and other relationships among project costs.

- Planned Value at Completion is defined as the sum of the original Planned Value at Completion and Approved Change Orders.
- A potential term, Earned Value to Complete, is defined as the difference between the Planned Value at Completion and the Earned Value to Date.

Earned Value to Complete shows how much of the remaining planned cost has to be earned to complete the activity.

- Cost Estimate to Complete shows how much planned and forecasted work needs to be done to complete the activity. The sum of Actual Cost and Cost Estimate to Complete shows the Cost Estimate at Completion.
- A difference between baseline and current schedule shows a difference between the contracted schedule and the most likely schedule to complete the activity.
- At the beginning of the project, the Actual Cost is zero and the Cost Estimate at Completion is equal to the Cost Estimate to Complete. We can note that the period To Date is equal to zero and, hence, the period from To Date to Current Plan Completion is equal to the estimated duration of the project. Consequently, the initial Cost Estimate to Complete from that period becomes the Cost Estimate at Completion. As the project goes forward and we update the project status, progress, and forecast, then the updated Actual Cost and Cost Estimate to Complete indicates the current Cost Estimate at Completion.
- Although there are other formulas for Cost Estimate to Complete, many studies suggest the use of the CPI to improve the forecast of Cost Estimate to Complete and Cost Estimate at Completion.

After the project's Cost Estimate to Complete has been calculated, we must define a new start for Cost Estimate to Complete (Fleming 1988, 207–217). It will show the development of the cost management plan from the "To Date" stage to the next date when the cost management plan is reviewed and updated. We have three alternatives that differ based on the management's approach to Cost Variance and Schedule Variance. Suppose management decides to continue the Cost Estimate to Complete from the Actual Cost to Date and, at the same time, the chosen alternative differs from the contractual cost and schedule plan. In that case, the project team must get necessary approvals via Change Orders before changing the baseline cost plan. If the Cost Estimate to Complete continues from the Planned Value, or Earned Value at Data Date, then the above equations for the Cost Estimate at Completion must change accordingly.

All the above formulas are just standard calculations for cost management data. After the reader becomes conversant with the elements of the calculations, it is necessary to learn and gain mastery in the use of the project management software chosen for the project. The cost module of the software package usually contains many automated procedures that simplify and improve cost calculation.

Besides, there are analytical tools that help assess project values from a statistical point of view instead of assessing project values based on traditional project performance metrics (Prieto 2012).[114]

Earned Schedule

An earlier discussion in this chapter was about the application of the schedule variance, schedule performance index, and predicting the time duration of the project.

Besides, there are new ideas for using project cost in project management. Lipke proposes the use of the Earned Schedule as a suitable and project duration–specific method for calculating project variances and indexes. The Earned Schedule concept uses traditional Earned Value cost to determine how over the course of project and at a specific time point can time-increment of the Planned Value the identical Earned Value occurs (Lipke March 2003[115]; Lipke Summer 2003[116]; Lipke Winter 2004[117]).

Traditionally, in a cost-based schedule, the Schedule Variance shows the difference between the Earned Value and Planned Value. Analogically, in a time-based schedule, the Schedule Variance shows the difference between the Earned Schedule and Actual Time, or the time difference between the horizontal projection of the earned value and the planned value. Lipke uses the same analogy to develop other metrics, as the Schedule Performance Index and Independent Estimate of (project) Duration. The following equations illustrate the above concept:

Schedule Variance (Time-Based) = Earned Schedule (ES) – Actual Time (AT).

The above Schedule Variance shows how many units of time the project leads or lags vis-à-vis the expected level of performance.

114 Prieto, Bob. "Generalized Analysis of Value Behavior over Time as a Project Performance Predictor." *The Measurable News* Issue 04 (2012): 1, 4–10. http://mycpm.org.

115 Lipke, Walt. "Schedule Is Different 1st Part." *The Measurable News* (March 2003): 10–15. http://mycpm.org.

116 Lipke, Walt. "Schedule Is Different 2nd Part." *The Measurable News* (Summer 2003): 31–34. http://mycpm.org.

117 Lipke, Walt. "Connecting Earned Value Cost to the Schedule." *The Measurable News* (Winter 2004): 1, 6–16. http://mycpm.org.

Schedule Performance Index (SPI Time-Based) = Earned Value Schedule (ES) / Actual Time (AT)

The Schedule Performance Index shows how the project planned time is progressing each period of the project's actual (elapsed) time.

Independent Estimate of (Project) Duration (IED) = Planned (Project) Duration / (SPI, Time-Based).

An independent estimate of project duration shows the project duration estimate using the time-based SPI.

If the Earned Value schedule is located between the Previous Period (P) and the Actual Time (AT), and where AT = P + 1, then

Earned Value Schedule (ES) = Number of Completed PV_P Time Increments (Previous Period) + AT, where

AT: 1 = A\$1: A\$2

AT = A\$1 / A\$2 = $(EV_{AT} - PV_P) / (PV_{AT} - PV_P)$

EV_{AT} – Earned Value Cost (at the Actual Time)

PV_P – Planned Value cost (at the Previous Period)

PV_{AT} – Planned Value Cost (at the Actual Period)

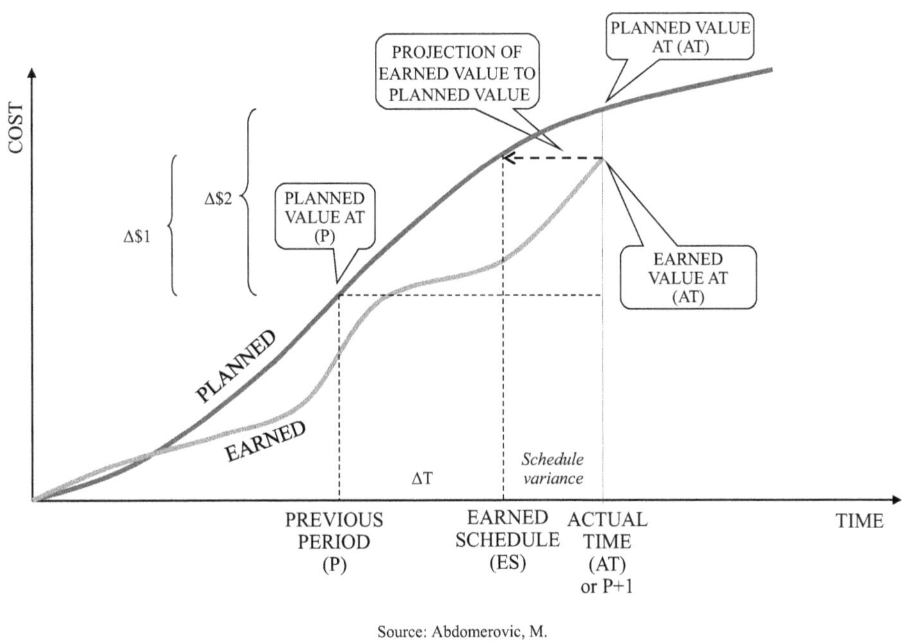

Figure 3.5: Earned Schedule

However, controversial discussions have occurred over using the project timeframe as the basis of calculations, particularly for calculating Schedule Variance, Schedule Performance Index, and Independent Estimate of (project) Duration. New works on this subject reveal that the Earned Value schedule theory suffers from some of the same deficiencies as traditional metrics do. The authors observe that though the Earned Schedule theory is useful for analytical purposes, it is still not the best of tools for assessing project schedule performance (Jacob 2006[118]). Besides, a purely graphical assessment of the Earned Schedule runs the risk of straying far from the reality, since factual cost values are not discrete and metrics among the values become insignificant and unpredictable (Figure 3.4).

Jacob and Kane developed a comprehensive method for forecasting the duration of an activity by the SPI unique to the activity and applying the method that forecast possible changes to the planned duration of the project (Jacob and Kane 2004, 1, 11–17).[119]

> Most recently, Lipke has used a scientific approach to discuss the possible conditions under which the Schedule Performance Index (time-based) may remain an accepted practice as well as a predictor in the process of forecasting the schedule duration (Lipke 2019, 21–30).[120]

Nevertheless, network diagraming methods can be used as a precision scheduling tool to show gradual changes in project schedule regardless of the project's cost dynamics. Therefore, we can use Lipke's time-based metrics only as a supplementary tool for predicting the PDM schedule.

Cost-Estimating Constraints

Cost-estimating constraints are associated mostly with the optimal project duration and contracting for project development.

The proposed period or when and where we should undertake the project may shape project costs. The most important project timing characteristics relate

118 Jacob, Dave. "Is Earned Value Schedule an Unreliable Indicator?" *The Measurable News* (Fall 2006): 15–21. www.mycpm.org.

119 Jacob, Dave, and Michael Kane. "Forecasting Schedule Completion Using Earned Value Metrics." *The Measurable News* (Summer 2004): 1, 11–17. www.mycpm.org.

120 Lipke, Walt. "Earned schedule forecasting method selection." *The Measurable News* Number 01 (2019): 21–30. http://mycpm.org.

to planning the cost of capital, available technology, major procurements, available contractors, and risks associated with cultural factors at the project location. The project's proposed timeframe is beyond the project team's influence, so we must focus on completing the project as required.

The proposed time duration or how much time is necessary to complete the project must consider the project cost and the cost of the project's product. If the project duration changes, then, in most cases, the project cost will change as well. Figure 3.6 Optimization of Project Time and Cost shows the client's view, and we can see that the minimum project cost C_3 is achieved if the project time duration is close to $T_{3.}$ Those optimal results usually occur during usual work conditions; however, the optimal point could slightly move left or right because of the effect of project getting completed correspondingly at an earlier date or a later date. Usually, the client chooses an optimal project completion date and establishes an incentive scheme for completing the project at an earlier and penalties for the delay in completing project, that is, completing the project beyond the planned date of completion. If the client requires an earlier project completion date, the performing organization must deploy additional resources and increase the project cost. If the premium for earlier project completion rises faster than the gain from the earlier completion of the project, the client will reduce the premium. If the negotiated incentives cannot cover the contractor cost for threshold resource requirements, then the project reaches point $T_{1,}$ where a reduction of project duration is no longer feasible. Delaying the project completion date causes an increase in project cost because the project's product comes late to the market and causes loss of revenue and profits. If penalties for delayed project completion increase slower than the project costs, the client will increase penalties. If negotiated penalties cannot cover the loss of revenue on account of delayed completion of the project, then the project reaches point $T_{2,}$ where project delay is no longer acceptable. The cost estimate in this period, from the project initiation to its closure, is known as the original budget. It is a synonym for the original Planned Value at Completion.

The proposed costs and time duration of the project are often subject to various contingencies. The most common are contingency planning and scenario planning. Contingency planning is always quantitative and is used to protect the project against risks of schedule, cost, insurance, or others during project development. However, scenario planning is always related to narration and a holistic and nonmathematical forecasting to plan a possible strategic scenario for the future (Ford 2020).[121]

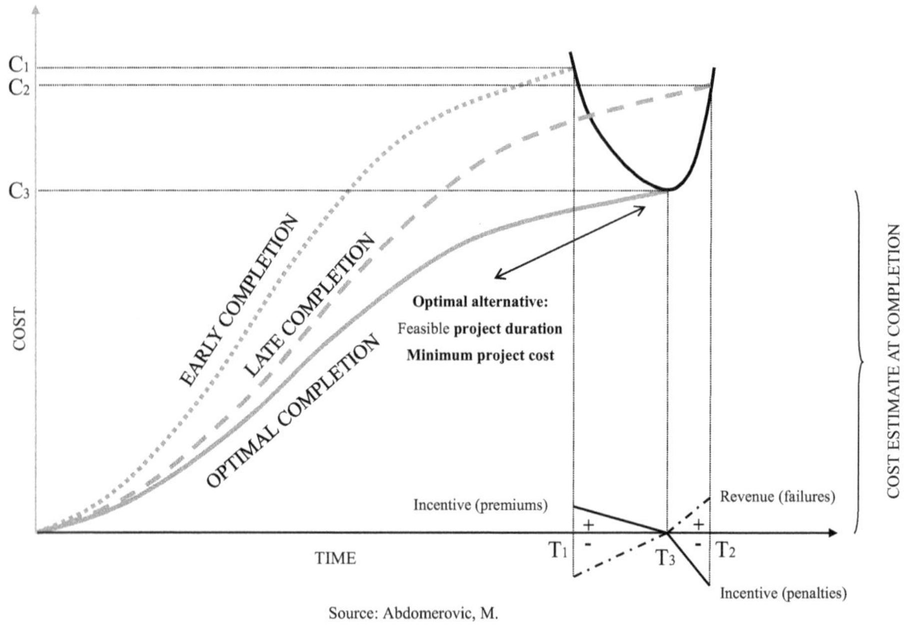

Figure 3.6: Optimization of Project Time and Cost

The project's contractual conditions that regulate relationships with project stakeholders should get special attention during the cost-estimating process. Regarding this requirement, we must consider the client's and contractor's views.

- The client view, where we identity two extremely different cases, depends on the contract between the client and the contractor. If the contract type is "cost-plus," then the client should have a system capable of controlling each line item in the contractor's estimate and payment application. In this case, a client must understand the contractor's cost management system. This type of contract usually occurs with new technology, where the time factor is most important. However, if the project develops under this contract, the client must also have an incentive scheme to boost schedule, cost, and technical performances for the project end items. It will lead to a

121 Ford, Steve. "Contingency Planning vs. Scenario Planning." *PM World Journal* Volume IX, Issue VII (July 2020): www.pmworldjournal.com.

more meaningful and realistic development of the project. If the contract is a "fixed-sum" type contract, the client should have a reliable system for assessing the contractor's bid, including an estimate of change orders and cash flow projection. Otherwise, the client could face a chronic imbalance of money which also affects other contracts. This type of contract is common for well-known technologies with well-defined, detailed specifications and directions from the client and good responses from prospective contractors. For this type of contract, the client does not need contractor cost reports. As with other types of contracts, an incentive scheme can also help speed up the project and improve project development.

- Contractors' views about contracts vary depending on their own expectations about the type of work they need to perform. If it is a "cost-plus" contract, then the contractor must perform work as specified by contract, minimize project duration, and earn maximum incentives. Suppose it is a "fixed-sum" contract, then the contractor should try to minimize their cost to achieve a greater difference between the contract's fixed price and the cost of performing work specified by the contract, including the cost of approved change orders. To achieve this goal, the contractor must have better control over their work, which depends mostly on the contractor's project management system.

It is a well-supported opinion that the quality of the contract can make or break the project. A fair contract can compensate for project development problems, including changes in material, labor prices, project objectives, or marketing conditions. If the contracting parties do not anticipate unexpected needs and the ground reality of the project in terms of its feasibility, then the project team's effort could prove ineffective and the project unsuccessful.

Case Study

Many in engineering, construction, and government projects have recognized the relevance of the Earned Value method. However, the Earned Value is used only occasionally in the payment application process.

In setting the scope for the presentation of the application of earned value to accelerate the payment application process, it is necessary to do the following:

- Reduce the number of terms circulating in today's publications and practices dedicated to the payment application process.
- Orient the example toward principles widely applied to practice. For example, the Baseline Planned Value at Completion is always equal to the Original Planned Value at Completion plus Change Orders.
- Present the change order in the project plan as an activity or group of activities with all the standard time and cost attributes. Each change order shows the magnitude of changes between the Original Planned Value at Completion and Baseline Planned Value at Completion. So, each change order must include its own Original Planned Value at Completion, Baseline Planned Value at Completion, Earned Value, Actual Cost, and others.

Besides, it is necessary to relate the meaning of general project management terms (PMI's PMBOK Guide) with practice-oriented terms (AIA G-Forms, 2004).[122] The analysis of the terminologies helps understand the ordinary meaning of data, regardless of their sources and use by different project management communities. Here are some of the common terms described in project management glossaries and their synonyms described in the G702 and G703 standard forms:

- Planned Value at Completion (Original Plan) is a synonym for the Original Contract Sum (Form G702). The costs are from the period of signing the contract.
- Planned Value at Completion (Baseline Plan) is a synonym for the Scheduled Value (Form G703) and Contract Sum to Date (Form G702). All three costs show the updated contract amount.
- Planned Value at Completion Variance is equal to Planned Value at Completion (Baseline Plan) minus Planned Value at Completion (Original Plan). Planned Value at Completion Variance is a synonym for the Net Change by Change Orders [G702]) since the Net Change by Change Orders (G702) is equal to the Contract Sum to Date minus Original Contract Sum.
- Earned Value to Date is a synonym for the Total Completed and Stored to Date (G702 and G703). Both costs show how much of the planned work has been accomplished by a specific date.

122 AIA G-Forms. *AIA's Documents G702 and G703*. American Institute of Architects, Downloaded March 2021: www.aia.org.

The terminologies and basic calculations relevant to the payment application process are shown in Figure 3.7 AIA and PM Terminologies.

The payment application process starts when the performing organization and the client sign the contract. When signing the contract, the performing organization uses a project master plan and contract line items to develop a contract schedule and cost plan. Such a form of contract schedule and cost become a part of the project's original plan, the Original Planned Value at Completion.

After a time, the client may change the initial Original Planned Value at Completion by issuing Change Orders. As a result, the Change Orders show the differences between the Baseline Planned Value at Completion and the Original Planned Value at Completion for the current period. This difference is known as Planned Value at Completion Variance. The Change Orders can be positive, which increases the Baseline Planned Value at Completion, or negative, which decreases the Baseline Planned Value at Completion. As Change Orders could be negative, its current Planned Value, Earned Value, and Actual Cost could be negative too.

To compile the project status, progress, changes, and forecast, we must include approved Change Orders and pending Change Orders. Those changes must have different cost account codes and activity codes.

Very often, some internal agreements need to change without changing the scope of the work. For example, an in-house design department might need extra resources to complete requirements, or a bad installation might require additional work and material. Although the client does not accept such changes, the performing organization must include them to compile the project status, progress, causes, and forecast.

We assumed for this example that activity for internal Change Orders could have as an input the Actual Value/Cost only. As we do not have a baseline Planned Value at Completion for such activity, we have no Earned Value and Planned Value Variance either. However, charged Actual Value/Cost will result in negative Planned Value to Complete for such activity. That means all remaining work must be accomplished with a decreased cost of Planned Value to Complete, or we must use a contingency amount. Internal Change Orders must also have different cost account codes and activity codes.

As mentioned earlier, this case has been calculated and presented first by (Primavera 1993)[123] project management software and repeated with later

123 Primavera P3 1993. *Project Planner for Windows – Reference.* Primavera System, 1993. www.primavera.com.

versions. All versions, including Primavera/Oracle 2019, have an alternative set of rules for calculating project cost, or we can develop custom rules. For this example, we can do the following:

- Link Original Planned Value at Completion and Baseline Planned Value at Completion. It means changing both costs for the same amount and we need to update one of them.
- Link Remaining Duration and Schedule, Percentage Completed. It means that change in one variable will affect the other.
- Set Planned Value at Completion Variance equals the Baseline Planned Value at Completion minus Original Planned Value at Completion.
- Set Original Planned Value to Complete equals the Baseline Planned Value at Completion minus Actual Value/Cost.
- Allow a negative Cost to Complete.

In addition to cost rules, it was necessary to explain the meaning of costs and exchange information between different systems.

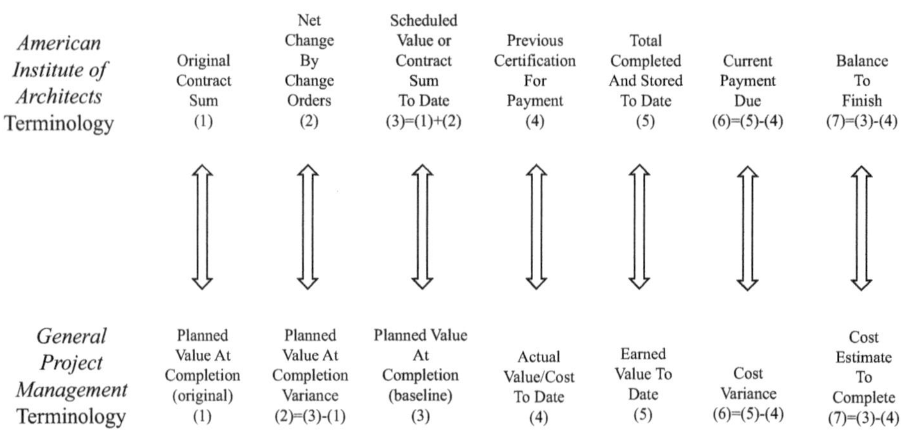

Source: Abdomerovic, M.

Figure 3.7: AIA and PM Terminologies

Figure 3.7 AIA and PM Terminologies contains two rows that describe cost terms for two systems currently used in practice. Most of the figure's columns are generated by Primavera project management software, and only a few columns relevant for the payment application process are a part of AIA's system. For example:

- The first row shows that the Balance to Finish is used to calculate the difference between Scheduled Value (Contract Sum to Date) and Previous Certificate for Payment. As the Previous Certificate for Payment is derived from the Earned Value in a previous period, we can say that Balance to Finish is synonymous with Cost Estimate to Complete shown in the second row.
- The second row shows the key project management costs relevant for both the payment application process and the project management process. Note that the column Cost Estimate to Complete calculates the difference between Planned Value at Completion (baseline plan) and Actual Value/ Cost to Date. Therefore, Cost Estimate to Complete shows how much money we must spend towards completing the project, and this cost is calculated in the same way as in the AIA system's Balance to Finish. We can also observe that the two systems have different cost names only if we analyze the calculations for other costs. However, the meaning of the costs is the same.

We use AIA and PM terms with identical meaning in order to generate Primavera reports and accelerate the payment application process. These terms are as follows:

- PM's Planned Value at Completion (baseline) has been defined in G702 as Contract Sum to Date and in G703 as Scheduled Value.
- PM's Planned Value at Completion Variance has been defined in G702 as Net Change by Change Orders.
- PM's Earned Value has been defined in G702 and G703 as Total Completed and Stored to Date.

After receiving substantial data from the project management software system, the forms G702 and G703 are sent to the accounting office to finalize the payment application process. Substantial parts of AIA's G702, and most of the details in AIA's G703, are generated by the Primavera project management software system and shown in Figure 3.8 Project Summary as of January 19, 2004.

	Start Date	Duration	Finish Date	% Completed	Planned Value At Complete (original) (1)	Planned Value At Complete Variance (2=3-1)	Planned Value At Complete (baseline) (3)	Actual Cost To Date (4)	Earned Value To Date (5)	Cost Variance (6=5-4)	Cost Estimate To Complete (7=3-4)
Project 30095											
	16 Aug 02 A	654	18 Mar 05	47	13,160,515	161,603	13,322,118	5,124,225	6,263,891	1,139,666	8,197,893
Project Management											
	16 Aug 02 A	654	18 Mar 05	62	690,000	0	690,000	358,699	430,333	71,634	331,301
Key Milestones											
	10 Sep 02 A	637	18 Mar 05	30	100,000	0	100,000	0	30,000	30,000	100,000
Electrical Engineering											
	02 Oct 02 A	498	22 Sep 04	75	341,860	0	341,860	227,669	255,520	27,851	114,191
Mechanical Engineering											
	10 Sep 02 A	440	08 Jun 04	99	263,400	0	263,400	260,400	260,400	0	3,000
Software Engineering											
	20 Sep 02 A	498	10 Sep 04	78	1,129,095	0	1,129,095	884,464	884,464	0	244,631
Installation											
	11 Aug 03 A	230	28 Jun 04	43	10,252,140	0	10,252,140	3,339,396	4,480,464	1,141,068	6,912,744
Acceptance Testing											
	29 Jun 04	116	17 Mar 05	0	117,000	0	117,000	0	0	0	117,000
Documentation											
	10 Sep 02 A	545	04 Nov 04	20	267,020	0	267,020	53,597	53,685	88	213,423
Change Orders											
	25 Nov 03 A	136	10 Jun 04	-81	0	161,603	161,603	0	-130,975	-130,975	161,603

Source: Abdomerovic, M.

Figure 3.8: Project Summary as of January 19, 2004

We use the project management software system to generate Change Order Details as shown in Figure 3.9 specifically for some of the rows in Figure 3.8 Project Summary as of January 19, 04.

Start Date	Duration	Finish Date	% Completed	Planned Value At Complete (original) (1)	Planned Value At Complete Variance (2=3-1)	Planned Value At Complete (baseline) (3)	Actual Cost To Date (4)	Earned Value To Date (5)	Cost Variance (6=5-4)	Cost Estimate To Complete (7=3-4)
All Change Orders										
25 Nov 03 A	136	10 Jun 04	-81	0	161,603	161,603	0	-130,975	-130,975	161,603
CO No: 2										
25 Nov 03 A	1	25 Nov 03 A	100	0	-63,689	-63,689	0	-63,689	-63,689	-63,689
CO No: 8										
25 Nov 03 A	1	25 Nov 03	100	0	-62,091	-62,091	0	-62,091	-62,091	-62,091
CO No: 3										
25 Nov 03 A	1	25 Nov 03	100	0	-5,195	-5,195	0	-5,195	-5,195	-5,195
CO No: 7										
19 Jan 04	20	19 Feb 04	0	0	28,263	28,263	0	0	0	28,263
CO No: 9										
19 Jan 04	1	19 Jan 04	0	0	-17,978	-17,978	0	0	0	-17,978
CO No: 10										
19 Jan 04	10	29 Jan 04	0	0	10,454	10,454	0	0	0	10,454
CO No: 1										
19 Jan 04	1	19 Jan 04	0	0	-100,831	-100, 831	0	0	0	-100, 831
CO No: 6										
19 Jan 64	92	25 May 04	0	0	130,323	130,323	0	0	0	130,323
CO No: 5										
19 Jan 04	103	10 Jun 04	0	0	242,347	242,347	0	0	0	242,347

Source: Abdomerovic, M.

Figure 3.9: Change Order Details as of January 19, 2004

The cost shown in the column Previous Certificate for Payment, Figure 3.7, should not decrease because this cost has already been paid. However, suppose a situation arises when the Current Payment Due has to be reduced. In that case, we must decrease the percentage expended at a particular activity, which will decrease Total Completed and Stored to Date. As Current Payment Due equals the Total Completed and Stored to Date minus the Previous Certificate for Payment, this situation will show a negative cost.

Although there are different procedures to complete a payment application, the reader may find the following steps useful:

- Decide how line items for scheduled costs should be broken down or summarized to make a reliable and straightforward payment application. Ensure that this content complements the cost accounting system of the performing organization and that the client accepts the structure as a basis for approving the payment application.
- Analyze the project management software and understand what data can be obtained directly and what custom data items must be generated.

- Use Original Contract Sum to fill in the G702. Use the details of the Original Contract Sum for cost accounting purposes to track changes of the contract.
- Before we set a new data date and record time progress, we should enter the Actual Value/Cost, which for this case study is equal to the Earned Value.
- Progress of the project to a new data date and determine the current Earned Value for the current period can be used to complete the G702 and G703 for the current period.
- Determine the current payments due for invoice processing.

In particular, the Earned Value methodology and the project management software system should be a basis for producing a reliable and straightforward application and certification for payment. The Earned Value shows details of work accomplished as of the data date, including Change Orders. Therefore, there is no simpler way to prove how much work has been completed as of the data date and how much work has to be completed after the data date. The Earned Value shows the project progress; therefore, related application and certification for payment results are reliable and without subjective distortion. The results are efficient because the value "completed and stored to date" is already calculated for the performance report as "earned value"; therefore, the payment application procedure can immediately use this data. The reader wishing to apply this process and adopt PMP features should spend about a week to study the source document and computer procedure on this subject (Abdomerovic 2004).[124] Automating and accelerating payment application without glitches promotes trust and incentives for all the contractual parties.

124 Abdomerovic, Muhamed. "Contract Payments and Earned Value Cost." *The Measurable News* (Summer 2004): 25–33. www.mycpm.org.

4

Best Practice in Project Management Planning

Introduction

In the architecture–engineering–construction (AEC) industry, the term "best practice" generally refers to a method or task implemented for an increased chance of success when managing construction/capital projects. At the 2011 National Construction Forum, the Best Practice work-stream identified that inconsistent implementation of best practices in the AEC industry impacts project performance (NAC 2014, iii).[125]

Best practice in project management planning (PMP) covers project managers' visions and skills to develop and implement the project management plan. For more than a decade, the AEC industry has been experimenting and developing the Integrated Project Delivery (IPD) method that seeks to integrate people, systems, business structures, and practices across the whole project. Although IDP recognizes that increased planning efforts contribute to project success with

125 NAC, 2014. *Best Practice Work Stream Feasibility Report.* Publication 2014-2. The National Academy of Construction, Retrieved June 25. 2020. www.naocon.org.

an emphasis on participants' collaboration (AIA IPD 2017),[126] it does not guarantee smooth teamwork or promise to resolve differences among team members (Manata, Garcija, Mollaoglu, and Miller 2021).[127]

In more practical terms, a best practice project management plan should explain the following:

- What are the theoretical and methodological bases for the development and implementation of the project management plan?
- What is the appropriate level of detail needed in the plan in order for it to successfully develop, implement, assess, accept, get paid, use, maintain, and derive benefits from the work defined?
- How do details and their attributes control the results at the higher levels of the project and company's business management?
  How many dollars did we earn for each dollar paid by the data date?
  How many dollars did we earn for each dollar planned to be spent by the data date?
- How much should we invest and how long (project timeline for completion) would it take to complete the plan?
- What are the trends for costs and schedule?
- What are the contingency reserves spent or still available?
- What risks have been addressed, currently identified, and their potential removed?

The above information is essential for project activities, work packages, contracts, internal agreements, stakeholders, periods, and other structural constructs. It is way beyond our capacity to autonomously gather, process, and use such information to manage the project. So, we must have work-related knowledge and responsibilities assigned for each team member and a capable project manager who can integrate the many steps in the process of developing and implementing the project management plan.

126 AIA IPD. *Integrated Project Delivery.* Chicago, IL: American Institute of Architects & American Institute of Architects California Council. 2017. www.aia.org.

127 Manata, Brian, and Angelo Joseph Garcia, and Sinem Mollaoglu, and Vernon Miller. "The effect of commitment differentiation on integrated project delivery team dynamics: The critical roles of goal alignment, communication behaviors, and decision quality." *International Journal of Project Management* Volume 39, Issue 3 (April 2021): 259–269. https://sciencedirect.com.

The project management plan is the statement of responsibilities for project contents and the principal interface between the client and the contractor. The client looks at the project management plan as an instrument for the continuous monitoring of the progress vis-à-vis project contracts and forecasting long-term revenue for project products; the longer the project development, the less the income from project products. The contractor looks at the project management plan as a tool for continuous balancing of contractual requirements and resource productivity; the prolonged resource deployment at a particular project will lead to reduction of revenue for each resource utilized. Therefore, the best practice in PMP supports the win-win deal for both the client and the contractor.

Development and implementation of project management plan depend on understanding the project contents, including the technological and management works, planning environment, contractual requirements, needs of project stakeholders, fundamental planning skills, responsibilities, current and potential risks, planning information, and others.

The Project Management Team of Client Company, the Management of Client Company, and the Management of Performing Company collaborate in all of these aspects in various ways depending on the role they play in project implementation. For example:

- The client company's project management team uses company standards for project management and sets general requirements for PMP. Team members of the client company reach a consensus about stakeholders' needs and expectations for the plan's information.
- The client company's management sets requirements for information about project phases and upper project business structures. Client company managers help integrate the project into their company to carry out businesses that devolve around that project. They also oversee the transition of project from one phase to another, including the transition of resources and authorities.
- The performing company's management follows guidelines for the development and implementation of the project management plan. They are directly involved in preparing general contracts and subcontracts and oversee the process of achieving planned resource allocation and outcomes of project activities and works.

Steps in Project Management Planning

The parties with the most stake in the project continuously deal with data analysis, relationships between various factors (including human resources), and synthesis of the various phases of PMP. Such efforts help define the general view of project plan and work to be carried out for the project. Next, step by step, the different project team players improve and fine-tune the project plan until the project's original plan and responsibilities for implementing the project plan are approved and accepted. They then carry out and follow-up reviews on activities covering the key aspects of the plan, including the following: changes made to project plan components; comparison of the various attributes of project plan components in their original, baseline, and current forms; understanding the causes for variances; updates to the project plan; and suggestions to be made to steer management actions to take the project forward.

This might sound simple, but is not because none of these steps happen automatically given the potential for delays in collecting data. The above notions are core parts of both the project technological contents and project management processes managed by professionals with expertise in different fields. Although it is a clear possibility that conflicts of opinions will arise in planning and implementing the project, because of the differences in the nature of work experiences and the varied interests of the project team professionals. Such conflicts must be resisted and it should be ensured that project managers make valuable contributions to developing and implementing effectively the project management plan.

Development of Project Management Plan

A project management plan is a complex document representing an integral object of related requests, structures, domains, stakeholders, objectives, contracts, specifications, drawings, decisions, and other exceptionalities. It involves carrying out processes based on several disciplines:

Project management, including scope, time, resources, cost, quality, procurement security, benefits, finance, integration, and so on

Technology management, including construction projects, information technology projects, area development projects, and so on

General management, including social environment and social entities, system analysis, return on investment analysis, benefits analysis, sustainability, cost accounting, and so on

To facilitate a common understanding and general agreement in relation the project plan among project participants, we must ensure that project planning processes are carried out at the lowest level of project scope structure—the activity level. Such an approach to planning requires that activities and their attributes contain clear, sufficient, and reliable information.

Project Requirements.

Understanding client requirements is essential for developing the integrity, reliability, and applicability of a project management plan. Here are some client's instructions that the performing organization must follow:

- Apply customer templates to identify project calendars, activity type, description, unit of measure for activity duration, identification of project resources, resource calendars, unit of measure, and unit cost for each resource.
- Use open–start and open–end activities only for the project start and project completion milestones; however, if other open-starts or open-ends are a reality, they should get constraint dates.
- Practice and gain familiarity and mastery in using the Precedence Diagram Network (PDN), the prescribed computer operating system, and the project management software.
- Apply the primary logic of project management plan to deal with schedule values items; apply secondary logic to accommodate submittals and significant events for purchase, fabrication, safety, delivery, test, storage, installation, or handover.
- Phase, quantify, and calculate the value of significant material and equipment, all the way from requirements for specification documentation to customer acceptance test.
- Quantify and calculate the value of minor material and equipment.
- Show the details of important safety and security issues, agreements, or values in the project management plan.
- Display in the project management plan all defined works, including temporary works such as electrical and water supply, sanitary work, office building, security system, protection fences, roads, parking areas, and so on.
- Keep a detailed record of each unusual event, change orders, field order, delay, advance, or claim; explain impacts and pursue the resolution of issues potentially arising from such impacts.

- Document and approve each resequencing of activities and planned durations, including change of lead/lag durations, decreased positive float, or change in resource assignment and availability.
- Inform the client, respond immediately, and facilitate any change to work, conditions, or project plan.
- Use the project calendar to update and distribute results in relation to the project management plan; determine the status, progress, changes, forecasts, and payment requests and get necessary approvals.

Suppose the performing company has a problem in fulfilling the project management plan requirements. In that case, the client may appoint a consultant to work with the performing company and deduct the consultant's fees from the payments made against invoices raised by the performing company.

Introductory Meeting.

The planning process's introductory meeting should occur within a week after the performing company visits the site and officially receives the tender. The client representative should conduct the introductory meeting and address the client's profile, project technology, deliverables, timeframes, site facilities, communications, safety, emergency measures, signage, and environment. Besides, they will address problematic areas and events, priorities, requirements, responsibilities for PMP, including timely, reliable, and sufficient reporting.

The performing company's project manager accepts contractual requirements and responsibilities, emphasizing the importance of work coordination, workers' requirements for safety and protection at the work site, equipment and materials, and other common interests relevant for PMP.

The performing company's project planner should explain the timetable proposed for developing and implementing the project management plan and the reporting structure and routine to be followed by various contractors, including at the management level. They ask project stakeholders to specify what they want to see in printed and softcopy reports, for example, items to cover in reports and selecting, grouping, and sorting information that each stakeholder would like to see in reports. In the live session, the project planner simulates reporting views and gets some feedback and impressions about the manager's needs; next, they present the report structure and inform the audience about the steps to be taken to comply with client requirements. They must be prepared to answer any questions about the interaction between technology management and project management, overlaps among project components, the required level of details, and why the suggested project planning approach is the right choice.

In most cases, during the discussion, the project planner uses real-life example to provide a big picture on the project plan (see Figure 4.1 Project planning, Key Contracts, Manager's View). Thus, the project planner shows how the performing company's project manager retains control over the project plan and ensure their thoughts are communicated to and understood properly by the project team members before they start developing a project management plan.

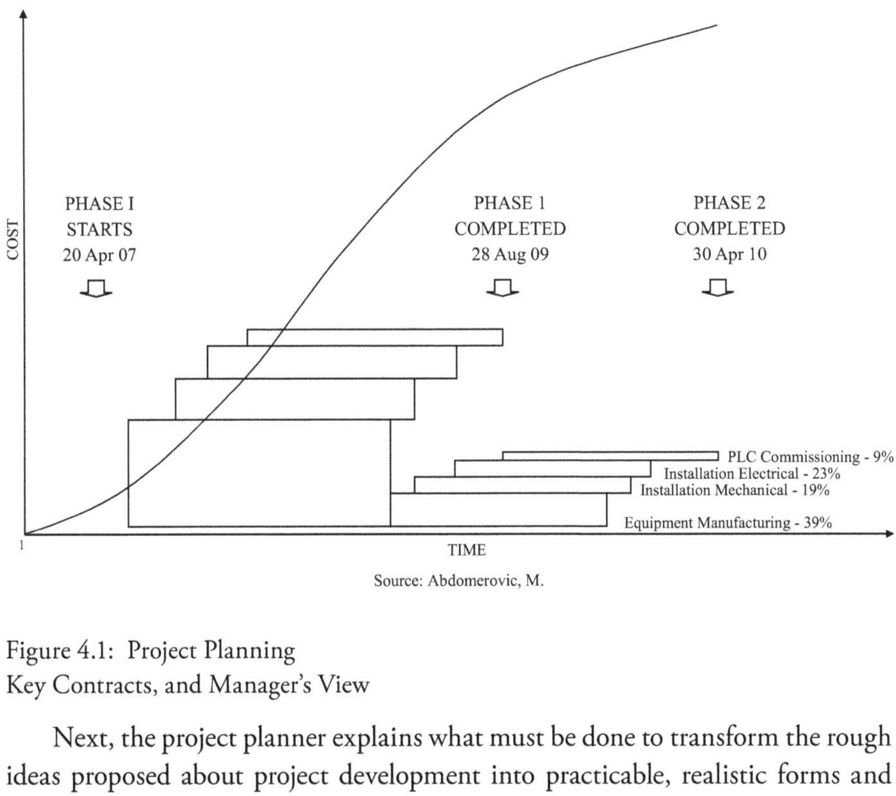

Figure 4.1: Project Planning
Key Contracts, and Manager's View

Next, the project planner explains what must be done to transform the rough ideas proposed about project development into practicable, realistic forms and present them in a comprehensible form in project management reports. Figure 4.2, Management Summary, provides a comprehensive interpretation of the project team's requirements in developing the project management plan illustrated in Figure 4.1.

Activity Description	Start Date	Finish Date	Baseline Value At Completion (1)	Current Schedule % Complete To Date (2)	Earned Value To Date (3=1*2)	Baseline Value To Date (4=1*6)	Value Variance To Date (5=3-4)	Baseline Schedule % Complete To Date (6)
PROJECT	20 Apr 07	30 Apr 10	350,032.72	89	311,294.82	324,870.55	-13,575.73	93
Phase 1	20 Apr 07	28 Aug 09	291,366.96	97	281,805.02	291,366.98	-9,561.96	100
PLC Commissioning	05 Nov 07	19 May 09	23,689.12	83	19,751.74	23,689.12	-3,937.38	100
Equipment Manufacturing	20 Apr o7	06 Dec 08	125,201.64	100	125,201.64	125,201.64	0.00	100
Installation Electrical	13 Jul 07	21 Apr 09	76,814.47	94	72,447.53	76,814.47	4,366.94	100
Installation Mechanical	21 May 07	14 Jun 09	53,476.75	98	52,219.11	53,476.75	-1.257.64	100
Steel Installation	01 Jun 07	22 Dec 08	12,185.00	100	12,185.00	12,185.00	0.00	100
Phase 2	08 Aug 08	30 Apr 10	58,665.74	50	29,489.80	33,503.57	-4,013.77	56
PLC Commissioning	13 Mar 09	14 Dec 09	6,407.66	0	0.00	1,815.68	-1,815.68	28
Equipment Manufacturing	05 Sep 08	10 Jul 09	20,586.16	74	15,326.35	13,335.78	1,990.57	63
Installation Electrical	20 Sep 08	12 Oct 09	15,706.48	36	5,610.10	8,324.18	-2,714.08	53
Installation Mechanical	22 Sep 08	04 Sep 09	12,859.44	50	6,413.75	7,770.73	-1,356.98	61
Steel Installation	11 Aug 08	10 Jul 09	3,106.00	69	2,139.60	2,257.20	-117.60	73

Project Status: Project schedule and cost are within approved Performance Measurement Baseline. Although negative Value Variance indicates work deficiency, however, it is completely part of non-critical activities and minor disputes.

Management actin: Further delay of PLC Commissioning (Phase 2), caused by Electrical Installation delay, have to be watch closely. The details have been discussed at the Construction Manager and distributed.

Source: Abdomerovic, M.

Figure 4.2: Management Summary

Project planer clarifies how the management summary (see Figure 4.2) report comes out of complex and integrated project contents constituting as many as 8,000 activities with a mammoth 100,000 attributes. To understand such requirements, we must revisit our initial notions about the PMP trajectory.

There are similar requirements from project stakeholders, who need intervallic reports about the status, progress, changes, forecasts, and causes of the project management plan's key components. Typical users of reports are the board of directors, CEOs, or presidents of both the client organization and the performing organization and the project business manager, regional managers, capital project managers, technology division managers, project managers, functional managers, team/contract leaders, or supervisors. Although the reports are brief and do not run beyond a single page, they must still be reliable, sufficient, and comprehensible enough to receive managers' attention.

A well-prepared and well-conducted introductory meeting will support managers to use their professional expertise to effectively carry forward the project management plan to its successful implementation and conclusion. Such discussions also involve defining and finalizing the more specific and detailed steps, specifically in relation to operations and deployment of resources, involved in developing and implementing the project management plan.

Basic Terminology.

The project team compiles basic terminologies; generates reports simulating the project functions as may happen in real time, giving due consideration to potential challenges or delays in the implementation; and works toward arriving at a common understanding of the terms used in the project management reports to be submitted. Such terminology comes from glossaries presented by the client, the performing organization, contractors, and software applications prescribed for PMP. A lot happens at this stage, but primarily the goal is to get consensus among stakeholders about specific definitions of some terms which can be defined and interpreted in multiple ways, often very different from the meaning to be derived based on how they are used in the current project; about how we define, forecast, and calculate cost estimates at the completion of the project; and about dealing with approved or pending change orders, payment, claims, and so on. It is better to maintain a dictionary of synonyms for terms that agree with how they are used by the customer and in the industry.

Project Works.

Develop a work breakdown structure (WBS) for each project phase and show how project work is structured and specified. The structure will show several levels where each lower level contains more detailed work elements. The levels may include the project, project phases, deliverables at each phase of the project, work contracts for each deliverable, and work packages within each such contract.

We assign direct costs for project works through the cost of all resources necessary to accomplish activities forming part of the work package. Those costs are planned, controlled, authorized, and paid for at the lowest level of the work defined—at the level of individual task or activity as proposed in the project management plan.

Responsibility for Project Works.

Develop organizational breakdown structure (OBS) for the performing company and show how to organize, manage, and/or implement the different sub-plans of the project management plan. For example, OBS levels include the performing organization, departments within the project-performing organization, including a department for relations with crucial contractors; teams within each department; and persons within each team. Usually, one or more work packages, including all cost accounts within packages, are assigned to individual responsibility. Assignment of cost accounts to the individual responsibility happens after securing the contracts and before the start of the cost-accounting process.

Organizational breakdown structure serves at some point to assign project organization's indirect costs. Indirect costs are planned, controlled, and authorized at a specific level of management and shown as a part of the hammock activities specified in the project management plan. The specifications of indirect cost for a group of activities include the following:

- Indirect costs over a defined period, such as project management office costs during the development and implementation of the project management plan
- Indirect cost directly proportional to some direct cost, such as the equipment freight costs which are absorbed in the cost of the equipment

Project Master Plan.

Develop and submit a project management master plan; show the big picture on how work is expected to be done and the method and tools to be used to develop the plan further. The master plan is a proposal that covers the higher-level components of the project that can be developed later to become a part of the schedule value items or activities. For example, it can show contracts for each phase of the project, along with duration, cost, and the relationships between the contracting parties or entities. It can also show the milestones, duration of contingency, and any specific contractual requirements. The basic assumption here is that the master plan's components and attributes are robust enough to meet the outcomes envisaged for the original plan.

A better approximation of the project master plan to the future original plan's summary results can be achieved if the client company develops a master plan for the forthcoming contracts and work packages specified in those contracts. This plan must be based on proven past practices to structure the project work, calculate the duration of the whole project, and estimate the overall project cash flow. Here, the performing company must work with potential contractors to clarify the contents and cost accounts for work packages and simplify the planning process. They must also negotiate for creating highly flexible relationships within a work package and among work packages to simplify work preferences and update the project logic.

A project's master schedule is of prime significance in carrying out mega projects. There is enough literature showing strong arguments on how an integrated project schedule should look like and function and how its master plan must cover fundamental requirements, including the dynamic of megaprojects (Chang, Hatcher, and Kim 2013).[128]

128 Chang, Artemis, and Caroline Hatcher, and Jai Kim. "Temporary boundary

Schedule Value Items.

The term schedule value item is synonymous with project activity; whereas the schedule value items represent the contract elements, the activities represent project planning network elements.

Project team must assist prospective contractors in going through the master plan and ensure schedule value items for work packages are clear and easily understood. Project team should assign at least one schedule value item for each work package. The initial number of schedule value items should be in proportion with the scope weight factors for each of the schedule value items. A joint effort between the client company, performing organization, and the prospective contractor is needed because resources for specified work can be planned, implemented, measured, and paid for only on the basis of schedule value items.

Activity List.

Project team must work closely with prospective contractors to analyze network planning diagrams for work packages of project contracts and define the timeframe for accomplishing the work of each packages. The manager at the performing organization must complete the following tasks:

- Break down voluminous schedule value items into more activities and related attributes
- Use a renewed list of activities of the work packages and related schedules to update the contents of the project's master plan

Relationships among Activities.

Work closely with contractors and technology managers to establish relationships among work packages. Those relationships may initially evolve only at a higher structural level, which is the work package level. When conditions allow, the relationships will emerge at the most detailed level of the work defined, which is the activity level.

Some activities with a long duration may be convenient at some point; however, such activities barely relate to other activities and, hence, must be developed in more details. This concept is core to relationships among project activities.

objects in megaprojects: Mapping the system with the Integrated Master Schedule." *International Journal of Project Management* Volume 31, Issue 3 (April 2013): 323–332. www.elsevier.com/locate/ijproman.

To progress from the stage of network diagram for the work package to stage of planning and firming up the work package, we must develop clear attributes for activities slated for completion under each work package. For example, to get a time management plan for the work package, we must define the time estimate for each activity within the work package. As time estimates are based on the detailed specification of work and resource availability, we must consider estimating standards, databases (Means 2019),[129] (WinEst 2017),[130] or other key factors such as the history of of project duration, project conditions, and expert opinions. The more detailed is the breakdown of work package contents to project activities, the more accurate will be the estimate of activity attributes and the work package as a whole. Sometimes we need to relax the relationships among activities using the pair of start-to-start and finish-to-finish activities as an alternative for finish-to-start activities or using the progress override logic for activities.

To progress from development of plans for each work package to the development of plans for the whole project, we must establish relationships among work packages. Relationships among work packages are not always simple and can cause unlikely results or loops in the project. We must gradually approach these relationships, starting from the most apparent relationships, and calculate results and then proceed to the next relationship until we reach the project planning objectives defined in the project's master plan.

We must devote exceptional attention to the development of a project network diagram for big projects or programs. In such cases, we should develop a series of standard work packages with flexible attributes and use them to continuously improve the project management plan.

Duration and Cost for Activities.

The duration and costs for completing activities depend on how detailed and accurate are the project specifications and resource calendars, including the length of work shift, number of work shifts within 24 hours, holidays, and number of workdays per week. Before signing the contract, the contractors must ensure the following happens:

- Make available estimates on duration, resources, or cost of resources for each activity. Although a contractor cannot always provide resource estimates for each activity, or even for each work package, the contractual

129 Means. *Building construction cost data*. Kingston, MA: R. S. Means Company, 2019.

130 WinEst. *Cost estimating solution.* WinEstimator, 2017. www.winest.com.

provisions should provide a procedure to deal with the total number of resources assigned to a specific work. For example, from the daily estimated presence of mechanical installers and expected daily output of installers measured in length, weight, pieces, and so on, we can get a measurable time and cost estimate for a mechanical installation plan.
- Define the procedures to be followed for the various material planning activities, including the specification, procurement, storage, installation, testing, commissioning, acceptance, and payment schedule for materials.
- Analyze possible results in relation to the time and cost components of major activities and other scenarios including market conditions, timing of money, resource availability, time- and cost-estimating databases, overheads and profits, and other time and cost issues.
- Evaluate the payment system and its relation to the project management plan. Ensure that the contract includes sections related to the payment process, retentions, and nonpayment; work timings—number of working days/number of working hours in each shift or day; change orders, and so on.

Each activity with its estimated duration and cost becomes a part of the database for project progress tracking, payment processing, and recording the actual costs incurred.

Alignment of Project Structures.

Companies in project management business usually have a concrete structures for operations and human resources. If we look at a structure as an isolated organization, then everything may appear acceptable. But problems arise when different structures do not match. To reduce problems resulting from diversified project structures, the manager of the performing company must do the following:

- Understand the structures of general cost accounting standards and project cost accounting practice. Talk to managers and understand the level of detail they want to see in the project management plan and what are their views about the process of transferring the actual cost from the general cost accounting function to the project cost accounting function.
- Understand the structures of the project cost–estimating and project cost–budgeting systems. Ascertain the possibility of doing a project cost estimate and project budgeting at the activity level or distributing cost estimates to project activities using the activity weight factor.

- Understand the structures of the organization of project work and people. Assign codes to project activities and their attributes and simulate the required reports

Control Levels.

Inconsistency in project structures calls for consensus among key project stakeholders about planning levels for project operations. For this purpose, the project manager of the performing company must lead action in fulfilling the following requirements:

- Analysis of contents and the level of control over operations
- Developing contents to match the requirements of operational control
- Propose and maintain a common operational-level interface or point of communication where information is exchanged specific to a contract and between different contracts

Key stakeholders should achieve consensus about project structures and control levels for project operations determined in the course of developing the project's master plan.

Integrated Project Management Plan.

Now is time to simulate project reporting as well as calculate and control results across the whole project and between the project structures. For this purpose, we must have a standard routine to do the following:

- Design the required reports and identify the data source for the reports
- Set milestones and simulate project development
- Add constraints in relation to essential resources or cost of the resources and simulate project development
- Use hammock activities to add indirect costs and simulate project development
- Review and amend the project's critical path, duration, resource distribution, and cash flow, where needed and appropriate
- Assign activity codes and use them for selective reporting
- Summarize project plans at the WBS and OBS levels and as defined in the master plan of project management
- Check the responsibilities assigned for each of the milestones to be achieved

- Summarize project at the control account plan level and balance results with the assigned responsibilities
- Check incentive schemes in the project management plan and understand their relationships with the project documents
- Check the procedure for releasing change orders and documentation for changes in conditions, scope, cost, and time specified in the project plan
- Check the claims procedure, especially its compliance with documentation that a court of law or a legal body may accept
- Define and specify the data needed for project update, data collection methods, and the personnel or entity to carry out the data collection
- Develop a list of possible events and contingencies that could happen but have not yet been shown in the project plan

Once you get the picture on the acceptable scope, time, cost, or cost of a resource plan, it must be discussed, fine-tuned, and accepted as the original project management plan. At this time, you must have defined quantities for authorized works and authorized works for which the costs or prices are yet to be finalized.

Setup of Initial Baseline.

After we finalize the original project management plan's value at completion and save it as the first version of the baseline and current project management plan, the core documents on the plan for project implementation will be made available. The project team must accomplish all the above steps before hosting the project implementation conference, issuing the project management plan, and confirmation to proceed with the project implementation.

Implementation of Project Management Plan

Confirm the status of documentation and conditions before proceeding with the implementation of the project management plan; for example, check the availability, security, safety, accessibility, and inspection reports for locations; secure availability and approval of current documentation; check availability of required resources and deployment plan; and learn about the procedure for managing any unforeseen challenges or delays in the implementation process.

Once the implementation has begun, the project manager must handle the now-active plan of implementation and its dynamics cautiously and decisively. We can better understand the project plan's implementation if we shadow a typical day of construction manager and project planner, which are the two key roles in PMP.

Construction manager is at the site by 7 a.m. to study the project documentation and the work that should be performed during that day; at 8 a.m. they conduct meetings with contractors' representatives to review issues and give directions for work; at 9 a.m. they conduct a meeting with their project team to review issues and give directions for work; at 10 a.m. construction manager visits the construction site; at 12 a.m. they go on a lunchbreak with the project manager and/or client representative or a contractor to wind down, discuss, and resolve work issues; at 1 p.m., back from the lunchbreak, they analyze what and how much work have been accomplished against the work schedule for the day; at 2 p.m., the construction manager meets specific individual members of the project team (client representative, project manager, contractor, member responsible for safety and security, chief accounting manager, negotiator for procurement of material and equipment, designer, planner, quality controller, etc.) to discuss issues, receive information, and give direction; at 3 p.m. they visit the project site again to know the status of work progress and prepare for the next day's meeting at 8 a.m. The construction manager is the last to leave the office, usually at about 6 p.m., with their headphones still on that will keep them busy for a while.

The project planner occasionally joins the construction manager during visits to the construction site to scrutinize the plan and discuss the differences in the level completion of actual work against the work that was planned. They collect data daily, simulate results, present issues, and receive directions the next day at morning and noon meetings, at 9 a.m. and 2 p.m., respectively. The project planner conducts weekly meetings on Friday, from 10 a.m. to 2 p.m., which includes contractors' representatives, to review and confirm the data collected and preliminary results about the weekly status of work progress, discuss any changes to be managed, review the forecast for schedule value items, and fine-tune or improvise on the contractors' plans. Participants of the meetings distinguish work related to noncritical activities from work related to critical activities in order to assess any possible changes or deviations from the operational requirements specified in the original project plan. In reviewing critical activities, the meeting attendees must consider resource requirements and availability and other conditions that keep the project schedule steadily moving as per the schedule planned. Since the number of noncritical activities is 7–9 times bigger than the number of critical activities, it is the number of noncritical activities that has the most influence on, and hence determines, the project's earned value and estimates of the cost of completion. At the meetings, project team members, contractors, and functional representatives filter available information, discuss deviations between the progress planned for and the actual progress, introduce new requirements, remove or modify existing requirements, and review the need for changes to be made to the critical path floats trends and other prevalent issues. The weekly meeting uses daily meeting records, site visits, assessment of results, and project plan updates. The project planner prepares a weekly report of work status, progress, changes, and forecast for the project plan and its components. The project planner meets construction managers each Friday at 4 p.m. to discuss current planning issues, weekly reports and receive information before publishing the current plan.

Daily meetings and visits to site are essential for keeping stakeholders and project teams focused on the more important issues. At these meetings, the personnel responsible update and authorize project documentation. They mark changes by pen and sign them off, so that updated documentation is ready for use, and discuss the causes for any specific issues encountered that day. The key topics of meetings are safety and operational issues such a work of short-term schedule to be completed. The basic meaning of the construction manager's daily commitment is to provide competent supervision and certainty in project development. A comprehensive and updated project management with an itemized list of current issues, personal notes, and other documentation helps the construction manager to closely and effectively monitor work progress and address and resolve issues quickly.

Daily meetings are mostly about "improvisation" on short-term themes defined and governed by the project management plan. Muirhead and Simon perfectly cover this: "we had a plan but knew from the start that the plan was not going to be perfect … we would need to be highly flexible" (Muirhead and Simon 1999, 193).[131]

The term *daily project meetings* may be deemed similar in meaning to the term "agile" cooperative teamwork on incremental planning and delivery. However, daily project meetings are different; their objectives are to resolve immediate or urgent issues and optimize the outcomes envisaged in the project management plan.

131 Muirhead, Brian, and William Simon. *High Velocity Leadership: The Mars Pathfinder Approach to Faster, Bette, Cheaper.* New York, NY: HarperCollins Publishers, 1999.

Data Gathering.

The project team members discuss the most current data about the project management plan during the daily meetings. At least twice a week, the project manager invites key contractors to attend the meetings in order to assess the status, progress, causes, changes, and forecasts on work. The attendees review activities that took place in the previous two weeks, especially in light of whether there have been violations of provisions in the contract. Also reviewed are items such as activity start date, finish date, remaining duration, relationships, progress, time estimate revision, delay in progress, as well as any addition, deletion, or modification of activity attributes and related documentation.

The meeting devotes significant amount of time and attention to review the status on both approved and pending change orders, claims, and approvals to be confirmed between the performing organization and the client organization as well as the approvals to be received and confirmed between the performing organization and its contractors. Although these issues do not surface frequently or reach an alarmingly bigger proportion, the costs of change orders barely amount to 5% of the contract value, and claims for compensation to offset the cost of implementing change orders are sporadic. However, failure to process changes and claims in a timely manner may cause issues to even drag beyond the project's completion.

Narratives, including further steps and related responsibilities from the meeting, are recorded, reviewed, and distributed to the participants and archived.

Updating Procedure.

Once the project enters the implementation stage, we must keep the project plan up to date. In real time, project activities and their attributes change over time, and we need to manage changes systematically. Each update to project management plan includes current plan and often the baseline plan but rarely the original plan.

Updating procedures and related PMP software need time to test and adequately update projects. The key is to understand the relationships between current and baseline plans and the results of project updates. There are three principles for updating project plans:

- We cannot go back in time; nothing can change in any plan before the "time now" date.
- Nothing can change in the baseline plan without approved change orders and procedures for updating the project.

- Anything can change in the current plan after the "time now" date; however, any change that leads to changes in contractual conditions must pass through the change-order procedure.

Before the start of the updating procedure, we must know the following:

- Manager's view of changes in the plan
- Client's view of changes in the plan
- Parties interested in the results of updating the plan
- Requirements for updating the plan
- Routines for updating the plan
- Features of the project management software package to deal with updating the plan
- Reflection of updates to plan on the current plan and the baseline plan

We can update the baseline project plan in two ways—as a standalone plan or within the current plan.

- The baseline project plan update as a stand-alone plan relates to selected data. We may need to analyze some variances between baseline and original project plans or between baseline and current project plans by excluding some of the project or activity data.
- To update the baseline project plan within the current plan depends on a project management software package's functions and a basic understanding of the project's time, resource, and cost variables.

The current project plan is always updated as a standalone plan. There are different procedures for updating the current project plan. All of them assume that the project "data date" must progress to the "time now" date from the previous period. After we set the new data date, it is necessary to do the following:

- Consider the actual situation for each activity in progress or those completed following on the previous update. It includes the actual start of activity, percentage complete, expected completion date, quantity or cost of resources spent, and other activity data. Assuming that project works and resources are distributed evenly across the entire duration of the activity, we can assess both the time elapse and the time remaining. In updating the current project plan, we may include the pending change orders which may not show up yet in the baseline plan.

- Consider the differences between baseline and current project plans. It includes continuously checking the baseline and current activity's attributes: durations, start and finish dates, elapsed duration, remaining duration, lead and lag times, contracted amounts, contingency changes, approved change orders, pending change orders, work completed and billed, work completed but not billed yet, work erroneously billed, or accounting adjustment of bills. We must check all the above prior to publishing the project status, progress, changes, and forecasts.

The original plan gets updated when we deal with massive project development modifications that require significant changes to the project scope, cost, and schedule.

Project Management Plan after the Update.

The documents for the updating procedure apply to a specific accounting period of the project that has already been concluded and its conclusion conveyed through the reports submitted. Assessing the project periodically helps to provide up-to-date information on the scope, time, resources or cost of resources, and other attributes in light of the baseline project plan and the current project plan. We may observe the following in this process:

- The baseline project plan is an earlier and approved picture of the current project plan that has been changed by implementing the approved change orders. The baseline plan is used as a benchmark to compare it with the original plan and the current plan.
- The current project plan is continuously monitored because it includes both the approved and pending change orders and daily changes and updates that do not affect the project contracts. It reflects the most recent status, progress, changes, or forecast of project scope, time, resource or cost of resources, and other attributes. It changes in every update period and is likely approved before the start of the next period starts.

The above steps emerge from established practice described in Chapter 8section Updating project management plan.

Every new experience is influencing and shaping steps that are later used for more reliable planning worldwide. This includes the numerous examples provided and discussed in the past literature:

- The process between client and contractors before or following contract award or before/after a major change to the contract (Kuehn 2011, 197–221)[132]
- Narratives about modern, demanding business world, need to meet the ground reality via investing in collaboration, teaming, agility, unlearning, and simplicity of communication to succeed in the "new normal" (Taylor 2021, 1–4)[133]
- Perceptions about and dimensions of project benefit management and have an impact on the success of the project and its business strategies (Carlos and Kunc 2015, 1–41)[134]
- The different actors and entities playing key roles in computerizing a multi-project environment include network administrators, database administrators, operations executives, project control coordinators, program managers, project managers, resource/cost managers, team leaders, and team members (Maharana 2020, 3–5)[135]
- Sense-making in relation to the causes of unexpected events and adapting over time to different conditions and deal with expectations and changes (Kutsch, Djabbarov, and Hall)[136]

132 Kuehn, Ursula. *Integrated Cost and Schedule Control in Project Management.* Vienna, VA: Management Concepts, 2011.

133 Taylor, Peter. "Make Your Business Agile: A Roadmap for Transforming Your Management and Adapting to the New Normal." *PM World Journal* Volume X, Issue V (May 2021). www.pmworldtoday.net.

134 Carlos Eduardo Martins Serra, and Martin Kunc. 2015. "Benefits Realization Management and its influence on project success and on the execution of business strategies." *International Journal of Project Management* Volume 33, Issue 1 (January 2015): 53–66. https://sciencedirect.com.

135 Maharana, Dibyaranjan. *Oracle Primavera P6 Professional Project Management, Release 19.* Coppell, TX, 2020.

136 Kutsch, Elmar, and Ibrat Djabbarov, and Mark Hall. "How managers frame and make sense of unexpected events in project implementation." *International Journal of Project Management* In Press Version (May 2021). https://sciencedirect.com.

Reports and Records in Project Management Planning

Project Reports

A lot of activities are involved in selecting, grouping, sorting, formatting, and presenting PMP reports— For example, a report selected by mechanical engineering task activities selected activities are grouped by type of mechanical work, sorted by activity number within the type of mechanical work, formatted in the alphabetical table and presented as a printed report is one of many. Managers, stakeholders, contractors, interest groups, team members, sub-contractors, or individuals may select standard reports; group them by type of activity, level of completion, level of criticality, or factored values; and sort them by technological and management attributes. The reports may use a numeric table, narrative table, plain graph, intelligent graph, or in a format combining all of these features, and be shown in different versions, such as printed reports, on-screen, audio files, or audiovisual media content embedded in the report's digital version. Project reports provide many advantages to the user, including the following:

- Focus on sufficient and straightforward information extracted from the content of integrated PMP
- Understand the PMP attributes
- Explain project status, progress, forecasts, and changes and help improve the decision-making process
- Update and publish current actions and responsibilities for project works
- Facilitate proactive communication of mutual interests between parties in order for them to cooperate and contribute effectively to achieving the project plan's objectives

Reports must always provide structured information with the highest possible quality and integrity of data. An average project planner spends on quality control of report about 25–30% of the total time available to develop and maintain high-quality reports. After compiling work results and presenting them in a commonly used, standard and coherent form of report, the project planners should not stop at that but continue to assess and improve the reports periodically. Next, project managers must analyze the project reports prior to publishing.

There are different ways to generate and maintain project reports. The reader may find the following steps useful:

- Design project reports and show in them the information relevant for the intended recipients of the reports
- Structure reports around specific points of control and address the responsibilities for project's attributes.
- Ensure project reports complement client needs and show how the project gets managed for all stakeholders and ensure the performing company understands how the project has to be governed and monitored.
- Record time progress and get Earned Value, including Earned Value for Change Orders.
- Document Change Orders for each contract and calculate their impact on scope, schedule, and cost of the project.
- Compare contractors' requests for payment with related Earned Value and send approved requests to project cost accounting for payment.
- Ensure that information on the internal Change Orders in the performing organizations is listed as a separate category.
- Make a narrative summary of reports for top management, explain variances, and suggest management actions.
- Ensure the implementation of management decisions is reflected on project reports.

The subsequent reports are standard requirements, and the project planner should discuss the reports during regular meetings.

Short-Term Report.

The short-term project management plan report is usually updated and published weekly. It provides the most detailed versions of activities currently in progress, about to begin, or about to be completed. The activity list reflects the scope of work, status, progress, or forecast and may serve as a backup in the approval of payment requests or advance payment. The report shows the following:

- Selected activities, which have or should have started, progressed, or completed within a four-week period, which covers one week before the data date and three weeks after the data date.
- Selected activities are grouped by contracts.
- Grouped activities are sorted by contracts and early start date.
- Activities are illustrated in a form that combines the bar chart and columns. The bar chart contains current and baseline timeframes. Columns include the current early start date, late finish date, total float, baseline,

and current percentage completed, as well as a summary of these items where applicable.

The reports should be delivered at least one hour before the start of the weekly meeting in order to help attendees read and understand the information presented.

Report on Earned Value.

The report on earned value is usually updated and published at the beginning of the last week of each month. In the case of large delivery orders or major change orders, the plan needs to be updated and reissued as required. It provides the project manager and contractors a most detailed view of the activities and dates specified in the project management plan, including milestone dates and revisions resulting from approved change orders. The report features the following:

- Selected activities, usually all project activities and resources or cost of resources as would apply to those activities.
- Selected activities are grouped based on contracts.
- Grouped activities are sorted by contracts and percentage of completion
- Activities are presented in a combined bar chart and column format. The bar chart should contain current and baseline time plans. The columns should include the current early start date, late finish date, total float, planned value, earned value, actual value, baseline, and current percentage completed, as well as their summarized values if applicable. Besides, the columns area should contain schedule and cost variances and other available metrics.

After the publication of the updated earned-value report, the performing organization's project manager and client's project manager assess the report. When the client completes the review and approves the earned-value report, the client project planner sends complete documentation and payment application for the current month to the client's accounting office. The payment application process must have a detailed procedure about what we consider as earned. For example:

- When was the advance payment released and deducted from the earned value?
- When was the retention withdrawn and released?

- What percentage of the delivered equipment considers as earned, and when the equipment is earn 100%?
- How should the approved positive or negative change orders be included in payment applications?
- What kind of standard industry forms should we use for payment applications?
- What are the names and meanings of the terms used to review earned value and payment application processes?

It is good practice to deliver reports at least two days before submitting the payment application.

Stakeholders Report.

The stakeholder's project management plan report is usually updated and published monthly or when required. It provides for project stakeholder manager the deliverables and related contracts of their interests. The report illustrates:

- Selected activities, usually a stakeholder's project activities.
- Selected activities are grouped by deliverables.
- Grouped activities are sorted by deliverables, contracts, and finish dates.
- Summarized contracts within each deliverable in column format. Columns include the baseline and current values, the early start date, late finish date, earned value, actual value, estimate to complete value, percentage completed, schedule and cost variances, and other metrics.

Stakeholders should get the reports two days before the stakeholders' meeting.

Figure 4.3 shows an excerpt from stakeholders' reports used for assessing the status, progress, and forecasts for project deliverables.

Top Decision-making Report.

The project management plan report for decision-makers is usually updated and published monthly or on request. It provides for the project manager a single-page summarized list of project phases and related contracts. The report expresses:

- Selected activities, usually all project activities.
- Selected activities are grouped by phases.
- Grouped activities are sorted by phases, contracts, and finish date.

	Completion Date	Budgeted Cost (BC)	Cost At Completion (CAC)	Budget Variance (BC-CAC)	Planned To Date (PV)	Earned To Date (EV)	Paid To Date (AC)	Cost To Complete (CAC-AC)	Cost Variance (EV-AC)	Schedule Variance (EV-PV)
United States	12-Nov-99	109,706,749	109,026,178	680,571	105,395,104	101,448,447	97,299,529	11,726,649	4,148,918	-3,946,657
Alabama	11-Aug-99	12,497,403	11,851,323	646,080	11,678,789	11,188,686	10,995,203	856,120	193,483	-490,103
Mobile	11-Aug-99	7,291,807	7,758,938	-467,131	7,216,807	6,651,704	7,137,940	620,998	-486,236	-565,103
Montgomery	02-Apr-99-A	5,205,596	4,092,385	1,113,211	4,461,982	4,536,982	3,857,263	235,122	679,719	75,000
Florida	13-Oct-99	17,244,697	14,882,200	2,362,497	15,633,683	15,161,686	13,505,345	1,376,855	1,656,341	-471,997
Jacksonville	26-Mar-99-A	5,261,374	4,323,386	937,988	4,648,754	4,723,754	4,061,053	262,333	662,701	75,000
Winter Springs	19-Mar-99-A	5,181,107	4,480,754	700,353	4,635,271	4,710,271	4,292,227	188,527	418,044	75,000
Apopka	13-Oct-99	6,802,216	6,078,060	724,156	6,349,658	5,727,661	5,152,065	925,995	575,596	-621,997
Indiana	27-Nov-98-A	6,795,214	6,901,794	-106,580	6,624,396	6,697,288	6,679,771	222,023	17,517	72,892
Evansville	27-Nov-98-A	6,795,214	6,901,794	-106,580	6,624,396	6,697,288	6,679,771	222023	17,517	72,892
Kentucky	29-Sep-99	18,429,503	18,146,350	283,153	17,875,646	16, 990,433	15,384,654	2,761,696	1,605,779	-885,213
Elizabethtown	17-Jul-98-A	4,592,949	4,454,201	138,748	4,501,073	4,576,073	4,422,283	31,918	153,790	75,000
Crestview Hills	29-Apr-99-A	6,775,868	6,976,676	-200,808	6,672,844	6,752,844	6,759,932	216,744	-7,088	80,000
Louisville	29-Sep-99	7,060,686	6,715,473	345,213	6,701,729	5,661,516	4,202,439	2,513,034	1,459,077	-1,040,213
Maine	02-Oct-98-A	6,124,859	6,248,334	-123,475	6,049,699	6,124,699	6,143,410	104,924	-18,711	75,000
Kennenbunk	02-Oct-98-A	6,124,859	6,248,334	-123,475	6,049,699	6,124,699	6,143,410	104,924	-18,711	75,000
Texas	17-Nov-99	41,483,056	42,536,679	-1,053,623	40,480,874	38,153,638	36,239,736	6,296,943	1,913,902	-2,327,236
Carrollton	25-Mar-99-A	7,169,998	7,195,790	-25,792	6,892,776	6,967,776	6,974,783	221,007	-7,007	75,000
Richardson	28-Jul-99	8,346,824	8,451,711	-104,887	8,714,751	7,950,351	7,118,482	1,333,219	831,859	-224,400
Grapevine	22-Jun-99-A	8,125,416	8,317,792	-192,376	7,900,383	7,975,383	7,259,197	1,058,595	716,186	75,000
Houston	12-Nov-99	8,429,519	8,182,990	246,529	8,257,512	6,617,605	5,810,866	2,372,124	806,739	-1,639,907
Sugar Land	28-Jul-99	5,686,687	6,009,835	-323,148	5,611,687	4,923,758	4,925,308	1,084,527	-1,550	-687,929
Kingwood	30-Mar-99-A	3,724,612	4,378,561	-653,949	3,643,765	3,718,765	4,151,090	227,471	-432,325	75,000
Virginia	12-Aug-98-A	7,132,017	8,459,498	-1,327,481	7,052,017	7,132,017	8,351,410	108,088	-1,219,393	80,000
Virginia Beach	12-Aug-98-A	7,132,017	8,459,498	-1,327,481	7,052,017	7,132,017	,8,351,410	108,088	-1,219,393	80,000

Source: Abdomerovic, M.

Figure 4.3: Project Performance Report

- Summarized contracts within each phase in a combined bar chart and column format. The bar chart contains current and baseline plans. The columns should include the current early start date, late finish date, planned value, earned value, estimate at completion value and variances, and their summarized values for the project.

The updated decision-making report of the project management plan should never be more than a single page of analytic data and single page of narratives explaining the data. Project planner usually designs and compiles this report on request.

As-built Report.

As-built project management plan reports are requested, specified in detail, and published before the contractor requests retention. After the completion of all contracts and due activities, the contractor submits an as-built plan showing the actual start and finish dates, logic, cost, earned value, retention, and other items required by the contract. This report also provides supplementary documents for the handover of completed works and closeout procedures for the contract. The report pictures:

- Selected activities, usually all project activities and subcontract activities.
- Selected activities are grouped by contracts.
- Grouped activities are sorted by contracts, subcontracts, and finish dates.
- Summarized subcontracts within each contract presented in a combined bar chart and column format. The bar chart should contain current and baseline plans. At the same time, columns should include current start and finish dates, planned value, earned value, actual value, schedule and cost variances, retention for each subcontract, as well as summarized values for the contract.

After the publication of the as-built project management plan report, the contract manager and project manager assess the report. The assessment process must address the data for each subcontract; completed works; built-in materials and equipment; safety issues; and the causes, impacts, and claims for compensation for issues arising from time extension and cost overruns of the project management plan. When the review process is completed and requests for retention are approved, the client releases retention to the contractor and closes the contract. After this point, the contractor releases the retention to subcontractors.

Most of the above reports may add on narratives that debate the structure, contents, key results, and recommendations to users, including the following:

- Status and forecasts for critical resources
- History of changes, status, progress, or forecasts for critical activities
- Problem areas and action required
- Conditions to achieve contract dates
- The need for exceptional management actions
- Current and anticipated delays and causes of delays
- Impacts of delays on activities, milestones, and completion dates
- Current claims and forecast of outcomes
- Critical activities among contracts
- Change of duration and logic for activities
- Pending requests for information, change orders, permits, and other issues not observed from the report

When the project is completed and all planning data are replaced with actual data, we can analyze the project's financial performance, assess project success, and document the lessons learned.

It is not rare that a lack of knowledge prevails because of oversimplifying the project management reporting requirements or reducing PMP options. Such an approach hides the causes of results, reduces performance metrics to pure statistics for high-level components of the project, and delays management decisions and consequently makes them irrelevant.

n contrast, today we have new technologies that can be deployed to improve the quality and precision of the project management reporting process. There are new visualization tools available in the market today which can help us arrive at a better understanding of the time and space concepts in the context of project management. From end to end, the user can do instant data collection and use commands to view the project status up to the very second they view the screen; it comes from fully integrated systems, continuous flow of information from one system to another knowledge-based system, and reliable predictive analysis that handle large amounts of structured and unstructured data (Ghorbant 2019, 13–22).[137]

137 Ghorbani, Shohreh. "Top 5 cutting-edge project controls technology trends and forward-thinking strategies to foster innovation." *The Measurable News* Volume 2019, Number 02 (2019): 13–22. http://mycpm.org.

The project reports are complex documents and need a systematic approach. But even properly developed and maintained project management reports are limited and are not a substitute for, but only support, practical management actions.

Project Records

Project records are documents, meeting minutes, approvals, certificates, textual, audio, or graphical submittals, and other information relating to work, materials, products, assemblies, and equipment that the contractor is required to accumulate during construction and convey to the owner for use before final payment and project closure (Means 1991, 444).[138] The project records must be organized for easy identification and filing.

Project records are closely related to project management plan, and project team members must train themselves and develop knowledge and expertise to handle the project recordkeeping process efficiently and in a timely manner to benefit future projects. Some industries are regulated entities that help project participants preserve the history of project conditions, events, changes, problems, security, and safety cases. The records include contracted works, work required, unapproved requirements, and unrequired work. Project records show the date, location, and responsible performer, the list of everything needed for work, staff mobilization, equipment and materials delivered, resource availability, work development, and results indicating the level of quality in the work carried out.

The record shows what was completed by the observation date, completed as planned and paid for, delays and interruptions, erroneously completed works, time and cost incurred to carry out repairs, punch list, and so on. Project records also contain specific information about weather conditions; specific work conditions; the types and numbers of personnel assigned to work in the project; expected working hours; idle time and the causes for downtime or idle time; equipment, material, and tools at the disposal of the project team; and information on any unusual situations, incidents, concerns, and remedial actions. There are various tools that may help with organizing project information. For example:

138 Means. *Illustrated Construction Dictionary.* Kingston, MA: R. S. Means Company, 1991.

- CSI's Master Format helps to organize, code, and communicate project documents. It is particularly beneficial for assessing building products and the environment (CSI Master Format 2020).[139]
- CSI's Uni Format helps to organize building information through its lifecycle as the project design gets finalized. It is particularly beneficial for project teams to work efficiently and coordinate better in the early stages of the project's documentation process (CSI Uni Format 2020).[140]

Both project records of past activities and the project reports on the actual performance as well as deviations against the original plan will immensely help improve the team members' understanding and knowledge about the project management plan.

Activity Record.

The activity records show daily observations of project work that should be in progress. The observation is documented by the contractor's technology-oriented representative who is the supervisor of the mechanical installation process. The report lists specific activities and events observed; date and time of observation; accessibility of work location; availability of specified materials, equipment, and employees; and deviations or omissions from the targets as recorded in the project documents, remedial action taken to resolve such deviations, and implementation of changes. The activity record helps the project team member understand how activity results comply with the project plan and requirements and documentation of various project activities, including approvals, changes, claims, and so on.

Test Record.

The test record shows the periodical observation, examination, evaluation, and testing of product or work to measure its compliance to the physical or chemical characteristics proposed and agreed between the client and the project organization, as well as the descriptive specification documented by the contractor's technology representative designated as the quality-control supervisor for the mechanical installation process. The report contains data for specific work, materials, structural elements, equipment tested, date and time of testing, location,

139 CSI Master Format. *CSI's Maser Format Standard,* Alexandria: Construction Specification Institute, 2019. www.csiresources.org/standards.

140 CSI Uni Format. *CSI's Uni Format Standard,* Alexandria: Construction Specification Institute, 2019. www.csiresources.org/standards.

phases, and quality control in the test methods carried out. The test report helps project participants know how the testing results fall below, deviate, meet, or exceed the technical specifications, industry standards, and local bylaws and regulatory standards.

Control Record.

Control record shows how documented and undocumented works, materials, or equipment, as well as changes to works, have been managed and recorded; how contract documents are released, maintained, and their application supervised; whether work location could be reached easily and on time; what reports and records are not supervised as they should be; and actions needed to improve work results. The control report is assessed occasionally by the client's representative, who is designated usually as the contract manager at the client's end. The assessor uses project documentation and established procedures and methods to supervise works and revises the performing company's activity and test records. CSI's master form helps organize, code, and communicate project documents. Numerous standards recognize it for the assessment of building products and the environment.

Plan Record.

Plan Record shows how the project management plan is regulated, developed, updated, and applied. Plan report helps project participants to know how site operations reflect project management plan; how material, equipment, and labor time for an activity have been utilized to update the project management plan; how the plan supports the management of changes to the contract; how often does the project planner visit the site location to discuss planning issues; and how communication between project participants refer to project management plan. The client's contract manager compiles the plan record, informs the project contractor about issues, and offers effective perspectives and suggests remedial actions where needed.

Quality in Project Management Planning

Several sections, examples, and case studies of this book highlight the relationship between the project management plan's requirements and project team members' skills in creating, developing, and periodically updating the plan. So, we can understand the level of quality in the project management plan by assessing the methodologies, skill sets, and project activity–specific knowledge of the project team members. Otherwise, we cannot regard the project plan as a document that helps organize project work and people and properly update the plan.

Methodologies and Skills

The assessment of methodologies used by and the skill sets of the project management team member indicates their competence in PMP and the quality of the project management plan itself which they are expected to deliver. For example, we can assess their competence in managing the following documentation:

- Notes on bylaws, standards, and specifications for project works imposed by the client, by legal institutions and regulatory bodies at the place (e.g., host country) where the project happens, and by the performing organization
- Notes on organization and oversight of reports and records about the project work
- Notes on organization and oversight of requirements for PMP
- Notes on the organization of development and the approval of a project management plan as well as its conditions which were agreed upon and expected to be fulfilled by all parties involved in the implementation of the project
- Records of the status, progress, and forecasts of the contract schedule value items
- Records on how change orders were handled and claims for compensating additional work, project overruns, and additional expenditure arising from carrying out change orders and field orders
- Records and reports generated during the PMP processes
- Records of qualitative and quantitative inspections carried out during the project work
- Records of the payments made for the completed project tasks or activities
- Record of the relationships between earned-value reports and payment application
- Records of current project plans and the actual project work carried out

Quality assessment of methodologies and skills in technology management may additionally qualify a project management team member. However, the technology-oriented project team member must show the capability to apply that knowledge in developing and implementing the project management plan.

Maturity Path

The maturity path for developing and implementing a project management plan is similar to the ones already seen in new disciplines. This path starts from misunderstanding and lack of management support for a new discipline and to later embrace it as an essential part of the company's management and cost-saving tool (Crosby 1979, 21–34).[141] It typically takes 5–10 years or even 15 years to reach a desired level of maturity in PMP.

Project management planning (PMP) is widely taught and researched in undergraduate and graduate schools, postgraduate studies, professional associations, educational organizations, and in government offices which are closely related to project management. The assessment of project management team member's maturity path points to the member's competence in PMP and the quality of the project management plan they may develop. For example, we can assess their competence by considering the following criteria:

- Earns formal education
- Attends project management courses and seminars
- Builds team spirit and trust in PMP
- Recognizes the requirements of project business
- Develops project objectives and project master plan
- Uses advanced technology features and functions of the prescribed project management software
- Leads the development and implementation of the project management plan
- Coordinates technology management and project management
- Evaluates and negotiates project contract plans
- Compiles values from the scope, time, integration, or other segments of the project management plan
- Compiles values from the finance, human resources, safety, cost accounting, industry regulations, or other general management areas
- Integrates the project plan within the project business plan
- Presents a project plan to different functional and management levels
- Performs competently in various management positions and in projects of various sizes and types which use a wide range of technologies

141 Crosby, Philip. *Quality is free.* New York, NY: A Mentor Book, 1979.

The project team members' methodologies, skill sets, and maturity path continuously improve through project management meetings. Such meetings shape the competence of as well as inspire project team members to demonstrate optimum efficiency in their work. Most such meetings are recurring events allowing the participant to prepare for the meeting and demonstrate their competency. Each meeting must contain the project's name, dates of the meetings, meeting's themes or central topic, documentation, participants, and action plans. For example:

- The introductory meeting addresses and clarifies the PMP policy, requirements, and expectations, including partial, substantial, and final occupancy plans. Participants discuss the PMP methodology, software, reporting procedures, reports, structures, payments, submittals, tests, and workplace inspections. Besides, the introductory meeting addresses the industrial relationships, labor agreements, stakeholders' interests, negotiations, relationships, team works, conflict resolutions, decision-making, project facilities, safety, security, environment protection, communications, and so on.
- The contract progress meeting addresses and reviews any question concerning the status, progress, changes, causes, outstanding issues, new alternatives, materials, products, work processes, equipment, subcontracts, and forecasts for the project contract or any part of the contract. Those meetings may address observations made during the site visit, information from fact-finding missions, photographs, updates, publication time, and contents of the project's contract management plan. Besides, the contact progress meeting regularly compares the current contract management plan with the baseline version of the plan and reviews supporting narratives, advice, comments, and concerns related to the plan's status on its progress, problems and their resolutions, forecasts, safety at the workplace, quality control, payment processes, and funding issues.
- The project management plan's recovery meeting aims to address any changes or questions related to the project plan, contract, assumed conditions, planned resources, labor and equipment productivity, and the contractor's analysis and recovery behind changes. Those meetings may address the review of written recovery statements describing the cause for delay, problems, and the contractor's actions to make progress and match the plan. It may include improving information quality and precision, training, site conditions, coordination for resources, cutting idle time for

people and equipment, more efficient activities' overlaps, sequences, additional resources, minimum reworks, and waste of materials.

In the context of the foregoing discussions about these meetings, we must know the competency and role of a project team member in explaining the issues and making the meetings a fruitful endeavor and contributing to successful outcomes of the meeting. Team members should prepare questions and answers for the meeting and take meeting notes. After the meeting, team members inform staff and discuss the decisions made that affect most of them and items related to individual responsibility. Team members should delegate activities, inform the manager, and follow-up on future actions finalized during the meeting.

Career Path in Project Management Planning

Developing and implementing a project management plan is essential for shaping the project team members' career paths. A brief description of key roles for developing and implementing a project management plan may help understand the project team members' interests and opportunities. In turn, this can help design a framework for education in PMP.

In general, a project management trainee who is eager to embark on an ambitious career journey will be willing to confront decades-old positive and negative experiences. In this context, a lack of understanding about career paths, technical skills, or knowledge needed for teamwork are just a few problems. People are usually involved in project management based on their own interests about the career paths they want to embark on (Havermans, Van der Heijden, Savelsbergh, and Storm 2019, 346).[142] Most project management trainees believe they can succeed in project work; however, they need to possess solid technical skills to succeed in a formal project management role (Burga, Leblane, and Rezania 2020, 154).[143] Although project trainees receive support from formal and informal sources, there

142 Havermans, Liselore, and. Beatrice Van der Heijden, and Chantal Savelsbergh, and Peter Storm. "Rolling into the profession: Exploring the motivation and experience of becoming a Project Manager." *Project Management Journal* Volume 50 (June 2019): 346–360. www.pmi.org.

143 Burga, Ruben, and Joshua Leblanc, and Davar Rezania. "Exploring Student Perceptions of Their Readiness for Project Work: Using Social Cognitive Career Theory." *Project Management Journal* Volume 51, (2020): 154–164. www.pmi.org.

should be a specific way or formal mechanism that helps project team members understand and access career opportunities (Ringhofer, Keegan, and Huemann 2019, 476).[144] Here are brief work descriptions for some project team members.

Project Manager

The project manager may be the owner of the project or owner's or the management's representative dedicated to complete the project adhering to pre-specified requirements and standards as well as managing unforeseen challenges with the potential to cause deviations from the goals of the project plan. The project manager's primary responsibility is to negotiate project contents and contract with the performing entity. Besides, they assess and evaluate changes, claims, incentive schemes, liquidate damages, and payments to be made for the work completed. For this purpose, they lead, promote, supervise, and approve the project management plan's development and implementation. The following activities summarize the work of the project manager:

- Collects information about project objectives, strategies, local politics, key stakeholders, and financing
- Reviews specification and actions for the development and implementation of a project management plan
- Keeps under control the project scope definition, contracts, and objectives
- Contacts client regarding changes to the project scope and their impacts on project cost, time, performance, and expectations
- Contacts company management regarding relationships with key stakeholders and expectations specified in the plan
- Contacts design company regarding the content and timing for project documentation,
- Contacts the general contractor regarding the content and timing for work packages and related schedule value items
- Contacts procurement department, with special attention to items that need a longer lead time to procure

144 Ringhofer, Claudia, and Anne Keegan, and Martina Huemann. M. "Who Supports Project Careers? Leveraging the Compensatory Roles of Line Managers." *Project Management Journal* Volume 50 (2019): 476–486. www.pmi.org.

- Works closely with project team members to develop and maintain control over the project scope, cost, cost factors, performance reporting, and project changes
- Understands the payment process, including payment for stored materials, installed materials, contracted line items, price variations, change orders, fees, services, retention, claims, rejected works, and other payments
- Takes responsibility for the assessment of planned and completed works and the timing of the payment process

However, the project manager's actions may depend on their personality or mindset. Some authors argue that besides knowledge and experience, project managers with a unique personality (both male and female) make better decisions in ambiguous conditions (Cohen, Ornoy, and Keren 2013).[145] Besides, project managers' individual commitments to the project and their personal connections outside the project context may allow a deeper insight into human aspects of project work (Brochner 2021).[146]

Some project managers may not be good team builders; they look at project management team members only as a group of skilled and sophisticated software users, which restricts from fully grasping the importance of a team member's role in the project. Imagine a simple project, a 5,000 sq. ft. apartment building, for which the architectural design has already been developed and updated by an architect well-versed with using AutoCAD software and having sufficient working experience in healthcare projects. Or the project plan is developed and updated by a mechanical well-versed with the use of software such as Primavera/Oracle and with solid experience in working in power plant projects. Both the architect and the planner will deliver insufficient project documentation.

So, a reliable approach in this case depends on the following. First, the project manager must understand the contractual requirements for project planning documentation; second, project manager has working knowledge about the current project, solid experience working in similar projects, and has the ability to communicate with peers. Both the manager and team members must understand

145 Cohen, Yuval, and Hana Ornoy, and Baruch Keren. "MBTI Personality Types of Project Managers and Their Success: A Field Survey" *Project Management Journal* Volume 44, Number 3 (June 2013): 78–87. www.pmi.org.

146 Brochner, Jan. "Construction project management fiction: Individual values." *International Journal of Project Management* In Press Version (May 2021). https://sciencedirect.com.

the limitations of project planning documentation and must possess the ability to jointly manage changes to documentation caused by changes and glitches in requirements, conditions, decisions, workmanships, and unpredictable events. Only then we can move forward to think about the unique personality traits of the project team members.

Project Planning Manager

The project planning manager is a professional who is recognized as a specialist in the organization and involved in creating and maintaining all services or carrying out all relevant actions under their responsibility during the course of developing and implementing the project management plan. The following list of activities are a recap of the different tasks to be completed by the project planning manager:

- Coordinates with the project manager in all aspects of the development and implementation of the project management plan
- Develops a procedure to gather, cluster, integrate, process, and disseminate data such as the scope, cost, time, and other information related to the development and implementation of the project management plan
- Analyzes the project documentation and structures the project codes according to organization's general instruction for assigning codes
- Analyzes project management's winning strategy and sets the project planning objectives
- Organize or perform actions for the development and implementation of the project management plan
- Compiles original, baseline, and current plans and gets approval from the management or the relevant decision-makers at the higher levels to whom they report
- Develops control levels and reports for each stakeholder
- Updates project plan and reports on the status, progress, forecasts, and changes in the attributes of the project management plan
- Maintains and stores the project management plan records for auditing purposes

Cost Accounting Manager

The cost accounting manager is responsible for providing project and project business management with general financial records and various cost reports to stakeholders and functionaries across the whole project and as defined in the project management plan. The following activities outline the work of the project cost accounting manager:

- Understands the process of project cost accounting and cost coding
- Aligns project budget structure with project cost management structure
- Understands the process of costing and costing differences
- Understands contract's clauses related to payments
- Operates payment application processing for the project works completed
- Collects, verifies, splits/summarizes, and distributes the actual project cost according to the budget structure
- Designs and produces contract cost accounting report by including contract amount, approved changes, approved payment applications, the amount paid, retentions, actual cost, and other project accounting requirements for each cost account category of the contact
- Identifies and reports to the project manager any problem related to cash flow and other issues such as delayed payments, advance payments, suspended payments, or wrongly released payments
- Follows the procedure for closing out the contract's cost account

Cost-Estimating Manager

The manager responsible for cost estimating in the project is the closest partner of the project manager in developing a cost management plan for the project. They make cost estimates and translate them into an applicable structure in PMP and secure its intended application. The following activities are carried out and monitored by the project's cost-estimating manager:

- Defines cost-estimating stages and related level of documentation
- Bases the cost-estimating structure on the project's cost management structure and master plan
- Leads cost-estimating and bidding processes during the course of the development of the project management plan
- Conducts review meetings periodically to decide the final cost estimates for the project against which contract or subcontract bids will be assessed

- Follows estimates of realistic cost, maximum management reserve, and minimum gross profit margins to win bids
- Considers contractor's cost estimate for change orders during the implementation of the contract
- Participates in the payment application process and assesses the contractor's account and contractor's account with its subcontractors

Quality Manager

The quality manager's objective is to observe work results and issue a controllable set of guidelines that will provide acceptable and financially viable work products according to specifications, inspection, and payment processes. Their actions provide excellent results for normal conditions; otherwise, a problematic issue may require the involvement of other professionals and project managers. The following activities describe the work of the project quality manager:

- Analyzes project quality standards, regulations, requirements, and expectations for project quality management
- Analyzes the balance between the required quality and the cost to fulfil the specific functions and successfully retain the features of the work product
- Understands what each schedule value item in the contract is and how its quality should be planned, assessed, measured, and reported
- Complies with the project and industry requirements to define, inspect, approve, reject, order minor rework, or accept schedule value items
- Leads action in quality planning and quality control for a major part of the project management plan
- Assures that the quality plan results in improved quality of each schedule value item, contract, and project
- Maintains the level of quality of the product which can be purchased, used, and maintained safely under normal conditions and requirements

Risk Manager

The risk manager's job is to protect project assets from losses by continuously monitoring and taking actions to prevent potential hazards in the project; other activities include the identification and elimination of high risks to assets or insure assets to protect them from high-level risks. The risk manager is also responsible for taking actions to promote the chances for the project's success. The following activities recap the work of the project risk manager:

- Starts work as early as possible, during the pre-investment phases of the project and before the start of the development of the project management plan
- Analyzes potential risks and opportunities by identifying and estimating the cost of risks and other impacts
- Assesses the probability of risk occurrence, causes of risks, quantification and qualification potential damages arising from risks; creating performance bonds for risks; taking actions that creates opportunities and benefits the whole project
- Discusses risks and potential benefits at weekly project meetings and informs project the manager of any changes in plan due to upcoming risks or challenges or opportunities in the course of the project
- Pays special attention to assessing project performance, trends, and consequences regarding project contractual agreements during the implementation of the project management plan
- Initiates corrective actions, change requests, mitigation options, and risks response plan to lessen the impact of risks
- Update the list of risks and list of opportunities by assessing changes in the plans for estimating and mitigating risks and actions to promote opportunities

Procurement Manager

The procurement manager monitors the whole process of procurement, right from when an item is requested to the point where it is delivered to the user. They analyze the procurement process to identify the lowest possible cost, optimal functions, acceptable quality of the products to be purchased and identify how safely a product can be procured. The following activities summarize the work of the project procurement manager:

- Understands procurement strategies of project management business and the project
- Understands procurement documentation contents, including the technical documentation, contracts, warranty, and responsibility
- Analyzes the political and financial conditions in relation to procuring products and the timing of procurement, as well as reviews the suppliers

record in terms of cost and quality to choose the best supplier of the products to be purchased
- Analyzes statement of work as well as the planning sequence for selection, pricing, negotiation, specification, and procurement of work items
- Participates in developing and finalizing the procurement contract and participates in the bidding process
- Analyzes the procurement plan, payment plan, and users' readiness to accept and maintain procurements cost-effectively
- Coordinates actions in moving the items purchased along the trajectory starting from the procurement source, that is, supplier, to the last stage where the items purchase are delivered to the end user

The development of basic project management skills is a long but rewarding process. For example, you want a project planner who understands the project's technological processes, management processes, contracts, management requirements, design, and procurement documentation. You may also ask the project planner to compile these processes and documentation into a simple, sufficient, and reliable one-page report for senior managers. Ideally, such a person would have a graduate degree, two years of experience in the relevant industry, five years of experience in preparing cost estimates and project timeframes, competence in using the required project management software, and having the right personality traits and attitude that work best in the project environment. They may lead action and deliver consistent project planning documentation that is as reliable as any other professional document in the project.

The career path in PMP is a complex yet promising space (Google 1).[147] In a short but insightful article, Williams discusses the emerging trends, tools, and resources, as well as plans for changes that project management professionals need to understand to perform at the optimum level. The author gives examples of modern methods, project and operational data analysis, use of artificial intelligence technology, management of growing connectivity, block-chain technology of opinions, and other technologies important for improving career development and responding to current project business needs (Williams 2019).[148]

147 Google 1. *Project management schools: Statistics, Professional trends, Educational trends, Faculty salaries, Schools by state, Related links.* Google, May 2021. www.google.com.

148 Williams, Rob. "Fortifying your career in 2020 and beyond." *The Measurable News* Volume 2019, Issue 02 (2019): 9–12. http://mycpm.org.

The career paths for team members cannot be considered in isolation, outside the project team, which is the central social entity in the project; it accomplishes project work and delivers values to organizations. So we must understand the relevant issues about project team meaning, professional development, terminology, trust-building among team members, organization, creativity, performances, effectiveness, teaming, and others to deliver more than the sum of individual-level contributions (Dalcher 2018).[149]

In Chapter 5, Project Management System Logic, I will present the system logic steps that spring from the collection of general project management system contents. The best-practice steps and system logic steps complement one another and mingle and flow together into an updated system to develop and implement the project management plan.

149 Dalcher, Darren. "The wisdom of teams revisited: Teamwork, teaming and working for the common good." *PM World Journal* Volume VII, Issue IX (September 2018): www.pmworldjournal.net.

5 Project Management System Logic

Introduction

This chapter and the next are intended for advanced courses in project management planning (PMP) and facilitating connections with sponsors and entrepreneurs. Audience for the chapters belongs to several groups of the project management community:

- Postgraduate students who understood well the first four chapters in this book and are seeking a career in project management education
- Educators interested in teaching a scientific process and bringing a new perspective to PMP
- Researchers interested in understanding and handling a general collection of the project management systems and their logics
- Entrepreneurs keen to learn more about project management system's logic in terms of creating lasting business opportunities
- Owners of the collection of project management system knowledge who would like to learn new perspectives about system knowledge

Chapter 5 is an overview of project management system knowledge and perspectives about improving PMP. For this purpose, the chapter includes a discussion about the following themes:

- General collections of project management system knowledge
- The PMBOK Guide as a potential archetype of general project management system knowledge
- Handling of project management system knowledge and its logic
- Project management system logic as a template for the project management plan
- Processes for handling changes to system logic and project management plan

The above audience and themes may transform the nature of project management, its system knowledge, research, education, planning, and business.

A general collection of project management system knowledge encompasses various standards—the Project Management General Standards, Organizational Standards, Quality Standards, Scheduling Standards, Earned-Value Standards, Risk Standards, and others that impact the understanding about project management.

The messages from Project Management General Standards and the organizations dedicated to developing the project management profession, although similar, improve the compilation of project management in their own ways. For example:

- PMBOK Guide, Project Management Institute of USA (PMI), describes the sum of knowledge within the project management profession.
- APM BoK, Association for Project Managers of UK (APM), defines the role and influence of personal experience and knowledge in project management.
- IPMA Competence Baseline, International Project Management Association of Zurich-Switzerland (IPMA), describes the expected competences of project manager, who is a professional well-versed planning and controlling a project.
- P2M Bok, Project Management Association of Japan (PMAJ), outlines how project management can best stimulate innovation and improve business value.
- Other international and national standards and associations established to facilitate global project management.

In 1995, Curling wrote an influential Editorial and Introduction for the special issue of the *International Journal of Project Management*, where he discussed the international "body of knowledge" status and perspective. While most of his views continue to be influential and inspiring, this is what he said about the project management body of knowledge:

Project management practitioners do not have a universally accepted framework for assembling the knowledge associated with the practice of project management. (Curling 1995, 67)[150]

Contributing authors to the special issue of *IJPM* presented insights about framing, developing, and using a body of knowledge associated with project management. In his "Criteria for a Project Management Body of Knowledge," Widman presents enduring visions for developing and maintaining a model of the project management body of knowledge:

Ideally, sound criteria should lead to a model of the PMBOK, which enables the contained knowledge to be organized so that it can be examined systematically and its scope can be evaluated. (Wideman 1995, 72)[151]

From the beginning of the pursuit of learning about how to model project management knowledge, the readers develop various views about project management. Some of the issues get general acceptance, while some continue to remain significantly challenging and unresolved.

Morris et al. come closer to the applied research line probing the existence of a common discipline associated with project management practice that can facilitate discussions on project management. They assert:

In the end, however, most people working in the subject do believe that there is a generic discipline that is core to the practice of project management across a very wide range of industries and applications and that, as a result, it is worth trying to define what this core is. (Morris, Patel, and Wearne 2000, 156)[152]

As ideas for assembling and systematically examining project management knowledge evolve, the fundamental question emerges—can people and

150 Curling, H. David., 1995. "Editorial." *Introduction, International Journal of Project Management*, Volume 13, Issue 2, 67–70.

151 Wideman, R. Max. "Criteria for a project management body of knowledge." *International Journal of Project Management* Volume 13, Issue 2 (1995): 71–75. www.elsevier.com/locate/ijproman.

152 Morris, Peter, and Marsh Patel, and Stephen Wearne. "Research into revising the APM project management body of knowledge." *International Journal of Project Management,* 18 (2000): 155–64. www.elsevier.com/locate/ijproman.

organizations influencing project management knowledge see the possibility of the emergence of a generic discipline that is core to that knowledge? Answers to this question aren't straightforward. Some researches see dealing with the knowledge management part of the project as similar to acquiring knowledge in other areas of project management structured and described in the PMBOK Guide (Gasik 2011).[153] In contrast, recent research argues that the continuous study of the knowledge aspect of the project can provide clues to improving both the project knowledge and the project as a whole (Payne, Roden, and Simister 2019).[154] In practice, the overwhelming examples show that PMP may be an indispensable discipline to help understand project management system knowledge.

The history of project management knowledge, from the age of scientific initiatives in the early 1960s to its general acceptance in the early 1980s, reasonable development by today, and the controversies in its current trends, shows the core of project management knowledge. The remarkable development of the PMBOK Guide reflects the historical perspective. It shows that PMP could be a generic discipline for systematically examining system knowledge and its logic. It was a sparkling point for further search.

Many discussions were necessary to recognize the collection of general project management system knowledge as the project and identify its contents to understand its logic. Among commercially available project management systems, I found that the PMBOK Guide's revised editions from 1996 to 2017 comply with the requirements of the study because they:

- are well-structured and continuously updated
- differ substantially from other project management systems by the relational output/input characteristics
- show that PMP is a substantial part of the project management system knowledge

Let's learn more about the PMBOK Guide capacity to expose and use its logic for various purposes, including a systematic approach to PMP.

153 Gasik, Stanislaw. "A Model of Project Knowledge Management." *Project Management Journal* Volume 42, Number 3. (April 2011): 23–44. www.pmi.org.

154 Payne, Judy, Eileen Roden, and Steve Simister. "Through the knowledge lens: Knowledge Management adventures in project-land." *PM World Journal* Volume VIII, Issue IX (January 2019): www.pmworldjournal.com.

To follow, the reader of the notion should recall some earlier sections (Chapter 1: Basis for Project Management Planning).

The PMBOK Guide

I ask myself if it is possible to write criticism painted by admiration when facts tell other stories. At the same time, I do not want to damage the work of others. If I show a less-than-favorable judgment in discussing the PMBOK Guide, it is because I have always intended to understand better the PMBOK Guide than any of it purposes, objectives, organization, or promotion. All I want to show is that a collection of project management system knowledge, and so the PMBOK Guide, can reach a massive population of average managers if its contents are developed systematically and its logic is made simple and visible.

Past of the PMBOK Guide

The PMBOK Guide started in the late 1980s. It came into being through project management, a rather ambiguous concept at that time. Yet, PMP, as a specific characteristic of the PMBOK Guide, keeps a background role. Continuum of genuine relationships between PMP and project management system knowledge characterize the contents of the PMBOK Guide's revised editions.

In the foreword by Mary Devon O'Brien, the Project Management Body of Knowledge (PMBOK) was developed as a document in 1988 to identify and describe the major knowledge areas—the framework—of project management (Wideman 1991, i).[155] The document builds around the framework, glossary, the eight project management functions (scope, quality, time, cost, risk, human resources, contract/procurement, and information/communication), integration management, project lifecycle, and stakeholder satisfaction.

The document from 1988 has been developed in the succeeding editions of the PMBOK Guide. The process of managing changes to a project or system, description of relationships between processes, and base of relationships in the form of output/input gains significance and attracts particular interest in the pursuit of understanding the PMBOK Guide and its logic.

155 Wideman, Max. *A framework for project and program management integration.* The PMBOK handbook series Volume No 1. Upper Darby, PA: Project Management Institute, 1991. www.pmi.org.

The process of managing changes began well (Wideman 1991, ii, VII-3, 4, 5). Later, the PMBOK Guide's revised editions made the notion arguable (PMI 1996, 28, Figure 3.1)[156] or ambiguous (PMI 2017, 562, Figure 2.1).[157] Wideman wrote:

Perhaps the first step is to recognize that learning about project management is learning about a process—the process of managing change. (Wideman 1991, ii)

The PMBOK Guide's description of the relationships between project management processes was an excellent introduction to project management system logic (PMI 1996, 31; PMI 2000, 33).[158] Later, edition after edition the "flow diagrams" were presented that made the relationships between project management processes visible (e.g., PMI 2004, 47[159]; PMI 2008, 47[160]; PMI 2013, 73[161]; PMI 2017, 82).

The PMBOK Guide's unique notion, the base of relationships in the form of output/input, categorizes the PMI's PMBOK Guide as the systematic knowledge and keeps its competitive advantage over other project management bodies of knowledge (PMI 1996, 41; PMI 2000, 42; PMI 2004, 79; PMI 2008, 73; PMI 2013, 65; PMI 2017, 71). Let's look at the summary of references that show when and how the PMI Teams describes the output/input characteristics of the PMBOK Guide in terms of system logic.

Although the PMBOK Guide initially describes the output/input notion at the "core processes" level, it clearly shows an avenue for developing and maintaining project management system knowledge (PMI 1996, 30–35; PMI 2000, 32–37). Diagrams and associated texts for PMBOK Guide's later editions (e.g., Third Edition—PMI 2004, 42; Fourth Edition—PMI 2008, 42) imply that relationships between process groups occur at the output/input level. Fortuitously,

156 PMI 1996. *A Guide to the Project Management Body of Knowledge (PMBOK® Guide) 1996 Edition.* Newtown Square PA: Project Management Institute, 1996.

157 PMI 2017. *A Guide to the Project Management Body of Knowledge (PMBOK® Guide) Sixth Edition.* Newtown Square PA: Project Management Institute, 2017.

158 PMI 2000. *A Guide to the Project Management Body of Knowledge (PMBOK® Guide) 2000 Edition.* Newtown Square PA: Project Management Institute, 2000.

159 PMI 2004. *A Guide to the Project Management Body of Knowledge (PMBOK® Guide) Third Edition.* Newtown Square PA: Project Management Institute, 2004.

160 PMI 2008. *A Guide to the Project Management Body of Knowledge (PMBOK® Guide) Fourth Edition.* Newtown Square PA: Project Management Institute, 2008.

161 PMI 2013. *A Guide to the Project Management Body of Knowledge (PMBOK® Guide) Fifth Edition.* Newtown Square PA: Project Management Institute, 2013.

the PMI Staff acknowledges the output/input notion using the X1.3 rules for handling inputs and outputs (PMI 2017, 640–641). However, perfect conditions for developing project management system logic postpones, which delays the way when fewer pages mean more systematic contents of the PMBOK and its long-lasting credibility stays intact.

The PMBOK® Guide has disseminated project management knowledge successfully for decades. It is one of the most preferred references for studying, lecturing, researching, and practicing project management.

Unique features of the PMBOK Guide are also subject to continuous analysis and are a point of reference in books and journal articles. Many discussions have taken place that compared the systems, acknowledged the differences, and understood Curling's ideas about the general body of knowledge. For example, Crawford et al. discuss some of the above by comparing the GAPPS body of knowledge with other standards (GAPPS 2007)[162]:

A high level of alignment was found with the [GAPPS's] 48 categories [topics] and other corpora [standards], although this was of varying consistency. (Crawford, L. et al., 2007, p.15)[163]

The above observation shows the commonalities among project management systems. It is invaluable. But some parts of this study show that making comparisons and identifying relationships between the standards could be well beyond our capacity. Let's consider the PMBOK Guide and the GAPPS in more detail.

The PMBOK Guide provides guidelines for managing individual projects (PMI 2008, 3), whereas the GAPPS helps conclude whether a project manager can perform competently (GAPPS 2007, 9). Although both standards have the same mission, we cannot compare the two or relate one with the other. While the PMBOK Guide has reached the level of particles and gains characteristic for consistent comparison and relationships to other systems, the GAPPS did not use such features and, consequently, like other systems, miss the opportunity to become a substantial part of an international body of knowledge. If we try to identify GAPPS topics within the contents of PMBOK Guide's Fourth Edition,

162 GAPPS 2007. *A Framework for Performance Based Competency Standards for Global Level 1 and 2 Project Manager.* Sydney, Australia: Global Alliance for Project Performance Standards, 2007. www.globalpmstandards.org.

163 Crawford, Lynn, and Julien Pollock, and David England. "How standard are Standards: An Examination of Language Emphasis in Project Standards." *Project Management Journal* Volume 38, Number 3 (September 2007): 6–21. www.pmi.org.

we can find that the GAPPS topics (GAPPS 2007, 41) scattered throughout the different levels and structures of the PMBOK Guide contents:

- The Scope Management, Time Management, and some other GAPPS topics reside in the knowledge areas level of the PMBOK Guide (PMI 2008, 103, 129).
- Change Control, Project Closeout/Finalization, and some other GAPPS topics reside at the process level of the PMBOK Guide (PMI 2008, 93, 99).
- Business Case, Requirements Management, and some other GAPPS topics reside at the input or output level of the PMBOK Guide (PMI 2008, 75, 109–111).
- Information and Communication Management, Negotiation, and some other GAPPS topics reside within the tools and techniques sections of the PMBOK Guide (PMI 2008, 87, 227).

Therefore, the technical side to studying a general project management system requires standard terms hidden in details, output/input, or particles of system contents. It is the condition to understand the contents of a project management system and its relationships with other systems.

The PMBOK Guide is a widespread and flourishing project management content. The Project Management Institute (PMI) standards and guideline publications have been developed through a standards development process based on voluntary consensus (PMI 2017, Notice). They cover the generally recognized project management contents and provide essential details on how they can help project management. The PMBOK Guide's earlier editions contain two substantial parts:

- Part 1—A Guide to the Project Management Body of Knowledge (PMBOK Guide)—is structured at the top level by project management knowledge areas (integration, scope, schedule, cost, quality, resource, communications, risk, procurement, and stakeholders).
- Part 2—The Standard for Project Management—is structured at the top level by project management process groups (e.g., initiating, planning, executing, controlling, and closing). The contents of processes specified in Part 2 are identical to those described in Part 1.

Although Part 1 and Part 2 have different top-level structures, both parts end with the same processes and, consequently, the same sets of inputs and outputs. It is the explicit system thinking.

The PMBOK Guide's experience was a success; its management initiated, organized, acquired, filtered, and disseminated an enormous collection of project management knowledge. There is unwavering interest in the PMBOK Guide, commonly for the Project Management Professional certification, education, and research; however, its system logic remains unrealized, causing the risk of not utilizing the competitive advantage and, in turn, lose the opportunity to promote new business ventures.

The present of the PMBOK Guide

The PMBOK Guide's Seventh Edition is a novelized view of flourishing project management knowledge. It's been exciting to read comments evolving in real time during the compilation of PMBOK Guide's Seventh Edition. Here are some early thoughts related to the PMBOK Guide's Seventh Edition Exposure Draft that facilitate the analysis of its published edition. Pirozzi believes that the PM's "fresh approach to the profession" will drastically change the PMP Certification process and PMI's reference texts (Pirozzi 2020).[164] Shepherd expects the PMI Staff to make significant changes to its terminology and presentational aspects (Shepherd 2020).[165]

When we have the new edition of the PMBOK Guide's Seventh Edition, it would be interesting to see how the PMI Staff can deal with the above and other concerns. Let's see briefly how the PMBOK Guide's Seventh Edition responds to readership's and stakeholders' requirements to advance the PMBOK Guide by improving its contents, credibility, readability, information, practicality, and recognition (PMI 2021, vii–viii).[166]

164 Pirozzi, M. 2020. "On the Subject of PM Standards, People and Community, Letter to the Editor." *PM World Journal*, Vol IX, Issue III, (March 2020). www.pmworldjournal.net.

165 Shepherd, M. 2020. "On the matter of Project Management Standards, Letter to the Editor." *PM World Journal*, Vol IX, Issue XII, (December 2020). www.pmworldjournal.net.

166 PMI 2021. *A Guide to the Project Management Body of Knowledge PMBOK Guide Seventh Edition and the Standard for the Standard for Project Management*, 2021, Project Management Institute Inc., 14 Campus Boulevard, Newtown Square, PA 19073-3299.

The PMBOK Guide's Seventh Edition consists of new terms and views practiced within the Agile community, along with restructured, renamed, and summarized knowledge from PMI's earlier editions challenging the way we think project management is supposed to look. The Standard for Project Management Body of Knowledge and A Guide to the Project Management Body of Knowledge are two essential parts of The PMBOK Guide's Seventh Edition. In everyday terminology, I can recognize the following:

- The Standard for Project Management Body of Knowledge as a charter for the project management office
- A Guide to the Project Management Body of Knowledge as an outline for PMP

The Standard for Project Management Body of Knowledge describes the value delivery and project management principles that may influence the behavior of people involved in projects. For this purpose, the standard refers to the following:

- Stewardships and responsibilities for project activities
- Project teams and collaborative behavior to accomplish shared objectives
- Stakeholders that proactively and positively influence the success of the project
- Value and outcomes that show quantitative and qualitative contributions to business objectives
- System thinking that helps manage the interacting and dynamic conditions of the project
- Leadership behavior that facilitates individual and team needs toward common objectives
- Tailoring processes to cope with the project's unique contents and requirements
- Quality that reflects expectations of stakeholders and meets common objectives
- The complexity that we must structure and weigh its components to reduce the negative impact
- The risk that should be disambiguated and assessed all the time to promote opportunities and minimize negative impacts
- Adaptability and resilience to deal with fluctuating project conditions

- Change resulting from project outcomes creates new conditions and behavior to deal with the updated state of the project

A Guide to the Project Management Body of Knowledge describes the domains of project performance achieved by people's activities and behaviors. For this purpose, the guide brings up the following:

- Stakeholders' performance domain that assumes that stakeholders collaborate based on common interest
- Team performance domain that requires creating conditions that motivate individuals to contribute to teamwork
- Development approach and lifecycle domains assumes launching the method and dealing with project phases to understand project contents
- Planning performance domain holds a system to plan project deliverables and outcomes
- Project work performance domains consider constructing processes for handling activity resources
- Delivery performance domain assumes accomplishing the activity scope, quality, and other attributes to be achieved
- Performance measurement domain considers assessing and maintaining acceptable project performance
- Performance uncertain domain deals with activities and functions associated with threats and opportunities that the project team identifies, evaluates, and manages

Besides, The Standards for Project Management and A Guide to the Project Management Body of Knowledge, the Appendices, Glossary, and Index help understand the PMBOK Guide's Seventh Edition.

The PMBOK Guide's Seventh Edition leans to Agile standpoints of the short-term investment, presented through appealing readability, along with a collection of other project management themes and terms. It shifts from the global process-based practice to a principle-based standard focused on "intended outcomes rather than deliverable" (PMI 2021, x). The notion is the main difference between narratives that guess the upcoming short-term outcome and global practice that measures status, progress, and forecasts by documenting what to do and why we should do what we do for the project.

The good news is that all options complement one another in the short term period looking in isolation. Therefore, "nothing in this edition of the Standard for Project Management or Guide to Project Management Body of Knowledge negate alignments with the process-based approach of past edition" (PMI 2021, xi). This promise should operate by the PMIstandard+™, "an integrative digital platform that incorporates current, emerging, and future practices, methods, artifacts, and other useful information" (PMI 2021, xii).

Besides, the PMBOK Guide's Seventh Edition maintains the above notions through an extended definition of project management, stating that the project team can achieve the outcomes using prescriptive, hybrid, and adaptive approaches (PMI 2021, 3–4). The all-inclusive system is a great challenge, as the PMI Staff are expected to and will continue to update its fundamental, process-based idea in future editions.

The Standard for Project Management and A Guide to Project Management include an ever-fresh view of terms and approaches. But this may not be all that transparent and clear. For that reason, the PMI Staff of the PMBOK Guide's Seventh Edition should reevaluate the transparency of terminologies used. For example:

- How planned and actual metrics for scope, time, cost, change orders, claims, benefits, unusual requirements, and conditions of project deliverable differ from metrics for customer-defined outcomes of Agile deliverables?
- How planned and actual metrics for an organization's structural system component differ from the outcomes for an organization's governance system component?
- How terms established and practiced for decades—Feedback (Chapter 5, Figure 5.3), Lead Time Chart (Chapter 7, Santora 1963, 734–736),[167] and Integrated Performance against the Baseline (Chapter 3, Fleming and Koppelman 2006, 111–125)[168]—differ from the PMBOK Guide's Seven Edition's Feedback (PMI 2021, 3, 161), Lead Time Chart (PMI 2021, 189), and Project Performance Domains (PMI 2021, 7–129)?

The PMI Staff of the PMBOK Guide's Seventh Edition should promote clarity in the application processes which, though in practice for generations, have been perceived differently. For example:

167 Santora, A. V. *The Encyclopedia of Management,* Edited by Carl Heyel. New York: Reinhold Publishing Corporation, 1963, 732–39.

168 Fleming, Quentin, and Joel Koppelman. "Start with 'Simple' Earned Value on All Your Projects." *The Journal of Defense Software Engineering.* 2006, 16–19.

- How do the project's monthly results on project completion differ from the Agile short-term investment outcomes on Agile open-ended completion?
- How can we focus on business and social outcomes rather than deliverables when the deliverable and its attributes precede and define the outcomes?
- When should we replace the project's structural estimate of what to do in the next period with the Agile estimate of the upcoming short-term outcome?

Formally, the PMBOK Guide appeared to have independent competitiveness governed by output/input characteristics. We see now it may also be enhanced by the inclusiveness of popular matters. How can we deal with these new challenges?

The Perspective of the PMBOK Guide

Let's start the discussion with the fundamental question. If the PMI Staff cannot recess the development of what you're doing for a period of your professional life, then who will?

Taking a break from developing traditional output/input levels, the PMI Staff are instead promoting equal opportunity for contributing to the future editions of the PMBOK Guide. So, let's think about the breaks in process-based opportunities:

- An extended break in developing the PMBOK Guide's output/input may cause unexpected difficulties during its updating.
- Pausing the PMBOK Guide's development at the output/input levels may promote ambiguities and illusions about understanding project management.
- Novelizing the PMBOK Guide, the average scholars lose the chance to research the Guide, and practitioners may not apply the Guide.
- By resting the development of the output/input features in the PMBOK Guide, we may simplify education but cannot provide answers to contemporary project management questions.
- Reducing the PMBOK Guide's output/input development may undermine the growth of actual project system knowledge and its fundamental needs.

The PMBOK Guide without systematic development of output/input may explain how great ideas of the PMBOK 1991, and the PMBOK Guide 1996 complicate by flow diagrams, novelize by Agile language and end. However, if we know where the project management knowledge, including the PMBOK Guide, is coming from and when and how it began to flourish, we may know where it should go and, in turn, participate in its ongoing development and transition.

Principle-based handling of project management system knowledge alone may inhibit the recognition of process-based project management. Even if we continue to compile already impressive project management system knowledge and explain its components, its problems do not stop. For example, without output/input characteristics, users cannot systematically add, delete, or modify pieces of project management system knowledge. They will not be able to move project management system knowledge from the general collection to applying its logic to PMP.

As we know, the comprehensive structure of the PMBOK Guide content provides equal opportunity for sustaining its contents, credibility, practicality, and recognition. It means the PMBOK Guide processes' lowest level should end with unique output/input sets, regardless of the selection and organization of its higher levels, knowledge areas, or performance domains. A comprehensive structure for known and knowable system contents can help in the following ways:

- Simplifies the compilation, control, implementation, and maintenance of the PMBOK Guide.
- Explains fuzziness inherent in project management systems and shows the PMBOK Guide's logic close to its hypothetical meaning, distinct visualization, and recognized handling.
- Justifies new requirements for change and localizes the changes within the contents of the PMBOK Guide.
- Shows the level of practice we choose and opens discussions about what we could have missed in the PMBOK Guide and how to get better next time.
- Reduces the gap between an impressive collection of the PMBOK Guide's project management knowledge and its application.
- Moderates the gap between students' certification exams for system knowledge and the actual project management needs.
- Connects generations of project management followers educated to think globally and those who work at the input/output levels of the PMBOK Guide.

The PMI Staff have abundant material to promote systematic and rational views of general collections of project system knowledge alongside certification-centered contents. Otherwise, it isn't easy to make sense of all this accumulated knowledge.

The PMI Staff should see the future of the PMBOK Guide as a tool that helps to understand with ease the diversified readership and strategic opportunities. Longer pauses in developing output/input characteristics may cause longer-lasting problems in the creation of future versions of PMBOK Guide and professional standards since it they are the only measurable indicators of changes to their predecessors and help the readership gain the systematic advantage of the PMBOK Guide compared to other professional certification standards. The output/input characteristics enable comparison and creation of links among standards and the development of universal system logic that may become the primary source for various standards, services, and PMP practices. Besides, output/input characteristics enable the systematic testing and evolution of the PMBOK Guide regardless of changes or reconstructions of its upper levels.

Understanding the relationships between project management plan and project management system knowledge enhances the project manager's competency. In addition, the skills to produce or understand a project management system logic will move the project manager from preoccupation with the short-term plan to comprehensive analysis, relationships, synthesis, and updating of project management system logic, project management plan, and, consequently, a short-term plan.

We live in a world of unprecedented technological innovations and the transformation of social entities' efforts to tackle new challenges. Although the simple solution providing short-term narrations cannot be proven before facts arrive, the ideal of doing so appeals to many novices in project management. So, we should have answers to the following questions: How has general project management knowledge been thought? What was the objective of educators? Why is it so common to hear that practice differs from education? Why does ambiguity prevail the comprehensiveness and appeal to a mass of project management certification contenders, which vary widely depending on project needs?

The challenge for readership is to keep the new PMI's orientation toward principle-based and process-based project management. We hope contributions to its output/input characteristics will last long enough to justify the PMBOK Guide's status, changes, and competence. For example, the "Project Cost Management Overview" (PMI 2017, 232) and similar overviews would be sufficient until a full-blown supplemental publication is published which includes the system logic. It will better explain the concept and avoid its early replacement. But how can we seize the opportunity?

Rules for Handling System Knowledge

This section deals with the project management's second order (PM-2) which may serve as a methodological example for handling general collections of project management system knowledge:

- Developing and implementing project management system logic
- Facilitating the relationships among different project management systems
- Using system logic to improve the system approach to PMP

A general collection of a project management systems is a complex matter; it may include many

- areas (feasibility, sustainability, finance, investment, organization, growth, employment, planning, security, usage, maintenance, others)
- levels (system, processes, outputs/inputs, particles, others)
- attributes for each level (description, relations, codes, others)
- explanations for each attribute (dictionaries, professional glossaries, journal articles, books, others)
- paradigms (traditional structure, current structure, narratives, narrative rationality, mid-level pragmatism, others).

The idea to model a collection of the project management system is critical for understanding its complexities, especially to explain the complexity inherited in a project management system, the model close to its hypothetical meaning, distinct visualization, and the time needed to fulfil handling needs. If we study the project management system at the output/input levels or their parts and particles, then system logic will emerge from the sphere of ambiguity. Consequently, the reader can discuss or apply the system as this is the viable alternative to explain a system model. The lowest-level system structure—the particle attributes—is not systemized yet, whereas the upper-level system structure—the processes—leads to vague relationships among project management system components.

To reach new consumers, serve as an outline for PMP, and connect to a mass of average managers and planners, the project management system knowledge must be analyzed in detail and derive comprehensible practical meanings. For this purpose, we must compile application-oriented rules to examine, debug, and simplify the contents of project management system knowledge. The rules for the handling of project management system knowledge are divided into three categories:

- Rules for relating the particles of system logic or condition that control how a particle is related to its predecessors and successors
- Rules for developing the chronological sequence of particles or conditions that allow the incremental explanation and improvement of system logic, in the step-by-step procedure for the system's entire contents
- Rules for verifying system logic or conditions to identify, debug, sense, and use system logic as an outline for developing and implementing the project management plan.

The whole process is similar to the forward pass through the network planning diagram (Chapter 2: Forward Calculation). Relationships begin by identifying each process's outputs resulting from open–start sets or defined inputs. We move forward by relating the outputs of the commencement processes to identical inputs of the succeeding processes. The critical output/input relationship becomes one that completes the input requirements of the succeeding processes. After completing all relationships, all outputs of critical output/input relationships and open-end outputs become critical. An ultimate path from the commencement particle to the completion of the last particle implies the completion of all other system particles.

Rules for Relating Particles of System Logic

We must reassess the notion that project management processes connect the outputs they produce. For this purpose, we must establish rules for relating outputs/inputs or particles for the most detailed element of a system structure (Figure 5.1). Here is a brief description of the key rules:

- There are three types of system particles, the relational outputs/inputs, the open-start inputs, and the open-end outputs. The outputs comprise the relational particles and open-end particles, and the inputs comprise the relational particles and open-start particles. As the project management system overlaps with other disciplines, open-start particles may relate to other disciplines' open-end particles. In contrast, an open-end particle may relate to the open-start particles of other disciplines.

- Relationships within a particular knowledge area are established by relating the process outputs and inputs. They are observable by moving forward from the first process group to the last process group of a particular knowledge area.
- Relationships among two or more knowledge areas are also established by relating the process outputs and inputs. We can move forward within the same or different process groups within a single area of knowledge or multiple knowledge areas.
- Suppose there are more processes with input requirements from another process. In that case, the output particle relates to the succeeding process's input requirements.

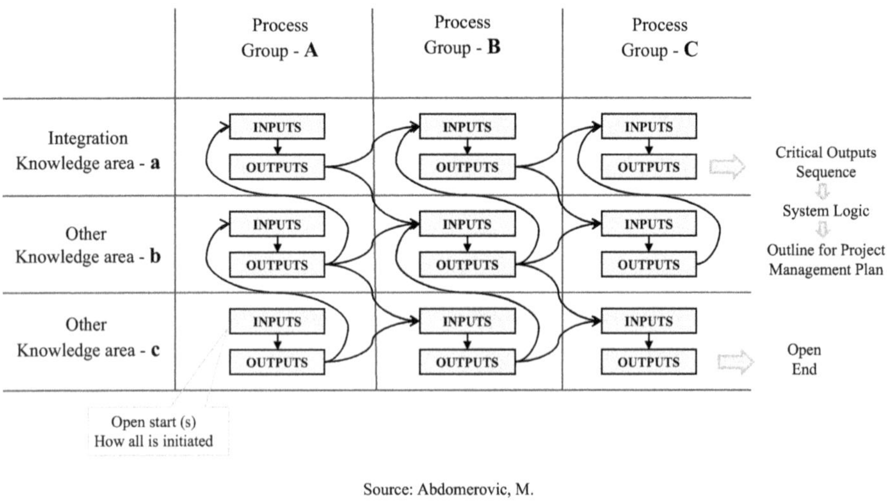

Figure 5.1: Relationships of System Particles

- A particular set of input requirements always precede the development of unique output particles. Different sets of input requirements must always result in different output particles. Therefore, there are no two or more same particles in a system; otherwise, the disambiguation process must continue.
- There are no identical input requirements for two or more processes; otherwise, each particle's distinctive characteristic is defective.
- There is a process where none of the particles from other processes constitute a substantial part of the development of its output particles, and then at least an open-start input to such a process is required.

- If two or more processes contain open-start or open-end particles, output/input chains indicate an intermediate result.
- A particle from the area of integration in project management cannot relate to other knowledge areas' input requirements in the same process group.
- If neighboring processes from the same process group and the same knowledge area do not have at least one relational particle, they are combined into a single process.
- The number of processes is not limited; however, each group must have one process.

Let's see some examples of how relationships occur in the project management system logic of the PMBOK Guide's Fourth Edition. Figure 5.1 shows how:

- The relationship "Aa" to "Bb" relates the outputs and inputs within the different knowledge areas and other process groups. For example, the output part of the project management plan relates to and changes inputs in several succeeding processes: Direct and Manage Project Execution, Perform Quality Performance, Acquire Project Team, Develop Project Team, Manage Project Team, Distribute Information, Manage Stakeholder Expectations, and Conduct Procurement. The processes that receive the input "Project management plan" generate outputs for the "Project management plan updates" in the above processes.
- The relationship "Ca" to "Cb" is related to the outputs and inputs within the same knowledge area and different process groups. For example, the Project Quality Management area contains output the Project management plan updates from the Executing Process Group that changes input Project management plan in the Monitoring and Controlling Process Group.

By applying the rules to each particle of the project management system's contents, we have reached the first stage on the way to system logic. This stage shows how the system's particles control project management processes. Consequently, the control of processes automatically passes to control process groups and all higher levels in the system. After this stage, a system's state is powered with a dynamic feature and is ready for reconstruction using appropriate contents and conditions. Suppose there is a reasonable need to replace a particle within the system contents. In that case, we can reconnect the particle to the existing input requirements, split the particle and reconnect its parts to existing input requirements, split some input requirements, and observe a different set of resulting particles or introduce new input requirements or even a new process. Such an analysis can sense the system contents and the position of the particle or particles.

Rules for Developing Sequence of Particles

After the contents of the system particles are related, we must have rules to develop the sequence for the particles of the system content. The following rules summarize the analysis of how the system's outputs emerge or happen sequentially:

- If an output from a process is an input to another process, then the preceding process and the succeeding process are related by the relational output/input.
- If there is a process with all inputs defined, where at least one input is the relational output/input, the process succeeds.
- An output from the preceding process can be related as an input to several succeeding processes.
- The critical succeeding process is the one that has all of its inputs defined, including at least one relational output/input from the preceding critical process.
- The outputs revealed from critical processes create the critical outputs sequence of system particles.

By applying the above rules to each particle of a project management system's contents, we have completed the second stage on the way to system logic. The stage shows a step-by-step route for analyzing, relating, synthetizing, or updating the system contents. Figure 5.2 illustrates a summary of the Initiating and Planning Processes of the PMBOK Guide's Fourth Edition.

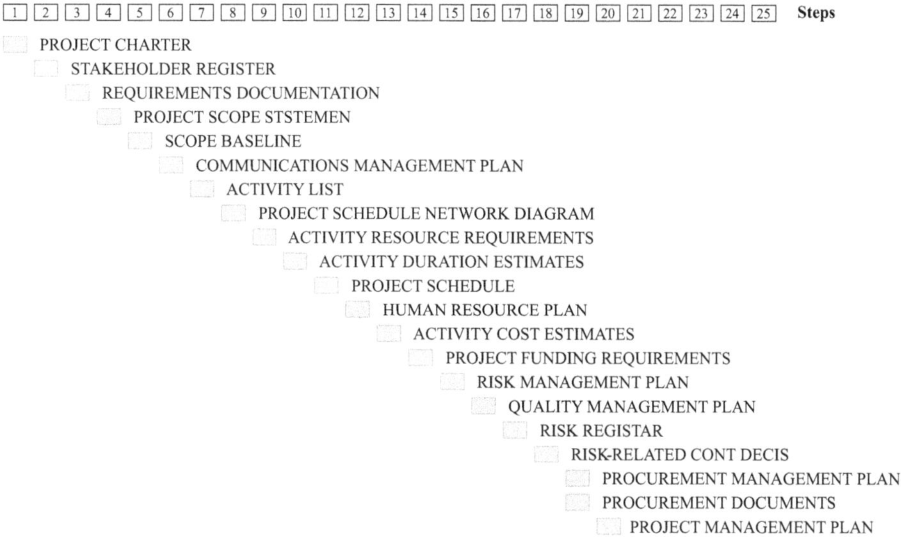

Source: Abdomerovic, M.

Figure 5.2: Critical Outputs Sequence

Let's now take a look at some examples of differences between approaches to PMI's PMBOK Guide.

The contents of the project management system knowledge as would be explained by the narrative approach may end up with ambiguous explanations of the functions of the project management system. The narrative approach's problem is the endless discussions about whether a particular answer for a system is superior to other reasons. However, the structural approach to project management system knowledge simplifies discussion about the system. For example, the approach to developing the project management plan has changed with each edition of the PMBOK Guide:

- Changes that were incorporated in the editions published between 1996 and 2000 were rather minor and indicate a smooth transition.
- The project management plan's developments and revisions from the 2000 edition to the Third Edition were massive. Besides different approaches to developing a project management plan, none of the Third Edition's input sets and only three output sets were the same as the 2000 edition.
- Developing the project management plan from the Third Edition to Fourth Edition turned back to the logic similar to the one used in the 1996 and 2000 editions.

Therefore, it is impossible to control the volume, explanation, or meaning of narratives about changes. However, using a structural approach to analyze system contents and contents relationships, we reveal the unique and integrative system logic for the above three PMBOK Guide's editions and simply compare the steps in their logic. By comparing the critical outputs' sequences in the PMBOK Guide's revised editions, we can explain why their logic is different and how we can improve historical perspectives (Abdomerovic 2009, 228–230[169]; Abdomerovic 2005, 148–151[170]; Abdomerovic 2002, 167–168).[171]

If updating the general project management system knowledge, including the PMBOK Guide's editions, does not follow a logical sequence, it may require massive reconstructions. So, structural explanation and consequential disambiguation and updating a collection of project management system knowledge are the first steps to understanding the project management system knowledge and its potentials.

A common expectation is that the system's complexity gradually decreases from its holistic form to structural form. For this purpose, we must break down each ambiguous part of the system's contents until the stage where we understand and define its unique meaning (Descartes 1952, 54–60).[172] For example, the output 6.3.3.3 Project documents updates have three particles, the Activity lists, Activity attributes, and Resource calendars (PMI 2008, 145). Those particles can relate the output 6.3.3.3 Project documents updates to processes 6.3 Estimate Activity Resources, 6.4 Estimate Activity Duration, 6.5 Develop Schedule, as well as 7.2 Determine Budget and explain five missing links:

- The particle Activity lists of output 6.3.3.3 Project documents updates can relate to the input 6.4.1.1 Activity lists.
- The particle Activity attributes of output 6.3.3.3 Project documents updates can relate to the input 6.4.1.2 Activity attributes.

169 Abdomerovic, Muhamed. *Brainstorming The PMBOK® Guide Fourth Edition.* Louisville, KY: Project Management Publications, 2009.

170 Abdomerovic, Muhamed. *Brainstorming The PMBOK® Guide Third Edition.* Louisville, KY: Project Management Publications, 2005.

171 Abdomerovic, Muhamed. *Brainstorming The PMBOK® Guide Second Edition.* Louisville, KY: Project Management Publications, 2002.

172 Descartes, Rene. *Rules for the Direction of the Mind.* In: Hutchins, Robert, Editor in chief, Great Books of the Western World, Volume 31. Chicago, IL: Encyclopedia Britannica, 1952.

- The particle Resource calendars of output 6.3.3.3 Project document updates can relate to the inputs from 6.4.1.4 Resource calendars, 6.5.1.5 Resource calendars, and 7.2.1.5 Resource calendars.

The disambiguation process should reach the other parts of the system typically presented in narrative forms—as social environment, social entities, project business strategy, governance, complexity, or other project components. Improving the conversation between structuralism and holism to explain system contents and logic may have a growing impact on the project management system's understanding and application potentials.

We have the term *activity* which describes the most detailed component of project contents and the term *particle* which describes the most detailed component of project management system contents. I understand activity as a part of a technological cluster, in which activities and their attributes explain the project plan. Symmetrically, a particle is a part of a system cluster in which particles and their attributes explain the system logic. Each time the system particles' definitions improve, the system or intelligent approach to the project management plan also improves correspondingly.

A collection of project management system knowledge should go through comprehensive analysis and expose system logic to move from the stage of improvement to a final standard document needed by many managers and planners. The first view of system logic will give a chance to improve the logic by connecting it to the documentation of real-world projects. Such an approach can move project management system knowledge toward the how-to guide, as piling the system knowledge alone in a general manner won't suffice for learning purposes.

In the case of large projects, programs, or sustainable business opportunities, where strategic project management has increased its role, the rules for the compilation of system logic may differ. As the project work package is built by activities, deliverables by work packages, the building of programs for projects, and other program components. Suppose characteristics of large projects are such "that we do not find in the classical theory of project but are core to describing the various aspects we encounter on these projects" (Prieto 2015, 32).[173] In that case, we must compile a set of expected processes with likely inputs and outputs to express various conditions and adapt the system logic to large projects. Besides,

173 Prieto, Bob. "Project Management Theory of Large Complex Projects." *PM World Journal* Volume IV, Issue VI (June 2015). www.pmworldtoday.net.

we must also understand the social environment and entities of the specific project, program, and project business to enhance the system logic.

Rules for Verification of System Logic

Before we use system logic as an outline for the improvement of best practice in PMP, or development of project management plan from the scratch, we must identify the following:

- The unique set of required system processes
- The unique collections of inputs and outputs for each process
- The unique set of output particles in a system
- The unique contents of each particle
- Relationships for all required particles
- Particles required for the specific situation.

Answers to the above questions need time. If a system is practice-oriented, then its logic must also test and validate relationships between particles or what experts think about system logic. I discussed a rationale for system logic and available results with project management professionals. By putting together the topics covering during the discussion, it was possible to filter the answers and debug interruptions and loops in the system logic of the PMBOK Guide's editions.

Besides, we must be genuinely convinced that the system logic can be proven easily. Still, this phase of the work has often been a subject of narrative arguments, also based on factual project documentation, which can affect the system logic at any time. For example, the output "11.1.3.1 Risk management plan," of the process "11.1 Plan Risk Management" (PMI 2008, 276–279) cannot be delivered before completing Step 15 as specified in existing contents (Figure 5.2). Some experts think that substantial risk plan and project feasibility elements, including local resources availability, social environment, social entities, climate, and the responsibilities for risks, will be known much earlier, in the project planning process's front-end phases. And so, system logic may have several levels of decision points that ultimately reach the purview of decision-makers involved in developing the project management system logic. Without the system logic and critical outputs sequence, the above observations may not come to fruition.

By applying the above method of verification to processes and particles of a project management system's contents, we reach the third stage of system logic. This stage adds some practical aspects to be considered before applying the system logic.

Overall, adhering to the above rules will facilitate measurable and meaningful access to project management system knowledge. The rules can help accomplishing the following tasks:

- Analyze any collection of project management system knowledge and understand its contents
- Reveal and apply system logic as the perfect form of content to enhance the efficacy of PMP and update it with best system knowledge
- Understand and manage the changes made to a collection of project management system contents
- Stay informed continuously in regards to the features and functions of current system knowledge and use its system logic whenever a new opportunity arises
- React better and in a timely manner to any changes in project conditions and requirements
- Expose project development logic in a way that is comprehensible to an average user

As implied by the PMBOK Guides (PMI 1996; 2000; 2004; 2008–2017), the substantial meaning of project management system contents emulates the essence of PMP contents. Therefore, we can use a particular project management system's logic to enhance the efficacy of PMP. At the same time, the reader should acknowledge that the development and updating of system logic:

- does not question or modify statements given in the collection of the project management system
- comments on system's statements only when necessary to continue with explaining the system logic.

In the context of the foregoing topics, editors and peers routinely ask me why I am talking about the PMBOK Guide's Fourth Edition when its Sixth and Seventh Editions are already published and are in active use in the field. There are several reasons. This book intends to illustrate how system knowledge reveals its system logic in general and makes the critical output sequence understandable for an average user. I have explained in three books and several journal articles that developing and updating project management system logic applies to any collection of project management system knowledge.

But this exercise is not routine; it requires about one week of analysis to understand the procedure and several months of research to reveal the logic of project management system knowledge. We will discuss this issue in Chapter 6 since all of those efforts have enormous implications for the potential of project management; however, making such efforts becomes a risky mission if there is no support from the system knowledge owner or from the entrepreneur's willingness to take initiatives to strengthen the PMP process in their organization.

Relationships between Process Groups

The project management plan or system logic change over time and must be updated. For this purpose, we must understand project management processes, relationships between processes, and exchange of information between processes.

While the PMBOK Guide's revised editions' contents show continuous progress in collecting and organizing what is generally known as project management system knowledge, the presentation of project management processes needs some updates. In particular, the PMBOK Guide's revised editions need slight correction to present a useful model of this sort (PMI 1996, 28; PMI 2000, 31). Later editions of the PMBOK Guide present similar notions as an ambiguous model (PMI 2004, 40; PMI 2008, 40; PMI 2013, 50; PMI 2017, 562). For example:

The PMBOK Guide's 2000 edition project management processes are organized and presented as five main groups of processes: Initiating, Planning, Executing, Controlling, and Closing (PMI 2000, 31; Figure 3.1). If we follow the associated text that explains the relationships among central process groups, we can observe the following:

- The text associated with Figure 3.1 does not assume the control process group's relation to the executing process group. However, Figure 3.1 does. In reality, the executed work has to be controlled and its outcomes or results sent to the planning team to update the plan and continue with plan execution or initiate new action. Therefore, the relationship from process groups to executing processes groups has to be deleted.
- Project management processes consist of discrete and sequential information that provides the intelligence needed for a single piece of a project defined by an activity or a portion of an activity. The same notion applies

to a single piece of system defined by the system particle. Therefore, the expression "in a Phase" should be deleted from the title of Figure 3.1. There is no direct iteration of a project's or system's higher levels (phases, processes, process groups, contracts, deliverables, or other information clusters). Iterations among higher levels come from synthesizing information from the most detailed components of the project or the system.

PMI's Figure 3.2 Overlaps of Process Groups in a Phase (PMI 2000, 31) and Figure 1.5 Example of Process Group Interactions within a Project or Phase (PMI 2017, 555) are examples of common glitches in project management literature. Figure 3.2 may show any structural component of the project or project management system, except for a single piece of information defined by project activity or system particle. As mentioned earlier, sequential feedback processes are performed for a specific project activity, or system particle, or only of portion either the activity or the particle, defining overlaps and interactions among the project or system components at higher levels. Therefore, understanding and applying overlaps and interactions between project management process groups need a new explanation. In reality, most practices see solutions in a single feedback model supported by additional tools.

In this book, I have developed the Figure 5.4 Management Feedback by applying the most elementary form of feedback control system (Doyle, Francis, and Tannenbaum 1992, 31–32).[174] For this purpose, I added my comments in brackets to help the reader understand the general feedback terminology used in the implementation processes of the project management plan. Let's start with the definitions for the three modules of the basic feedback mechanism:

- Module controller to generate the plant's input [in project management, we can call this the planning process]
- Module plant, that is, the object to be controlled [e.g., work on hardware, software, process, or information; in project management, we can call these the executing processes]
- Module sensor, measures the output of the plant [in project management, we call these the controlling processes]

174 Doyle, John, and Bruce Francis, and Allen Tannenbaum. *Feedback Control Theory.* Mineola, NY: Dover Publications, 1992.

We can see from Figure 5.3 that each module in the central process groups has two inputs—one internal and one external and one output. I interpreted these general notions to project management as follows:

- r—reference or command input [release of the original project management plan]
- v—sensor output [outcomes of controlling processes for work results]
- u—actuating signal, that is, plant input [release of current and baseline project management plans]
- d—external disturbance [results from force majeure and a range of project environmental factors or management issues]
- y—plant output and measured signal [work results and change requests]
- n—sensor noise [disputes related to work performance measurements, quality control measurements, work acceptance, payments for accepted work, change requests]

For example, the construction crew's output (y) from the executing process group is fed back through a quality-control output (v) from the controlling process group to compare with the planned input (r). The planning process group then takes the difference between the planned data and output (v) to change the input (u) in an updated plan for the construction crew and optimize the construction crew's output. But to approach this routine, we must first know the processes within each process group, and second, all relational outputs and inputs that form causal chains and transfer information from the preceding process to the succeeding process of the system continue progressing within this feedback cycle until the stage where the last activity is accomplished.

Figure 5.3 illustrates the summary of the Planning, Executing, and Controlling processes in general. The processes are related to the most detailed component of a system or project attributed by any measurable data. All higher levels of the system or project are just systematic summaries of related details. The Initiating and Closing processes are used for actual projects arbitrarily when needed in order to initiate or close a single component or a group of components. We can use the procedure to improve our understanding of the project management processes, management feedback, and project or project management system knowledge in most situations.

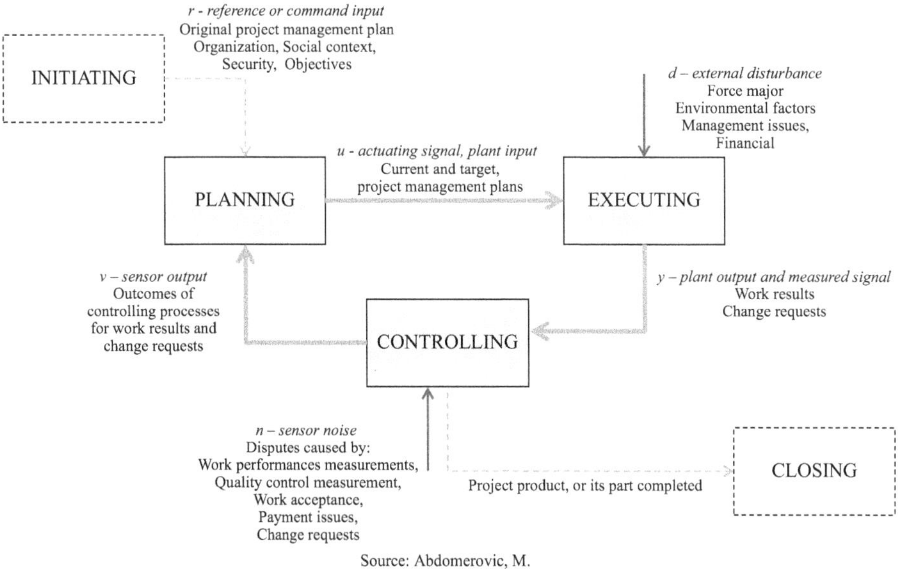

Figure 5.3: Management Feedback

A practice-oriented form of project management feedback is presented in Figure 1.10, elaborated daily in various forms by many project management team members.

Interest in understanding the feedback and connections among different aspects and topics does not fade. Some researches go beyond the standard practice of examining the role of mental models in project management feedback (Abdel-Hamid 2011).[175] A recent study of complexities in the construction industry, including in PMP, provides helpful references which can be applied and explored in future research in this area (Liu, Le, Hu, Xia, Skitmore, and Gao, 2019).[176]

175 Abdel-Hamid, Tarek K. "Single-Loop Project Controls: Reigning Paradigms or Straitjackets?" *Project Management Journal* Volume 42, Number 1 (February 2011): 17–30.

176 Liu, Mingqiang, Jun Le, Yi Hu, Bo Xia, Martin Skitmore, Xianyi Gao. "System Dynamics Modeling for Construction Management Research: Critical Review and Future Trend." *Journal of Civil Engineering and Management* Volume 25, Issue 8 (2019). 730–741. https://doi.org.

Extracts from Case Study

The continuous improvement of PMP contents starts with analyzing and resolving disagreements over project management system contents, answering what, why, and how we add, modify, or delete a specific issue in a collection of project management system contents. After understanding this process, the system contents and its logic can become a perfect database for PMP. Such system logic comprises two parts:

- The first part explains the process of developing the project management system logic, which improves the contents of a project management plan. For this purpose, the reader must understand the contents of the Initiation and Planning process of the PMBOK Guide and must have working experience in using methods such as Work Breakdown Structure (WBS), the Critical Path Method (CPM), or the Precedence Diagramming (PDM). This part of system logic contains 20 steps. For this exercise, I will describe the focal points of Step 5.
- The second part explains the process of implementing the project management system logic, which improves the contents of the implementation of the project management plan. For this purpose, the reader must understand the Executing, Controlling, and Closing processes of the PMBOK Guide and have working experience with the feedback method (FM), in addition to having working experience in using WBS, CPM, or PDM methods. This part of system logic contains 15 steps. For this exercise, I will refer to the main points of Step 31.

Analyzing a general collection of project management system content requires that each step of system logic has a unique position within the critical output sequence. For this purpose, the reader needs to examine all direct and surrounding conditions for each step and record comments that explain the situation and step's position. The reader can use the comments to fine-tune the steps of system logic and contribute to updating the general collection of project management system content. However, we should avoid decorating the system logic with particles outside the selected system knowledge collection unless we speak about a specific project or contribution to system knowledge.

A real-life project does not pass through the first or second part of the system logic. Both parts systematically improve the prescriptive and pragmatic contents for the current project management system knowledge. In continuation of the process, the real-life project uses the improved system knowledge. As a general collection of project management system knowledge gets updated, its system logic becomes an updated outline for the project management plan.

Development of Project Management System Logic

The development of project management system logic has two perspectives—system development and project application.

The system development perspective shows the methodological steps involved in developing the project management system contents for the Initiating and Planning process groups illustrated in Figure 5.2. The project application perspective helps develop a project management plan or improve the best practice in project management plan development using the Critical Outputs sequence of the Initiating and Planning process groups. Let's briefly introduce the Information Technology (IT) Changes project and illustrate the contents of Steps 5 in the Critical Outputs sequence.

The IT Changes project is the primary objective of the insurance business operating for more than three decades. The company management team has issued requirements for a study titled "Insurance Business Forecast for the Next Decade." The study has shown that the population growth, the future change in communication with customers, and the relationships between forecasting events are the basis for expanding client capacities. The client management has recognized the importance of improving communication with customers and initiated the IT Changes project. For this purpose, the client management issued a request to the Project Management Office (PMO) to develop a "Project management plan" for the new project.

To fulfil the management's request, the PMO uses processes defined in the PMBOK® Guide, Fourth Edition and its system logic presented in the form of Critical Outputs sequence (Figure 5.2). Here are the contents and comments for Step 5 of the Critical Output sequence and an example of its application.

Contents of Step 5.

The process Create WBS (PMI 2008, 104) contains three inputs that are independent or already defined in the preceding steps:

- Project scope statement
- Requirements documentation
- Organizational process assets.

The outputs from this process are the WBS, WBS dictionary, Scope baseline, and Project document updates. We need the WBS as an input for two processes, the WBS dictionary as an input for two processes, the Scope baseline as an input for several processes, and the Project document update as an input for process Plan Communications.

The next critical output in the above process is the Scope baseline since it delivers the inputs for the next critical process, the Plan Communications. Here are some comments that help understand the conditions surrounding Step 5:

- The output Project document updates include component "approved change requests" as a possible output in this process. However, the approved change requests output is not defined within the output set of this process.
- The output Scope baseline should be renamed Scope management plan. Some outputs refer to suffice baseline, the Scope baseline, Schedule baseline, and Cost performance baseline, which cannot be used before the project management plan is compiled since we are only at Step 5 in the developmental trajectory of the project management plan.

Example for Step 5.

Although listed as a unique output, the Scope baseline includes, either directly or indirectly, the following components:

- Project scope statement
- WBS
- WBS dictionary.

A key document here is the WBS, which provides a deliverable-oriented structure of the project scope. This structure must confirm the deliverables defined in the project scope statement and identify work packages within each deliverable. Furthermore, the project manager must distribute information (identifier, description, schedule dates, budget, quality parameters, and staff assignments) for each work package.

Figure 5.4 shows one part of the WBS for the IT Changes project. The WBS shows five levels. Since the structure contains many work packages, it is impossible to fully describe the entire project within a brief document with reasonable number of pages. Therefore, only the project's WBS's main features are illustrated by selecting one item from each level and dividing it into its lower-level components. The levels shown as part of the WBS are as follows:

- Project level, which is IT Changes.
- Deliverable level, which contains the following deliverables: Software, Hardware, and Building; this level is absorbed into the Project level.
- The work package level contains the following work packages: Applications Network and Education. This level is absorbed into the Deliverable level.
- Activity level contains the following activities: Maintenance, Design, and Implementation; this level is absorbed into the Work Package level.
- The resource center level contains the following resource centers: System analysis, System structure, and Programming. This level is absorbed into the Activity level.

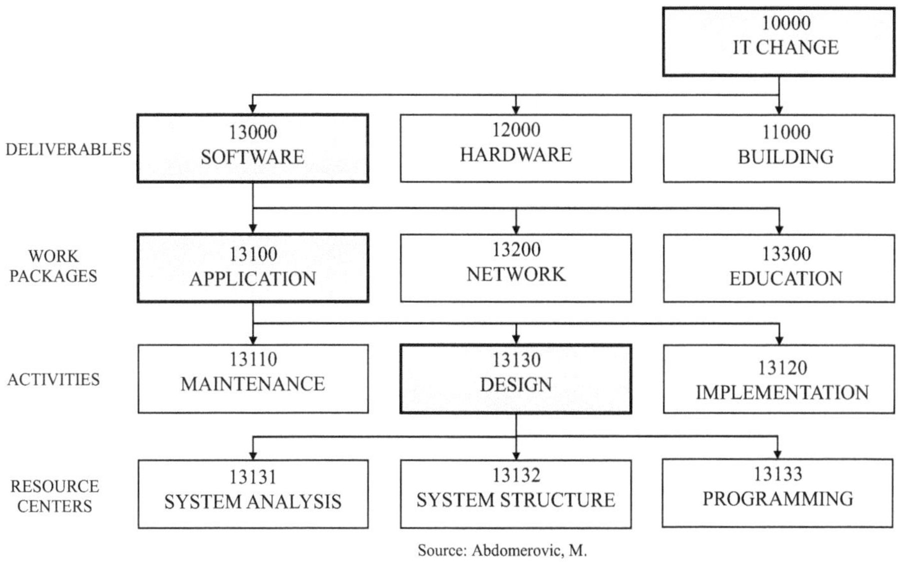

Figure 5.4: Project Scope Baseline and Work Breakdown Structure

The example used in this book shows the following vertical path of the WBS: from the Project (IT Changes) to Deliverable (Software) to Work Package (Applications) to Activity (Design) to all of the design activity's Resource Centers (System analysis, System structure, and Programming).

The WBS dictionary is another form used to show the project structure. It could be the only choice for a big project and operational purposes. Besides basic data presented in the WBS, a WBS dictionary usually contains the cost account codes, cost amount, start and finish dates, and the WBS number for each line item.

The Development of Project Management System Logic ends with Step 20 and the output, the Project Management Plan. Figure 5.5 shows the summarized data for the project and its deliverables for the IT Changes project, Data Date of August 8, 2008. The report is from the beginning of the project, Step 5, when the progress columns of the report are not affected. The columns of the figure are pretty much a part of the standard reports:

- Start Date—the date an activity can start after the completion of the steps preceding it
- Duration—the amount of time needed to complete an activity
- Finish Date—the date an activity can be finished without delaying the succeeding critical activities
- The Percentage Complete—the proportion of the cost for an activity that has been completed
- Planned Value at Completion (Original)—the planned cost for an activity that defines the project work which should have been completed as per the original plan of activity
- Variance in the Planned Value at Completion—the difference between the planned value at completion (baseline) and planned value at completion (original) for an activity; the difference shows the value of the approved change orders for an activity
- Planned Value at Completion (Baseline)—the planned cost for an activity that defines project work that should have been completed as per the baseline plan for an activity; planned value at completion (baseline) is well known as the planned value at completion
- Actual Cost—the actual cost for an activity that defines the project work that has been completed on the date of performance measurement
- Earned Value—the planned cost for an activity that defines project work that has been completed on the date of performance measurement
- Cost Variance—the difference between the actual and planned costs for an activity that defines project work and has been completed on the date of performance measurement
- Planned Value to Complete (Current)—planned cost for an activity that defines project work which should have been completed between the date of performance measurement and the completion of activity as per the current plan; planned value to complete as specified in the current plan differs from the planned value to complete as specified in the baseline plan by the value of the pending change orders; planned value to complete based

on the current plan is well known as a cost estimate to complete; however, if there is no change order, or a change order whose approval is pending, then planned value to complete as per the current plan is the same as the planned value to completion as per the baseline plan; planned value to complete (baseline plan) is well known as the planned value to complete.

Start Date	Duration (months)	Finish Date	% Complete	Planned Value At Completion (original) (1)	Planned Value At Completion Variance (2=3-1)	Planned Value At Completion (baseline) (3=1+/- ACO)	Actual Cost To Date (4)	Earned Value To Date (5)	Cost Variance (6=5-4)	Planned Value To Complete (current) (7=3-4+/- PCO)
Project 30095										
4 Aug 08 A	23	30 Jun 10	0	15,000,000	0	15,000,000	0	0	0	15,000,000
Building										
04 Aug 08 A	17	19 Dec 09	0	12,000,000	0	12,000,000	0	0	0	12,000,000
Hardware (delivery)										
4 Jan 10	2	26 Feb 10	0	2,000,000	0	2,000,000	0	0	0	2,000,000
Software										
5 Jan 09	18	30 Jun 10	0	1,000,000	0	1,000,000	0	0	0	1,000,000

ACO – Approved Change Orders
PCO – Pending Change Orders

Source: Abdomerovic, M.

Figure 5.5: Project Management Plan, Project Report, Data Date—August 8, 2008

Implementation of Project Management System Logic

There are two vantage points from which to view the implementation of project management system: system implementation and project application.

The system implementation view shows the methodological steps involved in implementing the project management system contents of general project management system knowledge; the steps in the contents of Executing, Controlling, and Closing process groups. The project application view helps with implementing a project management plan or improving the best practice in the implementation of project management plan. Figure 5.3 illustrates the implementation of the project management system logic. The figure shows the basic chronological order, step by step, of feedback processes that change each activity in the project management plan while it passes through the central process groups. This part of the system logic starts with the original project management plan and ends with the completion of the project product in its totality or its partial completion. Let's briefly introduce the contents in Step 31 of the Critical Output sequence and its relationships with the IT Changes project.

When the client's PMO is engaged in updating the project management plan, it must collect data about changes to project activities and must have a procedure for updating the project management plan. It must know how the output from the preceding process groups is related to the succeeding process groups and what this relationship produces.

The project management plan changes while its activities pass through the various process groups. The implementation of project management system logic starts with the project management plan that belongs to the planning process group (Figure 5.2, Step 20). It ends with the output—the final product, service, or result—that moves to the Closing Process Group. Although updating the project management plan with Executing Process Group (Steps 21–24), Monitoring and Controlling Process Group (Steps 25–31), Closing Process Group (Steps 32–33) are not part of this book, some examples may help the reader get a basic idea of of this process. Here are the contents in Step 31 of the Critical Output sequence and an example of their application.

Contents of Step 31.

The process report performance (PMI 2008, 266) contains five inputs that are independent or already defined in preceding steps.

- Project management plan
- Work performance information
- Work performance measurements
- Budget forecasts
- Organizational process assets.

The outputs from this process are the Performance reports, Organizational process assets updates, and Change requests. The next critical outputs in the sequence are Performance reports and Change requests.

Example for Step 31.

The performance reports show project status, progress, and forecast. The information is derived at the activity level and then summed up at higher levels, including the project level. The information usually comes from measurable data, scope, schedule, and cost data found in the project plan. Performance reports are essential for explaining project status, progress, and forecasts. For example, we can see from Figure 5.6:

- How does the baseline project plan differ from the original project plan?
- How does the new scope estimated for "Design" activity reflect other values in the Approved Change Orders?
- Why does the schedule for the Change Orders, which begins after the original date for "Design" activity, not change the overall baseline project schedule presented in Figure 5.5?
- How much has the baseline or currently approved project plan progressed "To Date" compared to the "should be" progress as defined in the original project plan? From Figure 5.6, we can calculate and find that the "Design" activity is 2% behind the original plan and the baseline project plan's Percentage Complete for the "Design" activity is 18%—Earned Value × 100 / Planned Value at Completion (baseline). The original Percentage Complete should be 20%—Earned Value × 100 / Planned Value at Completion (Original). It should be clear that the Planned Value at Completion (Baseline) contains approved estimates, that is, Approved Change Orders, so we can use it to calculate progress by To Date. However, the Planned Value at Completion (Current), or its synonym Cost Estimate at Completion, may contain estimates that are not approved, that is, Pending Change Orders; therefore, we cannot use it to calculate progress by To Date.

Besides, Figure 5.6 shows the summarized data for activity Design and its Resource centers for the "Information Technology Changes" project, Data Date of April 30, 2009, close to completion period of the project, which is Step 31. We can analyze project performances and understand how the change brings the project's expected future performance in line with the plan and reduces future negative project performance probability. In relation to this project and its payment recorded on April 30, 2009, we can see from Figure 5.6 the following changes:

- Total payments for project Design (i.e., Actual Cost) reached $80,000, Accepted work (i.e., Earned Value) reached $50,000, and Due payment for this period (i.e., Cost Variance) reached a favorable value of $30,000.

- Payment records for different deliverables have different cost performance metrics, for example, plan to build shows progress, while "Software" shows an unfavorable variance.
- The project management plan updates must reflect approved changes to procurement documents, including the procurement management plan.

Completing Step 31 fills the input list of several other processes, including Monitor and Control Project Work, Monitor and Control Risks, and Administer Procurements.

The example presented illustrates the implementation part of the critical outputs sequence and helps understand the dynamics associated with the PMBOK Guide's Fourth Edition's critical contents. Besides, the results of the unique movement of the project management plan through management processes are indispensable for understanding the impact of each process and, consequently, improving the contents of project management feedback and project management plan implementation. The reader interested in the complete procedure, steps, and IT Changes application example should refer to the original documents (PMI 2008; Abdomerovic 2009).

After we compile the system logic, we speak about project management system knowledge only in terms of outputs/inputs and not in terms of the steps of the system logic that drive us to develop a project management plan for the actual project. Specific activities of the project management plan, and not system processes or system outputs and inputs, enter into the project management feedback loop that helps manage the project dynamics (Figure 1.10).

Performance Reports
Data Date: 30 Apr 2009 – *Activity Report*

Start Date	Duration (months)	Finish Date	% Complete	Planned Value At Completion (original) (1)	Planned Value At Completion Variance (2=3-1)	Planned Value At Completion (baseline) (3=1+/- ACO)	Actual Cost To Date (4)	Earned Value To Date (5)	Cost Varianc e (6=5-4)	Planned Value To Complete (current) (7=3-4+/- PCO)
Design										
5 Jan 09 A	12	18 Dec 09	18	250,000	25,000	275,000	80,000	50,000	-30,000	195,000
System Analysis										
5 Jan 09 A	3	31 Mar 09 A	100	35,000	0	35,000	35,000	35,000	0	0
System Structure										
2 Feb 09 A	2	31 Mar 09 A	100	10,000	0	10,000	10,000	10,000	0	0
Programming										
2 Mar 09 A	10	18 Dec 09	2	205,000	0	205,000	35,000	5,000	-30,000	170,000
Change Orders (Design)										
4 Jan 10	2	26 Feb 10	0	0	25,000	25,000	0	0	0	25,000

ACO – Approved Change Orders
PCO – Pending Change Orders

Source: Abdomerovic, M.

Figure 5.6: Performance Reports, Activity Report, Data Date April 30, 2009

6 Where Is Planning in (Project) Management Going Next?

Introduction

We must move from a narrative debate about what a general collection of project management system knowledge should do to the structural conclusion about what its system logic does. This notion may be the beginning of the enhancement of vast collections of project management system knowledge from increasingly novelized and sporadically related knowledge to simple and generally applicable system logic. The new addition to project management system knowledge can motivate numerous average users besides the producers and professional exam contenders. We may think here about the scholars who need a sustainable system perspective, the students who need career-oriented experience, the practitioners who need system guidelines to connect different project contents, or the average users who embrace convenient change, new technologies, and communication methods that are understandable and within their means, like credit cards, search engines, and smartphones.

The average user needs a straightforward explanation of what project management system knowledge brings up, what it means, and how they can use project management system knowledge. For this purpose, we must develop project management system knowledge to include distinctive particles, set in the simple figure, a particle ready for use, free of any narration. Otherwise, we cannot have systematic and user-oriented control of project management system knowledge.

There are several reasons why the narratives used in project management system knowledge should be flexible and simpler in the endeavor to develop project management system logic.

- System logic is a unique and integrated but hidden summary of project management system contents that show how system contents evolve. It comes into view as a result of relationships among the most detailed elements of project management system contents.
- System logic is the evidence of a consistent theoretical and methodological base of PMP. It shows that the development of project management system logic is in symmetry with the rules for developing the project management plan.
- System logic helps examine differences among project management systems. It provides insight into generally known elements of systems to understand the root causes of variations among systems.
- System logic helps understand the differences between requirements for PMP and limitations of the system contents. It proves why a project management system is or is not suitable as an outline for developing and implementing a project management plan.
- System logic helps avoid the increasing threat of irrelevance of ever-growing collections of general project management system contents. It proves how a particular system or its particles contribute to a cumulative project management system contents.
- System logic helps depart from a fuzzy explanation for overlaps among components and interactions between processes of a project management system contents. It shows that the particles of system logic govern the overlaps and interactions that take place within project management system contents.
- System logic is the objective history of the development of project management system contents. It helps understand the consequences of past, present, and future updates of system contents.

In the absence of references for the development and application of project management system logic, a list of observations may additionally help to explain the situation and view this applied research from a new perspective:

- When we develop and adopt a system to express the company's best practice, we assume specific contents, processes, and output/input chains of activities. Therefore, a practice-oriented system operates on the level of details; however, we rarely see such an approach for project management system's knowledge.
- There is an evident disconnection between expectations from practice and the narrative approach to explain project management system knowledge. Practitioners in various project management areas can structure problems and respond to requirements, while supporters of narrative project management systems rather talk in general terms and leave their systems unfinished.
- There are few scholars and professionals who are fully informed about the potentials of project management system logic. Yet, there is an evident rush for more sensational discussions about new systems, paradigm shifts, and project management reconstruction.

Are we realistic? We rarely comment on the negative designation of scientific project management planning as a source of a high application cost, causes of failed projects, lack of dynamism, lack of flexibility, and other substitutes in our arguments. And this is right. However, we repeatedly experiment with some narratives that inhibit the improvement and application of a general collection of project management system knowledge. And this doesn't seem right.

Symmetry of the Rules

We learned that the same methodological principles for developing and implementing a project management plan are applicable for developing and implementing project management system logic. It means that the methodological symmetry governs both the project management plan and project management system logic. In summary:

- The development of the project management plan (analysis, relationships, synthesis, and updating of project contents) is in symmetry with the development of project management system logic (analysis, relationships, synthesis, and updating of system contents). These symmetries must be acknowledged essential at this time for an explanation of the project management plan and project management system logic.

- As a result, the particles of the project management system (e.g., resource assignment) perform in a system as the activities of the project management planning (e.g., assignment of people, money, and machine) perform in an enormous number of projects around us.
- If we reorganize the structure of intermediate levels of project management planning contents or project management system contents, then the resulting project plan or system logic will not change. However, suppose we reorganize the activities of project management plan or particles of project management system logic. In that case, all upper levels, including the intermediate levels of project management planning contents or project management system contents, will change. It follows that activities control each project management plan's level and particles control each project management system's logic.

The same structural simplicity and integrity are rooted in the handling of both the project management plan and project management system logic. We use the same method to explain the overlaps among components and interactions between processes of system or project contents. Such conditions link the historical achievements and the new perspectives about PMP contents and project management system contents. Understanding the scientific methodology for PMP precedes developing project management system logic and understanding a general collection of project management system contents.

Producers and Users

Suppose we change the practical problems or conditions within a project management system knowledge by simulating the addition, modification, or deletion of particles or relationships among particles. In that case, we will get a different system logic. As each change must get a systematic explanation of the causes and justification of the change to the system logic, assuming responsibility for such a change is a significant challenge. So, it is essential that changes—as the extensions of project management system knowledge—count for professional leaders who have studied and resolved the problem and follow simple administrative procedures. What can we do with system logic revealed from a project management system contents?

The first wave of application of system logic may belong to scholars and graduate students, who may use system logic for debating and advancing the contents and procedures of developing and implementing a general collection of project management system knowledge. How many average scholars and students are willing to pay for the usage of updated system logic for an extended period? Not many. So, where is this trend taking us? Are the numerous average users really willing to participate in the process of updating and using the system logic? Yes, there are many who do that because such system logic will reflect collaborative and interactive views from many scholars, students, professionals, and a mass of end-users in active contact, who most likely prefer to generate, use, advance, and share benefits from participation. In the coming years, this ever-improving general collection of project management system knowledge may be the key to lasting improvement of PMP.

Let's see what Axel Bruns predicted; he addressed the development of new relations among producers and users and coined a new term for the approach, known as *produsage*. Here is a passage that describes this historical move:

The concept of produsage is such a term: it highlights that within the communities which engage in the collaborative creation and extension of information and knowledge that we examine in the book, the role of "consumer" and even that of "end-user" have long disappeared. The distinctions between producers and users of content have faded into comparative insignificance. In many of the spaces we encounter here, users are always necessarily also producers of the shared knowledge base; regardless of whether they are aware of this role, they have become a new, hybrid producer. (Bruns 2009, 2)[177]

Bruns develops a comprehensive procedure for his concept by describing the characteristics and principles of the idea: the path from usage to produsage, a tool kit to support produsage, commercial aspects of produsage, and thoughtful implication of the concept that will have an impact on our creativity, culture, and benefits offered by truly shared knowledge.

Readership interested in understanding the project management system knowledge and PMP may also need efficient and straightforward produsage options.

But spreading the book ideas should not stop at a produsage option. My vision is that the methodological base and observed symmetry should be the planning choice in different management areas and industries. Perhaps now is the best time to revise traditional distinctions between some management areas

177 Bruns, Axel. *Blogs, Wikipedia, Second Life, and Beyond: From Production to Produsage.* New York, NY: Peter Lang Publishing. 2009.

and attract new users to collaborate in the creation of a common methodological base. For example, the methodological base for developing and implementing a project management plan could drop its reference to a particular management branch. We may soon be talking about the development and implementation of the management plan. When will this happen, or is it already happening inside general management? Let's have a look at one of Drucker's early thoughts:

These three analyses—of activities, of decisions, of relations—should always be kept as simple and as brief as possible. In a very large and complex enterprise, the job may require months of study and application of highly advanced tools of logical analysis and synthesis. (Drucker 1970, 243)[178]

But to get a full spin, the next stage of similar material needs to combine, besides project management processes, all other processes from management areas related to the development and implementation of a management plan. It is feasible, too, because this is the path where planning in management, including project management, will soon be traveling.

Experience and Imaginary

Project problems are the usual preamble to launch a new project management idea. Sometimes, this packet also blames only the project management methods, not actors, for bad project results, while searching for a solution in other management areas. But other management areas, for example, global automobile production, which records extraordinary recalls that cost the automobile industry $40 billion/year (Wikipedia 2014, 9),[179] does not blame production management knowledge for bad results. Financial management, whose estimating models record historic disappointments (Taleb 2010, 44),[180] has Nobel laureates who are given high seats in management science. However, project management scholars still debate whether the PMP is fully recognized as a branch of general management. These are the fundamental reasons we must cite to assert that the methodological base for developing and implementing the project management plan, and its research and application, is in good condition but needs more education

178 Drucker, Peter. *The Practice of Management.* London, UK: Pan Books, 1970.

179 Wikipedia (2). *Product recall. Automotive industry.* http://en.wikipedia.org/wiki/Product_recall. Retrieved 6/10/2014.

180 Taleb, Nassim. *The Black Swan.* New York, NY: Random House Trade Paperbacks, 2010.

and research. Otherwise, we will endlessly be looking in other management areas to solve project management problems and sending confusing messages to the management world.

Is system logic a helpful avenue for research and application in project management? The answer is yes, given the new perspective of scientific PMP which enables us to develop system logic, live up to the vital needs from practice, and improve the project management plan and planning process. We repeatedly hear during project management assignments, reading, and talking to people that we can know about the project plan or system logic as much as we know about its structure. It means that understanding a system does not depend on how we design, organize, and describe the system, or project, what school or faculty it belongs to, what functions the system includes, or how we group and relate the functions or processes. However, it is essential to develop a system or project to the level of details, which is the only place to explain any project or system and debate its ideas fully. For example, at the level of generally known particles, the system reveals unique and integrative system logic that we can use in many ways: for the identification of new relationships between current system particles; introduction of new system particles; clarification of system purposes, advantages, disadvantages, and errors; explanation of system applicability to specific management areas, objectives, and levels.

This book demonstrates that we can reach the generally known particles of project management system knowledge and reveal their relationships to expose the system logic. Therefore, the reader should refer to this book for the following:

- A new application of fundamental theories and resulting methodologies of project management planning
- Observation of the symmetry of rules in the development of project plan and system logic
- Development of ideas to reveal, explain, and apply system logic.

Current Debates

The current debates on PMP relate to both the narrative and structural views. The narrative approaches are of significance for social scientists, whereas the structural systems are of prime importance for natural science and applied science. There is much discussion about the views and understanding about PMP: Do we need to understand only the details of the project or the whole picture of a project or both? What is a better way to understand project contents; how we handle the purpose and suitability of project management planning; how we take project dynamism, alternatives, and uncertainties in a project? In reality, these views are not mutually exclusive, and most project managers derived values from them over decades. For example, when a project management plan was disturbed by an unusual input, the project manager immediately conducts a brainstorming session to diagnose the whole problem, reduce the problem to critical issues, and narrate and follow up on the responses received from other end-users or stakeholders. In continuation, the project team develops a complete solution: structures and analyzes the situation, quantifies activities, excludes alternative relationships, and restarts regular updates of the project management plan.

Here are some distinguished perspectives that people use to explain their endeavor, including a project management system and project:

Traditional structural methods motivate generations of researchers to explain system contents by reducing a system to its components (parts, facts, information, and activities) and then understand a whole system by relating and synthesizing its elements. Descartes' *Rules for the Direction of the Mind* present reductionism, a structural method to discover science's truth. We should distinguish here two fundamental processes: the top-down or deductive process to rationally find out the objects laid down at the lower levels and reach those objects "that are simple" and clearly understood; and the bottom-up, or inductive process, used to compile, by carrying out "precisely similar steps," to reach or identify all the upper-level objects (Descartes 1952).[181] While reductionism gains a lasting recognition in natural science and applied science, it was never fully acknowledged for its importance in biological or social studies.

For a long time now, social scientists are experimenting with different ideas to explain social actions in a system. Weber emphasized the structures, characteristics, and understanding of society as observed by individuals. He attempted to explain social movements through the cause and effects of an individual's action. From Talcott Parsons' introduction to Weber's book, we can learn how Weber has related and understood the natural and social sciences processes.

One tendency of thought of his [Weber] time was to attempt to assimilate the science of human behavior as closely as possible to the natural sciences. By interpreting the later overwhelmingly in an "empiricist" manner, the result was to squeeze out all that was most distinctive in the traditional and common-sense

181 Descartes, Rene. *Rules for the Direction of the Mind.* In: Hutchins, Robert, Editor in chief, Great Books of the Western World, Volume 31. Chicago, IL: Encyclopedia Britannica, 1952.

treatment of human problems, notably the use of subjective categories. What Weber did was to take an enormous step in the direction of bridging the gap between the two types of science, and to make possible the treatment of social material in a systematic scientific manner rather than as an art. (Weber 1947, 11)[182]

The narrative method, which has been used in research to explain a system's contents by organizing and describing "holistic" purposes rather than "detailed" characteristics of its components, identifies and explains the difference between the narrative method and the structural method. Bertalanffy explains living phenomena as biological wholes (cell, organ, organism) or social wholes (individual, community, society). The author also acknowledges reductionism and holds that understanding the function of higher objects comes from the functioning of its components. This knowledge was a step ahead for a better understanding of the relationship between the system's social environment and the entities in that social environment. Bertalanffy wrote about how holistic ideas could lead to system theory:

The properties and modes of action of higher levels are not explicable by the summation of the properties and modes of action of their components taken in isolation [properties of any higher levels may not be found among the properties of their components]. If, however, we know the ensemble of the components and the relations existing between them, then the higher levels are derivable from the components [functional contribution of the components to the configuration and functioning of the whole]. (quoting from *Problem of Life*, 1952; Bertalanffy 1975, 152–153)[183]

Ackoff et al. have empowered Bertalanffy's idea with a measurable approach and showed how system thinking is related to society. The authors start from a holistic viewpoint of social science and suggest the concept should be quantifiable but not at the most detailed level of an activity that could be performed. Ackoff et al. deliver to readers a kit to deal with behavioral variables and develop measurable elements for a system.

In order to accomplish this study, it is necessary to provide idealized operational definitions and measures of functional concepts—definitions that provide standards in the same sense that the ateleologically oriented sciences provide

182 Weber, Max. *The Theory of Social and Economic Organization.* 1997. Glencoe, Il: The Free Press, 1947.

183 Bertalanffy, Ludwig. *Perspectives on General System Theory: Scientific – Philosophical Studies.* New York, NY: George Braziller, 1975.

standards for structural concepts (for example, length, density, and energy in physics). (Ackoff and Emery, 2008, 7)[184]

Carlsen and Pitsis present narratives in project studies and show how the experience and narrative capital enrich an individual's professional life.

Narrative capital is derived from experiences that people appropriate into their individual and collective life stories, retrospectively, as adding to a repertoire of accumulated learning and mastering, and prospectively, in terms of living with purpose and hope. (Carlsen and Pitsis, 2920)[185]

The current structural method, which is a different kind of reductionism, may comprise earlier thoughts. Weinberg thinks that statistical mechanics and mathematical deductions prove a structural approach in the previously resisted reductionism. He discusses examples from the science where a natural law, for instance, thermodynamics, gets full explanation later by "the form of a deduction using statistical mechanics methods from the details of what the system contains" (Weinberg 1992, 39–41),[186] or the physics of chaos, which holds that we cannot explain the whole in terms of the parts but that we may explain chaos by using "the mathematical deduction of the laws governing chaos from the microscopic physical laws governing the systems that become chaotic" (Weinberg 1992, 62). The following passage from Weinberg may illustrate current viewpoints of how we can approach the task of explaining the system content.

We would not pay much attention to a proposed autonomous law of macroeconomics that could not possibly be explained in terms of the behavior of individuals or to a hypothesis about superconductivity that could not possibly be explained in terms of the properties of electrons and photons and nuclei. The reductionist attitude provides a useful filter that saves scientists in all fields from wasting their time on ideas that are not worth pursuing. In this sense, we are all reductionists now. (Weinberg 1992, 64)

184 Ackoff, Russel, and Fred Emery. *On Purposeful Systems: An Interdisciplinary Analysis of Individual and Social Behavior as a System of Purposeful Events.* New Brunswick, NJ: Transaction Publishers, 2008.

185 Carlsen, Arne, and Tyrone Pitsis. "We are projects: Narrative Capital and Meaning Making in Projects." *Project Management Journal* (June 2020): Abstract. https://journals.sagepub.com.

186 Weinberg, Steven. *Dreams of a final theory. The Scientist's Search for the Ultimate Laws of Nature.* New York, NY: Pantheon Books, 1992.

Research in Project Management

Research in project management systems consists of continuous assessments of the flourishing views (PMI, 2017),[187] multi-perspective views (Kerzner 2017),[188] biased views (Rothman 2017),[189] practical views (Kueh, 2011),[190] multi-perceptive views (Lewis 2011),[191] balanced narrative views (Haines 2000),[192] complex theoretical views (Prieto 2015)[193] supplemented by philosophical actualities (Miyake 2005),[194] and project management views (Muirhead and Simon 1990).[195]

Researchers examine a communication framework for project management views. According to Bredillet's earlier thoughts, project management is in the pre-paradigmatic period, and the project management community builds a paradigm on or around the existing knowledge (Bredillet 2010, 6).[196] Hallgren examines as many as 61 papers published between 2007 and 2011. His work contains some recommendations on how to move from identifying the gap and improving existing knowledge to setting research questions and challenging existing assumptions

187 PMI 2017. *A Guide to the Project Management Body of Knowledge (PMBOK® Guide) Sixth Edition.* Newtown Square PA: Project Management Institute, 2017.

188 Kerzner, Harold. *Project management: A Systems Approach to Planning. Scheduling and Controlling,* 12th edition. Hoboken, NJ: John Wiley & Sons, 2017.

189 Rothman, Johanna. *Create Your Successful Agile Project.* Raleigh, NC: The Pragmatic Bookshelf, 2017.

190 Kuehn, Ursula. *Integrated Cost and Schedule Control in Project Management.* Vienna, VA: Management Concepts, 2011.

191 Lewis, James. *Project Planning. Scheduling & Control.* New York, NY: McGraw-Hill. 2011.

192 Haines, Stephen. *The System Thinking Approach to Strategic Planning and Management.* Boca Raton, FL: CRC Press, (2000).

193 Prieto, Bob. "Project Management Theory of Large Complex Projects." *PM World Journal* Volume IV, Issue VI (June 2015). www.pmworldtoday.net.

194 Miyake, Michiaki. "Management in a Digital Network Era. Reductionism and Holonic Management." IIST World Forum, (November 2005): www.cfiec.jp/wf/magazine/0387/0387.

195 Muirhead, Brian, and William Simon. *High Velocity Leadership: The Mars Pathfinder Approach to Faster, Bette, Cheaper.* New York, NY: HarperCollins Publishers, 1999.

196 Bredillet, Christophe. "Blowing Hot and Cold on Project Management." *Project Management Journal* 41, no. 3 (June 2010): 4–20. www.pmi.org.

and contributing to academia or practice (Hallgren 2012).[197] Bentahar and Cameron present relatively new research area of mixed qualitative and quantitative methods, along with detailed terms and conditions for the design, integration, and implementation of mixed-methods research (Bentahar and Cameron 2015).[198] Geraldi et al. noticed the lack of academic debates, disagreements, and provocative claims which were needed to develop better and more insightful theories within project studies (Geraldi, Soderlund, and Marrewijk 2020).[199] Current research and practice are not resistant to the above views. Here are some important topics on project management and communication framework:

- Shore identified and defined the systematic biases in the decision-making literature. These biases could explain in part the eight failed projects (Airbus 380, Coastal Guard Maritime Domain Awareness Project, Columbia Shuttle, Denver Baggage Handling, Mars Climate Orbiter and Mars Polar Lander, Merck Vioxx, Microsoft Xbox 360, and NYC Police Communication System). The findings suggest that the skills and techniques expressed in the rational view of project management may be insufficient to assure project success (Shore 2008, 13–14).[200]
- Berggren et al. stress the importance of the neo-realistic practice turn because criticism of planning approaches tends to lack grounded suggestions for effective managerial practices. Accordingly, the authors have found a way to use academic knowledge and practitioner experience to understand, reduce, and control project complexity. They think that this innovative practice has a capacity "to deal with the seemingly chaotic and emergent character of complex systems" (Berggren 2008, S111).[201]

197 Hallgren, Markus. "The Construction of Research Question in Project Management." *International Journal of Project Management* 30, no. 7 (October 2012): 804–816. www.elsevier.com/locate/ijproman.

198 Bentahar, Omar, and Roslyn Cameron. "Design and Implementation of a Mixed Method Research Study in Project Management." *The Electronic Journal of Business Research Method* 13, no. 1 (2015): 3–15. www.ejbrm.com

199 Geraldi, Joana, and Jonas Soderlund, and Alfons van Marrewijk. "Advancing Theory and Debate in Project Studies". *Project Management Journal*, Editorial (July 31 2020). https://journals.sagepub.com.

200 Shore, Barry. "Systematic Biases and Culture in Project Failures." *Project Management Journal* 39, no. 4 (December 2008): 5–16. www.pmi.org.

201 Berggren, Christian, Jack Jarkvik, and Jonas Soderlund. "Lagomizing. Organic Integration. and Systems Emergency Wards: Innovative Practices in Managing

- Many project management themes in Bredillet's work perceive the applicability of both the structural and narrative methodologies. He outlines significant schools of thought in several editorials that form a current understanding of project management and potential research. This work is of particular interest to the modeling school. The author repeats the importance of reductionism and reminds us of the social aspects of project management that are mostly associated with a holistic approach (Bredillet 2007, 3).[202] "Key idea of the school is to use hard and soft systems theory to model the project" (Bredillet 2010, 11).
- Saynisch draws a line between current thinking in project management (Project Management First Order, PM-1) and new interpretations of project management (Project Management Second Order, PM-2). The research program "Beyond Frontiers of Traditional Project Management" was founded to bring the theory of complex systems closer to real projects. The author explains the genesis, concept, system architecture, principles, methods, and the implementation of PM-2 in different project types and potential use of PM-2, along with integration aspects of PM-2 and various project management models (Saynisch April 2010[203]; Saynisch December 2010[204]).
- Hanisch and Wald propose to systematize the different structures of research perspectives on the basis of a literature review and to develop a research framework model integrating multiple theoretical perspectives and influencing factors. The research framework includes the design,

Complex Systems Development Projects." *Project Management Journal* 39, Supplement, (2008): S111–S122. www.pmi.org.

202 Bredillet, Christophe. "Exploring Research in Project Management – Nine School of Project Management. (Part 3)." *Project Management Journal* 38, no. 4 (December 2007): 2–4. www.pmi.org.

203 Saynisch, Manfred. "Beyond Frontiers of Traditional Project Management: An Approach to Evolutionary. Self-Organizational Principles and the Complexity Theory – Results of the Research Program." *Project Management Journal* 41, no. (April 2010): 21–37. www.pmi.org.

204 Saynisch, Manfred. "Mastering Complexity and Changes in Projects. Economy and Society via Project Management Second Order (PM-2)." *Project Management Journal* 41, no. 5 (December 2010): 4–20. www.pmi.org.

context, and goal to support different research perspectives and the development of strategies for further research (Hanisch and Wald 2011).[205]

- Contemporary studies in project management examine different paradigmatic perspectives. Following a theoretical discussion, Pellegrinelli et al. reviewed four sociological paradigms of sociological theory: the functionalist, the interpretive, the radical humanist, and the radical structuralist (Pellegrinelli and Murray-Webster 2011, 5).[206] The authors present the research methodology and objectives and the views from paradigmatic lenses for all four paradigms.
- Leybourne and Sainter promote new project management paradigm that adds flexibility to current analytical perspective. For this purpose, authors acknowledge that processes, tools, and leadership lead to the project's success. In contrast, standardizing rigidly and routinely the project organization, structure, culture, and performance metrics will only limit the chances of project's success and thus any changes proposed for the project should be brought in through negotiations and consensus where opinions are expressed in a subtle manner and not in an overbearing manner and team members and stakeholders demonstrate an embracing attitude toward improvisation of the plan through non-routine changes and activities (Leybourne and Sainter 2012).[207]
- Chang, A. et al. reiterate the importance of the Integrated Master Schedule (IMS) in complex projects, particularly as a summary of detailed project activities, organizational and social groups, and relationships across multiple levels. Authors consider a sense-making view that guides project stakeholders in shared understanding through uncertainty, complexity, and negotiation. Presented cases illustrate the role IMS in visualization and sense-making to manage megaprojects, which are typically long term and

205 Hanisch, Bastian, and Andreas Wald. "A Project Management Research Framework Integrating Multiple Theoretical Perspectives and Influencing Factors." *Project Management Journal* 42, no. 3 (April 2011): 4–22. www.pmi.org.

206 Pellegrinelli, Sergio. and Ruth Murray-Webster. "Multi-Paradigmatic Perspectives on a Business Transformation Program." *Project Management Journal* 42, no. 6 (December 2011). www.pmi.org.

207 Leybourne, Stephen, and Phillip Sainter. "Advancing Project Management: Authenticating the Shift from Process to 'Nuanced' Project Management in the Ambidextrous Organization." *Project Management Journal* 43, no. 6 (December 2012): 5–15. www.pmi.org.

face a high degree of complexity and uncertainty in their implementation (Chang, Hatcher, and Kim 2013, 323–332).[208]

- Chen-Yu Chang reminds that the current state of project governance literature is qualitative in nature. This research therefore represents a departure from tradition by developing a quantitative approach to the study of project governance (Chang 2015, 1). In principle, the central role of governance structures is to maintain the order of transactions. In the course of project implementation, order may be disturbed by random risks or opportunism-induced behavioral uncertainty. This research maintains that the concept of risk-bearing capacity can provide a coherent basis for integrating the decisions that happen at three levels—a. organizational, the choice of delivery; b. contractual, the choice of contract form; and c. financial, the use financial protection—and thus shed new light on the analysis of project governance (Chang 2015, 3).[209]
- Chow and Leiringer show that the materials used, in addition to serving as boundary objects that facilitate communication across knowledge boundaries, form part of a network that direct, controls, and manages the information flow among participants (Chow and Leiringer 2020, 1).[210] The challenges for main research exist in exploring how public engagement events can be managed to facilitate effective communication that contributes to a broader consensus on project value and in determining possible correlations between public engagement event outcomes and project outcome variables, such as project success and project efficiency (Chow and Leiringer 2020, 24).
- Prieto debates the specifics of large complex projects and promotes thinking beyond the usual theoretical bases for managing a diversified project.

208 Chang, Artemis, and Caroline Hatcher, and Jai Kim. "Temporary boundary objects in megaprojects: Mapping the system with the Integrated Master Schedule." *International Journal of Project Management* 31, no. 3 (April 2013): 323–32. www.elsevier.com/locate/ijproman.

209 Chang, Chen-Yu. 2015. "Risk-beating Capacity as a New Dimension to the Analysis of Project Governance." *International Journal of Project Management* 33, no. 6 (August 2015): 1195–1205. https://sciencedirect.com.

210 Chow, Vivien, and Roine Leiringer. "Public Engagement Events and the Management of External Stakeholders: Artifacts as Boundary Objects or Tools of Discipline and Control?" *Project Management Journal* (August 2020): https://journals.sagepub.com. 2020. www.pmi.org.

The author observes some equivalence between relativistic physics components and large complex projects and suggests that "the General Theory of Relativity provides a framework for rethinking our assumptions and approach to large complex projects" (Prieto 2020, 1–7).[211] Such original views must lead to new methodologies to deal with new challenges.

- Martinsuo argues that the traditional view of project value based on financial attributes is inadequate and proposes conducting studies based on the overall worth and benefits of the project to determine the project value. The rationale for this article emerges from the fluidity and ambiguity of the concept of project value and, at the same time, its tempting character attracts the attention of both practitioners and researchers, linking the temporary project with the owner's continuous operations, and potentially enabling the use of versatile approaches to assessing project success (Martinsuo 2020, 3).[212]
- The flourishing discipline of project management is creating new challenges in research. This work aims to stimulate debate on fundamental issues within project management research and activities and in supporting social and organizational disciplines. Authors suggest using an innovative review process to assess new ideas and promote new thinking in project management research (Geraldi, Soderlund, and Marrewijk 2020).[213]
- Viewing project complexity from a new perspective exploring how to pragmatically approach the design and development of a project plan can improve the ability to theorize project strategies. Authors discuss topics such as complexity theorizing, dualism, pragmatism as anti-dualism, construct of theorizing process, orders of theorizing, and levels of theorizing in project studies. The research recognizes new perspectives for future

211 Prieto, Bob. "A Deeper Look at the Physics of Large Complex Projects." *PM World Journal* IX, no. VIII (August 2020). www.pmworldtoday.net.

212 Martinsuo, Miia. "The Management of Values in Project Business: Adjusting Beliefs to Transform Project Practice and Outcomes." *Project Management Journal* (June 3. 2020). https://journals.sagepub.com.

213 Geraldi, Joana, Jonas Soderlund, and Alfons van Marrewijk. "Advancing Theory and Debate in Project Studies." *Project Management Journal*, Editorial (July 31 2020): https://journals.sagepub.com.

research at the mid-level by departing from the micro–macro divide and reach the third order of theorizing (Tywoniak, Ika, and Bredillet 2021).[214]

Applications of project management systems knowledge can improve best practices in PMP, continuous education for generally accepted project management processes, relevant technological processes, and current application software. It is priceless. The researchers and practitioners must also engage in the constant improvement of the project management system logic, which is key to identifying and understanding the ideal project management system contents and developing a systematic approach to PMP. Mutual interest may undoubtedly help us clarify views and contribute to better education and project results. And then, project business management can step up to promote the system approach to PMP. Otherwise, we may only get surprised when we see project management plans developed outside the boundaries of recognized project management systems.

Conclusion

It is no news that social science management categories (say behavioral) are related to "soft" or narrative methodologies. In contrast, natural and applied science management categories, perhaps material processing, describe "hard" or structural methods. Both narrative and structural techniques are recognized and used for decades to support project management. But the inability to integrate methodologies has only led to more buzzwords and endless discussions. We may see project going wrong or yielding outcomes different from those specified in the plan, structural methods failing to improve the results, or narrative techniques fail in putting in place remedial mechanism to prevent damages before they arrive. However, is also true that, instead of realistic views, only controversial views abound which overstate the problems encountered in project development and implementation. Thus, there is a need to develop robust methods that integrate applied science and social science management categories. For example, the measurable attributes (scope, time, cost, quality, risk, benefits, and others) are defined (identified, quantified, planned, implemented, assessed, paid, and updated) at the activity level and assigned to an individual who performs the activity. Such a

214 Tywoniak, Stephane, Lavagnon Ika, and Cristophe Bredillet. "A Pragmatic Approach to Complexity Theorizing in Project Studies: Orders and Levels." *Project Management Journal* 52 (April 2021): 298–313. www.pmi.org.

definition of an activity and its attributes enable the dynamic integration of each project's work and associated attributes to any project management structure level during the span or lifecycle of the project. Suppose we can similarly add, define, and assign to an individual the social attributes (let's say, behavior) and synthesize those extended definitions to higher project management structure (maybe team). In that case, integration of social attributes and their metrics is possible. Barseghyan's articles show one such model; the author argues that simple algebraic equations can mathematically represent the efficiency and productivity of human systems. He develops mathematical expressions that combine the number of people, their motivation, acting intensity and degree of rationality, quality and difficulty of the activity, people's errors, resource consumed, and the results for the activity (Barseghyan 2017[215], 2018[216], 2021[217]). If we can use this model to improve the human resource estimate for line items of current estimating databases, it would indeed be something new.

The project management system logic and project management plan show the state of a system at a moment of time, controlled by the methodologies presented. Relationships within clusters, consisting of the system particles and project activities, have characteristics of lineal chains within frontward-oriented network diagram. These relationships can change if we perceive different conditions. We are confronting a complicated relationship between other disciplines, unusual requirements within a profession, or emergent situations during the application of the current project management plan or the application of system logic in the project management plan. Such conditions may require creative yet cautious plans and steps to improve performance in activities lagging behind in the pursuit of the stated goals of the plan. At this point, we realize when does

215 Barseghyan, Pavel. "Elements of the Mathematical Theory of Human Systems, Part 1: Assessment of the Results of Human Actions and Activities Based on the Method of State Equations." *PM World Journal* Volume VI, Issue XII (December 2017): www.pmworldjournal.net.

216 Barseghyan, Pavel. "Elements of the Mathematical Theory of Human Systems, Part 2: Structural Mathematical Models of the Life of Humans Based on the Method of State Equations.". *PM World Journal* Volumr VII, Issue I (January 2018): www.pmworldjournal.net.

217 Barseghyan, Pavel. "Quantitative analysis of the efficiency and productivity of the activity of human system – Part 1: Graphical analysis of the nonlinear functional relationships between team productivity and team size." *PM World Journal* Volume X, Issue III (March. 2021): www.pmworldjournal.com.

PMP becomes an art, when does science address, and why do technology and management actors focus on, a remarkable platform of details to resolve issues.

7 Derivative Project Management Planning

Some projects have no plan, or the project plan is not updated. These projects practically transform into inaccurate requirements, unpredictable evolvements, and serious complications.

While we need a common understanding and skills for project management planning (PMP), we often see dissonance in the process of improvisation in managing project contents, organization, dynamism, performance, benefits, success, and so on. The confusion is associated with project team members responsible for creating innovative technologies and widespread start-up endeavors, where frequent changes in objectives and requirements are recognized characteristics. Emerging businesses usually sidestep the current PMP. They try to derive shortcuts—simple, convenient, motivating, quick, not necessarily with enhanced features for the PMP, but attractive for those in a hurry, who favor simple narrations over developing and acquiring strong skills. The risks of reinvention in PMP, however, are enormous.

The critics of the PMP system usually think in a fragmented rather than integrated approach. The promoters of the Critical Chain Method (CCM) contrast the current PMP by adopting production management planning, reconstruction of time estimates, and management of different buffers. The Agile supporters emphasize the sequence of short-term products as an alternative to the development of project contents and products. However, the best form of both the CCM and the Agile methods might only deliver predictable results for exceptional cases. If we need professional management of contents, relationships, dynamics, status, progress, changes, causes, and forecasts for the project, then the derivative PMP is suboptimal.

Both CCM and Agile promoters group and construct relationships among groups as a substitute for developing details and revealing relationships among details of project contents. Sometimes, promoters come from the project management realm not by demonstrating their planning competence but by raising the opportunity to convince students and customers that derivative planning is a convenient alternative. Incredible cheering with generally accepted slogans such as "adaptability," "motivated individuals," "collaborative work," "trustworthiness," "customer satisfaction," "optimal positive outcomes," "management of uncertainty," and other representative elements of the management idea becomes at times the pillar of promoters' rhetoric for derivatives.

Critical Chain Method

The critical chain is "the chain of steps that are constraint" (Goldratt 1997, 215).[218] The "Critical Chain" book is a business novel; it describes a case of product development management by applying principles and practice of product production management. To sail comfortably through a risky mission, the CCM novel students use the code of creative distraction; the novel's background scene consists of continuous contrasts with the current PMP. Whenever students need to conceive the next step in CCM, they construct some PMP problems. But this scenario which aims to create a new project management method does not go so smoothly.

The Critical Chain book's core is about management planning, primarily near a time management plan and some aspects of resource, contract, and financial management plan. The book's basic assumption contends "that the uncertainty existing in every project is the main cause for most problems." So, we must understand better "the safety [excessive time estimate] embedded in the planning of a project" that is intended to manage uncertainties. Other assumptions in the book pop up as the students from this novel confront specific issues in managing the projects.

218 Goldratt, Eliyahu. *Critical Chain.* Great Barrington MA: The North River Press Publishing Corporation, 1997. www.northriverpress.com.

The CCM gets started as a deterministic project management procedure, developed as a logical production management process, and finished arbitrarily. During this endeavor, the CCM students intend to find out "how to manage projects better." However, they acknowledge the real problems in their approach to project management and leave the scene without a viable solution.

To further explain CCM ideas, it is necessary to have a repetitive production project in mind, which going through continuous production after its development stage. The repetitive production project passes through the product development and production phases; the product development phase depends on project management knowledge, and the production phase depends on the production management knowledge. However, to open "another avenue" for the project's product development phase, the CCM promoters try to draw an analogy between project management and production management. But such an analogy is unfounded; project management knowledge helps manage unique endeavors, and production management knowledge helps with managing the repetitive effort.

In the following two sections, I will discuss the practicality of the CCM method, assuming that the reader is familiar with the current PMP.

Characteristics

Daniel Pullman, Chairmen and CEO of Genemodem, and Isaac Levy, the executive vice-president of engineering, discuss the difficulties in the timeline of product development that a project aims to accomplish. Pullman thinks more must be done to find a way to shrink the product development timeframe. He departs from current PMP to assess problems connected to the production project's development phase.

Richard Silver (or Rick) associate professor, is assigned with the responsibility of teaching a project management team at Genemodem on a subject where the current know-how does not deliver acceptable results. He realizes swiftly that the content and name of such a course would be project management. By presenting an alarming status of the current project management, Rick drives the class toward an unknown adventure to invent a method to manage the project better.

At the very beginning, Rick draws consensus among students that the time estimate of each step in the project contains a lot of safety aimed to deal with uncertainty in a project, yet, the safety somehow gets negated. The idea that inadequate estimate and safety in project planning doesn't allow us to cope with uncertainties inspires the students. To better understand the safety measures incorporated in a project plan, students must know how to estimate and use time and resources to implement safety at each step. They agree that production safety, stored in work in progress, waits in the queues to be used; then, according to their reasoning, most of the project safety embedded in the time estimate for each activity waits in queues to be used.

Later on, Rick discusses with students some elements and interpretations of the network planning diagram (NPD). For example, students try to answer questions about when to start on the other noncritical paths. If the project manager uses early start dates for project activities, they will have many activities on their list and lose focus as a result. In contrast, if the project manager uses late start dates for project activities, every activity becomes critical, and, in turn, the act of focusing on all activities indiscriminate will prove counterproductive and lead to waste of time. They soon recognized the need to develop a mechanism that enables a project leader to concentrate on essential issues. Besides, they thought that the current project progress measurement does not differentiate between the work done on the critical path and the work done on noncritical paths. Project team members also spent much time reinventing the methods and terms for managing floats, resources, and other PMP pillars.

The CCM book shows that Rick and students do not possess a theoretical and methodological knowledge about PMP. At the same time, we can see that CCM alone, or combined with Theory of Contents (TOC; Goldrat 1990),[219] does not give a systematic answer. Solutions have been available for many of the technical aspects debated in the class, even before the CCM came into project management practice. For example, the universal and continuously updated databases for an estimate of activity time and cost; the general set of rules for selecting, sorting, formatting, as well as disseminating of important information; computerized heuristics for resource aggregation, allocation, leveling, smoothing; critical path relaxing, and all for single project, group of independent projects, or programs, were incorporated into project management practice six decades ago.

Overview

Neither Rick nor his students recognize the current form of PMP "that exists in books and articles" (Goldratt 1997, 21). But sometimes, project management educators do not follow good examples from engineering or medical schools

219 Goldratt, Eliyahu. *Theory of Constraints.* Great Barrington MA: The North River Press Publishing Corporation, 1990. www.northriverpress.com.

where professional subjects are supported by practitioners who understand the scientific framework of the issue and work daily on challenging cases.

The CCM students repeated the stereotype that traditional project management is not working (Goldratt 1997, 12, 13, 23-27, 69-70, 72-73, 79-81, 133, 159, 233). The way to fix the problems in project management practice eventually led Rick and students to align their approach to production management knowledge (Goldratt 1997, 48, 49, 136-150, 158, 193, 234-237). Students thus recognized that CCM presents a new method for managing the developmental phase of the production project. The assumption that production projects' development phase can be based on production management knowledge was not reasonable, and the consequences of such flawed reasoning can be traced throughout the CCM book.

Rick and students search for arguments that inadequate time estimates and safety embedded in project activities impede the effective management of project uncertainties. Although different ways are used in practice to interpret time estimates (Goldrat 1997, 41-48), CCM students decided to uniformly reconstruct time estimates for project activities. For example, "to cut the original time estimate of the steps in half and use half of the trimmed lead time as a feeding buffer" (Goldratt 1997, 158) is a hard-sell. Ayers explained decades ago that reconstruction of time estimate for project activities requires a contractor, who understands the "economic time" of its resources and achieves competitive advantage through a better estimate of each project activity, as well as the organization and work skills of its people (Ayers 1984, 257).[220]

While discussing the "PERT diagram" (Goldratt 1997, 69) or "PERT chart" (Goldratt 1997, 158), the CCM students silently abandoned planning network methods and their features. By presenting PERT diagrams/charts (Goldratt 1997, 69, 158, 214, 218) in an arborescent form of graph, the CCM students sided with characteristics of LTC (Lead Time Chart), a "technique commonly used in the job shop, or when introducing new products into the fstudenty" (Santora 1963, 734-736).[221] For example, the Critical Path Method (CPM) project activity's "time duration" was renamed and used as the LTC's "lead time" (Goldratt 1997, 49, 118, 158). The CCM students use LTC for various purposes (Goldratt 1990, 66, 68, 69, 97, 99, 108, 158, 214, 218). But deploying such an inadequate method for new product development yields suboptimal outcomes.

220 Ayers, Chesley. *Specifications for architecture. engineering and construction.* New York, NY: McGraw-Hill Book Company. (1984).

221 Santora, A. V. *The Encyclopedia of Management,* Edited by Carl Heyel. New York: Reinhold Publishing Corporation, 1963, 732–39.

If we review the "PERT chart" and related texts of the examples (Goldratt 1997, 66), as well as its "Gantt chart" (Goldratt 1997, 68, 69), we can see how CCM students challenged the CPM floats and established a scene for the introduction of buffers. This process is wordlessly accomplished and illustrated as LTC without activity float, but with added time-loaded activities called feeding buffers (Goldratt 1997, 155, 157, 158). Students also reinvent the meaning for the total float of network diagram methods. We know there will always be a kind of management reserve for time or resources, but can the CCM reinventions of buffers handle it?

The transportation network diagram is appropriate for project planning, including the developmental phase of the production project. Yet, CCM students reasoning to include the ideal "product development time of roughly two years"' (Goldratt 1997, 5), as "any sizable project, is described by about one hundred steps," and the LTC method appears to be sound choice (Goldratt 1997, 232). While the project's complexity and uncertainty get reduced by an increased number of activities in current PMP, the CCM's 100 steps may not be sufficient for a realproject.

Using CCM to remove resource constraints and conflicts in allocation and identify the project's critical chain isn't an easy job either, because the class acknowledges the dynamic and unpredictable reality of developing the project in real time (Goldratt 1997, 218–221, 231–234). However, the students assume that once the company identifies the bottleneck, removes resource contention, and establishes a critical chain, it is sufficient to monitor buffers and get a project under control (Goldratt 1997, 235–237). By doing so, CCM's students would also have to abandon the systematic, proven, and simple calculation of CPM's critical path for resource-limited schedule under which independent activities take place following the resource calendars already incorporated into the plan. Therefore, the CCM approach does not either render resource management easier or make it correct. It is hard to accept that arbitrarily defined constraints can be substitute for the analytical procedure. Even if an arbitrary assignment of constraints happens, it is very unlikely that the CCM's critical chain will stay stable and an arbitrary decision will last.

The CCM doesn't have a workable concept for implementing the project management plan one way or the other. Although the CCM does incorporate a few ideas about project control and progress measurement (Goldratt 1997, 71–72, 162, 166), we cannot really see a clearly defined and proper project implementation mechanism other than the TOC's arbitrarily defined constraints and the CCM's fixed schedule. The CCM students often play with different forms and attributes of the project management plan (Goldratt 1997, 36, 41-50, 47, 48, 61, 1114–128, 119, 123, 149, 155, 236). However, they do not understand the functions, differences, or relationships between the project's original, baseline, and current plans.

We are not surprised to read the various comments about CCM in the journal articles, books, and in practice. Yet, it is also true that there isn't a single call for the replacement of current PMP. Here are some early comments:

- Trietsch has identified some primary sources that discuss the resource-constrained critical path much earlier before the CCM was reinvented and named as the critical chain. The author also notes that the CCM project buffer at the end of the LTC chart has the same function as project time contingency has in the CPM contract schedule (Trietsch 2005, 30–32).[222]
- Raz et al. notice that CCM uses just a new names forsome old-school notions because of which the critical chain would otherwise have been called the resource-leveled critical path. According to the authors, it may be that CCM was the first to describe the resource buffer; this, however, doesn't mean the invention is sound or easy to apply (Raz, Barnes, and Dvir 2003, 29-30).[223]
- Leach believes that the CCM is an important aspect of making continuous improvement to the Project Management Body of Knowledge. The author also acknowledges that the CCM departs from the PMBOK Guide and supporting literature. The CCM students manage buffers rather than project activities and open a different space to assess project status, progress, forecasts, and other project work metrics (Leach 1999, 39).[224]
- Patrick discusses how to use the TOC and the CCM to manage uncertain events in a project. The author presents his approach through a variety of

222 Trietsch, Dan. "*Why a Critical Path by Any Other Name Would Smell Less Sweet? Towards a Holistic Approach to PERT / CPM.*" *Project Management Journal* Volume 36, Number 1 (March 2005): 27–36. www.pmi.org.

223 Raz, Tzvi, and Robert Barnes, and Dov Dvir. "A Critical Look at Critical Chain Project Management." *Project Management Journal* Volume 34, Number 4 (December 2003): 24–32. www.pmi.org.

224 Leach, Larry. "Critical Chain Project Management Improves Project Performance." *Project Management Journal* Volume 30, Number 2 (June 1999): 39-52. www.pmi.org.

processes, tools, and techniques (Patrick 2001)[225] but doesn't draw a parallel between his approach and the earlier practices for the resolution of the same problems, for example, buffer management versus float management. Nevertheless, this work is useful for those determined to use TOC and CCM methods in project management.

- Herroelen et al. present a critical review of the relevant sources for elements, application steps, and software to be used in Goldratt's CCM project management method. They call this the Critical Chain Method Scheduling/Buffer management (CCMS/BM), Goldratt's TOC application for the project's product development phase (Herroelen, Leus, and Demeulemeester 2002, 48).[226]
- Cohen et al. acknowledge the acceptance of CCM in many multi-project organizations and describe CCM steps for single-projects and multiple-projects (Cohen, Mandelbaum, and Shtub 2004, 40-41). The authors also draw the reader's attention to the control mechanisms of the CCM and some other alternatives for multi-project management. The authors present hypothetical examples to show if the CCM is insufficient to control delays in projects, then alternative control methodologies "can give similar and sometimes better performance" (Cohen, Mandelbaum, and Shtub 2004, 48).[227]

Finally, we must ask why the CCM has incited enormous debates about its value. In this context, Trietsch has carried out a detailed analysis of the CCM. To quote from Trietsch a passage relevant to the context of discussion here in this chapter:

Arguably, in a field that had been established about 40 years before the publication of Critical Chain, the viable textbooks should have reflected accumulated

225 Patrick. Francis. 2001. "Critical Chain and Risk Management – Protecting Project Value from Uncertainty, (Parts 1-8)." *Focused Performance.* Retrieved Oct 22. 2013. http://focusedperformance.com/articles/ccrisk.html.

226 Herroelen, Willy, Roel Leus, and Eric Demeulemeester. "Critical Chain Project Scheduling: Do Not Oversimplify." *Project Management Journal* 33, no. 4 (December 2002): www.pmi.org.

227 Cohen, Izack, Avishai Mandelbaum, and Avraham Shtub. "Multi-Project Scheduling and Control: A Process-Based Comparative Study of the Critical Chain Methodology and Some Alternatives." *Project Management Journal* 35, no. 2 (June 2004): 39–50. www.pmj.org.

knowledge in the field, with the potential exclusion of esoteric material and very new contributions. But was this really the case? (Trietsch 2005, 33)

Few scholars and professionals recommend CCM as a general methodology for PMP. The CCM may apply to a small project with a sound and straightforward logic. It can be built on already developed models, or on a project carried out using mainly the company's own resources, which can be eventually clarified by the "hundred steps." No mega project discussed in the CCM book shows that CCM approach could deliver better results than the current form of PMP under similar conditions (Goldratt 1997, 23–24, 35–41).

After its big launch in 1997 and during the first two or three years, the concept of CCM looked promising. But from 2005 onwards, the attention given to it in practice and published literature was rather average and sporadic about its proclaimed features. There have been reports about its successful application, as well; however, strong criticisms emerged from both the academy and management professionals; as a result of such criticisms, the CCM is now almost forgotten. As we have seen, the CCM does not show how:

- pending and approved scope changes add to or subtract from the current and baseline plans
- actual work accomplishments during the current period compares to the baseline plan
- expected delays impact the project
- a change in development logic, as well as added, modified, and deleted activities and milestones impact the plan
- contract time, including all contract milestones, changes, and so on.

If the above parameters aren't taken into consideration, the project status, progress, and forecasts will not be manageable. If the CCM oversimplifies PMP, we cannot seriously consider the arbitrary cutting of time estimate, establishing bottlenecks, constraints, critical chain, and buffers in the CCM approach.

The CCM is not presented as a comprehensive methodology and cannot be integrated with a well-known and widely accepted PMP framework. It did not pass the test of its purpose and replace current PMP, including planning for the developmental phase of production projects.

Agile

Agile is a management planning method for short-term investment; it can be a part of management planning for discrete production, mass production, or carrying out a project. In common sense, Agile is the delivery of short-term investment product in terms of its negotiated features and functions. For this purpose, the Agile management planning aims to accomplish two continuous objectives: both deliver customer-defined product using short-term investment and focus on the next short-term product slated for release. Agile certainly is not about PMP that is related to the delivery of project investment product in terms of planned and actual metrics for project components.

The Agile product consists of technological phases for the short term, and the project product consists of technological phases for the whole project. Therefore, the Agile short-term investments phases are a synonym for project phases. Yet, the meaning and implications of the technological phrases differ substantially depending on whether they are used for Agile products or for project products.

Project phases represent the interface between project management and project business management. But we are stuck with irrational polarization around meaningless terms for phases, often terms like "Waterfall" or "predictive" in project investment phases, and terms like "the Agile" or "adaptive" in short-term investment phases. In summary:

- The top-down analysis and bottom-up synthesis for project planning contents define overlaps among the "predictive" phases of the whole project. We collect actual data to control the project phases' changes, including overlaps among project phases.
- Negotiation between the client and the performer defines the "adaptive" short-term planning contents. We collect actual data to control the short-term-phase changes, including overlaps within the short-term phases only.

Ironically, precisely the opposite happened, and the tagging of phases got reversed; the "Waterfall" project phases were completed simultaneously and "adapted" to project conditions (Chapter 1, Figure 1.1). The "Agile" short-term phases were concluded sequentially and "predicted" the subsequent short-term needs only (Chapter 1, Figure 1.2). The completed project phase, or a part of it, is used to update the whole project; however, we can use the completed Agile phase to determine the subsequent short-term phase. Daily project meetings for assessing work in progress have much in common with daily Agile conferences to evaluate the short-term phase. The results of daily project meetings reflect the whole project; however, daily Agile conferences have very little or no reflection on the open-end Agile endeavor. Therefore, accomplished and planned project investment phases, and not accomplished short-term investment phases, are the interface between project management and project business management.

The Agile services market is flourishing, and it is not easy to choose and communicate an analytical solution. Agile approaches are based on induction theory, reasoning from detailed facts to general knowledge; they incrementally deliver customer-defined value for short-time investments by climbing up to product completion. Some approaches elaborated the idea to operational levels to achieve product predictability (Schwaber and Sutherland 2016, 3–4).[228] In the meantime, the Agile promoters reduce or distort the current PMP's characteristics and redefine the meaning of its essential components. There are many unproven views about current project management:

- In current PMP The "type of project is operational only." In fact, the different phases of current PMP assure active and integrated relationships between operational levels of project management and strategic levels of project business management.
- In current PMP The "plan would remain unchanged for the project's duration." In reality, the project management plan consists of three components: the original plan that changes exceptionally, the baseline plan that changes through approved change orders, and the current plan that changes through approved and pending change orders. The revision of the project management plan is a standard process which was recorded for the first time six decades ago (O'Brien 1969, 36)[229] and it has been under continuous development and improvisation since then (Maharana 2019, 303–336).[230] The original plan's development takes approximately 30% of the planning effort while updating the baseline plan, and current plans take 70% of the planning effort.

228 Schwaber, Ken, and Sutherland, Jeff. *The Scrum Guide™, The Definitive Guide to Scrum: The Rules of the Game.* Scrum.Org and Scrum Inc., July 2016. http://creativecommons.org/licenses/by-sa/4.0/.

229 O'Brien, James. *Scheduling Handbook.* New York, NY: McGraw-Hill Book Company, 1969.

230 Maharana, Dibyaranjan. *Oracle Primavera P6 Professional Project Management, Release 19.* Coppell, TX, 2020.

- In current PMP "only those scope changes are approved where the existing baselines will not change very much." The truth is that the change orders process, including scope changes, is a regulated matter in dealing with project plan modifications. Change orders are issued for a contingency requirement to be fulfilled and are a part of the approved project budget and can also be modified any time depending on the project needs.
- In current PMP "each life cycle phase is completed before the next begins." It never really happens because phases generally overlap and continuously decrease resource consumption, lower the amount of efforts made, and shorten the lead times, over time, from the start to the end of the project. There will always be some design, procurement, acceptance for earlier specified works, or change orders, even for the project without a glitch.
- In current PMP "project status reporting alone consumes approximately 25% of the project budget." Without a doubt, the current PMP, including project status reporting, even in most complicated projects, will not exceed 2% of the total project budget.
- Current project management "does not assume additional work on the preceding phase once it is complete." There is no real example of this statement because we cannot go back in time. However, field-order and change-order procedures are well-established and standard industry practices. The process must be applied wherever and whenever work needs to be added, modified, or dissolved.
- Current project management "is generally rigid and does not acknowledge the actual situation." Suppose we ask people in engineering, construction, government sectors, and yes, in information technology, whether implementing project management plans and handling actual situations is a rigid process or standard daily routine. During project development, updating the project management plan does not differ from updating procedures for other documentation in the project, say the architectural, mechanical, electrical, contractual, and other documentation.
- "The Agile approach means less formal documentation and procedures." Changes in project scope, time, cost, contracts, and others are frequent and cause conflicts between contracting parties. Therefore, appropriate documentation must follow if a change occurs, and we should be careful when and what procedures, documents, reports, or records can drop out.
- The Agile processes use "feedback, rather than planning, as their primary control mechanism." There is a lack of understanding about project

management feedback and the implementation of the project management plan. For decades, the project management feedback has been, and continues to remain, a well-known part of implementing a project management plan and is unlikely to change soon.

- Current project management "is not applicable for research projects since future events uncertainty characterizes the research projects." Nothing can be farther from the truth; the current PMP indeed has the capacity to allow users to handle scope, time, costs, and other project attributes well in advance and control absolutely the process of determining and allowing when and what changes are to be made to the project under implementation.
- "Agile approach can better manage project uncertainty and frequent changes than the traditional approach." Indeed, the current project management has recognized procedures for handling project uncertainties and changes and assessing their impact. However, Agile does not have any procedure for managing uncertainties; it just welcomes change orders to cover all glitches resulting from inadequate planning and sometimes reconstructing seemingly completed and deployed in short-term investment phases.

Supporters of the Agile approach habitually use the project phases and project feedback to question the effectiveness of current PMP. The fundamental misperception for project phases and feedback is that the original project plan drives project development. However, it is critical to develop our understanding about the following aspects of the project:

- Understanding project phases (e.g., negotiation, design, production, installation, commissioning, and warranty) is essential for PMP because project phases link project management and project business management. Project management planning phases contain information about the project's original, baseline, and current plans, whereas the Agile phase contains information on short-term investment to be made as specified in the current plan. The differences are substantial and point to a lack of understanding about the functions of project management phases.
- Understanding project management feedback is critical for implementing a project management plan. Project feedback (planning, executing, controlling, and back to planning) involves implementing project management plans and managing changes under project conditions. The feedback

procedure affects project contents and changes the baseline and current plans, whereas the Agile feedback affects only the short-term investments and changes in the current short-term plan. In the current PMP, feedback management is an analytical procedure involving the whole project, whereas feedback in the Agile method is a arbitral procedure affecting only the short-term investments. The differences are significant and point to a lack of understanding about the project management feedback functions.

The following sections refer to the basics of the Agile approach. My comments within the sections will challenge the Agile method's practicality for a project, and project business, by comparing its key components with current PMP practices. For this reason, the reader should be familiar with the current PMP.

Characteristics

It has been many decades since the Agile idea first emerged in management practice. Renewed promise presented as a tool for short-term project planning created dilemmas initially; the Agile attracted many trainees to project management who understood the meaning of PMP through short-term planning only. As the Agile method does not address the whole project, project business, or strategic management of the company, its planning implications stay unknown.

The Agile models are developed in different forms and brand names and generally for situations where the whole system is unknown or not needed in full scale; yet, some immediate parts of the system are sufficiently defined and can serve as a nucleus for their subsequent development. Many sources assert that such an approach is essential for information technology projects, although it is unclear how Agile manages the project's future.

Those with working experience in current PMP will split the requirements into specific project phases and work elements within each phase and commit to assessing status, progress, changes, forecast, or other attributes of each work element and any project component and cluster of project components. However, those practicing Agile may roughly break down requirements to short-term investments that do not last longer than six weeks and work only on immediate short-term investment. They are not related to any status, progress, forecast, or other attributes of succeeding short-term investments. In reality, problems do not arise from the Agile orientation to short-term investment phases but arise instead from an insufficient understanding of the whole project.

Overview

Let's start with the architecture of the Agile movement by considering some views presented in its "manifesto' that summarizes the main principles of the Agile approach:

- Our highest priority is to satisfy the customer through early and continuous delivery of valuable software.
- Welcome changing requirements, even late in development. Agile processes harness change for the customer's competitive advantage.
- Deliver working software frequently, from a couple of weeks to a couple of months, with a shorter timescale preference.
- Business people and developers must work together daily through the project.
- Build projects around motivated individuals, giving them the environment and support they need and trust them to get the job done.
- The most efficient and effective method of conveying information to and within a development teamis face-tofac conversation.
- Working software is the primary measure of progress.
- The Agile processes promote sustainable development. The sponsors, developers, and users should be able to maintain a constant pace indefinitely.
- Continuous attention to technical excellence and good design enhances agility.
- Simplicity— the art of maximizing the amount of work not done—is essential.
- The best architectures, requirements, and designs emerge from self-organizing teams.
- The team reflects on becoming more effective at regular intervals, then tunes and adjusts its behavior accordingly (Agile 2013, the bullets mark added by the author).[231]

The term Agile reflects the above standpoints and meanings of the Agile Manifesto (PMI 2021, 235),[232] which differs from the project definition (PMI

231 Agile. *Agile Manifesto.* Agile Alliance, February 2001: www.agilemanifesto.org.

232 PMI 2021. *A Guide to the Project Management Body of Knowledge PMBOK Guide Seventh Edition and the Standard for the Standard for Project Management.* July 2021, Project Management Institute Inc., 14 Campus Boulevard, Newtown Square, PA 19073-3299.

2021, 245). The manifest emphasizes on the "early and continuous delivery" of software solution to the customer, "frequently" and within a "couple of weeks to a couple of months," where the delivered software represents at the same time "the primary measure of progress." As Agile does not look far enough in advance, measuring progress is relative; it relates to increments of a solution that may be changed or abolished as we learn more about upcoming increments. During the course of progress under the Agile method, the approach that "welcomes changing requirements" may be the price to pay for the lack of vision in specific areas or in project planning as a whole. The manifesto also highlights the importance of customers' continuous involvement in the incremental development of software, where "business people and developers must work together daily through the project" in open-end sessions. Such an approach shifts most of the responsibility to a customer for the solution, and the customer must think about what they want and whether they are willing to get collaborate continuously with the team of developers to achieve incremental results. The following statement of the manifesto best summarizes the open-end approach: "Simplicity—the art of maximizing the amount of work not done—is essential."

How do authors assess and measure the Agile values? Specifically, we must know where the project is heading before it is over, assuming there is no doubt about customer involvement and team capability. Let's have a look at some opinions, explanations, understandings, and impacts.

- Desaulniers and Anderson debate a perception about project management and Agile management and suggest selecting and using the most suitable process for a software development project (Desaulniers and Anderson 2001, 2).[233] The authors list the advantages of "adaptive" project phases; for example, the Agile applications "closely match customer requirements due to constant customer feedback" (Desaulniers and Anderson 2001, 3–4). However, they do not elaborate on how a fragmented system analysis typical with Agile management can trigger qualified feedback. How is the responsibility shared for the unknown project scope? How can the customer be informed about the project completion date and costs of changes?

233 Desaulniers, Douglas, and Robert Anderson. "Matching Software Development Life Cycles to the Project Environment." *Proceedings of the Project Management Institute Annual Seminars & Symposium.* Nashville: (November 2001). www.pmi.org.

- Nicholson describes software development methodologies that "have been traced back to 1957" (Nicholson 2013, 1),[234] as well as its current principles and practice (Nicholson 2013, 2). But after decades of application, the traditional PMP is tagged today as the "Waterfall" or "predictive" method and declared by some as inadequate for software development management. A strict, rigid step-by-step completion of activities in moving from one stage to another in software development is cited as a key reason for the inadequacy of traditional PMP in software development projects. The correctness of this view has never been proven. However, it resonated within the software development community, and a new concept with its definition encompassing descriptors such as "Agile" or "adaptive" became popular.
- Conforto et al. discuss the controversial stances of "predictive" and "adaptive" approaches in a review article. The authors lead readers through source references that describe a set of principles and practices of the Agile process and its end products. The research measures declared adaptive approach values while believing that a new approach can better manage project uncertainty and frequent changes than the traditional method. The research also lists opinions that misinterpret actual values, integrity, and the flexibility of the current PMP. However, the authors do not consider Agile management as a techniques "supported by the literature." Although Agile ideas can fulfil specific project conditions and requirements, the authors still question their values (Conforto, Carlos, and Amaral 2010, 73–80).[235]
- Oltmann thinks the traditional approach to project management that emphasizes on "thorough planning before executing the plan" is favorable for managing project contents. However, the Agile methods emphasize incrementalism over whole project planning by looking for an identifiable, short-term part of the project contents only, which is to be delivered to the customer over a specific period of time, which is usually several weeks (Oltmann 2013, 2).[236]

234 Nicholson, Laurence. "Agile in Project Management: A Brief Overview." *PM World Journal* Volume II, Issue IV (April 2013). www.pmworldjournal.net.

235 Conforto, Edivandro Carlos, and Daniel Capaldo Amaral. "Evaluating an Agile Method for Planning and Controlling Innovative Projects." *Project Management Journal* 41, no. 2 (April 2010): 73–80. www.pmi.org.

236 Oltmann, Jeff. "Agile vs. Traditional: An Unnecessary War." *PM World Journal* II, no. III (March 2013). www.pmworldjournal.net.

- Nee recognizes variation in companies, projects, cultures, conditions, and requirements that drive authors to adopt a blended approach to project management (Nee 2012, 1). The author argues that using traditional project management elements in an Agile situation is feasible (Nee 2012, 3).[237]
- The one approach essential for software development in future is that "We should define a project as far as we can and take into account customer requirements about the deployment of software segments." With this renewed process for continuous delivery of software, which first came into practice in 1968, Aguanno suggests that we should favor technological project phases over the incremental investment phases. The author gives an innovative look at the inevitable continuous development"—process, similar to the project's operations and maintenance phase (Aguanno 2013, 1–4).[238]
- Shenoy explains in detail the scope of the Agile project planning, progress reporting, and change management. The author repeats some stereotypes about the current PMP; however, he shows much understanding about the needs to improve planning in an Agile situation: "Yes, Agile Projects fail when they don't plan. And yes, Agile Projects need a plan." The author discusses some differences between the PMP and the Agile short-term segment planning, which may help communicate and reduce the gaps between the options (Shenoy 2019, 1–4).[239]
- In the review of Chin's book, Wideman quotes an email where Chin summarizes the environment of the Agile management.

Dynamic technology-driven environments, where customers often don't know, can't articulate, and/or are confused about requirements then, from the project manager's perspective, the requirements always appear to be changing, … Agile is something to consider. (Wideman 2006, 1)[240]

237 Nee, Nancy. "Finding the Right Blend: Sometimes Pure Agile isn't the Way to Go." *PM World Journal* I, no. IV (November 2012). www.pmworldjournal.net.

238 Aguanno, Kevin. "Continuous Delivery: The Ultimate Challenge for Software Development Managers." *PM World Journal* I, no. I (January 2013). www.pmworldjournal.net.

239 Shenoy, Ajay. "Common Misconceptions about Agile." *PM World Journal* VIII, no. X (November 2019). www.pmworldjournal.net.

240 Wideman, Max. "Book Review (Chin, Gary. Agile Project Management: How to Succeed in the Face of Changing Project Requirements. New York, NY: AMACOM,

- Rothman describes the current status, tools, and the Agile techniques, which are known aspects in incremental planning and delivering project products. For example, the author explains the "iteration" and the "flow" of Agile's two primary ways of incremental planning and delivery of project products. In the iteration-based Agile, a team works in time-boxes of the same duration, where each time box consists of standard technological phases for the project product's. In the flow-based Agile, a team works, in addition to standard phasing for the project productelement development, in time-boxes of required duration (Rothman 2017, 9–10).[241]
- Portman gives an overview of the Agile approaches which may help the user meet specific needs. The author discusses key methods, application levels, documentation, and communications within an Agile environment which may help gain a better understanding about this specific filed in management practice. The author extensively documents his article by source references and clarifies the Agile approach (Portman 2019, 1–11).[242]
- Einhorn et al. note that the success rate of business projects with an information technology component is unsatisfactory and cite reasons for the low success rate, such as wasteful expenditure running to billions of dollars annually. The authors give new insights into the management of information technology projects and found that business processes appropriately used throughout the project's lifetime may have a "major positive impact on the project success rate" (Einhorn, Marnewick, and Meredith 2019, 989).[243]
- Fink and Pinchovski reiterate that estimates of completion times in software development projects are often inaccurate, impede the fulfilment of project objectives, and eventually lead to the project's failure. The authors examine whether the human failure to estimate the relationships between

2004)." *Project Management Wisdom* (May 2006). http://maxwideman.com/papers/agile/intro.htm.

241 Rothman, Johanna. *Create Your Successful Agile Project.* Raleigh, NC: The Pragmatic Bookshelf, 2017.

242 Portman, Henny. "A bird's eye view on the agile forest." *PM World Journal* VIII, no. X (November 2019). www.pmworldtoday.net.

243 Einhorn, Frank, Carl Marnewick, and Jack Meredith. "Archiving strategic benefits from business IT projects: The critical importance of using the business case across the entire project lifetime." *International Journal of Project Management* 37, no. 8 (November 2019). 989–1002. www.elsevier.com/locate/ijproman.

increasing the speed in the completion of activities and ascertain correctly the time-savings achieved can enlighten our understanding of software development's decades-long time estimation problem (Fink and Pinchovski 2020, 99).[244]

- Tam C., et al. surveyed as many as 216 Agile practitioners and found that "team capability" and "customer involvement" are the main factors contributing to the success of ongoing Agile software development projects. Knowing which characteristics are significant to success, managers and teams can establish priorities, thereby improving project outcomes (Tam, Costa Moura, Oliveira, and Varajao 2020, 165).[245]
- Messai presents an overview of contracts and their perspectives in the application of the Agile method. The author reiterates the Agile values and principles in detail and elaborates on contract types that share and reduce risks in the entertainment business. While the approach describes clearly the cost and quality aspects, its description about the project schedule remains grey; all schedules are reduced to review points between each sprint to evaluate the project status and progress and forecast for completion in the next sprint (Messai 2019).[246]

The Agile promoters must understand how PMP can support incremental products and the whole project. Such an effort should start by adopting fundamental tools and techniques for analysis, relationships, synthesis, and updating the PMP contents. By retaining the pillars of the Agile method—the collaborative teamwork on incremental planning and delivering the project product's elements—users of the Agile method should also understand how to develop a vision for all project phases and iterations within and between phases.

244 Fink, Lior, and Barak Pinchovski. "It is about time: Bias and its mitigation in time-saving decisions in software development projects." *International Journal of Project Management* 38, no. 2 (2020): 99–111. www.elsevier.com/locate/ijproman.

245 Tam, Carlos, Eduardo Joia da Costa Moura, Tiago Oliveira, and Joao Varajao. "The factors influencing the success of on-going agile software development projects." *International Journal of Project Management* 38, no. 3 (April 2020): 165–76. www.elsevier.com/locate/ijproman.

246 Messsai, Sarra. "Agile Contracts: Effective Procurement for Enhanced Project Success in Entertainment Industry." *PM World Journal* VIII, no. II (February 2019). www.pmworldjournal.net.

Although Agile management is used for different purposes and is different from traditional PMP, it is a hybrid approach that mirrors PMP for each short-term product. Rothman's book already indicates that some of this is already happening (Rothman 2017, 9-10). In that case, we can find that each short-time increment of an open-end project reassembles the structure of the project's technological phases practiced in current PMP. Besides, the flow-based Agile method leans favorably toward the use of extended time-box duration for completing a specific work, which may be improved with current PMP.

We confront a wide range of situations where apparent misunderstanding or misinterpretation of facts may prevail and confuse the reader and escalate restlessness. How do we improve the system by "simplifying" PMP rather than continuously considering its origins, development, and features designed to handle short-term deliverables and project-end objectives? For example, some supporters of Agile management suggest that the long-distance plan is unnecessary because there are so many changes. However, the lack of continuous updating of whole project contents heightens the customer's inability to resolve accumulated project changes and better manage the open-end endeavor. Besides, the absence of overall project analysis, often caused by insufficient understanding of the customer's technological processes, will probably require a reconstruction of tangibles delivered in earlier periods. It may be a key concern with applying Agile management the and its narrow purposes for management of short-term investment.

If we subtract the promotional rhetoric from Agile management, we can see its capacity for management planning of short-term requirements and continuous delivery of short-term products. So, we may need Agile's short-term management to improve PMP, but only for creating a purposeful and systematic know-how. As a result, the definitions of project objectives and the governance of the next short-term investment may improve. It should be the platform for both promoting Agile management and extending suggestions for changes to its unproven promotional rhetoric.

While the Agile method helps cover the sequential short-term requirements, its primary value comes from raising the awareness about PMP. It is a necessary and helpful move; otherwise, some future projects may depend only on the intuition of project team members in creating and implementing the project management plan.

8 Notes, Integrated Definitions, Readings

Activity—Activity is the most detailed and unique element of project management planning (PMP) contents. Activity expresses specific technological or management work on hardware, software, service, process, or information in the project management plan. The performer will accomplish the work, or another party in the project will work for the performer as intended expressly or implicitly by the contract or agreement between parties. Activities are definite knowledge of project management contents and the building blocks of the project's higher structural elements and dynamic interactions and overlaps. We have differentiated and discussed several activity types in Chapters 1 and 2.

Different needs, requirements, and conditions of the project will result in the definition of various activities and their attributes.

Activity attributes—The activity attributes detail an activity defined and performed according to technological or management processes and documentation.

- Technological attributes include, for example, the activity description, relationships, duration, lead/lag time, milestones, resource types, quantity of resources, cost, unit of measure and cost for a unit of measure for each resource, and other technological attributes for activities. The attributes are end-results of technological processes and documentation, for example,

requirements, specifications, standards, regulations, contracts, product flow charts, prototype if any, payment requests, as-built documents, and others.
- Management attributes include, for example, the activity plans, status, progress, forecasts, codes, code values, cost accounts, and other management attributes for activity. The attributes are end-results of the management processes and documentation, for example, requirements, specifications, standards, regulations, contract, master plans, contract plans, work assignment and acceptance, pending payments, change orders, claims, reports, as-built plan, and others.

Other activity attributes include those of the social environment and social entities and unexpected and complex conditions. Those attributes, which may be covered by technological and management processes, are not generally known or systemized.

Activity codes—Activity codes are a general tool for managing project contents and contexts by selecting, grouping, summarizing, and formatting activities from project databases and other sources. For example, the activity's codes help produce many views of project structures, as WBS, CBS, OBS, and other project structures. As project client, stakeholders, managers, contractors, subcontractor, and other actors of the project are interested in different reports of project contents, it becomes a challenge to accurately define the activity codes.

The reports range from a single activity within a work package to an executive summary that includes all project activities. For example, as scope needs to combine with responsibility, we must give each activity the code values for both scope and responsibility. If an activity includes more than one responsibility, then the responsibilities are combined, or the activity requires to be split into multiple parts, then those parts are assigned to individual responsibility. Here is an example of a template for project activity codes and code values for each activity code:

Project structures
- Scope
  - Project
  - Deliverables
  - Contracts
  - Work packages
    - Activities for each work package
- Responsibility

Project manager
Architect/engineer
General contractor
Subcontractors
Team leader
Other structures (e.g., stakeholders, locations, fiscal periods)
Other substructures (e.g., project phases, virtual phases, Agile investment phases)
Activity code categories
Activity code values for each category

The above levels for project codes are applied selectively, depending on project management requirements and project size. In simple cases, we may need only two activity code categories, one for scope structures and one for responsibility structures.

Benefits management plan—Benefits management plan shows the documented explanation defining the processes for creating, maximizing, and sustaining the benefits provided by a project or program (PMI 2021, 235).[247]

Bottleneck (Critical Chain method [CCM])—Several projects are done by the same pool of people, and one of the skills is a bottleneck (Goldratt 1997, 193).[248]

Bottleneck buffer (CCM)—Time allowance aims to protect the bottleneck, the organization's overall performance (Goldratt 1997, 236).

Boundary object—A boundary object spans a group of objects with different viewpoints and indicates the collective limits that cannot be exceeded by any object included in considerations (Star and Griesemer 1989, Abstract).[249]

Burn chart—A graphical representation of the work remaining in a time box of the work completed toward the release of a product or accomplish a project deliverable (PMI 2021. 236).

247 PMI 2021. *A Guide to the Project Management Body of Knowledge PMBOK Guide Seventh Edition and the Standard for the Standard for Project Management.* Kindle Version, July 2021, Project Management Institute Inc., 14 Campus Boulevard, Newtown Square, PA 19073-3299.

248 Goldratt, Eliyahu. *Critical Chain.* Great Barrington MA: The North River Press Publishing Corporation, 1997. www.northriverpress.com.

249 Star, Susan, and James Griesemer. "*Institutional Ecology.* 'Translations' and Boundary Objects: Amateurs and Professionals in Berkeley's Museum of Vertebrate Zoology, 1907-39." *Social Studies of Science* 19, no. 3 (1989): 387–420.

Cadence—A rhythm of activities conducted throughout the project (PMI 2021, 235).

Causal premise—Part of the classical theory of a connection between cause and effect confirms the most common perspective for relationships among particles of the system logic and project plan activities. We present the project management system contents and PMP contents by a time-oriented network of particles/activities characterized by the following:

- Lineal relations during the development of project management plan; for example, activity "A" plan affects activity "B"; activity "B" plan affects activity "C," and so on until the last activity in a chain.
- Seemingly circular relations during the implementation of the project management plan; for example, activity "A" is in progress and gets updated through a sequence of management processes "a," "b," "c," and so on, and back to process "a" after progressing to the new data date and defining its status, progress, and forecast, including new conditions for the start of activity "B" (see Chapter 8, Updating the Project Management Plan)

New systems theory of causality tends to view soft relationships in a system by searching for analogies and similarities in the structure and process of changing levels and disciplinary domains (Ruben, cited in Ackoff and Emery, 2008, ix–x).[250]

Change order—A written authorization issued by the project designer or engineer and approved by the owner before any items have begun. It allows the contractor to change the original plans, specifications, or other contract documents or assumed conditions. Change orders are covered by contingency, which is part of the approved project duration and budget.

We treat a change order as a new activity with all the required attributes. When the data date moves, the new remaining duration is set for all activities and change orders in progress. If a change order is directly related to a particular activity, we add the value of the change order to the activity. If a change order is related to more activities, then its value can be distributed proportionally. If we deal with project scope reduction, then the negative change order's value decreases the project estimate at completion and affects one or more activities.

250 Ackoff, Russel, and Fred Emery. *On Purposeful Systems: An Interdisciplinary Analysis of Individual and Social Behavior as a System of Purposeful Events.* New Brunswick, NJ: Transaction Publishers, 2008.

Common terms—Various commercially available glossaries sometimes do not clearly distinguish key project management terms. For example, what should we prefer, for example, the plan versus schedule, planning versus scheduling, planner versus scheduler? I prefer the terms *plan, planning, planner* because these have a more general meaning than terms such as *schedule, scheduling,* and *scheduler.*

This subject is vast indeed, so we must agree first on how should we structure the planning terminology? For example, planning area (project, system), planning subject (practice, research), planning knowledge (scope, time, cost), the level sophistication of a plan (scientific, innovative, derivative), level of planning (master, contract, as-built), type of plan (original, baseline, current), and other planning structures.

Comprehensive dictionaries of PMP terms are key to gain a better understanding of the project management profession. Here are some volumes that contain good selections and descriptions of project management terms—Cleland and Kerzner (1985)[251]; Fleming and Koppelman 2000[252]; PMI (2001)[253]; GAO (2015)[254]; PMI (2017)[255]; PMI (2019)[256]; GAO (2020)[257]; and Wideman (2021).[258]

Complexity—Complexity is defined as "the quality of being complicated and compounded." (TransCreative Software 2021).[259] Complexity is a higher

251 Cleland, David, and Harold Kerzner. *A Project Management Dictionary of Terms.* New York, NY: Van Nostrand Reinhold Company, 1985.

252 Fleming, Quentin, and Joel Koppelman. *Earned Value Project Management,* Second Edition. Newton Square PA: Project Management Institute, 2000.

253 PMI 2001. *The Practice Standard for Work Breakdown Structure First Edition.* Newtown Square PA: Project Management Institute, 2001.

254 GAO 2015. *Best Practice for Project Schedules.* US Government Accountability Office: Publicly Released December 22, 2015. https://www.gao.gov/assets/680/674404.pdf. Presented by Kurian, Tijo, 2019: PM World Journal VIII, no. XI, www.pmworldjournal.net.

255 PMI 2017. *A Guide to the Project Management Body of Knowledge (PMBOK® Guide) Sixth Edition.* Newtown Square PA: Project Management Institute, 2017.

256 PMI 2019. *The Practice Standard for Scheduling Third Edition.* Newtown Square PA: Project Management Institute, 2019.

257 GAO 2020. *Cost Estimating and Assessment Guide: Best Practice.* US Government Accountability Office, GAO-20-195G, March 2020.

258 Wideman, Max. *Wideman Comparative Glossary of Project Management Terms.* 2021. www.maxwideman.com.

259 TranCreative Software. *WordBook. English Dictionary & Thesaurus.* iTunes Store. 2021. (Includes Web Contents http://en.m.wikipedia.org; http://mobile.answers.

stage of complicated; it is an extraordinarily difficult situation usually associated with big projects, poor governance, team members' behavior or skills, lack of adequate project processes, or paradigms. There are many discussions and explanations about complex systems and ideas to manage complicated and complex projects. For example:

- Saynisch draws a line between current project management (Project Management First Order, PM-1) and a new project management interpretation (Project Management Second Order, PM-2). The research program "Beyond Frontiers of Traditional Project Management" was founded to bring the theory of complex systems closer to real projects. The author explains the genesis, concept, system architecture, principles, methods, and the implementation of PM-2 in different project types and the potential use of PM-2, along with integration aspects of PM-2 and previous project management models (Saynisch April 2010, 5-21).[260]
- In the subsequent article, the author maintains his earlier view that project management for complex projects will be an all-inclusive concept for project management in the coming decades. Saynisch believes that PM-2 will act as an umbrella for the elements of the CPMCS (the Complex Project Managers Competency Standard—International Centre for Complex Project Management), ICB3 (the IPMA Competency Baseline), and PMI standards (PMBOK Guide, OPM3, Program Management, Portfolio Management; Saynisch December 2010, 17).[261]
- Williams et al. studied the project complexity and proposed project management practices to identify early warning signs in complex projects. The authors find that the early warning signs detected may be related to project processes or team members' behavior. Continued dialog and trust are critical both within and outside the team and the organizational support for

com; http://www.google.com. http://www.merriam-webster.com; http://www.wordreference.com).

260 Saynisch, Manfred. "Beyond Frontiers of Traditional Project Management: An Approach to Evolutionary. Self-Organizational Principles and the Complexity Theory—Results of the Research Program." *Project Management Journal* 41, no. (April 2010): 21–37. www.pmi.org.

261 Saynisch, Manfred. "Mastering Complexity and Changes in Projects. Economy and Society via Project Management Second Order (PM-2)." *Project Management Journal* 41, no. 5 (December 2010): 4–20. www.pmi.org.

critical assessment are essential to detect early warning signs. The authors conclude the research with a list of early warning signs (Williams, Klakegg, Walker, Andersen, and Magnussen 2012).[262]

- Stretton analyzed several studies on complications, complexities, and uncertainties in the program/project context and suggests a balanced approach. The author wrote that "traditional project management tools can still work well on complicated programs/projects—but not so well on complex programs/projects, with their elements of uncertainty" (Stretton 2017, 9).[263]

Constraint (CCM)—In resource constraints situation, the constraint is the longest chain of dependent steps (Goldratt 1997, 215).

Contingency—Cost contingency to cover the unpredicted cost in the project, and time contingency to cover the time loss resulting from unpredicted costs or other unexpected conditions. Contingency activity is situated at the end of the critical path.

Continuous delivery—The practice of delivering features increments immediately to the customer, often through the use of the small batches of work and automation technology (PMI 2021, 237).

Contract documents—All the written and graphic documents concerning the contract between the owner and contractor. Contract documents usually consist of contract forms, contract conditions, specifications, drawings, addenda, and contract modification. Bidding requirements precede contract documents; both contract documents and bidding requirements constitute bidding documents. If similar documentation is developed for exclusive use within an organization, we call it the agreement.

Contract types—There are many contractual relationships between parties involved in the project regulating the reimbursement for expenses incurred by vendors, contractors, subcontractors, or other such external stakeholders and service providers towards the fulfilment of their contractual obligations with the project organization. In all of the presented contracts, change orders and risk

262 Williams, Terry, Ole Klakegg, Derek Walker, Bjern Andersen, and Ole Magnussen. "Identifying and Acting on Early Warning Sign in Complex Projects," *Project Management Journal* 43, 2 (April 2012): 37–53. www.pmi.org.

263 Stretton, Alan. "Complication. complexity and uncertainty in program/project context." *PM World Journal* VI, no. III (March 2017). www.pmworldtoday.com.

management are standard features. Here are some well-known types of contracts used in the field of project management:

Cost-reimbursable contract places maximum cost of risk and full responsibility for all costs and profit or loss on the buyer. The buyer compensates the seller for the seller's allowable price (defined by the contract), and the seller earns their profit if the deliverables meet the specified performance criteria. We can distinguish here three approaches at least:

- The cost-plus and fixed-fee approach reimburses all legitimate supplier costs, including negotiated fixed fees earned upon the delivery of the end product.
- The cost-plus and incentive fee approach provides an initial negotiated baseline cost and fee that may change depending on the total permissible cost and fee.
- The fixed-price incentive approach provides an initial negotiated minimum baseline and maximum allowed cost. The supplier earns a profit as a factored value of subcontractor's accrued cost between the plus and minus changes from the baseline costs.

Fixed-price contract is the most favorable type of contract/subcontract, as it allows for determining and confirming a price that is not subject to adjustment in a later period. This type of contract places the maximum cost risk and full responsibility for all costs and profit or loss on the contractor/supplier. The bidding process always precedes this type of contract to obtain the best possible specifications and accomplishments in terms of the project's scope, cost, and timeframe for completion.

Netscher describes in more detail the contract types and subjects closely related to the contract documents. It may include the laws governing the contract, letters of intent, documents/records, client's obligations, project designer's obligations, managing contractor's obligations, change orders, claims, force majeure, insurance claims, resolving disputes, terminating the contract, and so on (Netscher 2014, 204–216).[264]

Contracts are a huge and highly complex subject, and the reader engaged in a real-time project should get more insights about them by studying standard contracts utilized in the government, public or private industrial/manufacturing

264 Netscher, Paul. *Successful Construction Project Management.* Subiaco, Australia: Panet Publications, 2014.

sectors, or other corporate entities. Besides, the reader should study classic references (Ayers 1984),[265] contemporary references, (Pickavance February 2013),[266] literature on comprehensive structures of contracts (Kotb, Abo Al Anwar, and Baraka August 2019),[267] and FIDIC's *Red Book* (Kotb, Abo Al Anwar, and Baraka September 2019).[268]

Control account plan—Control Account Plan or CAP describes management control points. Each CAP point is related to activities with specific scope, time, cost or cost of resources, cost accounts, and responsibility. The cost account manager reports to both the project manager and the functional manager.

Cost account code—Cost accounts codes help to plan and control project costs. Cost account code is usually assigned to each activity; however, we can assign a cost account code to a work package presented by a single-task activity or hammock activity. In that case, we cannot control the details of a work package. Each cost account code may be associated with one or more cost account categories. As a project involves many systems, associated structures, and control levels, the cost accounts help with identifying, categorizing, and managing such complexities. Besides, cost account codes must have clear relations with the company's general cost accounting system.

We use the cost accounts structure to assign each activity a cost account code in order to summarize activity cost for higher structure and control account plans. Cost account code is related to the lowest elements of the WBS and OBS structures. For example, if work packages describe the lowest level of scope definition, then each activity within a work package may contain a cost account code. Or to put it simply, we can present a work package by a single-task activity or hammock activity that spans a set of work package activities and assign a single cost account code to activity that represents the work package. But this simplification may miss the cost control of work package details. After setting the

265 Ayers, Chesley. *Specifications for architecture. engineering and construction.* New York, NY: McGraw-Hill Book Company. (1984).

266 Pickavance, Keith. "A New Construction Contract for the 21st Century" *PM World Journal* II, no. II (February 2013). www.pmworldjournal.net.

267 Kotb, Mostafa, and Mohamed Abo Al Anwar, and Haytham Baraka. "In-depth View on the Construction Contracts." *PM World Journal* VIII, no. VII (August 2019): www.pmworldjournal.net.

268 Kotb, Mostafa, Mohamed Abo Al Anwar, and Haytham Baraka. "The Main characteristics of FIDIC Red Book 2017." *PM World Journal* VIII, no. VIII (September 2019): www.pmworldjournal.net.

cost account code, we must associate it with cost account categories (e.g., labor, material, equipment, expenses, and subcontract). Here is an example of project cost accounts and cost account categories:

Activity (Task or Hammock)

Attributed to cost of resources, resources, or factored value of total resources where each cost or resource is assigned by the cost accounts including contract works, change orders, contingency, retainers, A/E fee, PM fee, permits, reimbursements, general conditions, raw materials, stationary equipment, movable equipment, furniture, overheads, profits, financing, land, insurance, and so on.

And each cost account is attributed to a cost account category including labor, material, equipment, subcontracts, expenses, and so on.

Cost accounting standard—The standard established under public law with the main objective of realizing consistency in cost accounting practice.

Cost breakdown structure—A structure in terms of costs and cost categories intended to manage project costs. In some instances, the structure must be consistent with cost accounting standards.

Cost of PMP—Cost of PMP is a highly contentious and much-criticized aspect in project management. Many studies reiterate that PMP is an important professional area and project cost-saving tool. Krazert and Houser review the cost of regulation of earned value management (EVM) and the cost of program management. The benchmark for estimating the cost of regulation of earned value management to the industry is 0.9% of the total program cost. The program management cost ranges from 10% for the contractor and 16.6% of the total program costs for the federal agency. Authors argue that "mature and quality EVM implementations, as a part of an overall approach to integrated program management, have cost savings that more than offset the cost of implementing and maintaining EVM." Besides, authors support the general understanding that "the effective application of integrated program management to any program or project requires planning, execution, performance analysis, and reporting whether or not EVM is used" (Krazert Houser 2006, 1, 7–9). The results of the above studies, one performed by a general contractor and the other by the federal agency, show that:

The quality or mature EVM implementations do not have an average higher total cost of integrated program management as compared with programs with low quality or immature EVM implementations. (Krazert and Houser 2006, 9)[269]

269 Krazert, Keith, and Joseph Houser. "Cost of Earned Value Management." *The*

However, the authors warn that the level of detail and discipline used by organizations and programs vary and, hence, the cost incurred for these activities will also vary between organizations.

Some examples show that even 1% of the total project cost for developing and implementing a project management plan is a cost-saving tool by producing better management information, understanding project trends, and keeping the project under control.

To draw some commonsensical assumptions from the above cost structures and results, we may look at an example of the construction project structure and related cost percentages:

A/E fees—7%
 Concept—2%
 Construction Documents—3.5%
 Permits—0.5%
 Documents implementation—1%
PM fees—4%
 Project management plan—1%
 Project manager and other staff—3%
Construction contract—74%
Equipment—5%
Contingency—10%

Reduced PMP is the problem because project results are correlated with spending on planning services. To be a project cost-saving tool, the average project planning service cost, excluding the salaries of project manager and his staff, should range from 0.25% to 1% of the total project cost. It depends primarily on the project type, size, and involvement of technology management and other professional services. The maximum percentage of total project cost for project planning service is related to high complexity and small-sized projects. For example:

- 0.75%–1% for refineries, petrochemical, chemicals, cleanup, baggage handling projects;
- 0.5%–0.75% for airports, dams, ports, bridges, hospitals, public transportation projects;

Measurable News (Fall 2006): 1, 7–9. www.mycpm.org.

- 0.25%–0.5% for banks, office buildings, shopping malls, schools, family housing projects.

Suppose the project management plan integrates the payment application process, cost accounting function, and ongoing financial risks and benefits analysis in relation to project costs. In that case, the service cost for PMP may range from 1% to 2% of the total project cost. When the total cost for PMP service is estimated, it should be distributed to managers and their staff as follows: 50% for project planning manager, 25% for technology manager, 7% for cost estimating manager, 7% for procurement manager, 4% for cost accounting manager, 3% for the quality manager, 2% for risk manager, and 2% for the project's administrative staff. The PMP service's total cost should be distributed as follows: 30% for the development of the project management plan and 70% for its implementation.

Cumulative flow diagram—A chart indicating features completed over time, features in other state of development, and those in backlog (PMI 2021, 238).

Daily standup—A brief, daily collaboration meeting in which the team reviews progress from the previous day, declares intentions for the current day, and highlights obstacles encountered or anticipated (PMI 2021, 238).

Design structure system—Steward explains how the Design Structure System (DSS) or flowchart of design information differs from critical path techniques and enhances the complex system's design planning. The author argues that DSS can be used to organize and develop an engineering plan and show information flow during the design work. It helps track the changes and impacts of any variable within the system and the schedule of work arising from such changes. Steward acknowledges that DSS does not replace the CPM but provides the preliminary analysis required before using the CPM (Steward 1981, 73).[270]

A flowchart depicts circular relationships and technological processes but not the technological plan. To transform the technological process into a technological plan, we must use a network planning diagram (NPD) besides the flowchart.

A circular causal premise for the relationships in an activity or group of activities is not an actual project's characteristic. When we talk about relationships in the project, we certainly think about linear, that is, sequential relationships that spring from the most detailed and knowable project content element, that is,

270 Steward, Donald. "The Design Structure System: A Method for Managing the Design of Complex Systems." *IEEE Transactions on Engineering Management* 28, no. 3 (1981): 71–74.

project activities. The activities or their parts are regularly assessed and updated at a data date. We cannot add, modify, or delete events before the data date; what happened before the data date is over, and we cannot go back to an earlier data date. Therefore, circular or the more-complex-than-circular relations cannot be an example for what happens in real-life projects in this context, and they should not be confused with updating of an activity while the project activities are subjected to review under the feedback loop on the data date.

When we initiate a situation that requires a change in plan, regardless of causes and time of occurrence, we have to deal with the plan's current conditions as of the data date. This situation can result in positive or negative change orders or field orders. If we developed a sequence of activities in more detail, we could minimize arguing about a circular flow of activities.

I was once required to use a fragmented form of design structure system. It was a complicated design project where several design disciplines used several types of design sequences that can be generalized as follows: "Program Data," "Conceptual Documents," "System Integration," "Preliminary Documents," "Final Documents' and "Final Check." This holistic sequence of activities involved ambiguous overlaps and circular considerations of work progress that obstructed the relationships among actions, updating procedure, justification of accomplished work, and payment requests. All of these problems point to the impossibility of using network diagrams as an alternative for the design sequence's "unavoidable" circular relationships.

We changed this later by introducing critical control points for the sequence, which improved the ability to assess the work accomplished and transition the design activity or a part of it to the next phase. For example, the end of the "Preliminary Documents" activity shows that:

- The due submittals are delivered.
- The long-lead item characteristics are specified.
- The layouts are completed.
- The drawings are 50% complete.
- The major catalog and structural attachments get approvals.
- The preliminary time and cost estimates for the project ranged from –10% to +25%.
- The major changes and decisions between the client and the project engineer are final.
- The work on the final documents of the project can proceed.

Better disambiguation of the design sequence has been achieved by breaking down each activity of the above design process into sufficient details and showing the exchange of information among performers. Such a linear sequence allowed for concurrent and controlled development of the design process and improved payment requests. Finally, this caused a holistic sequence of activities and circular or more-complex-than-circular causal premises to be wiped out from the design planning process.

DevOps—A collection of practices for creating a smooth flow of deliverables by improving collaboration between development and operation (PMI 2021, 239).

Effort types—In practice, the project measurement plan consists of three types of effort classified as follows: discrete effort, the level of effort, and apportioned effort. These efforts are summarized as follows:

- The discrete effort or task activity with a specific product or result earned through measured progress is calculated in three ways. First, as earning related to percentage of completion of an activity; second, as a 50/50 earning for activity in a timeframe comprising less than three periods—50% paid at the start of the activity and 50% paid after the completion of the activity, and third, 0/100 is earned for completing an activity with a timeframe comprising just one period, that is, 100% to be paid only after the completion of the activity.
- The level of effort or hammock activity allows for earnings through elapsed time rather than for performance; that is, project manager and staff, scheduling, contract administration, field engineering support, and others are usually paid based on elapsed time. Therefore, the level of effort has no schedule variance but can have cost variance.
- A task activity allows for earning through its direct relationship with other task activities. For example, fees for factory inspection are earned as a percentage of direct factory labor (Fleming and Koppelman 2000, 88-96, 168-168, 174, 185, 200).

Factual project documentation—It shows information identified in regards to project environments, contents, works, people, or products through documentary evidence. Both the narrative and structural approaches are equally crucial for recording and updating the documentation on project management contents.

Feasibility study—Feasibility study is a tool designed to prepare socially, technically, financially, and economically feasible projects.

Features—A set of related requirements or functionalities that provide value to an organization (PMI 2021, 240).

Feedback—Feedback theory has been applied in project management to handle how processes, primarily the planning, executing, controlling, and back to planning, are related to another by their outputs/inputs. The continuous and sequential exchanges of information between the processes apply to all activities during the implementation of the project management plan.

There is a variety of models that present the project management feedback processes. Today's feedback mechanism belongs to engineering and mathematics; it has roots in dynamic theory, feedback, or control theory that handles a dynamic system's behavior. A summary of thoughts and observations on this topic is presented as follows:

- The earliest idea that reminds us of project management feedback processes comes from Francis Bacon in our search. "The concept of PDCA [plan-do-check-act] is based on the scientific method, as developed from Francis Bacon's work (Novum Organum, 1620). The scientific method can be written as 'hypothesis'–'experiment'–'evaluation," or plan, do and check" (Wikipedia 2013).[271]
- According to Wiener, the "first significant paper on feedback mechanism is an article on governors, which was published by physicist Clerk Maxwell in 1868" (Wiener 1965, 11).[272] Maxwell became the first to produce an effective theoretical and mathematical analysis of a control system and can be considered the founder of feedback theory.
- Maxwell defines a feedback mechanism observing the governor, a part of the steam machine. Accordingly, "a governor is a part of a machine by means of which the velocity of the machine is kept nearly uniform, notwithstanding variations in the driving-power or the resistance." He developed a formal analysis and mathematical formulation for the governors, hoping to direct the engineers' and

271 Wikipedia (1). *Shewhart Cycle.* http://en.wikipedia.org/wiki/Shewhart_cycle. Retrieved 5/11/2013.

272 Wiener, Norbert. *Cybernetics or Control and Communication in the Animal and the Machine. Second edition.* Cambridge, MA: The MIT Press, 1965.

mathematicians' attention to such governors' dynamic theory (Maxwell 1868, 1).[273]

- Fayol, a great pioneer, gets the credit for the first definition of project management feedback. He was the first person who listed management functions as planning, organizing, command, coordination, and control. He also formulated several principles as guides for managerial actions (Mee 1963, 870).[274]
- Forrester (1918), the founder of system dynamics, a field closely related to feedback control theory, had made significant progress in modeling business systems. Forrester described the structure and principles of systems in industry and economy that involved technology and people. He was aware that system dynamics is an aspect of system theory. Forrester cautioned on "the difficulty in identifying and expressing the body of universal principles that explain the successes and failures of the systems of which we are a part" (Forrester 1968, 1/2).[275]
- The lasting and straightforward definition of feedback comes from Wiener: "when we desire a motion to follow a given pattern the difference between this pattern and the actually performed motion is used as a new input to cause the part regulated to move in such a way as to bring its motion closer to that given by the pattern" (Wiener 1965, 6–7). Wiener had also put much effort into analyzing and discussing social science, but he did not see much progress in this area (Wiener 1965, 164).
- Bale states that feedback principles in studies of living open systems are feasible. Accordingly, "in relation to the self-stabilizing and self-organizing nature of a system (i.e., cybernetic stability), the mutual causal effects of feedback have been recognized as invaluable tools for appropriately explaining the interaction observed in the relationships of a system with its environment" (Bale 1995, 18).[276]

273 Maxwell, James. "On Governors." *Proceedings of the Royal Society* Volume XVI, Number 100 (1868): 270-283. Retrieved 10/2/2011. http://seit.unsw.adfa.edu.au/staff/sites/hrp/historicalpapers/ongovernors.pdf.

274 Mee, John. *The Encyclopedia of Management*, Edited by Carl Heyel. New York, NY: Reinhold Publishing Corporation1 (1963): 865–71.

275 Forrester, Jay. *Principles of Systems*. Cambridge, MA: Productivity Press, 1968.

276 Bale, Lawrence. "Gregory Bateson, Cybernetics, and the Social / Behavioral Science." *Cybernetics & Human Knowing* 3, no. 1 (1995): www.narberthpa.com.

- Abdel-Hamid explores the interactions between technology and management activities and the role of mental models in project decision-making. The author "examines models of project planning and control, discusses some of their limitations, and proposes tools to address the associated deficiencies" (Abdel-Hamid 2011, 17).[277] "The model captures the richness and complexity of the NASA software development environment in great detail and uniquely integrates the engineering-type functions (designing, coding, and quality assurance) with the management-type functions (planning, controlling, and staffing)" (Abdel-Hamid 2011, 18). The author has observed how continuous monitoring of project status, progress, causes, and forecasts results in an adaptive and dynamic decision related to cost, schedule, and staffing strategies as a project progresses through the lifecycle. Abdel-Hamid recognized the nature of project management and the role of feedback in project management. He demonstrates how to derive environment-specific conditions and use computer simulation to improve decision-making in project management.
- Doyle et al. describe a theoretical approach to the feedback control system that we can use as a starting point in mapping project management feedback. The authors provide a basic concept of the feedback system (Doyle, Francis, and Tannenbaum 1992, chapter 3).[278] In Chapter 5, I added my comments to help the reader understand how the general feedback terminology is related to general management and PMP.

Feeding buffer (CCM)—It is a time buffer at the points where a feeding path merges with the critical path (Goldratt 1997, 158).

Graphs—Leonard Euler (1707–1783), a mathematician and philosopher, was born at Basel in Switzerland (Copes, Sloyer, Stark, and Sacco 1987, 54).[279] Euler is considered the founder of graph theory, a recognized mathematical field that is continuously advancing in theory and application.

277 Abdel-Hamid, Tarek K. "Single-Loop Project Controls: Reigning Paradigms or Straitjackets?" *Project Management Journal* 42, no. 1 (February 2011): 17–30.

278 Doyle, John, Bruce Francis, and Allen Tannenbaum. *Feedback Control Theory.* Mineola, NY: Dover Publications, 1992.

279 Copes, Wayne, Clifford Sloyer, Robert Stark, and William Sacco. *Graph Theory: Euler's Rich Legacy.* Providence: Janson Publications, 1987.

Euler's developed this method to find solutions for an old problem—the Konigsberg Bridges problem. Roper analyzes the Konigsberg Bridges problem and its solution, in Euler's own words. Here is Euler's question:

The question is whether a person can plan a walk in such a way that he will cross each of these bridges once but not more than once. (Roper, 2012, 15, quoting Euler)[280]

In a detailed analysis of the problem, Roper shows Euler's thinking in his quest to find a theoretical approach first:

But making an effort, however, of trying to find such an arrangement, we do well to consider whether its existence is even theoretically possible or not" (Roper 2012, 18, quoting Euler)

Euler's approach shows that the answer is negative for the Konigsberg Bridges problem and that his method can solve similar problems. Roper notes that Euler's "methods developed in the paper were pioneering for developing modern topology and graph theory" and describes the path from an empirical problem to graph theory (Roper 2012, 15-27). In continuation of this discussion, I will recap some of the graph elements to help the reader understand how the graph is related to the WBS and CPM.

A graph is defined with a set of points called nodes, or vertices, for example, the CPM events, and a set of lines called edges, or arrows called arcs, for example, the CPM activities, which connect pairs of vertices. There are different types of finite graphs oriented to problems in specific disciplines. The formulation of "tree" graphs [I] is the base for WBS and other similar structures (risk, decision-making) and the formulation of "transport" graphs [II] is the base for CPM and other network diagram methods. Accordingly:

- [I] A tree is defined as a finite connected graph with no cycles and possessing at least two vertices (Berge 2001, 152–164).
- [II] A transport network is a finite connected graph without loops (cycle or circuit, that is, feedback to past event, in which associated with each arc "u" is number—"c(u) ≥ 0"which we will call the capacity [activity attributes] of the arc u)(Berge 2001, 71–85).[281]

280 Roper, Duncan. "Euler and the Konigsberg Bridges: Some Lessons for the Philosophy of Mathematics." *School of Quantitative Methods and Mathematical Science. University of Western Sydney. Australia.* (Retrieved: April 2021).

281 Berge, Claude. *The Theory of Graphs.* Mineola, NY: Dover Publications, 2001.

Governance—The framework for directing and enabling an organization through its established policies, practices, and other relevant documentation (PMI 2021 240).

Holon—A "holon" is a relatively new term. It requires balancing opposite perspectives, individual and whole, short term and long term, and the front and the reverse. Miyake wrote:

At a certain stage in social and corporate development, it becomes vital to emphasize the relationship between the individual and the whole, the whole and the individual, and to act with an eye to harmony between the two. (Miyake 2005, 2)[282]

Human communications—Human communications can be classified into two broad groups; structural and narrative. Both forms of communication help explain the research and application paradigms. The following references remind us of some of the essential characteristics of structural and narrative forms of human communications.

The structural communication approach (epistemology, theory of knowledge) to usage, application, and methods has the following characteristics:

> Usage: We use a structural form of communication for events characterized by structural simplicity and comprehensiveness. Those events allow for argumentation, determination, quantification, analysis, and optimization.
> Application: Kurtz and Snowden bring additional thinking to the discipline of project management. The authors describe the Cynefin framework, a sense-making device that helps people make predictive action. The Cynefin framework has five domains:

- Ordered domain, known causes, and effects
- Ordered domain, knowable causes, and effects
- Unordered domain, complex relationships
- Unordered domain, chaos
- Domain of disorder.

We can apply the structural method of communication for domains where causes and effects are known or knowable. For the known causes and effects,

282 Miyake, Michiaki. "Management in a Digital Network Era. Reductionism and Holonic Management." IIST World Forum, (November 2005): www.cfiec.jp/wf/magazine/0387/0387.

the "structured techniques are not only desirable but mandatory" in this space. For the knowable causes and effects, "structured techniques are desirable, but assumptions must be open to examination and challenge" (Kurtz and Snowden 2003, 68–69).[283]

Methods: Deduce the problem's holistic view and understand its details. We can gradually approach the problem using the top-down analysis by detailing, examining, classifying, and relocating the activity cluster's components. The process is accomplished by the debugging and sensing components of the structure. Induce the problem's detailed information and understand its holistic view. We can approach the problem using the bottom-up synthesis by combining scattered details to recognize higher-level clusters and the problem's messages. The process is accomplished by the debugging and sensing components of the structure. Best results come from the combination of deduction and induction processes. Repeat the processes until the difference in contents between the analysis and synthesis becomes insignificant. Add to the components of the structure the descriptions that appeal to the user's sense. Test the structure in a real project.

The narrative communication approach (ontology, metaphysical reasoning) to usage, application, and methods have the following characteristics:

> Usage: We use a narrative form of communication for events characterized by holistic complexity and ambiguity. Those events allow for creating descriptions, stochastic variables, qualification, reasoning, and choice.
> Application: Here is a brief note how Kurtz and Snowden approach the domain of complex relationships, unordered domains, and the domain of disorder:

- For complex relationships, the authors suggest that the "narrative techniques are particularly powerful in this space."
- For the unordered domain, the decision model is to "act quickly and decisively, to reduce the turbulence, and then to sense the reaction immediately so that we can respond accordingly."
- For the domain of disorder, the key is in reducing the disorder "toward achieving consensus as to the nature of the situation and the most appropriate response" (Kurtz and Snowden 2003, 469–470).

283 Kurtz, Cynthia, and David Snowden. The new dynamics of strategy: Sense-making in a complex and complicated world. *IBM System Journal* 42, no. 3 (2003): 462–83.

Method: Using the methods for sense-making—the narrative database, convergence methods, alternative history. For example, we might prepare in advance a narrative database of relevant stories surrounding the issue, drawn from oral histories, collected anecdotes, published reports, historical documents, and the like (Kurtz and Snowden 2003, 471). For this purpose, we can also use Fisher's method of narrative rationality of good reason that adds elements of the structural approach to elevate the logic of reasons into the logic of good reasons (Fisher 1987, xii).[284]

Incentive schemes—The organization is interested in a product and wants to develop it within a given budget and timeframe and based on specifications and features that are desired for and expected of the product. If the contractor fulfills these conditions, the organization is prepared to pay him a reward negotiated between both parties (Vandeput 1972, 333).[285]

Integrative process—Combining and coordinating diverse (distinctly dissimilar or unlike) elements into a whole (TranCreative Software 2010).

Liquidated damage—An amount specified in a construction contract covers damages incurred by the owner due to the contractor's failure to complete the work within the time frame outlined in the contract (Means 1991, 345).[286]

Management reserve—Management reserve is a portion of the management budget for future use when an unexpected condition or a schedule value item cannot be covered by planned amount or contingency. Management reserve is not a part of the project plan but may serve as a short-term loan.

Material planning—Most material control points should show in the project plan as secondary logic, that is, standard equipment specified and procured from stocks (measuring equipment, transformers, pumps, pipes, reinforcements, concrete, fences, etc.). However, most supply chain activities belong to primary logic, when special equipment passes through design, prototype, fabrication, and procurement as unique components (e.g., conveyors, motor control panels, sliding paths, etc.). Material planning is an important area of the project plan and

284 Fisher, Walter. *Human Communication as Narration: Toward a Philosophy of Reason, Value and Action.* Columbia, SC: University of South Carolina Press, 1987.

285 Vandeput, L. "Incentive Schemes as a Contract Management Tool." *ESRO, 1972. Project Management and Project Control, 10th Summer School.* Frascati, IT: European Space Research Organization, (1972): 333–48.

286 Means. *Illustrated Construction Dictionary.* Kingston, MA: R. S. Means Company, 1991.

must be methodically explained and closely coordinated with technology, procurement, and contract management.

Mathematical deduction—Mathematical deduction is research conducted to establish truth by deduction from chosen axioms and explanations (Author unknown).

Overall project duration—Many parameters determine project duration; however, the project's type and cost are the most influential parameters. The generic table "Project Duration" contains project duration in workdays (5 days a week), depending on project type and project value. We can use the same table to get the time in calendar days (7 days a week), weeks, or months. To transfer the table into:

- Calendar days, multiply the duration by 1.4
- Weeks, divide duration by 5
- Months, divide duration by 22.

Cost estimate, $ (milions)	0.2	0.5	1	2	5	10	20	50
Project type				Duration (work days)				
Development								
Project Total	170	370	520	680	910	1100	1340	1800
Design	85	185	260	340	455	550	670	900
Construction	85	185	260	340	455	550	670	900
Medical								
Project Total	80	180	260	340	450	550	670	900
Design	25	60	85	110	150	180	225	300
Construction	55	120	175	230	300	370	445	600
Residential								
Project Total	70	150	220	280	380	460	560	750
Design	20	40	60	80	110	130	160	215
Construction	50	110	160	200	270	330	400	535
Commercial								
Project Total	60	140	200	260	340	410	500	680
Design	15	35	50	65	85	105	125	170
Construction	45	105	150	195	255	305	375	510
Industrial								
Project Total	50	120	170	230	300	370	450	600
Design	10	20	35	50	65	85	100	135
Construction	40	100	135	180	235	285	350	465

Source: Abdomerovic, M.

Figure 8.1: Project Duration

Example: Industrial Project, Cost US$1.5 million

- Project duration = 170 + (230 – 170) × 50 / 100 = 200 work days
- Design duration = 35 + (50 – 35) × 50 / 100 = 42.5 work days
- Construction duration = 135 + (180 – 135) × 50 / 100 = 157.5 work days

Suppose a type of project structure is built for deliverables or work packages within each deliverable. In that case, we can use the above table to estimate the duration for each work package. Next, relate the work packages and get the duration for deliverables and the project. The table data are good enough for the preliminary development of the project time master plan.

Overall project money flow—Many parameters determine the project's money or cash flow; however, the project's type and duration are the most influential parameters. The generic table "Cash Flow Projection" assigns a percentage of project budget costs that should have been completed at a specific time period or phase of the project. After the project time master plan is completed:

- Choose a curve that closely represents the patterns of of spending for the whole project or for the different parts of its structure.
- Get discrete cash flow value for a specific step by multiplying the budget and corresponding factor for the discrete step.
- Get cumulative cash flow value to specific time series by multiplying project budget and factor for cumulative value.
- Get project cash flow for each time unit by summarizing values from the most detailed structural parts of the project master plan.

Cost distribution										
Linear, uniform										
Time series	1	2	3	4	5	6	7	8	9	10
Discrete value	10	10	10	10	10	10	10	10	10	10
Cumulative time	10	20	30	40	50	60	70	80	90	100
Cumulative value	10	20	30	40	50	60	70	80	90	100
Linear, three steps										
Time series	1	2	3	4	5	6	7	8	9	10
Discrete value	19	19	19	19	6	6	6	2	2	2
Cumulative time	10	20	30	40	50	60	70	80	90	100
Cumulative value	19	38	57	76	82	88	94	96	98	100
Non-linear, early loaded										
Time series	1	2	3	4	5	6	7	8	9	10
Discrete value	7	19	25	19	9	7	5	4	3	2
Cumulative time	10	20	30	40	50	60	70	80	90	100
Cumulative value	7	26	51	70	79	86	91	95	98	100
Non-linear, midle loaded										
Time series	1	2	3	4	5	6	7	8	9	10
Discrete value	2	5	8	15	20	20	15	8	5	2
Cumulative time	10	20	30	40	50	60	70	80	90	100
Cumulative value	2	7	15	30	50	70	85	93	98	100
Non-linear, late loaded										
Time series	1	2	3	4	5	6	7	8	9	10
Discrete value	2	3	4	5	7	9	19	25	19	7
Cumulative time	10	20	30	40	50	60	70	80	90	100
Cumulative value	2	5	9	14	21	30	49	74	93	100

Source: Abdomerovic, M.

Figure 8.2: Project Cash Flow

Suppose a project structure is built for deliverables or work packages within each deliverable. In that case, we can use the above table to develop the cash flow for each work package. The table data are good enough for the preliminary cash flow projection of the project management master plan.

Outcome—An end result or consequence of a process or project (PMI 2021, 243).

Paradigm—Paradigm is the generally accepted perspective of a particular discipline at a given time. The terms *paradigm* or *pattern* come from the Late Latin *paradigm* and the Greek *paradeigma* (TranCreative Software 2010)**.** An ideal example Solomon (1992, 100).[287] In science's philosophy, the paradigm is associated with Kuhn's influential book *The Structure of Scientific Revolutions* (Blackburn 2008, 266).[288] At the beginning of his book Kuhn wrote:

In this essay, "normal science means research firmly based upon one or more past scientific achievements, achievements that some particular scientific community acknowledges for a time as supplying the foundation for its further practice." (Kuhn 1996, 10)[289]

The author also explains the various aspects and conditions of discoveries, anomalies, repeated failures, and others to fit ake scientific ideas within a scientific community.

Particle—A particle is the most detailed and unique element of project management system contents. It shows the general character of essential project management knowledge described or asserted in the actual project documentation. For example, the particle "resource assignment" can be found in the actual project documentation containing information about the assignment of people, money, space, and so on. Particles are the definite knowledge of the project management system and the building blocks of its logic and higher structural components. The level of particles is the only platform that can fully explain the contents, relationships, and dynamics of a project management system. Following is a summary of the different particles commonly found in the project plan:

287 Solomon, Robert. *Introducing Philosophy: A Text with Integrated Readings.* Fort Worth, TX: Harcourt Brace Jovanovich College Publishers, 1992.

288 Blackburn, Simon. *The Oxford Dictionary of Philosophy.* 2nd Edition. New York, NY: Oxford University Press, 2008.

289 Kuhn, Thomas. *The Structure of Scientific Revolutions.* Chicago, IL: The University of Chicago Press, 1996.

- The open-end particle shows an element of the project management system process that has not a successor relationship. However, the project management system overlaps other disciplines, and open-end particles may pertain to other discipline inputs.
- The open-start particle shows an element of the project management system process that has no predecessor relationship. However, the project management system overlaps with other disciplines, and open-start particles may also intervene in the other disciplines' outputs.
- The relational particle shows conditions when controlling how an output particle is related to an input particle or particles. Both the output and input particles must have the same name, contents, and properties to be relational. Relational particles always maintain the finish-to-start relationship.

Project management particles are limited in number and only known in a general way; however, there are many project management systems where a known set of particles can be generated in unlimited numbers. Different needs, requirements, and conditions will undoubtedly lead to the selection and modification of processes and input/output chains of particles. Imagine how many different types of houses can be built by standard building elements.

Particle attributes—A particle attribute is a detail of a particle defined in association with factual project documentation elements. A particle of project management system logic, for example, "resource assignment," can be associated with the real project documentation through the "assignment of people." Then particle the "resource assignment" and the factual project documentation "assignment of people" can be associated through their attributes too, that is, properties for the particle's "resource assignment" (e.g., unit of measure, qualification, working conditions, associated risk, hiring/reassignment policy) and symmetric elements of factual project documentation's "assignment of people" (e.g., name, carpenter, project site, site safety, full-time position).

As the system approach to PMP becomes more intelligent, its particles and attributes tend to be more detailed to accommodate an automated development and implementation of the project management plan. Such a plan will almost independently drive the daily process of project and project business management.

Besides, well-defined attributes are the most likely base for developing a general theory of management applicable to any type and complexity of the human endeavor, including project management.

Payment application—A formal written request for payment by a contractor for work completed on a contract and, if allowed in the agreement, materials stored on the job site or in a warehouse (Means 1991, 24, 410). The client should acknowledge that it has received the insurance certificate, payment and performance bonds, and a signed contract before the first payment request.

Pending change order—An estimate of expected cost and time that will change the project contract shortly. It is a synonym to "request only" for price and time needed to implement a change or "bulletin." Sometimes, the pending change order may include different values for the priced pending changes, as well as forecasted unpriced pending changes.

Priced pending change order cost account shows that an estimated cost will soon affect the project cost. Therefore, by its nature:

- The pending cost is shown at the Cost Estimate at Completion for specific changes not yet approved.
- The budget pending cost is always shown as zero because we do not know what changes are definite during budgeting. We assign to pending change order cost a separate cost account.
- The Actual Cost and Earned Value categories for the pending cost are always shown as zero because pending change orders' activities always come after the data date.
- The budget variance for a pending change order shows how much money is needed to finance anticipated project changes.

Performance measurement baseline—It represents the time-phased project baseline or baseline plan against which the project's original and current plans measure and report project status, progress, and forecasts.

Phases—Project phases define technological processes and who is responsible for accomplishing each phase. Project phases should not be confused with the sequence of Agile's short-term investment phases. Project phases are represented as cyclic and lineal models.

- Wearne presents a cyclic model. His approach consists of eight phases (Wearne 1973, 10-16).[290]
- Halbertsma presents a lineal model that is running for decades and, in most parts, stands the test of time (Halbertsma 1972, 204–207).[291]

290 Wearne, Stephen. *Principles of Engineering Organization.* London, UK: Edward Arnold Publishers, 1973.

291 Halbertsma, K. *The Phased Development of New Industrial Products.* In: Project Management and Project Control. Frascati: ESRO 10th Summer School, 1972.

Wideman clarifies project phases by his distinctive term, the "project life span" (Wideman 2004, 53–71).[292] Wideman's presentation of relationships between corporate, facility/product, and project lifespans are of particular interest. The author explains the hierarchy of project lifespans within a corporate project business structure (Wideman 2004, 65–66).

Archibald gives a comprehensive list that includes 10 project categories and 36 subcategories together with their phases. He emphasizes that these models provide a major starting point for applying systems thinking to manage projects (Archibald 2004, Part 1[293],(Archibald 2004, Part 2)[294]

Recently, more innovation has come into the development of project phases, which is a result of viewing and understanding the project as a sustainable endeavor.

Planning methods—Early scientific approach to project management plan consisted lists of activities with some notes about activity attributes.

Gantt method—The first scientific planning method came from Henry L. Gantt, a pioneer of modern management. The author's invention, known as the Gantt charts, represents significant planning improvements, including in project planning. His voluminous work includes over 150 titles, some of which became the bases for future research (Wallace 1956).[295] Although these first methods did not provide precise formulas or solutions, they did promote a more systematic approach to planning.

LOB method—In Goodyear and Rubber Company 1941 year, a graphic methodology for planning was developed and named the Line of Balance or LOB (Mundorff 1963).[296] LOB method was developed primarily for planning mass production. Later on, the method was applied to projects with repetitive operations in real estate and construction, for example, construction of similar

292 Wideman, Max. *A Management Framework for Project, Program and Portfolio Integration.* Vancouver, BC: Trafford Publishing (UK), 2004.

293 Archibald, Russell. "Part 1 Projects, Programs, and Portfolios." *Max's Project Management Wisdom, Guest Article,* (2004): www.maxwideman.com.

294 Archibald, Russell. "Part 2 Project Life Cycle Models." *Max's Project Management Wisdom, Guest Article,* (2004): www.maxwideman.com.

295 Wallace, Clark. *The Gantt Chart.* In: Maynard. H. B. Ed. Industrial Engineering Handbook. New York, NY: McGraw Hill, 1956.

296 Mundorff, George. *The Encyclopedia of Management,* Edited by Carl Heyel. New York, NY: Reinhold Publishing Corporation1 (1963): 420–31.

buildings as apartment blocks (NBA 1968).[297] Although there were other methods which were successfully applied in the second part of the 20th century, the LOB method hasn't lost its significance and value. The LOB method is still improving and is one of the most useful methods in planning for repetitive operations. We can also find excellent development and application of simulation models based on the LOB method. The primary objective of these applications was to cope with variability in production projects. The essential works and the developmental models built based on LOB and described by Fine are still active (Fine 1969).[298] Soon after, a very successful application of the LOB method combined with the network planning method was recorded. When a project included unique and repetitive segments, repetitive components, even when a planning framework is a network diagram, it was considered that the LOB method was the best tool for supporting project planning process for each repetitive component (Lumsden 1968).[299]

Network planning methods—In the late 50th of the nineteen century the project management discipline had developed the essential tools for developing and implementing the project management plan. It was the period that witnessed the framing the theoretical and methodical background of network planning methods to solve a broad spectrum of problems in project planning. The mathematical base of the network planning methods was the theory of graphs, particularly the transportation graphs. The first mathematical solutions proposed in the new approach to planning were linear programming and the use of the computer. This early period saw the development of network diagraming methods; in 1958-1959, the development of Critical Path Method (CPM) and Program Evaluation and Review Technique (PERT) was followed by the development of the Precedence Diagramming Method (PDM) in 1962.

Kelley gets the credit for advancing the preceding works and developing the CPM mathematical base into its present form (Kelley and Walker 1959).[300] In December 1957, six engineers applied the Kelley–Walker method to the planning and scheduling of a US$10 million chemical plant in Louisville, Kentucky.

297 NBA, 1968. *Programming House Building by Line of Balance.* London, UK: The National Building Agency, 1968.

298 Fine, Brian. *Management Game (Lecture notes at the University of Loughborough, UK).* Costain, Operational research department. London, UK: February 1969.

299 Lumsden, Philip. *The Line of Balance Method.* London, UK: Pergamon Press, 1968.

300 Kelley, J., and Walker, M. "Critical Path Planning and Scheduling." *Proceeding of the Eastern Joint Computer Conference* (December 1959): 160–73.

Shortly after, the project plan was updated and "required only about 10 percent of the original effort" (O'Brien 1969, 34–36).[301]

The PERT's research objective was to design a management control system for developing the Polaris missile system, a program whose activities were subject to a considerable degree of uncertainty, being widely spaced geographically. Experts from Lockheed (Young and Lennon) and Booz, Allen, and Hamilton accomplished most of their goals using the new planning method (Malcolm, Roseboom, Clark, and Fazar 1959).[302] Their key accomplishment was the recognition of uncertainty in relation to completion of activity as per time schedule and how to tackle time constraints in accomplishing a project task or activity (Moder and Phillips 1969, 1–14, 192–229).[303]

The CPM and PERT came to practice in the industry almost simultaneously, and we assume that they were developed independently. The arrival of these two methods triggered the development of other methods with similar characteristics. A well-known blend of elements from both methods is the PDM (Fondahl 1961, 1962).[304], (Fondahl 1962)[305]

The PERT research team directed by W. Fazar later developed a comprehensive and highly popular procedure for integrated planning and controlling project costs and time schedule. The system underwent further development and its application became more widespread since July 1962 (DOD and NASA Guide 1962, 9).[306]

301 O'Brien, James. *Scheduling Handbook.* New York, NY: McGraw-Hill Book Company, 1969.

302 Malcom. D. G., Roseboom. J. H., Clark. C. E, and Fazar. W. "Applications of a Technique for Research and Development Program Evaluation." *Operations Research 7* (1959): 646–69.

303 Moder, Joseph, and Cecil Phillips. *Project Management with CPM and PERT.* New York, NY: Van Nostrand Reinhold, 1964.

304 Fondahl, John. "A Non-computer Approach to the Critical Path Method for the Construction Industry," 1st Edition. *Stanford University, Department of Civil Engineering*, 1961.

305 Fondahl, John. "A Non-computer Approach to the Critical Path Method for the Construction Industry," 2nd Edition. *Stanford University, Department of Civil Engineering*, 1962.

306 DOD and NASA Guide. *PERT COST: Systems Design*. Office of the Secretary of Defense and National Aeronautics and Space Administration, 1962.

Fromm the early 1960 of the nineteen century, the CPM or PDM network diagram application dominated the project management plan development and implementation. Between the early 1980s and the present times, the PDM has become an exclusive project planning method. The principles of network diagraming, combined with other tools such as WBS and Feedback methods, became the cornerstones of, and were applied universally to, project and project business management.

Since the 1960s, the scientific development and implementation of project management plan have gradually gained prominence in PMP practice. Numerous published works describe the successful application of scientific approach to PMP. In general, the papers published 40 or 50 years ago document that the project management world has developed a tool that could improve the project scope, time, and cost.

While PMP is relevant to project success, the development and implementation of PMP tools are not being utilized in practice as much as they should be. Calls for a change followed the successful scientific project management application, and a new trend in project management became a reality. It was started based on observations that indicated that many projects had recorded massive overruns in terms of the scope, time, and cost. Statistics, case studies, and actions to improve the situations supported the need for change.

GERT method—We must also recall here the development of the Graphical Evaluation and Review Technique (GERT), which helps analyze network planning diagrams with stochastics characteristics (Pritsker 1966).[307] This method enables the user to load an NPD with activities describing all possible project development alternatives. It differed from the earlier methods—namely, the PERT, CPM, and PDM and led to an approach to planning where not all plan activities were needed to be accomplished to complete the project. The GERT enables the user to install several durations for each activity to calculate alternatives and based on them calculate the probabilities of completing the project.

Significant support for developing and applying scientific methods for project planning came with the use of computers and simulation models to better predict project outcomes. The application of simulation models was also proven essential to solve some stochastic problems which we thought mistakenly the PERT would easily resolve.

307 Pritsker, A. A. B. *GERT: Graphical Evaluation and Review Technique.* Santa Monica, CA, The RAND Corporation, 1966.

Current PMP methods are applicable and practical for any situation needed to engage resources during a specific period. The research and application of network planning methods have been flourishing while it has clearly been acknowledged that the project management now has a tool that helps develop and implement a more efficient and precise project management plan. Since then, these methods, combined with advanced computing and better approaches, represent the most significant paradigm to have occurred in the history of developing and implementing project management plans.

It took decades of developmental work for PMP to reach its contemporary. For example, evolution and lasting legacy of the earned value body of knowledge, from the PERT/Cost in 1962, followed by C/SCSC in 1967-1996 and the EIA-748D 2019 to Simple EVPM adopted for private industry (Fleming and Koppelman 2000, 25–33, 36–45, 141–149), is essential for project management. Many publishers cover the continuous development process and application of the earned value body of knowledge, for example, "The Measurable News," published by the College of Performance Management.

Continuous calls for PMP changes caused by misunderstandings and downsizing planning skills resulted in the continuous development of traditional methods (Trietsch and Baker, 2012).[308]

Program—A temporary organization established to cloud projects that develop their plans and relationships to align with plans of other projects in the program and outside the program. The complexity of individual projects and their relationships define the complexity of the program.

Project—"Any piece of work that is undertaken or attempted" (TransCreative Software 2010). A project is a dynamic mission defined by a time-oriented network of project activities and their attributes. The project is developed in a temporary organization that hosts a project management team to develop and implement a project management plan. A project organization can have different:

- Organizational names (project, project management service, project function, project department, project office, or project company)
- Services (project management, multi-project management, program management, project portfolio management, management by projects, operation and maintenance of project)

308 Trietsch, Dan, and Kenneth Baker. "PERT 21: Fitting PERT/CPM for use in the 21th century." *International Journal of Project Management* 30, no. 4 (May 2012): 490–502. www.elsevier.com/locate/ijproman.

- Typologies (centralized or decentralized)
- Models for project development (company-oriented model, a community of practice model, or third-party model)
- Relationships between project team and organization (collocated or virtual, permanent or outsourced project team).

Project organization begins when a project is formally authorized and the scope statement issued and ends when the project is handed over to the customer and the warranty expires.

Project buffer (CCM)—The project buffer is where we dampen the accumulated effects of all uncertainties (Goldratt 1997, 217).

Project management planning (PMP)—The act of the development and implementation of the project management plan. The project management plan is the organized, integrated, approved, and accepted project documentation, which helps manage dynamic conditions and actions related to project management contents and context. During this process, we usually deal with the following forms and values of different plans:

- Original plan—has the Planned at Completion attributes only.
- Baseline plan—has the Planned at Completion, Planned to Data Date, and Planned to Complete attributes.
- Current plan—has the Planned at Completion, Planned to Data Date, Planned to Complete, Earned to Data Date, Actual to Data Date, Estimate to Complete, Estimate at Completion attributes.

Project management and business management—Project management and business management may be closer than we thought. Drucker devoted much attention to analyzing and synthesizing general business (Drucker 1970). One of his statements summarizes, and which may have even ignited, the contemporary approach to the development of a management plan in general, including a project management plan:

There are three specific ways to find out what kind of a structure is needed to attain the objectives of a specific business: activity analysis, decision analysis, relations analysis. (Drucker 1970, 234–235)[309]

Drucker reminds us that "three analyses" should be applied to reveal the organizational structures the enterprise needs. The author observes that the

309 Drucker, Peter. *The Practice of Management.* London, UK: Pan Books, 1970.

activity analysis, decision analysis, relationship analysis, and synthesis need the "application of highly advanced tools of logical analysis and synthesis." Drucker doesn't specify or list the tools which we need; however, we would not be making a mistake if we assume that he was aware of the extraordinary power of the work breakdown structure and network diagramming the methods.

Suppose we consider the development of methodologies from the to late fties of the nineteen century to the present times and the scope of work to which Drucker referred. In that case, we should observe the symmetry between the development of the project management plan and business functions to accomplish the defined objectives. We may also find that the manufacturing projects' phases sound very similar to the manufacturing business's typical functions. Consequently, we can perceive how project and production management use the phases to connect with company business.

There is a strong belief in our community that project management is a part of general management. However, there is plenty of evidence to show that Drucker's approach to the analysis, relationships, and synthesis in the development of the management plan reassembles the analysis, relationships, and synthesis in the development of the project management plan. Although Drucker's approach does not discuss implementing a management plan, but highlights the feedback process which is a universal method and is equally applied in general management and project management.

Project management skills—Project management skills are the theme of this book since these are critical factors determining the project management's maturity in a company or organization.

Why is it that project team members do not often have the necessary skills? Can a skill-driven career attract young talents to commit to a long learning process? Are there experienced professionals to deliver the required training? Many scholars emphasize skills developments, and professionals in the field take it seriously.

- Besner argues that an extensive and well-known practice requires the use of specific tools and techniques to execute project processes (Besner et al. 2008, S123-S133).[310]

310 Besner, Claude, and Brian Hobbs. "Discriminating Contexts and Project Management Best Practices on Innovative and Noninnovative Projects." *Project Management Journal* Volume 39 (Supplement 2008): S123–S134. www.pmi.org

- Weaver notices the myth that anyone can schedule emerged. As a direct consequence of loss of skills, the importance of scheduling has dropped in most organizations and most projects run late (Weaver 2006, 8).[311]

Some studies discuss the general problems in regards to project management skills; however, the problem of lack of skills is real and should be addressed at the time of project feasibility study or much earlier.

Project management system—A collection of general project management system knowledge observed in various arrangements, contents, context, structures, and explanations of common messages.

Project management system logic—A common perspective for a collection of project management system knowledge in terms of principal mission, what the system knowledge brings up, what it means, and how we can use it. System logic holds the potential to drive general collections of project management system knowledge and transforms project management into a professional discipline.

Reductionism—Reductionism is an analytical method developed by Descartes. René Descartes (1596–1650)—mathematician, physicist, and philosopher—was born at La Haye in Touraine, France (Descartes 1952, ix–x).[312]

In *Rules for the Direction of the Mind* (Descartes 1952, 1–40), published 1629 in Holland, Descartes mostly describes reductionism, a method to discover the truth in science. He starts this journey to recognize a proposition that can be perceived and deduced in objects that enable understanding. He continues to "divide up each of the difficulties into as many parts as possible and learn the parental object. This orderly and continuous process ends when he arrives at the most simple objects we can observe 'clearly and distinctly'." The process then continues in the opposite direction, starting with the simplest objects and gradually reaches the level of the most complex knowledge through related objects and very similar steps. Descartes does not limit his method to a specific discipline or one of its domains.

I have summarized the rules for a quick insight into Descartes' method that may relate to some stages in the development and implementation of a management plan. The rules of the method are as follows:

311 Weaver, Patrick. "A Brief History of Scheduling." *Mosaic Project Services*, Australia (April 2006).

312 Descartes, Rene. *Rules for the Direction of the Mind.* In: Hutchins, Robert, Editor in chief, Great Books of the Western World, Volume 31. Chicago, IL: Encyclopedia Britannica, 1952.

- Rule I—The objectives of a unified methodology for searching truth in science come from the fact that the sciences are conjoined and interdependent.
- Rule II—Key differences between experience and deduction when approaching an object of the study and distinguishing the true from false.
- Rule III—Intuition that is based on evidence and needed for clarification of propositions, as well as deduction that derives its steps from known principles to the most simple facts are two complementary methods and "certain routes to knowledge."
- Rule IV—How two simple methods can lead the researcher progressively to "arrive at a true understanding" of the study.
- Rule V—How deductive processes "reduce obscure propositions step by step to those that are simpler" and then "ascend similar steps" and compile knowledge gathered in the preceding steps.
- Rule VI—How "certain truths can be known from others" and how the facts from this process can be organized in definite series.
- Rule VII—How matters of a completely deduced problem have to be "scrutinized" and how "enumeration" or induction of inventory has to be reviewed.
- Rule VIII—When we should stop analyzing a certain object of our study.
- Rule IX—How we can concentrate our attention on "what is easy and more readily understood" and then deduce one fact from another.
- Rule X—Why this method is easier to apply in disciplines with an established order and stay in close touch with numbers.
- Rule XI—How intuitive and deductive thinking works in understanding the associations between two propositions and "distinguishing … what is more or less relative."
- Rule XII—Topics of the method that have to be developed in more detail.
- Rules XIII, XIV, XV, and XVI show how a magnitude ("material body possessing extension and figure") of resolved problem can be determined from its facts and relationship to another already definite magnitude.
- Rules XVII–XXI show how a single proposition contains so many unknown magnitudes that they may all be subordinated to one another in succession, making a total magnitude equal to a certainly known magnitude.

Reductionism does not preclude emergent phenomena, but it does imply the ability to understand the emergent phenomena in terms of the process(es) from which it emerged (Reductionism, Wikipedia, Retrieved July 31, 2010).

Resource buffer (CCM)—A reminder for the resources, which doesn't change the elapsed time of the project (Goldratt 1997, 209).

Resource contention (CCM)—This means the same resource is supposed to be used in two different steps at a time (Goldratt 1997, 231).

Schedule of values—A listing of elements, systems, items, or other subdivisions of the work, establishing a value for each, whose totals equal the contract sum (Means 1991, 497). Schedule values are activities that describe the contents of the contract and help with carrying out activities such as planning, contracting, implementing, tracking, accepting, and paying for completed work.

Scientific historian's view—Many books use a narrative perspective to describe PMP. The *High Speed Velocity Management* by Muirhead and Simon is an exemplar narrative about implementing a project management plan. This book is a business novel and describes perfect examples from real project contents and context, known project management participants, real project actions, and success factors. For example, the following passage from this book may give the reader an idea about the context of discussions here:

[The Mars Pathfinder project] had come with neatly impossible constraints: go there at a fraction of the cost, do it in a fraction of the time, take risks but don't fail. (Muirhead and Simon 1999, front flap)[313]

The best part about this book is that it recognizes the interdependence between the structural and narrative approaches to PMP. Besides keeping a sense of the plan and adopting a plan to new situations that arise daily, we also need leadership excellence. Muirhead, the Mars Pathfinder project manager, has been aware that the project schedule is the critical framework for project success and managing such an extraordinary challenge.

Knowing there couldn't be any leeway in the schedule, I made up my mind that we would commit budget reserves as needed to help any manager in trouble keep from falling behind schedule. (Muirhead and Simon 1999, 41)

There is no general definition of the Faster, Better, Cheaper concept. While the idea defines structures, processes, relationships, and other analytics of traditional PMP, in its essence, this approach assumes widely accepted commitments to achieve gigantic goals. At the same time, Muirhead understands the limitation of the project management plan, which is just a leitmotif, not a faultless document. To cope with the unknowns, we must be ready to improvise on the theme.

313 Muirhead, Brian, and William Simon. *High Velocity Leadership: The Mars Pathfinder Approach to Faster, Bette, Cheaper.* New York, NY: HarperCollins Publishers, 1999.

It means updating the plan is a must, including usually avoided shots, preferential sequencing, lead/lag logic restraints, extended activity times, or imposed dates.

But in the world of Faster, Better, Cheaper, improvising should be seen as an inseparable part of [detail] planning, the other half of a complete process.… On Pathfinder, we had a plan but knew from the start that the plan was not going to be perfect, that when we met the enemy, we would need to be highly flexible. (Muirhead and Simon 1999, 193).

Specific calculations—There are calculation specifics for some activity attributes that we must test before applying the attributes. For example:

Budget—If a particular cost account resides on a single activity, all budgets for this cost account are assigned to that activity. Suppose a specific cost account resides in more than one activity. In that case, the proportion of each activity's budget should reflect the proportion of work for this activity. In general, if an activity has to be broken down into sub-activities for any reason, for example, planning, bidding, contracting, implementing, or controlling, then new activities must get appropriate attributes and values.

Estimate at Completion—Calculation of the estimate at completion depending on job progress and status for other cost categories:

- If the job did not start or a new estimate did not get completed, then the estimate at completion is equal to the budget. If we have a new estimate, then the estimate at completion is equal to the new estimate.
- If the job is in progress and a new estimate is not completed, then the estimate at completion is equal to the actual cost to date plus the remaining budget for the job. If a new estimate to complete has been made, then the estimate at completion is equal to the actual cost to date plus the estimate to complete.
- If the job is complete, then it is equal to the actual cost for the completed job.

The estimate-at-completion process is using all the above methods and other methods to produce a single value. During the project's progress, the method for calculating an estimate-at-completion cost is progressing too: from 0 (for a job not budgeted) to budget, to new estimate at completion, and, finally, to the actual cost for the completed job. There are many other very specific calculations for an estimate at completion, mostly depending on activity cost performance in previous periods.

Contingency—Contingency is a portion of the project budget held in reserve to finance the work changes due to unexpected problems and achieve the budget's original goals. Therefore, by its nature,

- the value for contingency is shown as a budget category because it is budgeted for unforeseen problems in the project and cannot be a negative value,
- its estimate at completion is always shown as zero because we estimate it to transfer its total value to re-budget other cost accounts in the project,
- its actual cost category and earned value category are always shown as zero because contingency resides at the activity after the data date,
- the contingency budget variance value is equal to the budget value (zero or positive value). It shows how much money is left in reserve to finance pending changes in the project.

We can distribute project contingency in two ways:

- Suppose the contingency is distributed to individual change orders (change order has the all attributes of a regular task activity). In that case, values for change orders add to the activities' budget and estimate at completion. Consequently, the contingency budget and the cumulative budget variance reduce the change order costs; the change orders estimate at completion are the same as in the budget, but the contingency estimate at completion is unchanged and stays zero while contingency budget variance is the same as in the contingency budget.
- Suppose the contingency is not distributed to individual change orders. In that case, the value for change orders spreads across many activities and adds to the project budget and estimate at completion. Consequently, the contingency budget and the cumulative budget variance reduce the change order costs.

After the contract is signed and real values are incorporated into the contract, the values of project cost accounts may not fit the budget. From that time to the job completion, the budget variance is calculated (budget minus estimate at completion) and balanced with contingency. Each "spending" of contingency will increase other cost accounts' budget value and decrease contingency budget variance. If the contingency has been exhausted, budget variances of other cost accounts show negative values, or there have been pending change orders that indicate negative values, it is then time for re-budgeting and compensating for cost accounts by using the management reserves.

So, contingency may change its value. For example, if a change order is negative, then the same amount of savings is made on contract cost and added to contingency. However, if a change order is positive, then the same amount of spending is made on contract cost and subtracted from contingency.

Pending Change Order—Pending cost estimates the anticipated cost that will soon affect the project's value. Therefore, by its nature:

- the pending value is shown under the estimate at completion category because it is estimated for certain changes not approved as yet.
- the pending budget category value is always zero; when the project gets the budget, we may not immediately know what changes are specific and where to transfer its estimate at completion.
- the values for pending actual cost and earned value categories are always shown as zero because the pending change order resides at the activity after the data date.
- the pending budget variance category value is zero or negative and shows how much money is needed to finance the anticipated project changes.

Sprint—A short-term interval within a project duration where a usable and potentially releasable increment of product is created (PMI 2012, 250).

State of the system—The term links to project management system contents and contents relationships as they are at the moment of observation.

Statistical mechanics—Statistical mechanics is the branch of physics that makes theoretical predictions about macroscopic systems' behavior based on statistical laws governing its component particles (TranCreative Software 2010).

Story—There are reminders to find the stories in a form that can be easily communicated and used to organize a database of project management facts. It is of special interest why Pells thinks that stories should come "from anyone and everyone working on the project" in order for them "to learn from other people … and mature in [their] capabilities and expertise" (Pells 2010, 1).[314] In his article, Pells uses the major project milestones as a source of project management stories and related questions to develop a story.

314 Pells, David. "Project Stories—the Largely Untapped World of Personal Experience & Lessons Learned in Project Management." *PM World Today* XII, no. IX (September 2010). www.pmworldjournal.com.

Story map—A visual model of all the features and functionality desired for a given product, created to give the team a holistic view of what they are building and why (PMI 2021, 250).

Story point—A unit used to estimate the relative level of effort needed to implement a user story (PMI 2021, 250).

Strategic and operational project management—Company's strategic project management is developed from company policy which also covers divisional views and responsibilities. According to Archibald, strategic project management consists of six important processes and related responsibilities:

- Select and authorize new projects and programs to be added to the organization's currently active project portfolios.
- Validate that each selected and authorized project and program properly support their currently approved strategic objectives.
- Prioritize all validated projects and programs within each established portfolio to allocate money and other key resources properly.
- Allocate key resources (money, skilled people, equipment, facilities, etc.) to each portfolio and each project and program therein.
- Establish the master schedule for each project portfolio, reflecting the established priorities and the approved allocation of money and other key resources to each project and program.
- Cancel or change the scope, schedule, and cost of approved projects and programs when such actions are required or justified (Archibald 2010, 3–4).[315]

After a comprehensive discussion of the above processes, the author notes that "five of the six strategic project management processes are the responsibilities of an organization's strategy managers and not its project/program managers" (Archibald 2010, 9).

As we see, strategic project management processes are outside the project; however, strategic requirements may significantly impact project and project management. Prieto notes that:

Strategic Business Objectives (SBO) become more important than requirements. In some instances, projects may be faced with emergent SBOs, especially

315 Archibald, Russell. "The Interfaces Between Strategic Management of an Enterprise and Project Portfolio Management Within the Enterprise." *PM World Today* XII, no. II (2010): www.pmworldjournal.net.

when "influencing vectors" cross the semi-permeable project boundary over an extended timeframe. (Prieto 2015, 26)[316]

Company operational project management as well as its more specific and measurable elements of management processes are developed in line with the organizational strategy. Archibald lists three crucial functions of operational project management and related responsibilities:

- Select and assign project and program managers.
- Design, select, and apply the best project lifecycle models for each project category.
- Select and implement the specific project planning, scheduling, executing, and controlling methods and software tools to be used (Archibald 2010, 4).

In turn, operational project management results may cause a reconsideration of the company's strategy and policy. Such a continuous exchange of information between policy, strategy, and operations for all projects and programs is developed through portfolio management, usually operated within the project management office.

Sustainability—Sustainability ideas in project management have emerged more than three decades ago and are mostly applied in big projects. For example:

- The UNIDO Manual for the Preparation of Industrial Feasibility Studies has organized project development into three key project phases: pre-investment, implementation, and operational (UNIDO ID/2006, 6).[317]
- The Brundtland Commission defined sustainable development as "the challenge of facing the future, and of safeguarding the interests of coming generations" (UN 1987, Chairman's Foreword).[318]

316 Prieto, Bob. "Project Management Theory of Large Complex Projects." *PM World Journal* IV, no VI (June 2015). www.pmworldtoday.net.

317 UNIDO ID/206. *Manual for the Preparation of Industrial Feasibility Studies.* New York, NY: United Nations International Centre for Industrial Studies of UNIDO, 1976.

318 UN 1987. *Our Common Future, Report on World Commission on Environment and Development.* United Nations, UN Documents, 1987.

Sustainability can be understood in a new way from the project management system's perspective, including the project lifespan or lifecycle. Hart argues that "thinking systematically, through the full range of challenges and opportunities is the first important step managers can take toward the creation of sustainable value" (Hart 2010, 87, 97–98).[319]

Brulin and Svensson discuss how we can achieve sustainability, the mechanisms for the sustainable development of projects, and disseminate project results to other areas. They wrote that "a result-oriented approach has to be based on an iterative learning system ... on joint knowledge formation in a global context and be based on theory and practice and being transparent" (Brulin and Svensson 2012, 2).[320]

Some project management thinkers take the challenge and write more specifically about "project management sustainability." Silvius et al. report an analysis of 56 case studies on the assimilation of sustainability concepts in project management. The authors question the scope of sustainability in the initiation, development, and management of projects. They found that "the way sustainability is currently considered shows the traditional 'less bad' approach to sustainability integration and not a more modern social responsibility approach" (Silvius, Schipper, Schipper, and Nedeski 2013, 1).[321]

Symmetry—Here are some excerpts from Weinberg's work addressing the symmetry in natural science that may give an insight in studying the exclusivity of methodological aspects of PMP:

- The symmetry principle is a simple statement that something looks the same from certain different points of view.
- The important symmetries are not the symmetries of things but the symmetries of laws (Weinberg 1992, 136–137).[322]

319 Hart, Stuart. *Capitalism at the Crossroads: Next Generation Business Strategies for a Post-Crisis World*, 3rd Edition. Upper Saddle, NJ: Prentice Hall (2010).

320 Brulin, Goran, and Lennart Svensson. "Sustainable Change in Large Projects." *PM World Journal* I, no. V (December 2012): www.pmworldjournal.net.

321 Silvius, Gilbert, and Ron Schipper, and Snezana Nedeski. "Sustainability in Project Management: Reality Bites." *PM World Journal* II, no. II (February 2013): www.pmworldjournal.net.

322 Weinberg, Steven. *Dreams of a final theory. The Scientist's Search for the Ultimate Laws of Nature.* New York, NY: Pantheon Books, 1992.

Time box—A short, fixed period of time in which work is to be completed (PMI 2021, 251).

Unexpected conditions—Unexpected conditions can arise from the complexity of project environment, objectives, politics, project management, project scope, financing, technology, qualified resources, coordination of related functions, contracts, stakeholders' interests, commercial and market conditions, decision-making, and other issues.

Unexpected conditions are scaling events from those that can be known to those that cannot be known. General intention to manage unexpected conditions is driven by analyzing specific situations and planning a contingency for unforeseen events. Just to mention a few models:

- Descartes shows how a single proposition contains so many unknown magnitudes that they may all subordinate to one another in succession, making the total magnitude equal to a specifically known magnitude (Descartes 1952, Rules XVII—XXI).
- Kurtz and Snowden describe a knowledge structure that can help understand unknown events by "relaxation of the assumptions" and a consensus of decision-makers to deduce the problem area. Their management approach assumes that events are the substance of a "structured process and uncertain conditions" within each domain described in more detail earlier (Kurtz and Snowden 2003, 469-470).
- Giezen favors the traditional approach, which is today typical in engineering and construction. He clears and summarizes this approach as follows: In engineering-based planning, uncertainty is reduced by cutting things into pieces (Giezen 2012).[323]
- Stretton discusses the list of elements in uncertainty management structures created and incorporated into project phases, project estimates, and project parties. The lists of elements within each structure can help reduce and better understand uncertainty in project/program management (Stretton 2017, 4–6).
- Merrett and Sykes argue that details are of prime importance in capital projects' economic and financial analysis because logical analysis alone

323 Giezen, Mendel. "Keeping it simple? A case study into advantages and disadvantages of reducing complexity in mega project planning." *International Journal of Project Management* 30, no. 7 (October 2012): 781–90. www.elsevier.com/locate/ijproman.

is insufficient to manage problems in this area (Merrett and Sykes 1971, xii–xiii).[324]

- Taleb is concerned only about events that we cannot predict, the Black Swan. He describes this by three factors: First is the *outlier*, named so because it lies outside the realm of regular expectations and because nothing in the past can convincingly point to its potential occurrence. Second, it carries an extreme impact. Third, despite its outlier status, human nature makes us concoct an explanation for its occurrence after the fact, making it explainable and predictable (Taleb 2010, xxii).[325]
- Tain thinks that changing the communication methods is helpful. Accordingly, adopting advanced technology can easily and quickly recognize patterns of surrounding events and help us act faster and better (Tain 2019).[326]
- Prieto explains a memorable term—*Black Elephants*. While Black Swan can have positive or negative implications, the Black Elephants have adverse connotations that people would rather avoid. The author argues that Elephants are not going away and that they should be recognized and dealt with early (Prieto 2020).[327]

Updating the project management plan—There are various approaches to updating the project management plan and protecting its data. Here is an example which describes a reduced automatic procedure:

Have the most recent file of the current plan, for example, CP01; the most recent file of baseline plan, for example, BP01; the working file of the current plan, for example, CP02; the working file of baseline plan, for example, BP02; the server backup file for the most recent current plan, for example, CP05; and the server backup file for the most recent baseline plan, for example, BP05. Backup

324 Merrett A. J., and Sykes Allen. *The Finance and Analysis of Capital Projects.* London, UK: Longman, 1971.

325 Taleb, Nassim. *The Black Swan.* New York, NY: Random House Trade Paperbacks, 2010.

326 Tain, David. "Capitalizing on Complexity in Modern Business Environments: A Network-Based Perspective for Projects and Organizations." *PM World Journal* VIII, no. II (February 2019). www.pmworldtoday.net.

327 Prieto, Bob. "Black Elephants." *PM World Journal* IX, no. VIII (August 2020). www.pmworldtoday.net.

CP01 to CP05 and BP01 to BP05; delete CP02 and BP02; copy CP01 as CP02 and BP01 as BP02. Consider the following:

- Baseline plan (before progress): Check options (*) Close baseline plan.
- Baseline plan (update progress): Set baseline plan equal to approved current plan before progress.
- Current plan (before progress): Check options (*). Close the current plan, then backup current and baseline plans as CP05 and BP05.
- Current plan (update progress): Spotlight the period between previous data date and the new data date. Update progress for activities within the spotlight. Run schedule after new data date. Collect data (locate contact persons, observe work progress, compile notes from recent meetings, and record percentage complete, start, and finish dates for activities). Delete unrealistic progress from activities where the update has automatically progressed. Check and compare the current budget with the baseline budget. Check and compare the results of current and baseline plans. Run schedule, observe results, fix percentage on tasks and summaries, and fix other changes. Open performance reports and compare the current plan's progress with its progress from the previous period, now the baseline plan.

Chose update options (*); for example, link remaining duration and schedule percentage complete, and subtract Actual from EAC. When quantities change use, use the current unit price to re-compute costs and check all three costs. Use the updated percentage complete against budget to estimate and check both. Link actual to date and actual this period. Link the budget and EAC for activities that have not progressed. Calculate variance as EAC – B. Calculating project cost values depends very much on selecting the update options, which we establish before developing the project plan.

Launch a new dated Backup folder; Copy CP05 and BP05 in the dated backup folder and working folder. Rename the copy in a working folder and post the renamed copy to the server. Backup CP01 to CP05, and BP01 to BP05. Delete CP02 and BP02. Copy CP01 as CP02 and BP01 as BP02.

When computing the percentage complete for summarization, the weighting factor is resource units. For planned value and earned value calculations, use budget from the current plan rather than budget from the baseline plan.

Keep a record of changes to scope, time, resource unit prices, cost, and other attributes for each update.

Value—The worth, importance, or usefulness of some elements or processes or products (PMI 2021, 251).

Value chart—A chart that tracks the rates at which the deliverables are provided, validated, and accepted within a predefined interval (PMI 2021, 252).

Value Delivery System—A collection of strategic business activities aimed at building, sustaining, and/or advancing an organization (PMI 2021, 251).

Variables of system contents—The system particles and relationships between the system particles are critical variables of project management system contents.

Bibliography

Aba, Wayne, David Pells, and Miles Shepherd. 2018. "Program Benefits Management: An International Best Practice the US Government Could Use." *PM World Journal* VII, no. VI (June 2018): www.pmworldjournal.net.

Abdel-Hamid, Tarek K. 2011. "Single-Loop Project Controls: Reigning Paradigms or Straitjackets?" *Project Management Journal* 42, no. 1 (February 2011): 17–30.

Abdomerovic, Muhamed. 1982. *Principles and Practice of Project Planning.* Sarajevo, BH: Energoinvest, Science and Research.

Abdomerovic, Muhamed. 2002. *Brainstorming The PMBOK® Guide* 2000 *Edition.* Louisville, KY: Project Management Publications.

Abdomerovic, Muhamed. 2004. "Contract Payments and Earned Value Cost." *The Measurable News* (Summer 2004): 25–33. www.mycpm.org.

Abdomerovic, Muhamed. 2005. *Brainstorming The PMBOK® Guide Third Edition.* Louisville, KY: Project Management Publications.

Abdomerovic, Muhamed. 2009. *Brainstorming The PMBOK® Guide Fourth Edition.* Louisville, KY: Project Management Publications.

Ackoff, Russel, and Fred Emery. 2008. *On Purposeful Systems: An Interdisciplinary Analysis of Individual and Social Behavior as a System of Purposeful Events.* New Brunswick, NJ: Transaction Publishers.

Agile. 2001. *Agile Manifesto.* Agile Alliance, February 2001. www.agilemanifesto.org.

Aguanno, Kevin. 2013. "Continuous Delivery: The Ultimate Challenge for Software Development Managers." *PM World Journal* I, no. I (January 2013): www.pmworldjournal.net.

AIA G-Forms. *AIA's Documents G702 and G703.* American Institute of Architects, Downloaded March 2021: www.aia.org.

AIA IPD. 2017. *Integrated Project Delivery.* Chicago, IL: American Institute of Architects & American Institute of Architects California Council. www.aia.org.

Akkermans, Jos, Maxwell Cipulu, Udechukwu Ojiako, and T. Williams. 2020. "Bridging the Fields of Careers and Poject Management." *Project Management Journal* 51 (April 2020): 123–134. www.pmi.org.

ANSI PMI-19-006-2019. 2019. *The Standard for Earned Value Management.* Newton Square, PA: Project Management Institute (PMI). www.pmi.org.

APM 2012. *APM Body of Knowledge 7th Edition.* Buckinghamshire, UK: Association for Project Management, (May 2012). www.apm.org.uk.

Archibald, Russell. 2004a. "Part 1 Projects, Programs, and Portfolios." *Max's Project Management Wisdom, Guest Article*(2004). www.maxwideman.com.

Archibald, Russell. 2004b. "Part 2 Project Life Cycle Models." *Max's Project Management Wisdom, Guest Article*(2004). www.maxwideman.com.

Archibald, Russell. 2009. "Five Decades of Modern Project Management: Where It Come From, Where It's Going". *PM World Today* XI, no. X (October 2009). www.pmworldjournal.net.

Archibald, Russell. 2010. "The Interfaces Between Strategic Management of an Enterprise and Project Portfolio Management Within the Enterprise." *PM World Today* XII, no. II (2010). www.pmworldjournal.net.

Arcidiacono, Giuseppe. 2014. "Use of Project Cycle Management in Project Selection Process: Evaluation of European Commission approach." *PM World Journal* III, no. III (March 2014). www.pmworldjournal.net.

Arumugam, Ramkumar. 2019. "Skills Every PM Needs in Managing a Millennial Workforce." *The Measurable News* no. 01 (2019). www.mycpm.org.

Audemar, Piguet. The Economist. December 19th 2015 – January 1st 2016. Ad.

Ayers, Chesley. 1984. *Specifications for Architecture. Engineering and Construction.* New York, NY: McGraw-Hill Book Company.

Bale, Lawrence. 1995. "Gregory Bateson, Cybernetics, and the Social / Behavioral Science." *Cybernetics & Human Knowing* 3, no. 1 (1995). www.narberthpa.com.

Barnes, Martin. 2013. "We Can and Should Raise the Standards." *PM World Journal* II, no. I (January 2013). www.pmworldjournal.net.

Barseghyan, Pavel. 2017. "Elements of the Mathematical Theory of Human Systems, Part 1: Assessment of the Results of Human Actions and Activities Based on the Method of State Equations." *PM World Journal* VI, no. XII (December 2017). www.pmworldjournal.net.

Barseghyan, Pavel. 2018. "Elements of the Mathematical Theory of Human Systems, Part 2: Structural Mathematical Models of the Life of Humans Based on the Method of State Equations." *PM World Journal* VII, no. I (January 2018). www.pmworldjournal.net.

Barseghyan, Pavel. 2021. "Quantitative analysis of the efficiency and productivity of the activity of human system – Part 1: Graphical analysis of the nonlinear functional relationships between team productivity and team size." *PM World Journal* X, no. III (March 2021). www.pmworldjournal.com.

Bentahar, Omar, and Roslyn Cameron. 2015. "Design and Implementation of a Mixed Method Research Study in Project Management." *The Electronic Journal of Business Research Method* 13, no. 1 (2015): 3–15. www.ejbrm.com.

Berge, Claude. 2001. *The Theory of Graphs.* Mineola, NY: Dover Publications.

Berggren, Christian, Jack Jarkvik, and Jonas Soderlund. 2008. "Lagomizing. Organic Integration. and Systems Emergency Wards: Innovative Practices in Managing Complex Systems Development Projects." *Project Management Journal* 39 (Supplement 2008): S111–S122. www.pmi.org.

Bertalanffy, Ludwig. 1975. *Perspectives on General System Theory: Scientific – Philosophical Studies.* New York, NY: George Braziller.

Besner Claude, and Brian Hobbs. "Discriminating Contexts and Project Management Best Practices on Innovative and Noninnovative Projects." *Project Management Journal* 39 (Supplement 2008): S123–S134. www.pmi.org.

Blackburn, Simon. 2008. *The Oxford Dictionary of Philosophy.* 2nd Edition. New York, NY: Oxford University Press.

Blomquist, Tomas, and Markus Hallgren, and Andreas Nilsson. 2010. "Project-as-Practice: In Search of Project Management Research That Matters." *Project Management Journal* 41, no. 1 (March 2010): 5–16. www.pmi.org.

Bredillet, Christophe. 2007. "Exploring Research in Project Management – Nine School of Project Management. (Part 3)." *Project Management Journal* 38, no. 4 (December 2007): 2–4. www.pmi.org.

Bredillet, Christophe. 2008a. "Exploring Research in Project Management – Nine Scholl of Project Management Research (Part 4)." *Project Management Journal* 39, no. 1 (March 2008): 2–6. www.pmi.org.

Bredillet, Christophe. 2008b."Exploring Research in Project Management – Nine Scholl of Project Management Research (Part 5)." *Project Management Journal* 39, no. 2 (June 2008): 2–4. www.pmi.org.

Bredillet, Christophe. 2010. "Blowing Hot and Cold on Project Management." *Project Management Journal* 41, no. 3 (June 2010): 4–20. www.pmi.org.

Brochner, Jan. 2021. "Construction Project Management Fiction: Individual Values." *International Journal of Project Management* In Press Version (May 2021). https://sciencedirect.com.

Bronte van der Hoorn. 2020. "Seeing the Bigger Picture: Conditions that Influence Effective Engagement of Project Executives with Visuals." *International Journal of Project Management* 38, no. 2 (February 2020): 137–151. www.elsevier.com/locate/ijproman.

Brown, Lewis, and Leslie Howard. 1966. *Principle and Practice of Management Accountancy.* London, UK: McDonald and Evans.

Brulin, Goran, and Lennart Svensson. 2012. "Sustainable Change in Large Projects." *PM World Journal* I, no. V (December 2012). www.pmworldjournal.net.

Bruns, Axel. 2009. *Blogs, Wikipedia, Second Life, and Beyond: From Production to Produsage.* New York, NY: Peter Lang Publishing.

Budeli, Lalamani. 2021. "Data Analytics to Improve Engineering Project Management Office (PMO) Performance: The Predictive Analytics Approach." *PM World Journal* X, no. III (March 2021). www.pmworldjournal.net.

Burga, Ruben, Joshua Leblanc, and Davar Rezania. 2020. "Exploring Student Perceptions of Their Readiness for Project Work: Using Social Cognitive Career Theory." *Project Management Journal* 51 (2020). 154–164. www.pmi.org.

Carlos Eduardo Martins Serra, and Martin Kunc. 2015. "Benefits Realization Management and Its Influence on Project Success and on the Execution of Business Strategies." *International Journal of Project Management* 33, no. 1 (January 2015): 53–66. https://sciencedirect.com.

Carlsen, Arne, and Tyrone Pitsis. 2020. "We Are Projects: Narrative Capital and Meaning Making in Projects." *Project Management Journal* (June 2020): Abstract. https://journals.sagepub.com.

Carmeli, Abraham, Avi Levi, Riccardo Peccei. 2021. "Resilience and Creative Problem-Solving Capacities in Project Teams: A Relational View." *International Journal of Project Management* In Press Version (May 2021). https://sciencedirect.com.

Carter, Carissa. 2012. "The Total Float Consumption Index (TFCI)." *The Measurable News*, no. 4 (2012): 17–20. http://mycpm.org.

Champy, James. 1995. *Reengineering Management: The Mandate for new leadership.* New York, NY: HarperCollins Publishers.

Chang, Artemis, Caroline Hatcher, and Jai Kim. 2013. "Temporary Boundary Objects in Megaprojects: Mapping the System with the Integrated Master Schedule." *International Journal of Project Management* 31, no. 3 (April 2013): 323–332. www.elsevier.com/locate/ijproman.

Chang, Chen-Yu. 2015. "Risk-beating Capacity as a New Dimension to the Analysis of Project Governance." *International Journal of Project Management* 33, no. 6 (August 2015): 1195–1205. https://sciencedirect.com.

Chapman, Robert. 2011. *Simple Tools and Techniques for Enterprise Risk Management.* New York, NY: John Wiley and Sons Limited.

Chapman, Robert. 2021. "Ineffective Risk Management and the Collapse of Carillion – An Update." *PM World Journal* X, no. III (March 2021). www.pmworldjournal.com.

Chow, Vivien, and Roine Leiringer. 2020. "Public Engagement Events and the Management of External Stakeholders: Artifacts as Boundary Objects or Tools of Discipline and Control?" *Project Management Journal* (August 2020). https://journals.sagepub.com. www.pmi.org.

Cleland, David, and Harold Kerzner. 1985. *A Project Management Dictionary of Terms.* New York, NY: Van Nostrand Reinhold Company.

Cohen, Izack, and Avishai Mandelbaum, and Avraham Shtub. 2004. "Multi-Project Scheduling and Control: A Process-Based Comparative Study of the Critical Chain Methodology and Some Alternatives." *Project Management Journal* 35, no. 2 (June 2004): 39–50. www.pmj.org.

Cohen, Yuval, Hana Ornoy, and Baruch Keren. 2013. "MBTI Personality Types of Project Managers and Their Success: A Field Survey" *Project Management Journal* 44, no. 3 (June 2013): 78–87. www.pmi.org.

Conforto, Edivandro Carlos, and Daniel Capaldo Amaral. 2010. "Evaluating an Agile Method for Planning and Controlling Innovative Projects." *Project Management Journal* 41, no. 2 (April 2010): 73–80. www.pmi.org.

Copes, Wayne, Clifford Sloyer, Robert Stark, and William Sacco. 1987. *Graph Theory: Euler's Rich Legacy.* Providence: Janson Publications.

Crawford, Lynn, Julien Pollock, and David England. 2007. "How Standard Are Standards: An Examination of Language Emphasis in Project Standards." *Project Management Journal* 38, no. 3 (September 2007): 6–21. www.pmi.org.

Crosby, Philip. 1979. *Quality Is Free*. New York, NY: A Mentor Book.

CSI Manual of Practice. 2004. *Project Resource Manual: CSI Manual of Practice*, 5th Edition. New York: McGraw Hill.

CSI Master Format. 2019. *CSI's Maser Format Standard*. Alexandria: Construction Specification Institute. www.csiresources.org/standards.

CSI Uni Format. 2019. *CSI's Uni Format Standard,* Alexandria: Construction Specification Institute. www.csiresources.org/standards.

Cuganesan, Suresh, and Maurizio Floris. 2020. "Investigating Perspective Taking When Infrastructure Megaproject Team Engage Local Communities: Navigating Tensions and Balancing Perspectives." *International Journal of Project Management* 38, no. 3 (April 2020): 153–164. www.elsevier.com/locate/ijproman.

Curling, D. H. 1995. "Editorial." *Introduction, International Journal of Project Management* 13, no. 2, 67–70.

Dalcher, Darren. 2015. "There Is Nothing So Permanent as Temporary: Some Thoughts on Adapting Project Structures." *PM World Journal* IV, no. VI (June 2015). www.pmworldjournal.net.

Dalcher, Darren. 2018. "The Wisdom of Teams Revisited: Teamwork, Teaming and Working for the Common Good." *PM World Journal* VII, no. IX (September 2018). www.pmworldjournal.net.

Dalcher, Darren. 2019. "Moving Beyond Project Delivery: Reflecting on the Life Cycle Concept as Way for Organizing Project Work." *PM World Journal* VIII, no. I (January 2019). www.pmworldjournal.net.

Deardorff, Dale. 2010. "Pracademic Project Management: The Art of Blending Optimism with Reality." *PM World Journal* IX, no. XI (November 2020). www.pmworldtoday.net.

Daniel, Eric, and Pierre Daniel. 2019."Megaprojects as Complex Adaptive Systems: The Hinkley Point C Case". *International Journal of Project Management* 37, no. 8 (November 2019): 1017–1033. www.elsevier.com/locate/ijproman.

Delisle, Julie. 2019. "Uncovering Temporal Underpinnings of Project Management Standards." *International Journal of Project Management* 37, no. 8 (November 2019): 968–978. www.elsevier.com/locate/ijproman.

Desaulniers, Douglas, and Robert Anderson. 2001. "Matching Software Development Life Cycles to the Project Environment." *Proceedings of the Project Management Institute Annual Seminars & Symposium*. Nashville (November 2001). www.pmi.org.

Descartes, Rene. 1952. *Rules for the Direction of the Mind*. In: Hutchins, Robert, Editor in chief, Great Books of the Western World, Volume 31. Chicago, IL: Encyclopedia Britannica.

Dinsmore, Paul, and Jeannette Cabanis-Brewin. 2005. *AMA Handbook of Project Management*. American Management Association.

DOD and NASA Guide. 1962. *PERT COST: Systems Design*. Office of the Secretary of Defense and National Aeronautics and Space Administration.

Doyle, John, Bruce Francis, and Allen Tannenbaum. 1992. *Feedback Control Theory.* Mineola, NY: Dover Publications.

Drechsler, Andreas, and Sophia Breth. 2019. "How to Go Global: A Transformative Process Model for the Transition Towards Globally Distributed Software Development Projects." *International Journal of Project Management* 37, no. 8 (November 2019): 941–955. www.elsevier.com/locate/ijproman.

Driessnack, John. 2019. "Earned Value Management Standards Structures: Part 1 – Why Three." *The Measurable News* 2019, 02 (2019): 34–38. http://mycpm.org.

Drucker, Peter. 1970. *The Practice of Management.* London, UK: Pan Books.

EIA-748D-2019. *EIA-748D Earned Value Management Standard.* NDIA, January 2019.

Einhorn, Frank, Carl Marnewick, and Jack Meredith. 2019. "Archiving Strategic Benefits from Business IT Projects: The Critical Importance of Using the Business Case Across the Entire Project Lifetime." *International Journal of Project Management* 37, no. 8 (November 2019): 989–1002. www.elsevier.com/locate/ijproman.

Euler, Leonhard. 1998. The Seven Bridges of Konigsberg, 1735. In: Roper, D. L. "Euler and Konigsberg Bridges: Some Lessons for the Philosophy of Mathematics." *School of Quantitative Methods and Mathematical Sciences.* University of Western Sydney, Australia.

Fayol, Henri. 1984. *General and Industrial Management, Henry Fayol* (Revised by Irwin Gray). IEEE Engineering Management Society. New York, NY: IEEE Press.

Fine, Brian. 1969. *Management Game (Lecture notes at the University of Loughborough, UK).* Costain, Operational Research Department. London, UK: February 1969.

Fink, Lior, and Barak Pinchovski. "It Is About Time: Bias and Its Mitigation in Time-Saving Decisions in Software Development Projects." *International Journal of Project Management* 38, no. 2 (2020): 99–111. www.elsevier.com/locate/ijproman.

Fisher, Walter. 1987. *Human Communication as Narration: Toward a Philosophy of Reason, Value and Action.* Columbia, SC: University of South Carolina Press.

FKI Logistex. 2002. *Stage – Gate Project Management Manual.* Louisville, KY: FKI Logistex.

FKI Logistex. 2005. *Business Project Model.* Louisville, KY: FKI Logistex.

Fleming, Quentin. 1988. *Cost/Schedule Control Systems Criteria: The Management Guide to C/SCSC.* Chicago, IL: Probus Publishing Company.

Fleming, Quentin, and Joel Koppelman. 2000. *Earned Value Project Management*, 2nd Edition. Newton Square PA: Project Management Institute.

Fleming, Quentin, and Joel Koppelman. 2006. "Start With 'Simple' Earned Value On All Your Projects." *The Journal of Defense Software Engineering* 16–19.

Fondahl, John. 1961. "A Non-computer Approach to the Critical Path Method for the Construction Industry," 1st Edition. *Stanford University, Department of Civil Engineering.*

Fondahl, John. 1962. "A Non-computer Approach to the Critical Path Method for the Construction Industry," 2nd Edition. *Stanford University, Department of Civil Engineering.*

Ford, Lester, and Delbert Fulkerson. 1956. "Maximal Flow through a Network." *Canadian Journal of Mathematics* 8 (1956): 399–404.

Ford, Lester, and Delbert Fulkerson. 1957. "A Simple Algorithm for Finding Maximal Network Flows and an Application to the Hitchcock Problem." *Canadian Journal of Mathematics* 9 (1957): 210–218.

Ford, Steve. 2020. "Contingency Planning vs. Scenario Planning." *PM World Journal* IX, no. VII (July 2020). www.pmworldjournal.com.

Forrester, Jay. 1968. *Principles of Systems.* Cambridge, MA: Productivity Press.

Frederiksen, Nicolaj, Stefan Christoffer Gottlieb, and Roine Leiringer. "Organizing for Infrastructure Development Programmes: Govering Internal Logic Multiplicity Across Organizational Spaces." *International Journal of Project Management* 39, no. 3 (April 2021): 223–235. https://sciencedirect.com.

Fulkerson, Delbert. "A Network Flow Computation for Project Cost Curves." *Management Science* 7, no. 2 (1961): 167–178.

GAO 2015. *Best Practice for Project Schedules.* US Government Accountability Office: Publicly Released December 22, 2015. https://www.gao.gov/assets/680/674404.pdf. Presented by Kurian, Tijo, 2019: *PM World Journal* VIII, no. XI. www.pmworldjournal.net.

GAO 2020. *Cost Estimating and Assessment Guide: Best Practice.* US Government Accountability Office, GAO-20-195G, March 2020.

GAPPS 2007. *A Framework for Performance Based Competency Standards for Global Level 1 and 2 Project Manager.* Sydney, Australia: Global Alliance for Project Performance Standards, 2007. www.globalpmstandards.org.

GAPPS 2020. *A Guide Framework for Leaderships in Complexity – Exposure Draft.* Sydney, Australia: Global Alliance for Project Performance Standards, September 2020. www.globalpmstandards.org.

Gasik, Stanislaw. "A Model of Project Knowledge Management." *Project Management Journal* 42, no. 3 (April 2011): 23–44. www.pmi.org.

Geraldi, Joana, Jonas Soderlund, and Alfons van Marrewijk. "Advancing Theory and Debate in Project Studies." *Project Management Journal*, Editorial (July 31, 2020). https://journals.sagepub.com.

Ghorbani, Shohreh. "Top 5 Cutting-Edge Project Controls Technology Trends and Forward-Thinking Strategies to Foster Innovation." *The Measurable News* 2019, no. 02 (2019): 13–22. http://mycpm.org.

Giammalvo, Paul. "Should We Challenge or Recall ISO 21502: 2027?" *PM World Journal* X, no. III (March 2021). www.pmworldjournal.com.

Giezen, Mendel. "Keeping It Simple? A Case Study into Advantages and Disadvantages of Reducing Complexity in Mega Project Planning." *International Journal of Project Management* 30, no. 7 (October 2012): 781–790. www.elsevier.com/locate/ijproman.

Goldratt, Eliyahu. 1990. *Theory of Constraints.* Great Barrington MA: The North River Press Publishing Corporation. www.northriverpress.com.

Goldratt, Eliyahu. 1997. *Critical Chain.* Great Barrington MA: The North River Press Publishing Corporation. www.northriverpress.com.

Google 1. *Project Management Schools: Statistics, Professional Trends, Educational Trends, Faculty Salaries, Schools by State, Related Links. Google*, May 2021. www.google.com.

Greene, Robert. 1998. *The 48 Laws of Power.* New York, NY: Penguin Putnam.

Greene, Stuart, and Natalya Sergeeva. 2019. "Value Creation in Projects: Towards a Narrative Perspective." *International Journal of Project Management* 37, no. 5 (July 2019): 636–651. www.elsevier.com/locate/ijproman.

Haines, Stephen. 2000. *The System Thinking Approach to Strategic Planning and Management.* Boca Raton, FL: CRC Press.

Halbertsma, K. 1972. *The Phased Development of New Industrial Products.* In: Project Management and Project Control. Frascati: ESRO 10th Summer School.

Hall, Daniel, and Richard Scott. 2019. "Early Stages in the Institutionalization of Integrated Project Delivery." *Project Management Journal* 50 (April 2019): 128–143. www.pmi.org.

Hallgren, Markus. 2012. "The Construction of Research Question in Project Management." *International Journal of Project Management* 30, no. 7 (October 2012): 804–816. www.elsevier.com/locate/ijproman.

Hanisch, Bastian, and Andreas Wald. 2011. "A Project Management Research Framework Integrating Multiple Theoretical Perspectives and Influencing Factors." *Project Management Journal* 42, no. 3 (April 2011): 4–22. www.pmi.org.

Harari, Oren. 2002. *The Leadership Secrets of Colin Powell.* New York, NY: McGraw-Hill.

Hart, Stuart. 2010. *Capitalism at the Crossroads: Next Generation Business Strategies for a Post-Crisis World*, 3rd Edition. Upper Saddle, NJ: Prentice Hall.

Hatfield, Michael. "The Coming Sea-Change in Project Management Science." *PM World Journal* II, no. I (January 2013). www.pmworldjournal.net.

Haupt, Eleonore. 2004. "The Wonderful World of Acronyms." *The Measurable News* (Summer 2004). www.mycpm.org.

Havermans, Liselore, Beatrice Van der Heijden, Chantal Savelsbergh, and Peter Storm. 2019. "Rolling into the Profession: Exploring the Motivation and Experience of Becoming a Project Manager." *Project Management Journal* 50 (June 2019): 346–360. www.pmi.org.

Herroelen, Willy, Roel Leus, and Eric Demeulemeester. 2002. "Critical Chain Project Scheduling: Do Not Oversimplify." *Project Management Journal* 33, no. 4 (December 2002). www.pmi.org.

Hetemi, Ermal, Alfons van Marrewijk, Anna Jerbrant, and Marian Bosch-Rekveldt. "The Recursive Interaction of Institutional Fields and Managerial Legitimation in Large-Scale Projects." *International Journal of Project Management* 39, no. 3 (April 2021): 295–307. https://sciencedirect.com.

Heyel, Carl, ed. 1963. *The Encyclopedia of Management.* New York, NY: Reinhold Publishing Corporation.

Hoffmann, David, Frederik Ahlemann, and Stefan Reining. 2020. "Reconciling Alignment, Efficiency, and Agility in IT Project Portfolio Management: Recommendations Based on a Revelatory Case Study." *International Journal of Project Management* 38, no. 2 (February 2020): 124–136. www.elsevier.com/locate/ijproman.

ICB 2006. *ICB – IPMA Competence Baseline. Version 3.0.* IPMA – International Project Management Association, 2006. www.ipma.ch.

ICB 2015. *ICB – IPMA Competence Baseline. Version 4.0.* IPMA – International Project Management Association, 2015. www.ipma.ch.

ISO/IEC 12207. *International Standard 12207-2008: System and Software Engineering – Software Life Cycle Processes.* ISO/IEC, 2008. www.iso.org.

ISO/AS 4817 2019. *Earned Value Management in Project and Programme Management.* Sydney, Australia: Standards Australia, August 2019.

Jacob, Dave, and Michael Kane. 2004. "Forecasting Schedule Completion Using Earned Value Metrics." *The Measurable News* (Summer 2004): 1, 11–17. www.mycpm.org.

Jacob, Dave. 2006. "Is Earned Value Schedule an Unreliable Indicator?" *The Measurable News* (Fall 2006): 15–21. www.mycpm.org.

Kelley, J., and Walker, M. 1959. "Critical Path Planning and Scheduling." Proceeding of the Eastern Joint Computer Conference (December 1959): 160–173.

Kelley, James. 1961. "Critical-Path Planning and Scheduling: Mathematical Basis." *Operations Research* 9, no. 3 (May – June 1961): 296–320.

Kerzner, Harold. 2017. *Project management: A Systems Approach to Planning. Scheduling and Controlling*, 12th Edition. Hoboken, NJ: John Wiley & Sons.

Kilpatrik, D.C., 1972. "Float Trend Chart: The Practical Application of Project Planning by Network Techniques." *The Third International Congress on Project Planning*, Stockholm.

King, Michele, and Robin Smith. 2019. "Concurrently Verifying and Validating The Critical Path and Margin Allocation Using Probabilistic Analysis". *The Measurable News* (2019.01): 31–47. http://mycpm.org.

Konstantinou, Efrosyni. 2015. "Professionalism in Project Management Redefining the Role of the Project Practitioner." *Project Management Journal* 46, no. 2 (April 2015): 21–35. www.pmi.org.

Kotb, Mostafa, Mohamed Abo Al Anwar, and Haytham Baraka. 2019a. "In-depth View on the Construction Contracts." *PM World Journal* VIII, no. VII (August 2019). www.pmworldjournal.net.

Kotb, Mostafa, Mohamed Abo Al Anwar, and Haytham Baraka. 2019b. "The Main Characteristics of FIDIC Red Book 2017." *PM World Journal* VIII, no. VIII (September 2019). www.pmworldjournal.net.

Krazert, Keith, and Joseph Houser. 2006. "Cost of Earned Value Management." *The Measurable News* (Fall 2006): 1, 7–9. www.mycpm.org.

Kuehn, Ursula. 2011. *Integrated Cost and Schedule Control in Project Management.* Vienna, VA: Management Concepts.

Kuhn, Thomas. 1996. *The Structure of Scientific Revolutions.* Chicago, IL: The University of Chicago Press.

Kurian, Tijo. "How to Write a Model Scheduling Specification Incorporating the GAO's 'Best Practice in Scheduling' Appendices." *PM World Journal* VIII, no. XI (December 2019). www.pmworldjournal.net.

Kurtz, Cynthia, and David Snowden. 2003. The New Dynamics of Strategy: Sense-making in a Complex and Complicated World. *IBM System Journal* 42, no. 3 (2003): 462–83.

Kutsch, Elmar, Ibrat Djabbarov, and Mark Hall. 2021. "How Managers Frame and Make Sense of Unexpected Events in Project Implementation." *International Journal of Project Management* In Press Version (May 2021). https://sciencedirect.com.

Laszlo, Ervin. 1973. *Introduction to System Philosophy.* New York, NY: Harper.

Leach, Larry. 1999. "Critical Chain Project Management Improves Project Performance." *Project Management Journal* 30, no. 2 (June 1999): 39–52. www.pmi.org.

Lewis, James. 2011. *Project Planning. Scheduling & Control.* New York, NY: McGraw-Hill.

Leybourne, Stephen, and Phillip Sainter. "Advancing Project Management: Authenticating the Shift From Process to 'Nuanced' Project Management in the Ambidextrous Organization." *Project Management Journal* 43, no. 6 (December 2012): 5–15. www.pmi.org.

Link, Philip. 1963. *The Encyclopedia of Management*, edited by Carl Heyel. New York, NY: Reinhold Publishing Corporation1, 1963, 748–52.

Lipke, Walt. 2003a. "Schedule Is Different 1st Part." *The Measurable News* (March 2003): 10–15. http://mycpm.org.

Lipke, Walt. 2003b. "Schedule Is Different 2nd Part." *The Measurable News* (Summer 2003): 31–34. http://mycpm.org.

Lipke, Walt. 2004. "Connecting Earned Value Cost to the Schedule." *The Measurable News* 1 (Winter 2004): 6–16. http://mycpm.org.

Lipke, Walt. 2019. "Earned Schedule Forecasting Method Selection." *The Measurable News* no. 01 (2019): 21–30. http://mycpm.org.

Liu, Mingqiang, Jun Le, Yi Hu, Bo Xia, Martin Skitmore, and Xianyi Gao. 2019. "System Dynamics Modeling for Construction Management Research: Critical Review and Future Trend." *Journal of Civil Engineering and Management* 25, no. 8 (2019): 730–41. https://doi.org.

Lopez, Claire. 2019. "How Performance Indicators and Maintenance Will Become Project Managers' Best Assets in the Industry 4.0." *PM World Journal* VIII, no. II (July 2019). www.pmworldjournal.com.

Lumsden, Philip. 1968. *The Line of Balance Method.* London, UK: Pergamon Press.

Maharana, Dibyaranjan. 2020. *Oracle Primavera P6 Professional Project Management, Release 19.* Coppell, TX.

Malcom, D. G., Roseboom, J. H., Clark, C. E., and Fazar, W. 1959. "Applications of a Technique for Research and Development Program Evaluation." *Operations Research* 7 (1959): 646–69.

Manata, Brian, Angelo Joseph Garcia, Sinem Mollaoglu, and Vernon Miller. 2021. "The Effect of Commitment Differentiation on Integrated Project Delivery Team Dynamics: The Critical Roles of Goal Alignment, Communication Behaviors, and Decision Quality." *International Journal of Project Management* 39, no. 3 (April 2021): 259–69. https://sciencedirect.com.

Martinsuo, Miia. 2020. "The Management of Values in Project Business: Adjusting Beliefs to Transform Project Practice and Outcomes." *Project Management Journal* (June 3. 2020). https://journals.sagepub.com.

Material Handling Industry of America. 2010. *Material Handling Equipment Manufacturing.* MHEM Industry. www.mhia.org/learning/marketresearch/forecast.

Maxwell, James. "On Governors." *Proceedings of the Royal Society* XVI, no. 100 (1868): 270–83. Retrieved 10/2/2011. http://seit.unsw.adfa.edu.au/staff/sites/hrp/historicalpapers/ongovernors.pdf.

McLaren, Matthew, and Martin Loosemoro. 2019. "Swift Trust Formation in Multi-national Disaster Project Management Teams." *International Journal of Project Management* 37, no. 8 (November 2019): 979–88. www.elsevier.com/locate/ijproman.

Means. 1991. *Illustrated Construction Dictionary.* Kingston, MA: R. S. Means Company.

Means. 2019. *Building Construction Cost Data.* Kingston, MA: R. S. Means Company.

Mee, John. 1963. *The Encyclopedia of Management*, edited by Carl Heyel. New York, NY: Reinhold Publishing Corporation1, (1963): 865–71.

Meredith, Jack, Scott Shafer, and Samuel Mantel. 2018. *Project Management: A Strategic Managerial Approach.* New York, NY: John Wiley and Sons.

Merrett, A. J., and Sykes. 1971. *The Finance and Analysis of Capital Projects.* London, UK: Longman.

Messsai, Sarra. 2019. "Agile Contracts: Effective Procurement for Enhanced Project Success in Entertainment Industry." *PM World Journal* VIII, no. II (February 2019). www.pmworld journal.net.

Microsoft Project. 2019. *Project Management Solutions.* Microsoft. http://microsoft.com/project.

Miterev, Maxim, Anna Jerbrant, and Andreas Feldmann. 2020. "Exploring the Alignment between Organization Designs and Value Processes over the Program Lifecycle." *International Journal of Project Management* 38, no 2 (February 2020): 112–23. www.elsevier.com/locate/ijproman.

Mitroff, Ian. 2018. *Technology Run Amok: Crisis Management in Digital Age.* New York, NY: Springer.

Miyake, Michiaki. 2005. "Management in a Digital Network Era. Reductionism and Holonic Management." IIST World Forum, (November 2005). www.cfiec.jp/wf/magazine/0387/0387.

Moder, Joseph, and Cecil Phillips. 1964. *Project Management wit CPM and PERT.* New York, NY: Van Nostrand Reinhold.

Momeni, Khadijeh, and Miia Martinsuo. 2019. "Integrating Services into Solution Offering in the Sales Work of Project-based Firms." *International Journal of Project Management* 37, no. 8 (November 2019): 956–67. www.elsevier.com/locate/ijproman.

Morris, Peter, Marsh Patel, and Stephen Wearne. 2000. "Research into Revising the APM Project Management Body of Knowledge." *International Journal of Project Management*18 (2000): 155–64. www.elsevier.com/locate/ijproman.

Muirhead, Brian, and William Simon. 1999. *High Velocity Leadership: The Mars Pathfinder Approach to Faster, Bette, Cheaper.* New York, NY: HarperCollins Publishers.

Mundorff, George. 1963. *The Encyclopedia of Management*, edited by Carl Heyel. New York, NY: Reinhold Publishing Corporation1 (1963): 420–31.

NAC, 2006. *A Compendium of Safety White Papers.* Position paper No. 6. The National Academy of Construction, Retrieved June 25. 2020. www.naocon.org.

NAC, 2014. *Best Practice Work Stream Feasibility Report.* Publication 2014-2. The National Academy of Construction, Retrieved June 25. 2020. www.naocon.org.

NBA, 1968. *Programming House Building by Line of Balance.* London, UK: The National Building Agency.

Nee, Nancy. 2012. "Finding the Right Blend: Sometimes Pure Agile isn't the Way to Go." *PM World Journal* I, no. IV (November 2012). www.pmworldjournal.net.

Netscher, Paul. 2014. *Successful Construction Project Management.* Subiaco, Australia: Panet Publications.

Nicholson, Laurence. 2013. "Agile in Project Management: A Brief Overview." *PM World Journal* II, no. IV (April 2013). www.pmworldjournal.net.

Oltmann, Jeff. 2013. "Agile vs. Traditional: An Unnecessary War." *PM World Journal* II, no. III (March 2013). www.pmworldjournal.net.

O'Brien, James. 1969. *Scheduling Handbook.* New York, NY: McGraw-Hill Book Company.

O'Brien, James. 1975. *Scheduling Handbook.* New York: McGraw-Hill Book Company.

Parsons, Talcott. 2012. *The social system.* New Orleans, LA: Quid Pro Books.

Patankul, Peerasit, and Aaron Shenhar. 2012. "What Project Strategy Really Is: The Fundamental Building Block in Strategic Project Management." *Project Management Journal* 43, no. 1 (February 2012): 4–20. www.pmi.org.

Patrick, Francis. 2001. "Critical Chain and Risk Management – Protecting Project Value from Uncertainty, (Parts 1–8)." *Focused Performance.* Retrieved Oct 22. 2013. http://focusedperformance.com/articles/ccrisk.html.

Payne, Judy, Eileen Roden, and Steve Simister. 2019. "Through the Knowledge Lens: Knowledge Management Adventures in Project-land." *PM World Journal* VIII, no. IX (January 2019). www.pmworldjournal.com.

Pellegrinelli, Sergio, and Ruth Murray-Webster. 2011. "Multi-Paradigmatic Perspectives on a Business Transformation Program." *Project Management Journal* 42, no. 6 (December 2011). www.pmi.org.

Pells, David. 2010. "Project Stories – the Largely Untapped World of Personal Experience & Lessons Learned in Project Management." *PM World Today* XII, no. IX (September 2010). www.pmworldjournal.com.

Pells, David. 2021. "Project Management Needs a Higher Purpose! Part 1: Introduction, the Perfect Storm, Crises & PM", *PM World Journal* X, no. I (January 2021). www.pmworldjournal.com.

Pickavance, Keith. 2013a. "A New Construction Contract for the 21st Century." *PM World Journal* II, no. II (February 2013). www.pmworldjournal.net.

Pickavance, Keith. 2013b. "A New Construction Contract for the 21st Century: Time Management." *PM World Journal* II, no. III (March 2013). www.pmworldjournal.net.

Pickavance, Keith. 2013c. "A New Construction Contract for the 21st Century: Risk of Change." *PM World Journal* II, no. IV (April 2013). www.pmworldjournal.net.

Pickavance, Keith. 2013d. "A New Construction Contract for the 21st Century: Cost Management." *PM World Journal* II, no. V (May 2013). www.pmworldjournal.net.

Pirozzi, M. 2020. "On the Subject of PM Standards, People and Community, Letter to the Editor." *PM World Journal* IX, no. III (March 2020). www.pmworldjournal.net.

PMI 1996. *A Guide to the Project Management Body of Knowledge (PMBOK® Guide) 1996 Edition.* Newtown Square PA: Project Management Institute.

PMI 2000. *A Guide to the Project Management Body of Knowledge (PMBOK® Guide) 2000 Edition.* Newtown Square PA: Project Management Institute.

PMI 2001. *The Practice Standard for Work Breakdown Structure First Edition.* Newtown Square PA: Project Management Institute.

PMI 2004. *A Guide to the Project Management Body of Knowledge (PMBOK® Guide) Third Edition.* Newtown Square PA: Project Management Institute.

PMI 2006. *Practice Standard for Work Breakdown Structures. Second Edition.* Newtown Square PA: Project Management Institute.

PMI 2008. *A Guide to the Project Management Body of Knowledge (PMBOK® Guide) Fourth Edition.* Newtown Square PA: Project Management Institute.

PMI 2013. *A Guide to the Project Management Body of Knowledge (PMBOK® Guide) Fifth Edition.* Newtown Square PA: Project Management Institute.

PMI 2017. *A Guide to the Project Management Body of Knowledge (PMBOK® Guide) Sixth Edition.* Newtown Square PA: Project Management Institute.

PMI 2019. *The Practice Standard for Scheduling Third Edition.* Newtown Square PA: Project Management Institute.

PMI 2021. *A Guide to the Project Management Body of Knowledge PMBOK Guide Seventh Edition and the Standard for the Standard for Project Management*, 2021, Project Management Institute Inc., 14 Campus Boulevard, Newtown Square, PA 19073-3299.

Portman, Henny. 2019. "A Bird's Eye View on the Agile Forest." *PM World Journal* VIII, no. X (November 2019). www.pmworldtoday.net.

Prieto, Bob. 2010. "Let's Build a 'Program'". *PM World Today* XII, no. VII (July 2010). www.pmworldtoday.net.

Prieto, Bob. 2012. "Generalized Analysis of Value Behavior over Time as a Project Performance Predictor." *The Measurable News* 1, no. 04 (2012): 4–10. http://mycpm.org.

Prieto, Bob. 2015. "Project Management Theory of Large Complex Projects." *PM World Journal* IV, no. VI (June 2015). www.pmworldtoday.net.

Prieto, Bob. 2020a. "A Deeper Look at the Physics of Large Complex Projects" *PM World Journal* IX, no. VIII (August 2020). www.pmworldtoday.net.

Prieto, Bob. 2020b. "Black Elephants." *PM World Journal* IX, no. VIII (August 2020). www.pmworldtoday.net.

Primavera P3. 1984. *Project Management and Control Software – Manual.* Primavera System. www.primavera.com

Primavera P3. 1993. *Project Planner for Windows – Reference.* Primavera System. www.primavera.com.

Primavera P3. 2005. *Primavera Project Planner.* Primavera. www.primavera.com.

Primavera P6. 2019. *Project Portfolio Management.* Primavera/Oracle. http://www.oracle.com/primavera.

Pritsker, A. A. B. 1966. *GERT: Graphical Evaluation and Review Technique.* Santa Monica, CA, The RAND Corporation.

Raz, Tzvi, Robert Barnes, and Dov Dvir. 2003. "A Critical Look at Critical Chain Project Management." *Project Management Journal* 34, no. 4 (December 2003): 24–32. www.pmi.org

Ringhofer, Claudia, Anne Keegan, and Martina Huemann. 2019. "Who Supports Project Careers? Leveraging the Compensatory Roles of Line Managers." *Project Management Journal* 50 (2019): 476–86. www.pmi.org.

Roper, Duncan. 2021. "Euler and the Konigsberg Bridges: Some Lessons for the Philosophy of Mathematics." *School of Quantitative Methods and Mathematical Science. University of Western Sydney. Australia* (Retrieved: April 2021).

Rothman, Johanna. 2017. *Create Your Successful Agile Project.* Raleigh, NC: The Pragmatic Bookshelf.

Rwelamila, P. D., and Neha Purushottam. 2012. "Project Management Trilogy Challenges in Africa – Where to From Here?" *Project Management Journal* 43, no. 4 (August 2012): 5–13. www.pmi.org.

Sanchez, Hynuk, and Robert Benoit. 2010. "Measuring Portfolio Strategic Performance Using Key Performance Indicators." *Project Management Journal* 41, no. 5 (December 2010): 64–86. www.pmi.org.

Santora, A. V. 1963. *The Encyclopedia of Management*, edited by Carl Heyel, 732–39. New York: Reinhold Publishing Corporation.

Saynisch, Manfred. 2010a. "Beyond Frontiers of Traditional Project Management: An Approach to Evolutionary. Self-Organizational Principles and the Complexity Theory – Results of the Research Program." *Project Management Journal* 41, (April 2010): 21–37. www.pmi.org.

Saynisch, Manfred. 2010b. "Mastering Complexity and Changes in Projects. Economy and Society via Project Management Second Order (PM-2)." *Project Management Journal* 41, no. 5 (December 2010): 4–20. www.pmi.org.

Schwaber, Ken, and Sutherland, Jeff. 2016. *The Scrum Guide™, The Definitive Guide to Scrum: The Rules of the Game.* Scrum.Org and ScrumInc, July 2016. http://creativecommons.org/licenses/by-sa/4.0/.

Sergeeva, Natalya, and Graham Winch. 2021. "Project Narratives That Potentially Perform and Change Future." *Project Management Journal* (March 2021). https://doi.org/10.1177/8756972821995340.

Shenoy, Ajay. "Common Misconceptions about Agile." *PM World Journal* VIII, no. X (November 2019). www.pmworldjournal.net.

Shepherd, M. 2020. "On the matter of Project Management Standards, Letter to the Editor." *PM World Journal*, IX, no. XII (December 2020). www.pmworldjournal.net.

Soderlund, Jonas, Shankar Sankaran, and Christopher Biesenthal. 2017a. "The Past and Present of Megaprojects." *Project Management Journal* 48, no. 6 (2017): 5–16. www.pmi.org.

Soderlund, Jonas, Shankar Sankaran, and Christopher Biesenthal. 2017b. "The Past and Present of Megaprojects." *Project Management Journal* 46, no. 6 (December 2017): 5–16. www.pmi.org.

Solomon, Robert. 1992. *Introducing Philosophy: A Text with Integrated Readings.* Fort Worth, TX: Harcourt Brace Jovanovich College Publishers.

Stackpole, Cyndi. 2008. "PMBOK Guide – Fourth Edition Changes – A Overviev." *Project Management World Today* X, no. X (October 2008). www.pmworldtoday.net.

Star, Susan, and James Griesemer. 1989. "*Institutional Ecology.* 'Translations' and Boundary Objects: Amateurs and Professionals in Berkeley's Museum of Vertebrate Zoology, 1907-39." *Social Studies of Science* 19, no. 3 (1989): 387–420.

Steward, Donald. 1981. "The Design Structure System: A Method for Managing the Design of Complex Systems." *IEEE Transactions on Engineering Management* 28, no. 3 (1981): 71–74.

Stretton. Alan. 2011. "Notes on Project/Program Typology." *PM World Today* XIII, no. II (February 2011). www.pmworldtoday.com.

Stretton, Alan. 2017. "Complication Complexity and Uncertainty in Program/Project Context." *PM World Journal* VI, no. III (March 2017). www.pmworldtoday.com.

Stretton, Alan. 2018a. "Responsibilities for 'project' Successes/failures?" *PM World Journal* VII, no. XI (November 2018a). www.pmworldtoday.com.

Stretton, Alan. 2018b. "Relating Causes of Project Failure to an Organizational Strategic Business Framework." *PM World Journal* VII, no.I (January 2018b). www.pmworldtoday.com.

Stretton, Alan. 2019a. "Representing 'other strategic work' in Addition to Projects in an Organizational Strategic Management Context." *PM World Journal* VIII, no. I (January 2019a). www.pmworldtoday.com.

Stretton, Alan. 2019b. "A Perspective on Project Success Levels in an Organizational Strategic Management Context." *PM World Journal* VIII, no. II (February 2019b). www.pmworldtoday.com.

Stretton, Alan. 2020. "Expanding from Conventional Project Management into Broader Types of Services in an Organizational Strategic Management Context." *PM World Journal* IX, no. VII (July 2020). www.pmworldtoday.com.

Sundqvist, Erik. 2019. "The Role of Project Managers as Improvement Agents in Project-Based Organizations." *Project Management Journal* 50 (June 2019): 376–90. www.pmi.org.

Tain, David. 2019. "Capitalizing on Complexity in Modern Business Environments: A Network-Based Perspective for Projects and Organizations." *PM World Journal* VIII, no. II (February 2019). www.pmworldtoday.net.

Taleb, Nassim. 2010. *The Black Swan.* New York, NY: Random House Trade Paperbacks.

Tam, Carlos, Eduardo Joia da Costa Moura, Tiago Oliveira, and Joao Varajao. 2020. "The Factors Influencing the Success of On-going Agile Software Development Projects." *International Journal of Project Management* 38, no. 3 (April 2020): 165–176. www.elsevier.com/locate/ijproman.

Taylor, Peter. 2021. "Make Your Business Agile: A Roadmap for Transforming Your Management and Adapting to the New Normal." *PM World Journal* X, no. V (May 2021). www.pmworldtoday.net.

Thamhain, Hans. 2013. "Managing Risks in Complex Projects." *Project Management Journal* 44, no. 2 (2013): 20–35. www.pmi.org.

The World Almanac. 2014. *The World Almanac and Book of Facts.* New York, NY: World Almanac Books.

Thomas, Janice, and Mark Mullaly. 2009. "Explorations of Values: Perspectives of the Value of Project Management." *Project Management Journal.* Project Management Institute. 40, no. 1 (March 2009): 2–3. www.pmi.org.

TranCreative Software. *WordBook. English Dictionary & Thesaurus.* iTunes Store. 2021. (Includes Web Contents http://en.m.wikipedia.org; http://mobile.answers.com; http://www.google.com. http://www.merriam-webster.com; http://www.wordreference.com).

Trietsch, Dan. "*Why a Critical Path by Any Other Name Would Smell Less Sweet? Towards a Holistic Approach to PERT / CPM.*" *Project Management Journal* 36, no. 1 (March 2005): 27–36. www.pmi.org.

Trietsch, Dan, and Kenneth Baker. "PERT 21: Fitting PERT/CPM for use in the 21th century." *International Journal of Project Management* 30, no. 4 (May 2012): 490–502. www.elsevier.com/locate/ijproman.

Troyka, Lynn. 1993. *Simon and Schuster Handbook for Writers.* New Jersey, NJ: Prentice Hall.

Turner, Rodney. 2006a. "Towards a Theory of Project Management: 'The Nature of the Project.'" *International Journal of Project Management* 24 (2006): 1–3. www.elsevier.com/locate/ijproman.

Turner, Rodney. 2006b. "Towards a Theory of Project Management: The Nature of the Project Governance and Project Management." *International Journal of Project Management* 24 (2006): 93–95. www.elsevier.com/locate/ijproman.

Turner, Rodney. 2006c. "Towards a Theory of Project Management: The Functions of Project Management." *International Journal of Project Management* 24 (2006): 187–89. www.elsevier.com/locate/ijproman.

Turner, Rodney. 2006d. "Towards a Theory of Project Management: The Nature of the Functions of Project Management." *International Journal of Project Management* 24 (2006): 277–79. www.elsevier.com/locate/ijproman.

Tywoniak, Stephane, and Lavagnon Ika, Cristophe Bredillet. 2021. "A Pragmatic Approach to Complexity Theorizing in Project Studies: Orders and Levels." *Project Management Journal* 52 (April 2021): 298–313. www.pmi.org.

UNIDO ID/206. 1976. *Manual for the Preparation of Industrial Feasibility Studies.* New York, NY: United Nations International Centre for Industrial Studies of UNIDO.

UN 1987. *Our Common Future, Report on World Commission on Environment and Development.* United Nations, UN Documents.

Vandeput, L. 1972. "Incentive Schemes as a Contract Management Tool." *ESRO, 1972. Project Management and Project Control, 10th Summer School.* Frascati, IT: European Space Research Organization (1972): 333–348.

Verzuh, Eric. 2016. *The Fast Forward MBA in Project Management.* New York, NY: John Wiley and Sons.

Walker, Derek, and Christopher Dar. "Frontinus – A Project Manager From the Roman Empire Era." *Project Management Journal* 42, no. 5 (September 2011): 4–16. www.pmi.org.

Wallace, Clark. *The Gantt Chart.* In: Maynard. H. B.. Ed.. Industrial Engineering Handbook. New York, NY: McGraw Hill, 1956.

Wearne, Stephen. 1973. *Principles of Engineering Organization.* London, UK: Edward Arnold Publishers.

Weaver, Patrick. 2006. "A Brief History of Scheduling." *Mosaic Project Services*, Australia (April 2006).

Weaver, Patrick. 2012. "Henry L. Gantt. 1861-1919. Debunking the Myths, a Retrospective View of His Work." *PM World Journal* I, no. V (December 2012). www.pmworldjournal.net.

Weaver, Patrick. 2013. "Where Did We Misuse of the Names Gantt and PERT Originated?" *PM World Journal* II, no. IV (April 2013). www.pmworldjournal.net.

Weber, Max. 1947. *The Theory of Social and Economic Organization.* 1997. Glencoe, Il: The Free Press.

Weinberg, Steven. 1992. *Dreams of a Final Theory. The Scientist's Search for the Ultimate Laws of Nature.* New York, NY: Pantheon Books.

White, Brenda. 1971. *Sourcebook of Planning Information.* London, UK: Clive Bingley.

Whyte, Jennifer, Angelos Stasis, and Carmel Lindkvist. 2016. "Managing Change in the Delivery of Complex Projects: Continuation Management, Asset Information and 'Big Data'."

International Journal of Project Management 34, no. 2 (February 2016): 339–51. https://sciencedirect.com.

Whyte, Jennifer, and Andrew Davies. 2021. "Reframing System Integration: A Process Perspective on Project." *Project Management Journal* 52 (March 2021). https://doi.org/10.1177/8756972821992246.

Wickwire, Jon, Thomas Driscoll, and Stephen Hurlbut. 1991. *Scheduling: Preparation. Liability and Claims.* New York, NY: Wiley Law Publications. John Wiley & Sons.

Wideman, Max. 1991. *A Framework for Project and Program Management Integration.* The PMBOK handbook series No 1. Upper Darby, PA: Project Management Institute. www.pmi.org.

Wideman, R. Max. 1995. "Criteria for a Project Management Body of Knowledge." *International Journal of Project Management* 13, no. 2 (1995): 71–75. www.elsevier.com/locate/ijproman.

Wideman, Max. 2004. *A Management Framework for Project, Program and Portfolio Integration.* Vancouver, BC: Trafford Publishing (UK).

Wideman, Max. 2006. "Book Review (Chin, Gary. Agile Project Management: How to Succeed in the Face of Changing Project Requirements. New York, NY: AMACOM, 2004)." *Project Management Wisdom* (May 2006). http://maxwideman.com/papers/agile/intro.htm.

Wideman, Max. 2011. "Interview. (Peter McBride. Agile Project Management: Answers to the Questions on the Basics)." *Project Management Wisdom* (December, 2011). http://maxwideman.com/guests/agile_pm/note.htm.

Wideman, Max. 2021. *Wideman Comparative Glossary of Project Management Terms.* www.maxwideman.com.

Wied, Morten, Nina Koch-Orvad, Torgeir Welo, and Josef Oehmen. "Managing Exploratory Projects: A Repertoire of Approaches and Their Shared Underpinnings." *International Journal of Project Management* 38, no. 2 (February 2020): 75–84. www.elsevier.com/locate/ijproman.

Wiener, Norbert. 1965. *Cybernetics or Control and Communication in the Animal and the Machine.* 2nd edition. Cambridge, MA: The MIT Press.

Wikipedia (2). *Product Recall. Automotive Industry.* http://en.wikipedia.org/wiki/Product_recall. Retrieved 6/10/2014.

Wikipedia (1). *Shewhart Cycle.* http://en.wikipedia.org/wiki/Shewhart_cycle. Retrieved 5/11/2013.

Williams, Rob. 2019. "Fortifying Your Career in 2020 and Beyond." *The Measurable News* 2019, no. 02 (2019): 9–12. http://mycpm.org.

Williams, Terry, Ole Klakegg, Derek Walker, Bjern Andersen, and Ole Magnussen. 2012. "Identifying and Acting on Early Warning Sign in Complex Projects." *Project Management Journal* 43, no. 2 (April 2012): 37–53. www.pmi.org.

Winch, Grahm, and Jonghyuk Cha. 2020. "Owner Challenges on Major Projects: The Case of UK Government." *International Journal of Project Management* 38, no. 3 (April 2020): 177–87. www.elsevier.com/locate/ijproman.

WinEst. 2017. *Cost Estimating Solution.* WinEstimator. www.winest.com.

Woodgate, Samuel. 1968. *Planning by Network: Project Planning and Control Using Network Techniques*, 2nd edition. London UK: Brandon System Press.

Xiaofeng Guo. 2019. "Enabling EVM to Benefit Big Science Projects: Success in Tailoring EVM." *The Measurable News*, 2019, no. 02 (2019): 23–27. http://mycpm.org.

Zerjav, Vedran. 2021. "Why Do Business Organization Participate in Projects? Toward a Typology of Project Value Domains." *Project Management Journal* 52, no. 3 (April 2021): 287–97. www.pmi.org.

Ziek, Paul, and Dwight Anderson. 2015. "Communication, Dialogue and Project Management." *International Journal of Managing Project in Business* 8, no. 4 (September 2015): 788–803. https://doi.org/10.1108/ijmpb-04-2014-0034.

Index

A

B

C

D

Q

R

S

T

U

V

W

www.ingramcontent.com/pod-product-compliance
Ingram Content Group UK Ltd.
Pitfield, Milton Keynes, MK11 3LW, UK
UKHW021836100926
8556IPUK00004B/367

9 781433 189340